THE

PAIN

The Struggle for
Civil Rights in
Tallahassee, Florida

AND THE

PROMISE

We lived there summer of 1954 –
summer of 1956
Summer of 1964 – 1967,
(summer?)

THE UNIVERSITY OF GEORGIA PRESS | ATHENS AND LONDON

© 1999 by the University of Georgia Press
Athens, Georgia 30602
All rights reserved
Designed by Louise OFarrell
Set in 10.3/14 Minion by G & S Typesetters, Inc.
Printed and bound by Maple-Vail
The paper in this book meets the guidelines for
permanence and durability of the Committee on
Production Guidelines for Book Longevity of the
Council on Library Resources.

Printed in the United States of America
03   02   01   00   99   C   5   4   3   2   1

Library of Congress Cataloging in Publication Data
Rabby, Glenda Alice.
    The pain and the promise : the struggle for civil rights
in Tallahassee, Florida / Glenda Alice Rabby.
        p.   cm.
    Includes bibliographical references (p.   ) and index.
    ISBN 0-8203-2051-x (alk. paper)
    1. Afro-Americans—Civil rights—Florida—Tallahassee—
History—20th century.   2. Tallahassee (Fla.)—Race
relations.   3. Civil rights movements—Florida—Tallahassee—History—20th century.   I. Title.
F319.T14R33   1999
975.9'88—dc21   98-44087

British Library Cataloging in Publication Data available

To Ted, for this and more

Contents

Acknowledgments

This book was "a long time a comin'," and many people provided me with help and encouragement along the way. I am deeply grateful to several good friends, particularly Jean Bryant, David Levenson, Stan Makielski, and Peter Ripley, who gave me valuable comments and advice at various stages of this work. I am also indebted to David Colburn and David Garrow, who reviewed an earlier draft of the manuscript and offered many incisive criticisms and suggestions. Valerie Jean Conner, my friend and mentor for over twenty years, contributed so much to this book and to my growth as a historian that I cannot adequately express my appreciation in these few words. My coworkers at the Postsecondary Education Planning Commission in Tallahassee, especially Marie Causey, not only tolerated "the book" but remained interested in it over the many years it took to complete. Thanks, guys. Thanks also to Tawanna Hays, who transcribed many of my interviews and who very patiently helped prepare the final manuscript. So many kind people helped me at the various libraries and archives where I did research. I must, however, single out the staff at the Florida State Archives in Tallahassee for their friendly and courteous assistance.

On a more personal note, my daughter, Elizabeth Caldwell Bowyer, my sister, Tommie Sue Rabby, and especially my mother, Margaret Elizabeth Caldwell Rabby, stood by me through this ordeal with characteristic caring and good humor. My late father, Joseph Glenn Rabby, always believed "his gals" could do anything. His faith helped keep me going through some tough times. More than anyone, my husband, Ted Chiricos, has been there from the beginning, serving as sounding board, critic, and chief supporter. I benefited not only from his shrewd observations and insights but from his unfailing interest and enthusiasm. Finally, I want to thank all of the people, the makers of history, who allowed me to interview them for this book. Although all mistakes and errors of omission are mine alone, this is their story. I hope that I have done it justice.

The Pain and the Promise

Introduction

Blacks first sought freedom in North Florida as runaway slaves in the mid-eighteenth century. Two hundred years later, in May 1956, students at Florida A & M University (FAMU) launched a bus boycott that brought the civil rights movement to Tallahassee and influenced the struggle for black equality throughout the South.

Modern Florida is rarely considered a traditional southern state because of its unique demographics and its rapid growth. In 1949, V. O. Key observed, "Florida is unlike other states of the South in many ways and, in truth, it is scarcely a part of the South. . . . it occasionally gives a faintly tropical rebel yell, but otherwise it is a world of its own." [1]

It would have been difficult however, on the eve of the civil rights movement, to persuade the state's 603,000 black residents to agree with Key's conclusion that Florida was different. Its culture, politics, and above all, its race relations, shared striking similarities with the rest of the former Confederacy. And nowhere did these similarities resonate more strongly than in North Florida.

Tallahassee, situated in the middle of the Panhandle just eighteen miles south of the Florida-Georgia border, shared many of the Deep South characteristics common to its neighbors. Like other places with substantial black populations (blacks in 1950 accounted for 34 percent of Tallahassee's population), Florida's capital city maintained close ties to a past that encompassed a slave-based plantation economy, a racist ideology, resistance to new attitudes, and a distrust of change. Above all, Tallahassee was a dual society, built on the presumption of white superiority, with laws and customs designed to perpetuate racial inequality.

Tallahassee, like other southern communities, was governed by a close-knit group of white men—attorneys, landowners, bankers, and businessmen—who controlled its economy, determined its politics, and guarded its social mores. Along with these so-called golddusters, the small city comprised middle-class "hominy huskers," working-class "depot greasers," and—at the very bottom, of course—blacks. Ignored by most whites, black society in Tallahassee was also stratified. By the early 1950s, Tallahassee supported a small black middle class of state workers, educators, clergymen, and independent entrepreneurs who were the leaders and spokespersons for the black community—three-fourths of which worked at low-paying, unskilled jobs.

Blacks in Tallahassee breathed the same air, read the same newspaper, paid the same taxes, shopped the same downtown stores, endured the same sweltering summers, and enjoyed the same mild winters as whites, yet they lived separate, unequal, and distinctly disadvantaged lives. Educated at underfunded and overcrowded schools, paid low wages, denied service at restaurants, barred from public recreational facilities, required by law to sit at the back of the bus, relegated to separate drinking fountains and restrooms, denied treatment at the municipal hospital, excluded from the library and other public facilities, shut out of the city's political and civic organizations, mistreated by the police, derogated by politicians, denied equal protection of the law, stereotyped by the newspaper, and forced to live in a restricted area of town, blacks enjoyed few of the choices and almost none of the privileges of their white neighbors.

Yet small and significant changes occurred in the early postwar years that fostered at least the perception of broader participation. Tallahassee, the seat of government for Leon County and the state, had moved away from the agrarian economy that dominated other Panhandle communities. The powerful city commission increased from three members to five, polling hours stretched from eight hours to twelve, and the insularity of the small town (population 27,237 in 1950) was yielding before an influx of newcomers who arrived to teach at the two universities or to fill the growing ranks of government jobs. Between 1950 and 1960, Tallahassee's population increased by 77 percent.

State government expanded employment opportunities for both white and black citizens, and the two universities, one black and one white, provided a social and intellectual counterpoint to the area's conservative mentality. Leon County's legislative representatives typified orthodox southern politicians. But the governor of the state, LeRoy Collins, a native and a resident of Tallahassee, was known as a progressive—someone whose vision looked out of the past to a future connecting Florida to the rest of the nation.

Yet many trappings of the small southern enclave clung to Tallahassee. These included a "good old boy" police department headed by a chief who sold eggs from the back seat of his patrol car and was rumored to sell moonshine in the dry county; a newspaper editor who, though not southern born, voiced the reactionary, paternalistic attitude of the majority of his readers; an antiquated judicial system that kept tight jurisdiction over local matters; and above all a society that imposed rigid segregation on every aspect of life.

Blacks in Tallahassee never ceased to fear violence and with justification. Although the capital city saw fewer racially motivated assaults and murders than other parts of the Panhandle, between 1900 and 1930 Florida had the highest number of lynchings per capita in the country. Tallahassee's most sensational act of vigilante violence occurred in 1937, when two black men accused of stabbing a police officer were forcibly taken from the Leon County jail by masked intruders, who drove them outside the city limits and then shot and killed them. Such a gruesome incident was considered an anomaly in Tallahassee. But wherever blacks lived, in Tallahassee or elsewhere in Florida, they experienced the same types of discrimination found throughout the South, and racial violence lurked close to the surface well into the postwar years.

In 1956, after years of acquiescence to laws and customs designed to reinforce racial inequality, blacks in Tallahassee attacked one of the most visible and humiliating symbols of racism in the city, the segregated public transportation system. Beginning with a citywide bus boycott—the third to take place in the South and arguably the most successful—Tallahassee's 10,000 black citizens united in an indigenous, nonviolent protest against segregation and persevered in their demands despite overwhelming opposition from whites. More important, the boycott was sustained without the considerable outside financial and moral support that poured into the more famous boycott in Montgomery, Alabama. To civil rights supporters throughout the nation, Tallahassee was proof that Montgomery was not an aberration and that black demands for full participation in American society would spread across the South, even into its small cities.

Tallahassee's bus boycott unleashed forces that for fourteen years would permeate the town, encompassing its institutions, its organizations, and the relationships between its residents. Few entities were spared the effects of legal challenges, direct action, mass protests, and individual acts of defiance, all seeking to wrest power from the exclusive control of whites. The struggle often took unexpected twists and turns, adopted different strategies, and absorbed new partners but was always reemerging. Blacks in Tallahassee sometimes united in the fight against inequality. At other times they were fractious and undecided about leaders, tactics, and expectations. At times, blacks underestimated the determination of the white community and its ability to preserve its hegemony and protect its interest. Small concessions made by whites to avoid social or economic disruption were occasionally mistaken for harbingers of change. Fresh manifestations of whites' naked duplicity periodically reinvigorated black protest. However, the struggle for black equality, never a linear, uninterrupted movement, was fueled by a constant belief in its inevitability.

good descrip

As in many other southern communities, new and more assertive black leaders emerged during the mid-1950s and early 1960s in Tallahassee to replace the black spokesmen who had personified the politics of black deference. Many new leaders were recent arrivals, and those who were longtime residents typically held jobs independent of white control.

While black protest did fundamentally change during the boycott in Tallahassee and afterward, one period of black activism cannot be said to have followed ineluctably from another. Still, it would be a mistake, as Adam Fairclough observed in Louisiana, to conclude that the direct action demonstrations of the postboycott era were unrelated to the black protests of the early postwar period.[2]

In Tallahassee, beginning in the 1930s, the local National Association for the Advancement of Colored People (NAACP), led by John G. Riley, investigated, documented, and protested the abduction and/or lynching of blacks throughout North Florida. In the late 1930s, the organization filed a successful pay equalization suit for teachers. By the mid-1940s, Tallahassee blacks had begun to petition the city government for specific benefits: better recreational facilities, improved housing, better treatment on the municipal buses, and funds for a black hospital. Finding themselves only marginally successful working alone, blacks enlisted the help of sympathetic whites to entreat favors from the city government. By 1952, after an eight-year campaign, a coalition of black and white ministers had persuaded the city commission to hire black policemen. Black protest had evolved into what one participant remembered as "appeals to the better element of the community to do things for us."[3]

The leadership that emerged during the 1956 bus boycott promoted a dramatic shift in the city's race etiquette and changed forever the way in which the two communities interacted. This shift stunned whites, who claimed that Tal-

lahassee before the boycott had been blessed with two staples of southern my-
thology, contented blacks and "good race relations." The boycott empowered
many blacks whose jobs kept them from publicly attacking the racist system
underpinning their community. Led by the Inter-Civic Council (ICC), a cross
section of ministers, businessmen, and professionals, the boycott gave voice to
an entire subordinate community and national exposure to its most effective
spokesman, Charles Kenzie (C. K.) Steele. Later, as first vice president of the
Southern Christian Leadership Conference (SCLC), Steele forged a link between efforts in Tallahassee and the national struggle for black equality. Unlike
many nationally known civil rights leaders, Steele never moved from the city
where he came to prominence or left the church he came to lead in 1952.

Just as the Tallahassee bus boycott played an important role in the early days
of nonviolent mass protest, students at Florida A&M were the nation's first sit-
in protesters who chose to serve out their jail sentences rather than accept bail.
Although the sit-ins originated in Greensboro, North Carolina, students in Tallahassee helped bring national attention to direct action as a significant, disrup-
tive weapon against segregation. Their decision to go to jail in protest against
segregation in March 1960 highlighted the harshness of southern race relations
and helped fuel interest in the civil rights movement across the country.

For the next three years, Florida A&M students led sporadic demonstrations
against segregation in Tallahassee with a fervent belief that courage, faith, and
reason could overthrow white intransigence. They were wrong. They nonetheless refused to concede defeat even after their belief in the goodness of America
had repeatedly been shaken and their trust in whites nearly destroyed. In 1963,
after a dramatic protest demonstration at the city's segregated theaters, student
demonstrators were convicted of willful trespass. When the verdict was later
upheld by the U.S. Supreme Court, it was the first time since the sit-ins began
that the high court had upheld the convictions of civil rights demonstrators.

Today, almost forty years after the sit-ins, it is difficult to imagine how virulent racism was in Tallahassee or how dangerous it was to challenge. Like their
counterparts in other cities with a black college or university, Tallahassee students were the "militants," the soldiers in the local struggle. Although FAMU
had an active student chapter of the NAACP, the city's direct action protest
strategies were initiated by the Congress of Racial Equality (CORE) established
at Florida A&M in 1959. CORE's foothold in Tallahassee was important. Few
chapters existed outside of the North and the border states in 1959. The presence
of a confrontational, interracial civil rights organization in North Florida, no
matter how small, boosted the morale of blacks throughout the South.

Two sisters, Patricia and Priscilla Stephens, both students at Florida A&M,
quickly emerged as leaders of CORE and as spokespersons for movement

activities and strategies at a time when women rarely served in either position. Virtually no civil rights activities in Tallahassee from 1959 to 1964 occurred without the participation of at least one of these two young women. Remembered by a FAMU dean as "the bravest blacks I have ever known," the sisters kept the movement in Tallahassee alive even when jail sentences and school suspensions dampened the demonstrators' spirits. Patricia Stephens stands "head and shoulders above anyone concerned with human rights in that little southern city," Richard Haley, a national officer of CORE, wrote of Stephens in 1964. "To the segregationist she symbolizes unbending pressure, the puzzling willingness to suffer, then return again to press. To the Negro community she symbolizes their greatest hope for the future." Glossed over in accounts of civil rights activities in the South and slighted in books about CORE, the story of the Stephens sisters affords an example of the inadequate treatment of women in civil rights literature.[4]

Women often stood at the forefront of the civil rights movement in Tallahassee—the arrest of two FAMU women students who sat next to a white woman prompted the bus boycott—but the struggle knew no gender, age, or even racial bounds. From the beginning, white students from Florida State University (FSU) were involved in civil rights organizations and activities. Though few in number, they, and later white faculty from FSU, were part of one of the earliest and most lasting interracial movements in the South.

Not only outsiders but a few white locals supported the black struggle for equality, swiftly earning the antipathy of their neighbors. The outsiders' support and participation, however meager, was important. It underscored the fact that in Tallahassee, as in many southern communities, there was widespread though by no means unanimous white opposition to black advancement. Indeed, in this community, as in many other areas, officials—city and county commissioners, the mayor, the city manager, local law enforcement officers, school board members, and judges—provided the most vehement denunciations of the civil rights movement, reflecting perhaps the mind set of their constituents but certainly not rising above it.

The active participation of whites in boycotts, pickets, and demonstrations delighted national officials of CORE, who remained deeply involved in the affairs of the local affiliate. Although CORE never had a large membership, it was the principal direct action organization in Tallahassee. The NAACP provided ongoing legal counsel, advice, support, and participants in a wide range of civil rights issues and court cases, as it had for many years.

The NAACP was constantly under attack in Florida by powerful whites who accused it of fostering racial divisions, supporting the overthrow of the government, and encouraging the spread of communism. Attacks increased after the

1954 school desegregation decision in *Brown v. Board of Education* and peaked two years later when the state legislature created the Florida Legislative Investigation Committee (FLIC) to examine the role of the organization in the Tallahassee bus boycott. The scope of the investigation quickly grew—no human rights organization was safe from the committee's scrutiny—but its attack on the NAACP never relented. Florida did not officially outlaw the NAACP, but because of persistent harassment and threats by the FLIC, the organization's membership dwindled, its treasury was drained, and its leaders diverted. Still, the NAACP maintained a significant presence in the civil rights movement in Tallahassee, particularly during the sixteen-year battle to desegregate the public schools.

Despite Steele's position in the SCLC, the organization did not intervene in Tallahassee during any civil rights protests as it did in Albany, St. Augustine, Birmingham, and Selma. Consequently, the city never received the national exposure of those "hot spots," but neither did Tallahassee experience the violence that wracked some areas targeted by SCLC or the disillusionment that affected the movement in Albany and St. Augustine after SCLC leaders pulled out.

Several local civil rights groups sprang up in Tallahassee, as well as affiliates of other human rights organizations, and despite some competition and internal dissension, they worked fairly well together. There was never a formal split between white and black members within the major civil rights organizations in Tallahassee as there was in some areas in the South, but a few separatist organizations committed to affirming "black power" gained a brief foothold in the community in the late 1960s. Later, black neighborhood community associations joined with the old civil rights groups to campaign for racial equality.

In 1964, after years of protest, Tallahassee was no longer totally segregated. But the community remained a bastion of racial inequality. The reasons were the city's Deep South, small-town heritage and a lack of interest in change on the part of those controlling the town. As a "government town," the business community in Tallahassee depended less on outside capital for economic development than did some cities in the New South where social disorder jeopardized investment growth. But local businessmen were not immune from financial pressure, as when a united black community forced a showdown between the bus company and city government in 1956, and later, when hurt by the lunch counter sit-ins, some merchants grudgingly supported the desegregation of those facilities. While businessmen never took the initiative in promoting desegregation, they were less hostile to the idea than the city's public officials. By 1963, the airport, the bus terminals, and lunch counters at the national chain stores had been integrated. Most locally owned stores, however, remained segregated until passage of the civil rights bill in 1964.

As William Chafe noted with reference to Greensboro, whites in Tallahassee managed, without substantial violence and within the bounds of apparent "civility," to make minimal concessions while maintaining absolute control of power and resources in the community. The paternalism that dominated white discourse—the "concern" for blacks, the dedication to their "welfare"—belied fierce resistance and an angry refusal to yield more than minimally to avoid disorder and maintain a facade of peaceful decorum.[5]

As we know, however, the effects of protest in Tallahassee and elsewhere in the South eventually brought the issue of race to the forefront of the nation's conscience and onto the federal government's agenda. Over the impassioned opposition of Florida's legislative delegation, the 1964 Civil Rights Act became law. Segregation was legally dead, and the road to black political participation was opened.

Upon passage of the Civil Rights Act, and of the Voting Rights Act the next year, Tallahassee's struggle for racial equality entered a new phase. The days of dramatic, inspiring demonstrations against legal segregation had ended. For many blacks, the public schools—a last bastion of white retrenchment and the symbol of two separate and unequal societies—had become the target of civil rights activism. School desegregation was a long, frustrating battle in court. But the stupefying procedures, dry legal opinions, maddening delays, complicated rulings, and subtle subterfuge could not mask efforts by the school board and district court to thwart integration and could not obscure the courage of the first black children who violated the "sanctity" of white schools.

After final integration of the schools in 1970, some of the benefits of the long civil rights struggle became palpable for blacks. Other benefits remained illusory. Like many southern communities that supported an active protest movement, Tallahassee failed to fulfill the hopes and bright promises of the movement. Employment inequity, economic subordination, and political powerlessness became the new civil rights issues that defied easy solutions in Tallahassee and across the nation. Yet despite the limitations of the civil rights movement, it prepared the way for a future that is still unfolding.

Four decades after the bus boycott, black life and race relations in Tallahassee have significantly changed for the better, especially in the voting booth, in the courtroom, and in the classroom. Many problems persist. But if Tallahassee, as the nation, has yet to achieve racial equality, the mid-century movement for civil rights underscored both the promise of protest and the pain of what is yet undone.

1   A Long, Long Step Toward Victory

On Saturday, 26 May 1956, three students from Florida A&M University boarded a crowded city bus for a short ride into downtown Tallahassee. Excited about an upcoming dance at the university, they planned to shop for patterns and materials to make new dresses for the special occasion. After dropping their dimes in the meter, one of the young women walked to the back of the bus and joined the other standing black passengers. Instead of following their friend, roommates Wilhelmina Jakes and Carrie Patterson sat down next to a white woman in the long, three-person seat behind the driver.

Cities Transit bus driver Max Coggins glanced in his rearview mirror and was startled to see the two black women sitting next to a white woman. Coggins turned in his seat and told Patterson and Jakes to move to the back of the bus. Jakes, who had previously sat at the front of the bus when there were no white passengers aboard, refused to move. Rising from her seat, she told Coggins that she and Patterson would leave the bus if their fare was refunded. The driver kept the money and again ordered the women to the rear. When the pair refused to comply, Coggins drove to the nearest service station, ordered all passengers to remain seated, and called the police.

Patterson and Jakes watched in amazement as three cars full of policemen arrived on the scene. The arresting officer told the women that if they wanted a ride so badly, he would give them one—to jail. At the police station Jakes and Patterson were charged with placing themselves in a position to incite a riot. They were told that they could make one phone call to arrange for bail and that otherwise they would be held behind bars.

Trembling, Patterson called a friend, who unfortunately was not home. As she lifted the receiver to make another call, a policeman snapped at her, "I said you could only make one call." At that moment, the friend who had remained at the back of the bus walked through the crowd of policemen and asked to talk to Jakes and Patterson. The two women asked her to call the counselor for off-campus students at Florida A&M, who in turn told Edna Calhoun, the dean of women, that Jakes and Patterson were in custody. Calhoun called Moses G. Miles, the dean of students, who went to the jail and posted a twenty-five-dollar bond for the women's release.[1]

When the bondsman arrived, he immediately asked Patterson and Jakes whether they were members of the Communist Party or whether an organization had paid them and "put them up" to sitting on the bus. They politely replied that no, they had merely wanted to sit on the bus rather than stand. Irritated, the bondsman launched into a lecture on proper race etiquette in Tallahassee. "Now even if I wanted to marry you girls I couldn't," he told Patterson and Jakes, "because you are black and I am white." Jakes assured the bondsman that they were not interested in matrimony but did want to leave the police station as soon as possible. After receiving further instructions in southern race relations, Jakes and Patterson were finally allowed to leave in the custody of Dean Miles.[2]

The next morning, J. Metz Rollins, a Presbyterian minister in Tallahassee, picked up the Sunday paper and stared in amazement at the front page. As he read the account of the women's arrests, Rollins felt a surge of hope and anticipation. Was there a chance that Tallahassee's black community might react with the same spirit and determination that had inspired the Montgomery bus boycott five months earlier? As a black minister in a denomination that was predominantly white, Rollins was well acquainted with both the white and the black communities in Tallahassee; consequently he feared that any anger over the arrests would eventually fade into resentment.

While Rollins prepared for morning services, Robert Saunders, Florida executive secretary for the NAACP, was meeting with Charles Kenzie Steele, a Baptist minister in Tallahassee and president of the local NAACP. Saunders, who lived in Tampa, had been contacted Saturday evening by a reporter who picked up the arrest story on the United Press wire service. Saunders immediately called Roy Wilkins, executive director of the NAACP, to alert him to the situation. Saunders then contacted Steele, who like most people in Tallahassee had not yet learned of the students' arrest. After speaking with the minister, Saunders flew to Tallahassee.[3]

Both Steele and Saunders thought that the young women were still in jail on Sunday morning, and the two men went downtown to post bond. Upon discovering that the students had already been released, the two men visited Jakes and Patterson at their home. Steele and Saunders voiced admiration and support, but no plan for an organized protest was discussed. Although Saunders had been told by Wilkins that he could "pledge the full support of the NAACP to do something about this situation," Tallahassee was considered "a weak civil rights town" by the national office and was thought to be incapable of sustaining any type of effective protest.[4]

The thirty-five-year-old Saunders, a native Floridian, had been involved in civil rights activities since his youth in Tampa. In 1952, after years of volunteer work for the NAACP, he was offered the position of state executive secretary to replace the slain secretary Harry T. Moore.

Moore, one of the state's most outspoken critics of racial violence, had spearheaded the campaign in the 1930s to win equal pay for black teachers, had launched voter registration drives under the banner of the Florida Progressive League and the NAACP, and had fought against discrimination and intolerance in Florida. On Christmas morning in 1951, he and his wife were killed when a bomb exploded in their home in the east central Florida community of Mims. Forty-five years later, the Moores' murders remain unsolved.[5]

NAACP membership in Florida plummeted after Moore's death. When Saunders took over the post, the Florida NAACP had only 1,500 members. Despite the organization's nonconfrontational methods of attacking segregation and racism—largely in the courtroom and through political protests to elected officials—to most whites the NAACP meant communism, revolution, foment, or at least "uppity" blacks. Consequently, most Tallahassee blacks did not openly support the organization.

While most Tallahasseeans spent their Sunday evening with little thought of Saturday's disturbance, Patterson and Jakes, whose address appeared in the paper, were crudely made aware of their growing notoriety. Around 5:30 P.M., after talking with George Thurston, a local reporter, about their arrests, Jakes answered a knock at the door and saw a cross burning near the house. Frightened, she phoned a male friend at Florida A&M, who came and brought the two women to the campus for safety.

That night, university president George W. Gore convened a selected group of student leaders, faculty members, and deans at his home. James Hudson, the university's chaplain, later recalled that Gore was "not at ease with what happened." Although he was very much concerned about the young women's situation, Hudson said, Gore had the interest of Florida A&M at heart and hoped "that somehow this incident might be contained."[6]

But the time had passed for containment. Students who had heard of the arrests held their own meeting Sunday night and decided to hold a campuswide rally and protest on Monday morning. Posters and flyers were made and were quickly distributed across the campus. To prevent further retaliation by whites, university officials instructed Patterson and Jakes not to attend the rally. No blacks outside the Florida A&M campus were contacted about the student meeting.

Early in the morning on Monday, 28 May, Reverend Rollins received a phone call from a FAMU student who told him to come to Lee Hall, where he would find something of interest. When Rollins arrived on campus, he found the auditorium filled with students. No professors or administrators were in sight. Broadus Hartley, president of the Student Government Association, angrily recounted the events of the last few days. The students quickly decided that the arrest of the two women constituted an affront to the entire university and that "they did not want to be humiliated any more." After a brief discussion, the students decided that "in light of recent events in Montgomery" they could do nothing less than boycott the city buses for the remainder of the school term. After singing the alma mater, the students poured out of the auditorium onto the campus.[7]

As the meeting ended, Daisy Young, at work in the nearby admissions office, heard a loud commotion and ran to the balcony of the building. Below she saw hundreds of students rushing onto the thoroughfare that ran through the heart of the university. When the first bus came through, students blocked it and asked all black passengers to get off and not to ride the buses until further notice. The passengers complied. The next bus to come through the campus, followed by a police car, was empty. Within twenty-four hours, a cross section of the Tallahassee black community offered support and leadership, but there would probably never have been a Tallahassee bus boycott if FAMU students had remained in their classes that Monday morning.

As in Montgomery, the catalyst for the Tallahassee bus boycott was the courageous defiance of women who refused to obey the laws of segregation. In Tallahassee, however, unlike Montgomery, there had been no recent arrests on the buses or plans to boycott the transportation system because of racial indignities. While Rosa Parks was actively involved in the NAACP, neither Jakes nor

Patterson belonged to the university's NAACP chapter or to any other civil rights organizations. The two young women seemed genuinely stunned that their actions had caused such a turmoil in the community. Jakes said she had felt "real upset that they were treating us like criminals . . . , like we weren't human beings." She and Patterson both decided simultaneously that no matter what the price, they could not walk to the end of the bus.[8]

Whatever may have compelled Jakes and Patterson to defy segregation laws, their decision ultimately altered race relations in Tallahassee. Both women found themselves subjected to threats and unwanted press attention even after they had returned to their homes for the summer break. Jakes's mother, who lived in Ft. Lauderdale, was afraid to let her daughter leave the house. Patterson also received threats by phone and through the mail at her family home in Lakeland. Ironically, both Patterson and Jakes came back to Florida A&M University for the summer quarter because they felt that they would be safer at the university than in their own communities. The two women were escorted around campus by university officials to shield them from possible retaliation.

By the morning of Tuesday, 29 May, the student-sponsored boycott had received substantial local news coverage, but in general, white leaders, city officials, and Charles Carter, a spokesperson for the bus company, seemed little concerned that the movement would spread to the larger community. Malcolm Johnson, editor of the *Tallahassee Democrat,* wrote that the two students "may have been impelled by a misunderstanding of what the United States Supreme Court ruled was their right in intrastate bus seating." The young women could hardly be blamed because the Supreme Court was so "vague," Johnson added. Furthermore, their dimes should have been refunded to avoid an "embarrassing, volatile incident." The most disturbing element in the whole situation, Johnson noted, was the "statement of the President of the Tallahassee Chapter of the NAACP that the boycott will be carried beyond the campus."[9]

Indeed, by Tuesday, the adult black community had begun to mobilize. Steele, a member of the black Ministerial Alliance, and James Hudson, the alliance president, decided to discuss the student boycott at the organization's regularly scheduled meeting that day. Attendance at the midday meeting swelled because of interest in the students' boycott and because Steele and Hudson had asked other prominent blacks who were not members to attend. Black businessmen and educators were among those who joined the ministers to debate the best course of action.

The group quickly reached a consensus that the existing segregation policies and practices of the bus line and city were humiliating and morally wrong. The bus company operated under a franchise similar to those of bus companies in many southern states, but the interpretation of the applicable ordinances varied in each community. The Tallahassee ordinance required the bus company to "make and enforce reasonable rules and regulations providing for the segregation of the human races when more than one race is transported on the same bus." The most obvious rule prohibited whites and blacks from sitting next to one another. Black riders sat from the rear of the bus forward to a white painted line, and whites sat in front of the line. Particularly galling to blacks were the requirements that they stand when a front row double or triple seat was occupied by one white person on predominantly black routes and that a black passenger had to relinquish a seat to a white passenger if the bus was full.[10]

Although the bus boycott had already started, a minority of blacks at the meeting were opposed to endorsing it at all, while others favored supporting the students as long as the boycott did not extend beyond the confines of Florida A&M University. As the debate dragged on, Rollins grew impatient and walked out several times. "It took us two hours to do what the students had done in twenty minutes," he later lamented. When the last opposition to the boycott was finally defused, the group appointed a delegation of nine men, headed by Rollins, to discuss their grievances with the city manager, Arvah Hopkins, and Charles Carter.[11]

The delegation was instructed to convey the committee's support of the boycott and to register general complaints about the treatment of blacks on the buses. The committee met first with Hopkins, who said he could do nothing about the situation without first consulting with the five-member city commission. In a brief separate meeting, Carter insisted that his bus company operated under a franchise and was bound by the city ordinance that mandated segregated public transportation.

The dismissive attitude of both Hopkins and Carter reflected more than just white paternalism. The committee, which had brought no written grievances to the meeting, admitted that it felt uncomfortable speaking for the whole black community and was wary of presenting specific demands at that time. Rollins told Hopkins and Carter that the committee would return later after meeting with a more representative number of blacks. In fact, a mass meeting to discuss the boycott was already scheduled for that evening at Steele's church.

Word of the meeting spread quickly. By 8:00 P.M., 500 people had jammed into Steele's church to hear the diminutive minister recount the events of the last few days. By the time he had called for a voice vote to support the student boycott, the outcome was in little doubt. In the emotionally charged atmosphere, the audience unanimously agreed to include all of Tallahassee in the boycott. A committee was then appointed to develop a set of demands to present to the city and to the bus company. The demands (soon dubbed the three-point plan) were: (1) seating on the buses would be on a first come, first served basis; (2) blacks were to be courteously treated by white drivers; and (3) blacks were to be hired to drive predominantly black bus routes.

Another important result of the night's meeting was the decision to create an organization to represent the black community during the boycott. Originally, both Steele and Saunders had believed that the NAACP should lead any organized boycott effort, but many local blacks feared that the organization's radical reputation among white Tallahasseeans would hamper negotiations with city officials. Others felt the need to "get the pressure off the people who somebody in the power structure could call the next day and say, 'listen, if you want to do so and so, you keep quiet.'" It was these blacks, among them professors and administrators at Florida A&M or Lincoln High School, who were known to whites as the leaders and spokesmen of their community. For years they had patiently and quietly negotiated with city commissioners and prominent citizens for funds or resources to improve conditions for blacks in Tallahassee.[12]

One Florida A&M professor and veteran of such polite protests, M. S. Thomas, suggested that an umbrella organization should be formed to direct boycott operations. The result was the Inter-Civic Council (ICC), the first protest organization in Tallahassee to represent a cross section of Tallahassee's black community: professionals, ministers, small businessmen, laborers, housewives, teachers, and domestics. Officers were elected and committees appointed, but anyone who came to the meetings and participated in the discussions was considered a member of the ICC. Officers and spokespersons were expected to consult with this body before issuing statements or negotiating with the city.

Although there were no women officers or spokespersons within the ICC, women did have important roles as members of the organization. Gladys Harrington, a FAMU employee, was its secretary. She was responsible for taking notes during meetings and for typing and editing press releases for the newspaper. Daisy Young provided clerical services for the ICC and served as a link between Florida A&M students and the boycott leaders. The venerable "mothers," prominent black women within the black churches, were placed in charge of raising the money to keep the boycott and the ICC alive. Other women were active as organizers and in more traditional roles as background support. Indeed the boycott would depend upon black women, particularly domestic workers, many of whom had difficulty getting to work without the buses and some of whom were fired for supporting the boycott.

From its inception, the Tallahassee bus boycott was influenced by the ongoing, well-known boycott in Montgomery. Not only were students and local blacks aware of the historic event, but the ICC was modeled after the Montgomery Improvement Association (MIA), which was leading the bus boycott in that city. The two organizations adopted identical demands. Tallahassee boycotters also embraced MIA's commitment to "nonviolence," a term not widely used or understood in 1956. Both organizations acted as voices of the black community, but their officers took responsibility for formulating and articulating the grievances and demands of the boycotters. Although differences between the two boycotts later emerged, whites in both cities claimed that local blacks were being coerced and led by outside agitators who had come to town to unsettle the city's "good" race relations.

C. K. Steele was elected president of the ICC. Four other clergymen, King Solomon Dupont, David Brooks, Metz Rollins, and James Hudson, the chaplain at Florida A&M, were elected officers. Grocer Dan B. Speed, mortician Elbert W. Jones, barber Eddie Barrington, and dentist M. C. Williams formed the rest of the executive committee. Apart from Hudson, ICC board members were self-employed businessmen or clergymen who were not economically dependent on whites. Not one of them was among those considered by whites to be spokesmen or leaders of the black community. And unlike an earlier generation of black leaders whose livelihoods as teachers and professors had depended on white patronage, ICC board members were less vulnerable to white retaliation and less willing to yield to traditional race etiquette. Whites were quickly unsettled by what they perceived to be a change of leadership and tone within the black community. As Malcolm Johnson succinctly noted two decades later, "the preachers took over from the teachers." [13]

At forty-two years of age, Steele had been in Tallahassee four years when he was thrust into a leadership position in the bus boycott. A native of Bluefield, West Virginia, Steele had spent most of his childhood in a nearby company town of U.S. Steel and Coal Corporation, where his father had been a brakeman on the motorcar that went down into the mines. The senior Steele's position was considered more skilled than that of most black company workers who loaded coal underground for one dollar a carload. Throughout his childhood, Steele's father, who had never attended school, was determined that his son would finish high school and college and would never work in the coal mines.

From earliest childhood, the young Steele had a consuming passion for preaching. Donning his long black overcoat, the boy climbed on the back of trucks or onto tabletops or chairs and regaled his family and friends with Bible lessons or sermons he had memorized from church or revival meetings. Even before he was baptized at age ten, his mother had nicknamed him the Preacher. In October 1929, when Steele was fifteen years old, his parents gave in to the boy's pleading and allowed him to preach his first sermon inside a church. That same year, Martin Luther King Jr. was born.

Steele and King first crossed paths some years later when Steele was attending Morehouse College in Atlanta and King, still a child, was winning oratorical contests sponsored by the Atlanta Baptist Sunday School's Baptist Training Union (BTU) Convention. After graduating from Morehouse in 1938, Steele moved to rural northeast Georgia, where he spent a restless year as minister of Toccoa Baptist Church. In 1939, Steele accepted the ministry at Hall Street Baptist Church in Montgomery, Alabama. Except for a four-year stint at Springfield Baptist Church in Augusta, Georgia, Steele remained at Hall Street until 1952, when he came to Tallahassee's Bethel Missionary Baptist Church. Four years later both Steele and King were the leaders of bus boycotts that were separate but similar.

Steele was obviously influenced by the Montgomery bus boycott. He referred to it in later years as "the handwriting on the wall for the South" and called Tallahassee's boycott "a little Daniel who came along and interpreted that handwriting." He greatly admired King for his ability to articulate black grievances and for his "impact on the great evils in the world." Steele regarded King's leadership in Montgomery as a catalyst for action. "Martin made the world hear," Steele recalled. "When he spoke, I spoke."[14]

Tallahassee was important to King and to other civil rights leaders for many reasons. In particular they were concerned to know how the boycott would end and what effect it would have on any other protests. In May 1956, only Montgomery had an ongoing civil rights boycott, and there was no guarantee that it would succeed. Tallahassee proved that Montgomery was not an aberration, that blacks could organize a sustained protest effort. But whether blacks in either city would succeed was still very much in doubt in the spring of 1956. There were still observers within and outside of civil rights circles who doubted the efficacy of attacking segregation outside the courtroom.

To help boycotters in Tallahassee, the MIA sent the Inter-Civic Council a cash donation. King himself came to the city to offer support and counsel on at least one occasion. Because of the hostile atmosphere in Tallahassee, King was ushered in and out of Steele's church in secrecy to avoid fueling white accusations that the boycott had been masterminded by outside agitators.

The national NAACP maintained a strong presence in Tallahassee throughout the boycott and sent the ICC $1,500 — its first donation — immediately after the boycott began. Director Roy Wilkins was ready to send the check to the local NAACP chapter, but Steele, who worried that the money would not arrive safely if it came into town addressed to the NAACP, asked him to send it via the black Atlanta Life Insurance Company, which was located in Tallahassee. Saunders stayed in Tallahassee during the initial negotiations with the city, and the NAACP continued to offer advice, legal counsel, and money to the organization, but local leaders were clearly capable of organizing and leading their own boycott and wanted to do so. Indeed, both Steele and other ICC leaders insisted that the Tallahassee boycott was an indigenous, independent movement with demands that exceeded those developed by the MIA. "Montgomery was not a spark plug for Tallahassee," Reverend K. S. Dupont declared years later. "Tallahassee was its own spark plug." It soon became obvious to Tallahassee whites that the boycott, regardless of its origins, leadership, support, or outcome, was only the first step toward change in the city's race relations.[15]

Even though the veneer of racial harmony shattered at the beginning of the boycott, Tallahassee whites maintained that the majority of blacks were content with segregation and would be back on the buses within a matter of days. Meanwhile, members of the ICC formed a transportation committee to ensure that boycotting blacks could get to work. They elected Dan Speed as chairman of the committee that one week later coordinated a carpool of sixty-five volunteer drivers. According to the "ICC Diary," riders were instructed on 10 June at a mass meeting not to pay drivers but to make "contributions" directly to the ICC, which would reimburse the drivers. Such advice suggests that from the outset boycott leaders were aware of city and state laws regarding transportation systems and took precautions to avoid legal retribution or confrontation with authorities.

It was of course impossible to avoid confrontation. Despite warnings from the ICC about the importance of observing all traffic regulations carefully so as to "avoid this expense on the part of the council," carpool drivers were repeatedly stopped by local police for routine traffic offenses. Steele, like King in Montgomery, was one of the first to be arrested. He was charged with speeding and running a stop sign on 30 May 1956. Unwilling to go to jail, Steele paid his thirty-five-dollar fine and continued driving in the carpool. Steele came to believe that the arresting officer, rookie Burl Peacock, had been chastised by chief of police Frank Stoutamire, who he felt wanted to keep publicity and martyrs to a minimum.[16]

Stoutamire, who described himself as a "law and order man," had become police chief in 1953, after serving as Leon County sheriff for over thirty years. Well known by blacks and whites alike, in part for his successful egg business and his tolerance of numerous violations of the county's dry ordinance, Stoutamire never had the reputation of being a harsh southern sheriff. Instead of relying on police brutality or public confrontations with blacks to undermine the boycott and later civil rights protests, Stoutamire chose to harass blacks more subtly and continuously through increased police surveillance, bogus arrests, and infiltration of black organizations. In Tallahassee, the decisions as to how to stifle civil rights activities were most often made behind closed doors, in the courtroom, and at meetings, not in the streets or in front of television cameras.

Perhaps in an effort to minimize the boycott's significance, the cases of Wilhelmina Jakes and Carrie Patterson were turned over to officials at FAMU, and the city dropped the charges against the two young women. Stoutamire told reporters that the action had been taken after a long-distance telephone conversation with city judge John A. Rudd, who was out of town. Although Stoutamire explained that the judge's decision was "routine" in cases involving college students, some blacks felt that Rudd had deliberately denied the ICC the chance to turn the incident into a "test case" in federal court, as had been done in Montgomery.[17]

But Jakes and Patterson had been arrested for inciting a riot, not for violating a segregation ordinance. In order to challenge Tallahassee's segregation laws in court, blacks needed a plaintiff to challenge segregation laws and the white community directly. Few people were willing to incur such risk. To engage in a protracted legal battle took not only money but also experienced, competent legal counsel. The NAACP was already involved in two major school desegregation suits in Florida, and the likelihood that a local segregation ordinance would be overturned in court seemed remote to many in the NAACP and the ICC.

Years later, Steele insisted that he had opposed filing a suit because the Montgomery case (which was already in federal court) would eventually settle all local segregation ordinances dealing with transportation. But the outcome of the Montgomery case was unknown in the spring of 1956, nor was it clear that judicial rulings that prohibited local segregation laws would end similar practices in other areas. Indeed, in April 1956, the Supreme Court upheld a federal court ruling striking down segregated seating on the city buses in Columbia, South Carolina. That ruling was ignored by officials in Montgomery. More important, in the first days of the boycott, it was not clear that Tallahassee blacks were ready to demand integrated seating on the buses.

During the first week of the boycott, there was no direct communication between the ICC and city officials. The local press reported details of the boycott and what was said each night at the mass meetings. City commissioners met and discussed the boycott but said little about it in public. Meanwhile, the ICC offered no written explanation of what "the right to be seated on a first come, first served basis" meant. By avoiding the term "nonsegregated seating," blacks gave whites the impression that a compromise over seating was possible. Indeed, the first come, first served policy was already being followed in several large southern cities; it meant simply that passengers of one race were not required to relinquish their seats to passengers of another race. Passengers of different races continued to be prohibited from sitting next to one another.

In their first public statement, black leaders said that they wanted a policy whereby "Negroes would not have to stand if seats were available." Bus manager Carter said there would be no changes in the seating policy until city ordinances mandating segregation were revoked. The bus company could not hire black drivers, he explained, because the city segregation ordinance forbade it. As for the ICC's request that bus drivers be more courteous, Carter maintained that his drivers were instructed to be polite to all customers, a remark that "amazed" blacks, most of whom could "relate some humiliating, embarrassing, degrading experience on a bus." City commissioners refused to comment on ICC demands before receiving them in writing.[18]

With negotiations nonexistent, editor Malcolm Johnson called for the formation of "a committee of leaders of both races to sit down and talk out these problems and difficulties as they arise and head off incidents instead of letting them become inflamed." Johnson took the idea for such a committee from Gilbert Porter, executive secretary of the segregated Florida State Teachers Association, who made the suggestion at a meeting of the association. Porter, who was the former principal of Lincoln High School, was a man well known by white leaders as a spokesperson for the black community. Johnson and Porter agreed that the "situation calls for responsible action by all citizens of both races."[19]

The next day "an unofficial committee" that included Porter, two ICC members, a white minister, the president of the Tallahassee chamber of commerce, and a white businessman met to "bring about formation of a permanent interracial council here to solve problems between the races at their outset by peaceable and orderly means." Any hope that the group would have an ameliorative effect on the boycott vanished when they agreed not to get involved because the bus boycott was a situation that had already "developed." Tallahassee's first interracial committee never met again.[20]

While they railed against the boycotters in private, commissioners were forced to take the boycott seriously because blacks had formerly constituted nearly 80 percent of bus patrons. With approximately 90 percent of the black community boycotting the city buses, revenue was sharply curtailed.

On 1 June, attorneys for the city and the bus company met with ICC lawyer Theries Lindsey in an "exploratory conference" to clarify the issues in dispute. Lindsey, a recent graduate of Florida A&M University Law School, was assisted in the case by NAACP attorney Francisco Rodriguez of Miami. Circuit court judge Ben C. Willis represented the city in the absence of attorney James Messer, and Charles Ausley of the prestigious Tallahassee firm of Ausley and Ausley represented the bus company's interest. Neither side would comment on the meeting except to say that the real sticking point was the seating provision. Specifically, what did the ICC mean by "first come, first served"? Lindsey announced that written demands would be presented to the city commission during its next special meeting.

Later in the same day, Ausley called Malcolm Johnson and asked him to convene a delegation of black leaders to discuss the situation with attorneys for the bus company. Such closed-door meetings were typical in Tallahassee. Indeed, blacks had discovered years before that few political decisions of any significance were ever made in Tallahassee without consulting a small number of prominent men in the community who might or might not be elected officials at the time. Although Johnson was not a native of Tallahassee (he was born in Idaho and lived in Canada before moving to Florida), he wielded as much influence in the community as elected commissioners and perhaps more. He readily agreed to convene the meeting in the offices of the *Democrat*.

Johnson telephoned Porter and asked him to bring three other people to the meeting. When Porter arrived that afternoon with thirteen black leaders, many of them members of the ICC, Johnson and the other whites were stunned. Instead of working out a compromise, the black delegation surprised Johnson and Ausley by insisting that the original resolution, including the ambiguous three-point plan, would stand until after another scheduled mass meeting.

Although the meeting in Johnson's office failed to resolve the boycott and did not undermine the leadership of the ICC, city commissioners resolved to make a final attempt to deal with the boycott behind closed doors. On Saturday, 2 June, commissioners met privately in the Capital City Bank with fifteen blacks of whom only one, Episcopal priest David Brooks, was a member of the ICC executive committee. Despite the secrecy surrounding the sub rosa meeting, word of it began to circulate in the black community.

Steele, who was out of town, returned to Tallahassee late in the evening of the same day without knowing of the meeting. The next morning, Steele preached a sermon on Judas Iscariot and the theme of betrayal. Members of the congregation thought that Steele was referring to the blacks who had attended the Saturday meeting. As a result, these people, many of whom had been well regarded in the black community, were labeled traitors.

Most blacks believed that Brooks, a close friend of Steele's, had told him about the meeting and had named the individuals who had attended it. Steele publicly and privately denied that Brooks had done so. Nevertheless, Florida A&M coach Alonzo ("Jake") Gaither, one of Florida's most popular personalities, refused to believe that Brooks had not told Steele of the Saturday meeting and was so incensed by what he considered Brooks's treachery that he refused to speak to the Episcopal minister for over a decade.

On 3 June (one day after the secret meeting), the city's proposals for ending the boycott appeared in the *Democrat*. In their "official statement," commissioners noted that a strict policy of courtesy to all bus passengers was already in effect. Second, contrary to what Carter had said, the employment of black bus drivers was a matter of bus management and did not involve the city franchise. Third, the bus manager had advised the city that it would begin to receive applications for such employment, "and in the event of a vacancy will give all such applications due consideration."[21]

Commissioners announced that they had agreed to a new "franchise interpretation," whereby they could accept the ICC's first come, first served principle. To commissioners this statement meant specifically and only that "no member of either race must give up his seat on a crowded bus to another race." The commissioners refused, however, to permit members of the two races to share a double or triple seat. In other words, blacks would have to stand if all other seats were taken except those next to a white person. Furthermore, black passengers on the two predominantly black routes would have to stand if a lone white passenger sat on the last vacant double or triple seat. Commissioners expressed their "hope that the controversy will be promptly terminated so that [bus] service may continue and that the tension may be eased and there be restored the harmonious and cooperative spirit between White and Negro citizens which has made this a progressive, happy community."[22]

When word of the city's position became public, ICC vice president Reverend King Solomon Dupont called the proposal "a step toward agreement." In the evening of the same day, 3 June 1956, approximately 1,000 blacks crowded into Steele's church for an ICC meeting and listened while Dupont explained the city's position. Before a vote could be taken on the city's proposal, Steele rose and announced that he would no longer accept segregation of any kind on the buses.[23]

Taking the podium, the minister castigated the city's compromise position and announced that from that point onward, black Tallahasseeans "want to sit anywhere they want to sit on the bus if they pay their fare, otherwise, they're willing to walk." The crowd voted unanimously to reject the city's plan. The ICC executive committee drafted a statement that called the segregated seating arrangement "economically unsound, humiliating, arbitrary, inequitable, inconvenient and morally unjustifiable."[24]

The individuals who attended the meeting approved a resolution (presented the next day to the city commission) insisting on the right of all bus passengers to "sit wherever they choose on any bus or busses." It demanded that all bus drivers constantly be reminded of their "never ending obligations to render courteous service and equitable treatment to all passengers regardless of race, creed, or color" and asked that the bus company hire black drivers. The resolution implored commissioners to make a "morally right decision" and add "new laurels to Tallahassee's illustrious name." Years later, Steele recalled that Tallahassee's demands at the meeting had exceeded Montgomery's. This recollection was partly true. Although the MIA still held to its original "modified segregation" demand, MIA attorneys had filed suit against bus segregation in

Mongtomery four months earlier. On 3 June, however, the outcome of the suit was still unknown.[25]

Commissioners in Tallahassee were not moved by the ICC's plea for moral leadership. Commissioner William (Billy) Mayo accused the organization of "ignoring the existence of segregation laws." Although it was clear that not riding the bus was a hardship for most blacks, Mayo told the *Democrat* that the bus company should not be required to continue running buses on a line where the passengers "do not wish to ride," but he hoped "the Negro citizens can settle this [dispute] among themselves and not be guided by outside influences."[26]

Editor Malcolm Johnson charged that the leaders of the boycott "have been unreasonable and have used ill-advised procedures" while engaged in "a struggle for leadership with more moderate elements of their race." He agreed with Mayo that the bus company had nothing to gain by operating empty buses and that perhaps "suspension or outright cancellation of the service will remove a source of strife and let things cool off."[27]

At their 4 June meeting, city commissioners refused again to alter the bus franchise. They took ten minutes to reject the newest ICC demands that called for "full integration" of the buses. Then they discussed a petition received from Cities Transit that described the losses being sustained by the company in the overall operation, particularly on the two predominantly black FAMU and Frenchtown routes. The petition asked for permission to discontinue the now unprofitable routes, and the city quickly agreed. The company's request came less than one week after bus manager Carter had told black leaders that he was not at all concerned about the possible loss of black bus patrons.

On 5 June, one day before the FAMU and Frenchtown routes were canceled, a panel of three federal judges struck down Montgomery's bus segregation ordinances as unconstitutional. News of the court's decision infused the Tallahassee black community with renewed faith in their own boycott. Just as the *Brown v. Board* decision had inspired hope among blacks throughout the South, this latest court action made racial progress everywhere seem inevitable.

On 6 June, Steele told the ICC that the new federal court ruling was a "long, long step toward victory in the war in which we are engaged with a great giant." Few knew that evening how long the journey would take or how formidable the giant could be.[28]

2   To Walk in Dignity

Although Tallahassee city commissioners remained opposed to bus desegregation after the federal ruling, they, like many southerners, cared less about seating arrangements on buses than they did about the consequences of admitting that segregation was morally and legally unjustifiable. White Tallahasseeans feared that the least capitulation to black demands would inevitably lead to the end of all segregated institutions and to the breakdown of all racial barriers. Unwilling to admit that local blacks were unhappy with segregation, whites accused outsiders and northern instigators of stirring up trouble and disrupting the town's good race relations.

The conspiracy theory was frequently propounded in the *Tallahassee Democrat* as the boycott wore on. Editorials denounced the "so-called leaders" of the black community who were influenced by "outsiders" and by NAACP "agitators" who sought fame and glory at the expense of racial harmony. Most whites refused to recognize that the more militant black leaders now spoke for much of the black community.

The fear of change, the reluctance to question long-standing beliefs and traditions, and the comfortable familiarity of a shared past and culture made it easy for whites to view the ICC and the boycott as threats to the social fabric of their community. But there was at least a precedent, however limited, for those who did not subscribe to a parochial view of the world. In the late 1940s, two organizations formed in Tallahassee and gave whites who were interested in international affairs an opportunity to meet and discuss concerns such as world peace and cooperation among nations. One was a branch of the World Federalist Organization, and the other was the Liberal Forum.

The prominent citizens of Tallahassee who belonged to or participated in the activities of the World Federalist Organization included Senator LeRoy Collins and Supreme Court justice B. K. Roberts. But by the mid-1950s, the school desegregation decision in *Brown v. Board of Education* had generated a red-baiting atmosphere throughout Florida. There remained little tolerance in the state for organizations that supported "interdependence" among countries and a stronger United Nations and World Court.

By the late 1950s, the only organization for whites with divergent political and social views was the Tallahassee Council on Human Relations. The council was a chapter of the Florida Council on Human Relations, an auxiliary of the well-known Southern Regional Council, which conducted research and held seminars on southern race relations. The Tallahassee Council on Human Relations was Tallahassee's first integrated civic organization. Council members (many of whom were FSU and FAMU professors) did little more than meet and discuss Tallahassee race relations, but the fact that black and white citizens were gathering on an integrated basis somewhere in the city was news in Tallahassee. The activities of the Tallahassee Council on Human Relations went largely unnoticed by townspeople because the group never took a public stand in support of the boycott or tried to intervene as a group on the boycotters' behalf.

Two council members who did more than merely discuss race relations were Clifton and George Lewis, members of two of Tallahassee's oldest and most respected families. George Lewis was president of the Lewis State Bank in 1956 when the boycott began. His energetic wife, Clifton Van Brunt Lewis, a former May beauty queen in Tallahassee, was prominent in numerous charitable and civic organizations. Because of their long tradition of attending musical and cultural events at Florida A&M University, and their participation in the Council on Human Relations, the Lewises were well known to blacks in the community.

When raising money for bail, fines, and other financial emergencies became a serious problem for boycotters, black leaders went to Lewis to ask for his help. As a result, blacks were able to go to the Lewis State Bank at 7:00 A.M., before normal business hours, to borrow or withdraw money from the bank to help finance ICC operations. When all other lending institutions closed their doors to black protesters, the Lewis State Bank remained open. George Lewis personally intervened to provide financial support for blacks who left Tallahassee after the boycott. Along with a few local whites, the Lewises continued to support black civil rights actively and were both privately and publicly contemptuous of intolerance and racism in Tallahassee.

Although the boycott and the ICC met with an enthusiastic response among blacks in Tallahassee, solidarity was elusive. To some blacks, the leaders of the boycott were jeopardizing the gains achieved during years of patient compromise and conciliation: a modicum of security and comfort within the confines of racial segregation. To take a non-negotiable stand against segregation, to challenge the foundation of southern society, seemed unnecessarily risky, even foolhardy. Consequently, white officials continued to turn for help to the well-known blacks who "had lived here long enough to realize that everybody, blacks and whites, were moving too fast." [1]

M. S. Thomas, who started the vocational education program at Florida A&M University, maintained years after the boycott that when he and other well-known blacks were seen talking to the city manager or commissioners, the rumor would spread that they were working behind the scenes to undermine the ICC. In reality, Thomas recalled, "we were using some of the techniques that had been worked out for a long time." There were no "Judases" in the boycott, Thomas insisted twenty-five years later. He and other older blacks were always a part of the bus boycott planning but remained quietly in the background doing the "basic thinking." [2]

But after Steele's speech on betrayal and the identity of those blacks who had met secretly with city commissioners on 2 June became public knowledge, older spokesmen like Thomas began to lose their leadership status. Two decades after the boycott, Steele was still saddened by the role that his sermon had played in creating a division in the black community. According to the minister, one of the members of the Saturday delegation, George Conoly, lost his business in Tallahassee as a result of a withdrawal of black patronage following the sermon.

Conoly, a member of the NAACP since the 1930s, a founder of the Tallahassee Civic League, and a member of the Council on Human Relations, was hurt and confused when he was labeled an "accommodator for the City of Tallahassee" in an article published in 1960 by two Florida sociologists. Conoly, who was teaching at Florida A&M at the time, could point to years of civil rights work in Tallahassee before the boycott. He was one of a very small number of blacks in the late 1940s and early 1950s who petitioned the city commission to support the hiring of black policemen and the improvement of black recreational facilities. He was a member of the Tallahassee NAACP in 1951, the year Harry T. Moore, then executive director, was murdered in his home.[3]

But Thomas's and Conoly's past contact with influential whites might have kept them from fully grasping the extent of blacks' determination not to compromise on the issue of full integration. ICC leaders considered Thomas, Conoly, and other conservative blacks "Jefferson Davis negotiators" who no longer spoke for the black community.[4]

As June wore on, city revenues and bus company profits continued to drop. Finally, on 12 June, the city commission granted a five cent fare increase to the bus line and began legal action to lower the amount of franchise tax paid from the company's profits. Before they agreed to reduce the tax, city commissioners stated publicly that they lacked the authority to alter the company's franchise. Now it appeared to the black community that commissioners were constrained only by their prejudices. As profits continued to drop, company officials became less concerned with desegregated seating and more concerned with financial solvency. The commissioners, however, remained firmly opposed to the seating demand, which they considered more important than a loss in city revenue. Thus, division between profit and policy began to drive a wedge between the bus company and the city.

With the loss of bus service hanging over their heads, city commissioners blamed the gridlock in negotiations on blacks who supported "complete integration." Malcolm Johnson called on the white people of the community to save the bus company by using its services. "A city the size and stature of Tallahassee would be handicapped in its industrial expansion program and in many other ways without bus service," Johnson wrote, "but that possibility is a definite threat."[5]

In an attempt to explain its position fully and to counter charges that the boycott was the work of outside agitators, the ICC published a full-page open letter to the community entitled "An Appeal to the People of Tallahassee for Moral Justice." Written by ICC executive board members, the letter assured whites that "the Inter-Civic Council of Tallahassee had its birth in the Church" and would always "be guided by high religious and moral principles." The letter reminded readers that black citizens were "loyal Americans" and that the current situation would never have happened "if all bus patrons were treated as Americans."[6]

On 25 June, city commissioners met at city hall with a coalition of ten prominent whites and ten hand-picked "old Negro leaders" to discuss possible solutions to the month-old boycott. Steele and Rollins, who were not invited to participate, sat with other ICC members in the audience. Commissioners, desperate to avoid the loss of the city's bus system, offered to amend the bus franchise so that there would be full integration on the predominantly black bus routes except for one three-person seat that would be reserved for white passengers only. Seats on the other routes, they insisted, would be segregated as in the past. When remarks from the floor were allowed, Steele and Rollins argued against the compromise, reasserting the ICC demand for open seating on all bus lines. The meeting ended with no solution in sight. Malcolm Johnson noted that boycott leaders "should now recognize that there will be no settlement on the basis of complete integration."[7]

Later that afternoon, M. S. Thomas, who had attended the meeting at the request of the city commission, issued a statement urging that "everything be done to keep the bus company from going out of business." He quickly added that he was not trying to reverse his race's progress, because he believed "all Negroes envision a time when they can discard their second class citizenship." Thomas urged the "moderates" of both races to find a solution. John Swilley, a professor and like Thomas a veteran of the older black leadership, told reporters that "down deep inside every colored person has the hope he can eventually be removed from second class citizenship," but boycotting a bus was "not the proper way to register a protest against something."[8]

But few blacks in Tallahassee agreed with Thomas and Swilley. Steele insisted that blacks were not blindly following a few "radical" leaders, as had been repeatedly suggested by the newspaper and city officials. "Nobody led the people off the buses," he insisted, "they came off themselves." In what would later become the rallying cry of the boycott, Steele said that blacks would rather "walk in dignity than ride in humiliation." Rollins, speaking at a mass meeting that same night, said he was tired of hearing about all of the things that had been "given the Negroes. The Negro has not been given anything that was not rightfully his," he said, and he wanted nothing more than "his just rights." He, for one, Rollins insisted, "would rather see the bus company go, than go back to a 'Jim Crow' system."[9]

Despite some internal dissension and defections, the boycott continued. More and more blacks saw their participation as a symbol of unity against white oppression. Loyalty to the boycott went beyond the demand to sit at the front of the bus; it symbolized a challenge to all the laws, customs, and traditions that imposed intolerable indignities. Most ICC leaders were educated men who had achieved some prominence within the community, but the boycott was kept alive by average citizens who had never made a speech or challenged a rule.

Such a person was Laura Dixie, who attended the first mass meeting and belonged to two committees of churchwomen working diligently to raise funds for the ICC and to keep the black community apprised of developing events and ICC strategies. Dixie was born in Chaires, Florida, a small community ten miles east of Tallahassee. Like many rural black children, she grew up playing with her white neighbors while her family enjoyed cordial relations with local whites. It was not until she was in elementary school that Dixie grasped the cruel and puzzling realities of southern segregation.

Day after day, she and some of her eighteen brothers and sisters walked miles to the local black grammar school. As they walked down the dusty country roads, the yellow school bus passed by, carrying her white neighbors to another school. Dixie's older sisters had to live in town with another family in order to attend Tallahassee's Lincoln High School. She was not angry at the time, Dixie recalls, but merely curious.

In the early 1950s, Dixie's curiosity about segregation turned to anger. As a mother, Dixie was resentful that her daughter rode the bus to a segregated school miles from home. She joined the NAACP in Tallahassee but remained essentially inactive until a specific encounter with bus segregation turned her into an activist. On the way home from work one day, several years before the boycott, Dixie boarded a city transit bus and sat down beside a good friend whose complexion was very light. Mistaking Dixie's friend for a white woman, the bus driver insisted that Dixie leave her seat. When she refused, he threatened to call the police. When the driver became more and more agitated, Dixie's friend calmly informed him that she knew Dixie and that, furthermore, she was not a white lady. Chagrined, the driver returned to his seat and drove on. Dixie got involved in NAACP activities.[10]

For Dixie and thousands of Tallahassee blacks, taking a stand against segregation was something they had to do. Nevertheless, as the months passed and the boycott continued, the protesters' unity was seriously challenged. If white leaders could not cajole people into riding the bus, they could and did intimidate those who depended on paychecks signed by white bosses. At the same time, by following, stopping, or arresting blacks participating in the carpool, the police maintained a steady harassment of the protesters.

By 30 June it was public knowledge that the bus company would shut down the next day. In the evening the ICC held a spirited meeting. In his address, Steele told cheering blacks that the transit company had chosen to shut down rather than "perform that which is economically sound, morally right and democratic." Later, plans to seek a franchise for a profit-making transportation system were discussed. Reverend Dupont assured council members that six station wagons, twelve drivers, a secretary, and two dispatchers would provide an adequate transit system for the city's 10,000 blacks. In response to a reporter's question, Commissioner Mayo said he had not "the faintest idea" whether an application for a franchise would be granted or denied. The commission issued a public statement regretting both the loss of bus service and the "fine Negro leadership" of the past, which had been replaced by a group "many of whom are newcomers to Tallahassee and who apparently have no feeling or responsibility to the community, the general public, or even members of their own race."[11]

City commissioners did more than complain about "newcomers" to Tallahassee. During June and July, the police department conducted an exhaustive investigation of the ICC and its leaders that eventually led to the infiltration of the organization. Chief investigator R. J. Strickland coordinated the inquiry. The "Confidential Report" containing "City Secrets not to be released without the approval of said officials and the Chief of Police" revealed how desperately the city worked to discredit ICC leaders, to fan dissension within the black community, and to link the boycott to Communist influences.[12]

Central to the report were the background investigations of C. K. Steele and attorney Theries Lindsey. The most controversial fact uncovered about Lindsey was that he had once been employed by the New Deal's National Youth Administration, which connection "may or may not be significant," Strickland wrote. "A similar bus boycott in Montgomery, Alabama, receives great support from the *New Southerner*," Strickland noted, "a publication edited by Don West, a well-known Fifth Amendment Left Wing Writer and published by Aubrey Williams, a former Director of the National Youth Administration and connected with many Communist front organizations." Strickland reported that he had recently seen West in Tallahassee. He provided a detailed biography of West and described the labor organizer's activities.[13]

Strickland provided even more detailed information on Steele whom he personally interviewed "under suitable pretext." The minister told Strickland that "this bus seating had a particular meaning to Negroes and that they have given it great and complete support." Moreover, while "many had suggested a compromise those who made the suggestion were booed down at a meeting." Steele told Strickland that blacks "do not intend to give in [on the] issue and will continue to insist that they be treated equally and without distinction."[14]

Strickland uncovered almost every detail of Steele's personal life, including his salary, his checking account balance, his credit rating, and the details of a "very expensive" car purchase, including the dates and amounts of payments. "I was unable to learn what cash he may have received on the refinancing," Strickland lamented. The Steeles, who had five children (a sixth child was born in 1960), owned no property (they lived in the church parsonage), but, Strickland noted, as a trustee of the church, the minister had negotiated a loan that had been duly repaid.[15]

The detective included the names of Steele's trustees, ICC leaders, and the minister's out-of-state contacts "for possible future intelligence purposes." During the police investigation, Strickland reported, "it was established that much of the encouragement of the boycott came from FAMU." He provided a dossier of Florida A&M employees who, according to "a confidential informant," were "rabid for integration and [were] encouraging students to take part in it." Interestingly, the ICC leadership had already identified three of the men—George Conoly, M. G. Miles, and John Swilley—as "conservative" blacks. Strickland included a separate memorandum on President George Gore and his wife, Pearl Winrow Gore.[16]

When Strickland was unable to turn up any negative information on Steele from an investigation of "credit reports, police records, veterans affairs, and marriage records," Chief Stoutamire directed him to go to Montgomery, where Steele had previously lived, and to conduct an investigation of the minister's activities in that city. Strickland provided Stoutamire with a report on the Montgomery Improvement Association, Martin Luther King, and other boycott leaders in that city. While "Communist influence is felt in the Alabama boycott," Strickland wrote, "it is clear that the boycott is not Communist in its present personnel nor in its appeal to Negroes." He provided a list of Communists known to the Alabama authorities whose mission it was to "foment Negro unrest." Strickland returned from Alabama with detailed information on other "subversive" organizations, including the Southern Conference Education Fund, the Southern Conference for Human Welfare, and the "Moslem Cult of Islam."[17]

At the conclusion of the lengthy report, Strickland provided a number of recommendations to the city that were specifically designed to undermine the bus boycott. The twenty-one recommendations were divided into categories directed to the legislature, the police department, the Tallahassee City Commission, and the press. The majority of the recommendations dealt with destroying the ICC carpool through state legislation governing such operations. Meanwhile, Strickland advised the city to set minimum requirements for operating motor pool activities that would clearly place the carpool in violation of the law. At the same time, he recommended that the police intensify their surveillance and harassment of drivers. The city was advised to subpoena all bank records related to the carpool while preparing "pretrial examinations of Steele, Speed, Hudson, *et al* to learn the extent of their participation and the extent of their operations." Meanwhile, "no further dignity should be accorded the Inter-Civic Council by granting it any recognition as the leader or spokesman of the Negroes." Finally, the press should "play down the trouble" and issue "conservative releases slanted to show concern for the public in the operation of unsafe and uninspected vehicles."[18]

While the city prepared for an ultimate showdown with the ICC, the buses stopped running. Meanwhile, the ICC's transportation continued to flourish even without a franchise. As summer wore on, criticism of the boycott, and the NAACP, became more intense. Governor LeRoy Collins publicly castigated the national organization: "If it [the NAACP] is interested in advancing the welfare of Negro citizens it should concern itself with other conditions of far more importance than where people sit on a bus. There are so many things which need to be done for the benefit of the Negro before it [desegregation] becomes possible." Collins's attitude was common among whites: once blacks proved they were worthy of being treated like citizens in a democracy, they would be accorded the rights of citizenship. This paradoxical logic, blaming blacks for their subjugated position in society but opposing their actions to transcend it, stymied meaningful racial dialogue and social progress.[19]

Many blacks in Tallahassee had the custom of going to town on Saturday to shop and meet with neighbors and friends. During the first week of July, police began to accuse groups of black shoppers of loitering and admonished them to move on and to clear the sidewalks. Steele found these tactics another subtle way of harassing blacks because of the carpool. On 8 July, Steele suggested that the bus boycott expand to include the city's business community. Steele accused the police of trying to run blacks out of the downtown area. They do not realize, he said, "that we are in town not to break laws, but to pay bills and give business and patronage [to] stores that are friendly to us. . . . If they continue their police intimidation it will finally become necessary for us to stay out of town and make other arrangements to other cities to spend what little money we have to spend."[20]

Three days later, when Steele walked into a mass meeting, the entire audience stood and applauded for over five minutes. "Every coward in the world should have been there to see how much the people love a man who stands up fearlessly for what he believes is right, and speaks his real sentiments irrespective of the cost," one participant wrote afterward. "In general, the people are very proud of their ministers."[21]

While Steele encouraged blacks to boycott unfriendly merchants, ICC member and FAMU professor Edward Irons urged the ICC to form a voter registration drive in the black community so that the city commission could be "called to account for its conduct." Thus the boycott began to assume a more multifaceted nature as it slowly evolved into a loosely organized movement.[22]

ICC members agreed that they must find some way to take their demands into the courtroom if permanent change was to occur. Steele hesitated to attempt a "test case" in Tallahassee over bus seating until the Supreme Court had ruled finally on the Montgomery bus boycott. Its decision, he reasoned, would settle the matter once and for all. Steele, like King before him, had grown to appreciate the value of civil disobedience. During mass meetings in late June 1956, blacks debated the possibility of using "civil disobedience as a technique for eradicating tendencies to relegate us to a subordinate position." Steele himself seriously considered "accepting jail instead of bail" but chose instead, along with the rest of the ICC, to "continue the protest as we are doing." To most adult blacks in Tallahassee, jail was not a place where leaders, thinkers, and money raisers could work effectively.[23]

On 10 July, after a joint meeting with members of the Tallahassee chamber of commerce, the commissioners announced that they would no longer negotiate "under any circumstances" with black leaders and that a new campaign inaugurated by white civic leaders to get the buses moving on revised routes was making "encouraging progress." On the same day, the commission denied the ICC a franchise to operate any kind of transportation system.[24]

Although the police could effectively thwart the progress and continuity of the carpool by harassing and arresting drivers on minor traffic violations, city officials searched for a permanent, legal way to break the operation. City attorney James Messer announced that a study of the carpool's operation showed that it violated state laws governing "public carriers." Even though passengers were not charged regular fares, Messer contended, the carpools were supported by contributions from passengers. Therefore the operation came under the laws governing "for hire cars." According to Messer, the ICC was violating state ordinances that required the drivers of public carriers to have special licenses, insurance, and tags. He asked Attorney General Richard Ervin to review the ordinances and issue an official opinion.

Despite continued threats, ICC members voted to continue the boycott. Theries Lindsey told participants, "As long as you're driving your own car, buying your own gas and picking up your friends and neighbors, I don't know of any law you're violating." Meanwhile, the police, apparently waiting for Attorney General Richard Ervin to confirm Messer's interpretation of the carrier law, stopped arresting carpoolers but continued the investigation.[25]

Tempers flared during the month of July as more and more ICC drivers were stopped, taken to the police station, questioned, and often forced to sign statements regarding council activities. Steele lambasted the police for "subjecting blacks to the 'third degree' for what were previously considered minor traffic violations." Chief Stoutamire denied any wrongdoing by the police department and maintained that officers were "just trying to do a job." On 2 July, a freelance photographer from *Life* magazine found a window in the building where commissioners were meeting, lifted his camera up to the sill, and snapped three pictures. Chagrined commissioners chased the photographer down in the street and made him destroy the film.[26]

Rancor abounded in the capital city in July as the Florida legislature met in a special session called by Governor Collins to devise ways to retain school segregation in Florida in light of the 1954 and 1955 school desegregation cases in *Brown v. Board of Education*. Collins, who had recently won a bitter Democratic primary against three more conservative opponents, had managed to avoid extreme racist rhetoric during the campaign without appearing to compromise his opposition to desegregation. Thus his election (a primary win was tantamount to election in the state) was considered a victory for racial moderation in Florida.

Disturbed by the drastic measures enacted by some southern states to defy the high court's desegregation decision, Collins was determined that the legislature would not lead Florida into "massive resistance." When the committee he had appointed to devise ways to "avoid race mixing" in the schools presented its recommendations, Collins believed he had found a legal way of avoiding integration for years.[27]

At the heart of the committee's segregation package were recommendations to strengthen the state's pupil placement law. First enacted by the 1955 legislature after the second *Brown* decision, the law authorized county school boards to assign pupils on the basis of "the health, good order, education and welfare of the public schools." Revisions to the law (including one that authorized school boards to classify students according to intellectual ability) breezed through the 1956 legislature. Lawmakers also passed a law prohibiting the integration of school faculties and granted the governor the power to proclaim a state of emergency and to use law officers to suppress disorder that might arise as a result of the desegregation "crisis." Once these laws (based on the committee's recommendations) had passed, Collins was ready for the legislature to adjourn. But lawmakers were not in a cautious frame of mind in the wake of the Tallahassee bus boycott and the school desegregation decisions.[28]

After a closed-door meeting with Tallahassee city commissioners on 24 July, Leon County representative Kenneth Ballinger announced that he would introduce a bill to outlaw unlicensed carpools during transportation boycotts. Legislation to make it unlawful for a state employee to take part in an organized boycott was introduced by another North Florida representative. Neither proposal passed. Other bills, including one to replace public schools with private ones, were debated (but were not enacted) by legislators determined to take an aggressive posture against the threat of desegregation. In one of the most far-reaching decisions of the 1956 legislature, lawmakers established the Florida Legislative Investigation Committee (FLIC) to delve into the "subversive activities" of the NAACP.

The idea for creating such a "watchdog" committee had been proposed three years earlier by senate president Charley Johns (author of the original pupil placement law) to investigate crime and gambling in the state. The measure was opposed by then governor Dan McCarty, Senator LeRoy Collins, and other legislators who were concerned that the adverse publicity would hurt the state's lucrative tourist trade and that such a committee could have legal repercussions and might lead to covert "witch hunts." But by 1956, statewide fears of integration outweighed constitutional issues or moral concerns. Governor Collins allowed the FLIC act to become law without his signature, in effect giving it his tacit approval. Although the new committee was given broad authority to investigate any organization (or individuals) that threatened the safety of Florida's residents, it was quickly dubbed the "NAACP Investigation Committee" by the press.

Two of the first people interrogated by Detective R. L. Strickland of the Tallahassee police, now the committee's chief investigator, were the originators of the bus boycott, Wilhelmina Jakes and Carrie Patterson. Both were summoned to the capitol in September 1957 and were asked whether a Communist organization or the NAACP had put them up to defiance of the segregation laws. When they denied this association, Strickland asked whether they could have gotten "such ideas" from having attended Bethune-Cookman, a historically black private college in Daytona Beach with a small integrated faculty. Unable to prove a conspiracy theory, Strickland ended his interrogation and took Jakes and Patterson on a tour of the capitol. He showed the two women where "democracy in action" took place. Neither was ever approached by the press or harassed by local whites again. Jakes graduated from Florida A&M in December 1957, and Patterson, the following June.[29]

The FLIC seemed the least of Collins's worries during the summer of 1956. Increasingly alarmed by the reactionary mood of several North Florida legislators, the governor repeatedly urged lawmakers to be reasonable and judicious and to limit any local legislation to matters of "real emergency." When it appeared certain that an interposition resolution (an attempt to declare the Supreme Court decision unconstitutional and of no effect in Florida) would pass both chambers despite Collins's opposition, the governor seized upon an arcane constitutional provision and dismissed the legislature. Stunned politicians accused the governor of chicanery, but many Floridians breathed a sigh of relief at the close of the special session.

Collins's actions revealed his distate for racial demogoguery, but more important, they reflected his fear that racial unrest would derail the state's economic development and expansion. But the governor's heart was still ruled by his southern roots, which often brought him into conflict with his vision for Florida's future. Even as he attempted to moderate the passions of lawmakers, Collins inflamed the angry mood in the capitol by denouncing boycott leaders as "outsiders" and statewide desegregation efforts as "a miscarriage of ambition."[30]

Collins's criticisms and accusations did little to dampen the spirits of the boycotters. The spirits of city commissioners however, were considerably dampened when the chamber of commerce and bus company management insisted on negotiating an end to the boycott. On 30 June, city commissioners told ICC leaders that they would amend the bus company franchise, permitting the company to employ black drivers for predominantly black lines. Furthermore, as they had earlier promised conservative blacks, the new franchise would permit open seating on predominantly black lines except for "a three passenger seat in front reserved for white patrons."[31]

The ICC was now in a difficult position. Conservative blacks urged members to compromise with the city commission to end the boycott, which was hurting poor working people more than anyone else. Steele, who was under increasing pressure from some members of his own congregation, agreed. The ICC countered with a proposal that black drivers be employed by the bus line within thirty days and that the ongoing seating controversy be decided by a committee of twelve white and twelve black members selected by the council.

Stunned, the city rejected the compromise. Commissioner Mayo explained that commissioners had done "everything we know how to do to approach the problem with ideas that would be acceptable to the white population of Tallahassee as well as the colored which certainly at this time do not include integration." Mayo struck a familiar theme of whites when he said that black leaders "proved they didn't want the boycott settled. They were determined to keep the boycott going."[32]

Bus company president Stetson Coleman declared that the boycott was "a put up job, an un-American activity." He chastised Tallahassee blacks for following the leadership of "relative newcomers who will no doubt move along someplace else," leaving more "moderate, old-time Negro residents holding the bag." But "the Negro who once accepted his seat at the back of an empty bus with humility has children who are moved back there now with a genuine sense of humiliation," Malcolm Johnson reminded white readers. "We have failed to recognize that we have helped a race along toward cultural maturity and now it wants to stand among men." Nevertheless, he added, "first class citizenship doesn't go with a seat on a bus. . . . it is attained by good conduct, by devotion to civic responsibility . . . and by clean and moral and healthy living."[33]

In mid-July, Cities Transit's management and the chamber of commerce jointly announced that bus service would resume on 2 August 1956, with smaller buses running new schedules on new routes. Bus manager Carter announced that the old Frenchtown and Florida A&M routes would be resumed only if there was demand. Business interests simultaneously undertook an extensive media campaign to encourage white Tallahasseeans to ride the bus. Free rides, juice, and newspapers were promised to prospective patrons. The city announced that anyone riding the bus would be guaranteed police protection. Blacks were welcome to ride the bus if they obeyed segregation ordinances.

On 2 August, the buses began operating under the new reduced schedule. Shortly thereafter Cities Transit Company hired black bus drivers for the routes between Florida A&M and Frenchtown. While Steele was pleased that the bus company had met one of the demands made by the ICC, he reminded city commissioners that "the crux of the problem was the seating arrangements for passengers on the buses." As long as seating arrangements remained unchanged, they [blacks] certainly "would not be willing to settle for the jobs of the few, while the many must still ride in humiliation and segregation." On 3 August, Steele announced the results of a mass meeting held the night before. "Our people voted that they will not be herded like cattle to the rear of the bus though driven by smiling Negro drivers." [34]

As the summer drew to an end, commissioners announced consideration of an ordinance prohibiting all carpools in the capital city. Before any measure was enacted, Attorney General Richard Ervin announced that the ICC carpool was in violation of the state "for hire" tag laws, thus making it unnecessary for either the city or state to pass antiboycott legislation.

Within three weeks of Ervin's decision, eleven persons had been arrested, including almost all prominent members of the ICC. On 24 August, three carpool drivers were arrested, including Bessie Irons, wife of Edward Irons, a professor at Florida A&M. Earlier, she had been visited in her home by two policemen, who demanded that she come down to the jail for questioning. Alone at night with two sleeping children, she refused but persuaded the officers that she would "come down voluntarily tomorrow." Steele was also arrested on the twenty-fourth and then was charged on 28 August with defying the so-called carpool law. [35]

On 27 August, Lindsey asked that the cases be referred to the state courts for trial, as the defendants had been charged under a state law and not a local one. Municipal judge John Rudd denied the request and told Lindsey, "I've been running this court for three years and this is the first time I've ever had an attorney tell me how to run it; either enter a plea for your clients or I'll forfeit the bonds and order their re-arrest." Lindsey, who was under investigation by the Florida bar for his civil rights activities, entered a not guilty plea and left to prepare his case. [36]

On 2 September, the Ku Klux Klan paraded in full hooded menace past Steele's parsonage on Tennessee Street. After the parade, while blacks held "the biggest prayer meeting in the city's history," some 400 Klan members attended a rally outside the capital city's limits, where speakers denounced the U.S. Supreme Court, outside agitators, and Governor Collins. Unintimidated, the ICC stepped up its voter registration campaign.[37]

In the weeks before the trial of the carpoolers, a campaign of overt harassment against the black community continued. Police officers followed blacks to ICC meetings and took down the license tag numbers of parked cars. Local whites threw rocks through windows of parked cars and shouted insults and threats of violence through open church windows and over phones in the middle of the night. Blacks identified as leaders by the newspaper found their automobile and life insurance policies suddenly and inexplicably canceled. Despite the harassment by whites, blacks continued to make sacrifices for the boycott. Reverend K. S. Dupont remembered years later that a number of black women offered him the deeds to their homes to pay for the bonds of those who were arrested.

Although the level of commitment to the boycott varied substantially within each black church, social group, or business, perhaps no institution was so rocked and divided by the boycott as Florida A&M, the place where it had started. From the inception of the boycott, university staff and faculty were in a precarious situation. Many were among the most educated and respected members of the black community and were expected to speak on behalf of that community. Although the all-black university seemed a welcome haven from white interference or domination in the mid-1950s, FAMU, the only state-supported black university in Florida, depended heavily on the goodwill of powerful whites. No one understood the situation better than George Gore, the institution's president.

Gore had become president of Florida A&M in 1950 after William Gray resigned amid charges of fiscal mismanagement. A native of Nashville, Tennessee, Gore held a master's degree from Harvard and a Ph.D. from Columbia University. In his inaugural speech, Gore committed the university to the goal of providing an education of high quality for any black who wanted one. Although the college presidency appeared to be the pinnacle of success, Gore suffered infuriating indignities. He was not able to use the restroom, for example, or to eat meals when he met with other members of the state's board of control. But like his predecessors, Gore believed that even within the confines of racism, he could expand and improve the facilities and programs at Florida A&M. Steadfastly loyal to FAMU and dedicated to its progress and its preservation, Gore was a university president first and a civil rights advocate second.

The boycott put him in an untenable position. Throughout the protest, Gore received unrelieved pressure from influential whites to limit the participation of FAMU students and faculty in the protest. Gore was also subject to the same demands from conservative blacks, according to Professor John W. Riley, a longtime friend of Gore's. Simultaneously, blacks involved in the struggle accused the president of being an Uncle Tom because he had not taken an active public stand in favor of the boycott. One prominent alumnus came to Riley and asked why Gore did not quit his job and "get out there and lead the boycott." Other critics insisted that the president had obliged some faculty to give up their civil rights activities or resign. Gore's supporters insisted that his sympathies were with the boycotters and with future civil rights demonstrators but that his position in the community made it necessary for him to take a cautious approach to changing race relations in the South.[38]

The cautious approach manifested itself in different ways. In late September, Gore appealed to all of the university's employees to "refrain from active participation in the bus boycott for the good of the institution." Gore's statement came after an ICC news release announced that the president had told employees at Florida A&M that they must stop any bus protest activity. According to the council, Gore told faculty and staff, "either you are loyal to the University or loyal to something out there: cast your lot with this ship or get off." Gore insisted that it was not his intention to restrict the rights of any individual, "but the situation is that our relations here in Tallahassee and throughout the state have worsened steadily and we are now in a precarious position with regard to our future."[39]

The president appealed to university people who were identified with the movement and asked them to "use discretion and to consider any actions they might take with regard to the future of the university." Revealing some of the intense pressure he felt, Gore added, "Some of our most loyal friends here have been reluctant to help us now and I am frankly worried about what will happen when our appropriation requests go before the next Legislature. It behooves all of us to keep our heads to keep this ship from going under."[40]

Some university employees could not, in good conscience, curb their protest activities. Economics professor Edward Irons recalled that Gore called him into his office during the height of the boycott and told him to "stop his activities in the ICC." Irons replied that he did not represent the university at the ICC and that he conducted his boycott activities after 5:00 P.M. The thirty-four-year-old professor told Gore that he wanted to "break the chains on the minds of these students that would permit them to aspire to achievements which they couldn't do with chains on their minds." Irons, who continued to participate in the protest, left the university soon afterward along with other disgruntled faculty members who had been active in the boycott. Those who left included the chairman of the political science department and the sponsor of the student chapter of the NAACP.[41]

Clearly Gore used economic reprisals to chastise those faculty members who got out of line. Those who left the university had been offered less than token annual raises despite exemplary academic service to the university. Two university employees who did not leave and who remained active throughout the 1960s were Daisy Young, who later became director of admissions, and James W. Hudson, who served as chaplain and chairman of the philosophy department. Hudson, who held a Ph.D. from Boston University, had begun teaching at Florida A&M in 1946. Neither received more than minimal raises during the long years of civil rights protest and activities, yet both remained active in the movement and never complained of the price they paid for their commitment.[42]

Although FAMU employees were divided in their loyalty to the bus boycott, it would be a mistake to assume that the rest of the black community wholeheartedly supported the boycott or the leadership of the ICC. Some Tallahassee blacks, including members of Steele's church, accused the minister of sabotaging the safety and security of the black community. Other ministers prominent in the boycott were under similar pressure; some, like Presbyterian minister Metz Rollins, were in a particularly difficult position.

Rollins had come to Tallahassee in 1953 at the request of the Presbyterian Church U.S. (popularly known as the Southern Presbyterian Church) to organize and lead the city's first all-black Presbyterian Church. The money to pay Rollins's salary, buy the property, and build Trinity church was to come from the church's General Assembly, the Presbytery of North Florida, and the First Presbyterian Church of Tallahassee. When the boycott began, Rollins's congregation was worshiping at a black elementary school, although a piece of property for the prospective church had been purchased and plans for the new building approved. By summer 1956, Rollins's leadership role in the boycott had raised the ire of the elders of the First Presbyterian Church. When several of them demanded that First Presbyterian Minister Davis Thomas tell Rollins to quit participating in the boycott, he refused. The young minister even persuaded the session of his church to increase First Presbyterian's financial contribution to Trinity temporarily after the North Florida Presbytery had discontinued its support. To the delight and dismay of the ICC, the combined youth groups of First Presbyterian, Trinity Methodist, and First Christian churches invited Rollins in late July to speak to the young people. The speech was entitled "The Role of the Minister in the Bus Boycott."

But by the fall of 1956, with the boycott still going strong and no end in sight, support for Rollins within First Presbyterian had evaporated. When pressure intensified from both the General Assembly in Atlanta and the First Presbyterian's Negro Work Committee, Rollins began to fear for the survival of his small church. In early October 1956, he submitted his resignation to Trinity's congregation. When the members refused to accept it, Rollins transferred the membership of Trinity to the United Presbyterian (Northern Church) and continued his leadership in the boycott.[43]

Not all black ministers remained as steadfastly loyal to the boycott and the nascent protest movement in Tallahassee as Rollins and Steele. George Conoly remembered that, as in the 1930s and 1940s, some preachers clung to the old adage "politics and religion don't mix." Some ministers were "just as scared as anybody else" during the boycott, James Hudson recalled. "We never had [their] unanimous support." Regardless of one's occupation, of course, it took tremendous courage to attack segregation, but to some blacks, even those who supported the boycott, ministers like Steele could just "pack up everything they own in one suitcase and leave."[44]

Conservative blacks, particularly educators, were under the most severe criticism from within their own community. Educator Gilbert Porter was so incensed at being called an Uncle Tom that he sent Steele a telegram and asked the minister to read it aloud at an ICC meeting. "After almost twenty years of taking a forthright stand for my race, and most of the time standing alone," wrote Porter, "it strikes me as being rather queer that my position and integrity should be questioned especially by any thinking person in Tallahassee. Please let it be known that all intelligent Negroes should be fighting for the same thing—First Class Citizenship Status. We want nothing less, although we may differ on technique—never on principle."[45]

By late July, as the city commission's inquiry into the personal lives of ICC leaders continued, the police hired an informant to attend ICC mass meetings and report on the organization's activities. From 31 July to 2 September, the informant gave city officials details on the meetings, including the names of the speakers, and the amount and sources of contributions. More important to city officials were signs of growing divisiveness among blacks over how financial contributions should be handled and whether the ICC should continue to hold out for full integration in the face of increasing hardship and pressure from whites.[46]

The informant's detailed minutes revealed that Steele and Rollins kept up a steady stream of pressure throughout the summer, pleading with blacks to remain off the buses and to contribute to the carpool operations. Donations to the ICC's transportation system increased, and by mid-August the organization owned six station wagons. As the city's activities against the carpoolers increased, speakers became more vehement in their denunciations of the white community. Meanwhile Detective R. J. Strickland continued to interview ICC leaders "under pretext."

After speaking with Dan Speed, Strickland reported that Speed and others were willing to meet again with city commissioners and get the buses back on the run but that Steele opposed such negotiations. Speed told Strickland that most of the extremists were "suitcase Negroes" who had come from out of town and had no real stake in the community. Later, Speed reported his conversation with Strickland to the ICC and assured members that he had only said "what [he] wanted to hear." Speed reported that his policy was "not to let your left hand know what your right hand was doing." [47]

At a mass meeting on 26 August, Steele accused white Tallahasseeans of being "unjust to the colored race and not wanting them to have anything to raise their standards of living, [or] participate in local affairs as any citizen should be able to do regardless of race, color or creed." Three days later, the minister denounced the police department as "an organized bunch of thieves who did not know what they were doing," and accused the force of "trying to make a living off the colored people." [48]

Steele also had harsh words for the blacks who had gone back to riding the bus. He called them "fools" and asked them not to come to any more meetings or to talk among themselves as to what had transpired at the previous mass meetings. At the same time, Reverend K. S. Dupont implored the audience not to ride the bus and stated that he would "die and go to Hell before he would ride the bus again." But despite the pleas of Dupont, Steele, Rollins, and others, blacks were returning to the buses in numbers large enough to erode solidarity and undermine the ICC's no compromise stance. According to a Cities Transit operations report included in the informant's report of 12 August, an average of 288 blacks a week (including students at Florida A&M) were riding the FAMU and Frenchtown routes. Even in Montgomery the boycott was not 100 percent effective, and defections were a source of bitter recriminations in both communities. [49]

By late summer of 1956, there was growing resentment among some blacks that the ICC had not effectively used or accounted for all of the contributions it had raised. Despite the expansion of the carpool transportation system of which he was chair, Dan Speed was criticized by some blacks, including Dean Moses Miles at Florida A&M, of encouraging blacks to return to the buses. Then on 29 July, a local black businessman accused Miles of withholding $700 of an $800 donation intended for the ICC treasury. Miles, who had previously exhorted blacks to dig into their pockets for contributions, denied that he had taken the money, which was a gift from the National Baptist Convention. The weeping dean claimed that if he had been given $800, then he must have lost it.

Miles's detractors, many of whom had been clamoring for a better accounting system (which he had opposed) were not persuaded of his innocence. It took Steele's leadership to help the situation. On 2 September, Steele told the audience that there was not one shred of evidence that Miles had failed to report the total amount of the outside donation. Moreover, Steele said, the accusation against Miles could have been "influenced by the white people [who] were trying to set up a trap to break up the ICC." Although Miles had vehemently denied taking the money, Steele announced that the dean had promised to replace the $700. But even Steele's words could not silence the dissenters (several of whom were not from Tallahassee), who now encouraged blacks to return to the buses. W. R. Perkins from Griffin School said he wished that the people would "go back to riding the bus, for some of them are going hungry and naked in order to come to these meetings and give their money away." [50]

Although the informant's minutes revealed that there were both minor and significant divisions within the ICC during the tense summer months of 1956, a majority of blacks remained convinced that the ICC leadership was doing the best job possible and that Miles's situation was an unfortunate or perhaps fabricated aberration. Both the boycott and the campaign continued, although not with the unanimity of spirit so high in the spring. By late September, internal disputes had been laid aside for the more important battles still ahead.

As black leaders struggled to maintain harmony within their community, ICC attorneys worked desperately to have the charges against the ICC dismissed or at least to have the case moved to a state or federal court. Suddenly, the city commission dropped the charges of violating the state's "for hire" tag law and immediately re-arrested the eleven ICC members and other drivers for operating a transportation system without a franchise. By charging blacks with violating a city ordinance, commissioners hoped to delay or circumvent the appeals process.

Meanwhile, Steele asked Governor Collins to investigate "persecutions by the city police" against Tallahassee blacks. The governor refused on the ground that blacks had been arrested to his knowledge only for violating franchise laws and that the best place to settle any such dispute was in a court of law. Blacks, skeptical that they would find justice in a Tallahassee courtroom, awaited their trial with growing apprehensions.

In a final pretrial motion, Lindsey, now assisted by NAACP attorney Francisco Rodriguez, filed for dismissal of the case on the ground that the defendants were operating the carpool not as a business subject to city licensing but as a protest against segregation ordinances. Consequently, the defense argued, the city of Tallahassee was denying the ICC the right of free speech and the equal protection of the law. Rudd denied the motion and declared that "integration and segregation" had nothing to do with the case. The judge announced that he intended to restrict arguments to whether or not the carpool was legal and would not hear arguments regarding segregation or integration.

In a last effort to avoid Judge John Rudd's municipal court, Lindsey and Rodriguez sought a temporary order restraining the city from trying the cases. U.S. district court judge Dozier DeVane refused to grant the order on the ground that the federal court lacked jurisdiction: he did not have the right, DeVane said, "to tell Judge Rudd he can not try these cases."

On 17 October the court began hearing the city's opening arguments. The city charged that the ICC maintained a successful commercial operation that actually competed with Cities Transit. Assistant City Solicitor Mark Hawes asserted that the transportation system was "no two bit operation" but a successful commercial venture that had netted over $8,000 in three and a half months. Some of the seventy-five witnesses called by the city were ICC members, who testified that they had contributed funds to the carpool at mass meetings. Although city police testified that they never saw money change hands between passengers and drivers, Hawes hammered at the ICC drivers until they admitted accepting donations from passengers.[51]

Chief Stoutamire told the court that Dan Speed confessed to him that he was losing money by providing gas to the carpool, yet city prosecutors maintained that the ICC had made a profit while forcing a legitimate company out of business. Bus company manager Charles Carter strengthened the city's case when he testified that his company's profits had dropped from $15,000 to $9,000 per month because of the boycott.

As more and more discomfited blacks were forced to "testify against [their] people," tensions in the segregated courtroom intensified. When Hawes asked boycotter Laura Flucas about her participation in the carpool, she refused to say more than yes or no. Finally, Judge Rudd ordered Flucas to answer "yes, sir," and "no, sir," even though there was no Florida law requiring witnesses to do so. Flucas bowed her head for a full three minutes before raising it and answering faintly "yes, sir." She continued, however, to infuriate Hawes. When the solicitor asked her whether she had accepted a ride with "Bessie Irons," Flucas replied that she had ridden with a Mrs. Irons but knew no one named Bessie Irons. Her response was similar when she was asked whether she had ridden with Ralph Coleman. Rudd dismissed her from the stand and told her to wait outside the courtroom.[52]

On 21 October, fifteen minutes after the last arguments were presented, Rudd handed down his decision. The judge, who claimed to have called on "Divine Guidance to arrive at a just decision," found all of the defendants guilty, sentenced them all to sixty days in jail, and fined each of them $500. The jail sentences were suspended, but the fines of $11,000 were to be collected. Rodriguez issued a memorandum ordering the ICC to "end any car transportation activity as long as the order of the judge [is] in effect." He and Lindsey announced that they would appeal to a higher court.[53]

The following day, the ICC formally abolished the carpool but voted to continue the boycott. Steele announced that, for Tallahassee blacks, "the war is not over; we are still walking." City commissioners were still fighting, too; at a 23 October meeting, they voted unanimously to cancel the franchise of the Economy Cab Company owned by two local blacks, one of whom had served as assistant transportation chairman of the ICC.[54]

Word of the city's successful injunction against the carpool and the prosecution of boycott leaders made its way to Montgomery, Alabama. There, on 26 October, city commissioners heard from local attorney John Kohn, who represented an "interested group of citizens" who opposed the MIA's carpool. Kohn described Tallahassee's successful efforts to destroy that city's carpool and urged commissioners to seek a similar injunction against the one operated in Montgomery by the MIA. Four days later the Montgomery city commission passed a resolution ordering the city attorney to file proceedings designed to "stop the operation of carpools or transportation systems growing out of the bus boycott."[55]

Meanwhile in Tallahassee, blacks who had relied on the transportation system began to walk to their jobs. Driving his daughter to school almost a week after the trial, Steele saw an early morning procession of black domestics walking to work. "It was an inspiration to me," Steele told a reporter. "We will not go back to segregated buses."[56]

Steele tried to raise the money necessary to pay off the fines. He capitalized on the national prominence that the trial had earned Tallahassee by late 1956 in the many fund-raising trips he took. Steele traveled north to tell the Tallahassee story and ask for donations. He sometimes preached five times on one Sunday in order to reach as many potential donors as possible. It took him over five years to raise the $11,000. Years later, Steele observed that it was a lot easier for someone of King's stature to raise money than for "an insignificant little preacher like me."[57]

Although his intentions were good, Steele was criticized by some blacks in the community for being out of town whenever a crisis erupted at home. And of course some local whites later claimed that black leaders profited monetarily from the boycott and other civil rights struggles and that they used other blacks for the sake of their own selfish ends. But most black leaders in Tallahassee gained in 1956 nothing more than increased threats of physical violence, property damage, loss of income, and strained friendships and community ties.

On 13 November 1956, the U.S. Supreme Court affirmed the lower court's decision and declared that Alabama's state and local laws requiring segregation on buses were unconstitutional. In Tallahassee, Steele felt that he had been right to avoid testing the city ordinance mandating segregated bus seating before the Supreme Court ruled on the issue. But the black community underestimated the determination of Tallahassee officials to maintain segregation despite the Supreme Court's decision. Once again, local laws and customs proved as powerful as the dictates of the nation's highest tribunal.

3 In the Wake of the Boycott

Immediately after the Court issued its ruling on the Montgomery bus boycott, Tallahassee officials worked furiously to circumvent the decree and limit its impact. Federal judge Dozier DeVane told local attorneys that the highest court had made all segregation laws "deader than a doornail" but that the pattern set by recent federal court rulings had left it up to the local courts to decide "when to hold the funeral." When the Governor's Advisory Commission on Bi-Racial Problems asked attorney Lewis Hall to "discuss the Tallahassee bus situation," he replied, to laughter, that he thought "the Supreme Court had decided that for us." Not convinced, Attorney General Richard Ervin maintained that laws outside Alabama must be specifically tested before they were considered invalid. Meanwhile, Mayor John Humphress appealed to all Tallahasseeans and the bus company to cooperate in maintaining segregation.[1]

ICC leaders were unsure of their next move. During the first week in December, Steele traveled to Montgomery to attend the "Institute on Nonviolence and Social Change" called in part by Martin Luther King Jr. to prepare black citizens of Montgomery for riding on integrated buses. Galvanized by King's opening address to the gathering of southern ministers and activists, Steele returned to Tallahassee eager to test the segregated seating ordinance.

On 20 December, federal marshals delivered the final court order to Montgomery city officials to desegregate their buses. That day, King and a small group of supporters rode through the streets of Montgomery at the front of the buses. In Tallahassee the bus segregation ordinances were still in effect. But without a viable, organized transportation system, the boycott could not continue. The ICC had two options: return to the buses and obey local segregation ordinances or insist that the Montgomery ruling applied to Tallahassee.

On December 23 the organization voted to end the seven-month-old boycott and to return immediately to the buses in a "non-segregated manner." At a mass meeting that night, the ICC passed out instructions on how to conduct the move back to the buses. Like the guidelines used in Montgomery, the instructions urged blacks to "sit more to the front of the bus, rather than to the rear," promised legal assistance for anyone arrested, and advised blacks to turn the other cheek if they were struck by disgruntled whites. "Remember," the instructions warned, "the carrying out of this part of our movement can make all the steps we have walked worthwhile or not."[2]

On 24 December, teams of black ministers and leaders of the ICC boarded the buses at designated stops across town. Metz Rollins and Dan Speed were both asked to move to the rear of the bus but remained seated and were ignored. Steele and two other ministers rode another bus without incident. On the Florida A&M and Frenchtown routes, other black riders sat at the front of the bus, but according to the *Tallahassee Democrat*, "Negro domestics were riding at the rear of the bus."[3]

Furious that both blacks and the bus company had ignored the mayor's request, city commissioners sent written instructions to Cities Transit demanding that it direct its drivers to maintain segregation on the buses or forfeit its franchise. But the financially strapped company had wearied of the politics of race relations. In a startling turn of events, attorneys for the bus company asked the federal court whether the Supreme Court ruling applied to their franchise and Florida laws. Not to be outdone, the city brought suit in circuit court to revoke the company's franchise if it continued to disregard the segregation ordinance.

The conflict between city officials and the bus company escalated on 27 December when Chief Stoutamire arrested bus manager Charles Carter and nine Cities Transit bus drivers for allowing blacks to sit near the front of the bus. This was an extraordinary incident, given that the bus franchise clearly prohibited blacks and whites from sitting together but did not strictly prohibit blacks from sitting at the front of the bus if they did not sit next to white passengers.

Nevertheless, although blacks and whites had not sat together, the company's franchise was suspended by the city commission. In retaliation, the bus company sued the city for $100,000 in damages. In its suit, the bus company claimed that as a result of the boycott the daily revenue from its operations had been reduced from $550 per day to a low of $117 per day, and the company declared that any further suspension of operations would put it out of business. Federal judge DeVane issued a temporary restraining order to keep the city from interfering in the bus operation until the issue had been settled in the courts. The judge maintained that "every city and state has the right to litigate these matters," although he refused to rule on the constitutionality of the bus seating ordinance.

The ICC moved to take advantage of the split between the city and the bus company. Dan Speed, now chairman of the "Ride the Bus Integrated" campaign of the ICC, announced that groups of blacks would board each available bus that afternoon and would occupy front seats. A "front ride demonstration" was planned for the afternoon of 27 December.

But when Speed, Steele, and sixteen other ICC leaders showed up at the corner of Monroe and Park Streets to board the next bus, they found a crowd of 200 whites, many carrying poorly concealed weapons, waiting for them. Steele, fearful that bloodshed was imminent, called off the planned ride. Determined not to back down and lose the momentum gained from the Supreme Court decision, Steele decided that individual blacks would continue to test the bus policy unannounced but that there would be no mass demonstrations (and no announcements of integrated rides) until emotions cooled.

Only a few people of either race rode the buses in Tallahassee during the tense days that followed; some blacks sat in the front, others in the back. There were no public incidents. Threats of violence against black leaders and increased damage to black property set the stage for what many considered to be an inevitable tragedy.

On New Year's Eve, the Leon County White Citizens Council passed a resolution asking Governor Collins to use his new emergency powers to take control of the buses. That same evening, shotgun blasts were fired into a grocery store owned by Cornelius Speed, a cousin of the ICC leader Dan Speed. Apparently, the vandals intended to destroy the ICC leader's property, which was located in another section of town.

Shortly before midnight, bricks were thrown onto the porch of the Steele home by a white youth who fled in a waiting car. Soon afterward, the car returned, and this time rocks were hurled through the living room windows. Fearing that a bomb might follow, Lois Steele gathered the sleeping children, including a six-week-old baby, and moved to the middle of the house. Steele then went into the bedroom to peer at the assailants. As he walked down the hall, he took a Smith and Wesson revolver out of a desk drawer. Steele was determined to defend his family, but he worried that any exchange of gunfire might result in a full-scale race riot in Tallahassee. Like King, Steele had a commitment to nonviolence that was based on practical expediency as well as on religious ethics.

As the hours passed, Steele became convinced that his tormentors were content to throw rocks and hurl verbal insults at him and his family. He put away the gun, cautioning the family to keep all the doors and windows closed and curtains tightly pulled. The next day, one of Steele's parishioners told the minister that he had overheard some white men discussing the incident at a downtown store. The men had evidently been hoping to turn the rock-throwing incident into something more violent. Armed and eager, they had waited through the night for Steele to reveal his position in the house by coming to an open window or door.

It did not take long for Steele's tormentors to become much bolder. Shotgun blasts and shattered windows broke the stillness of many January evenings and terrified Steele's children. Steele and his wife left the blinds full of bullet holes hanging on their windows for years after most people in Tallahassee had forgotten the boycott. Despite fearing for his family's safety, Lois Steele remembered, her husband had refused to curtail his activities even after repeated and varied threats of violence.[4]

On more than one occasion, undertakers responded to rumors and came to the Steeles' home to take the minister's body to the morgue only to find him alive and well and eating dinner. Neighbors continually told Steele that they saw the police, not white hoodlums, fire into his home. Some people claimed to have overheard their employers discussing plans to kill the embattled minister. Phone calls at all hours of the day and night interrupted the family's routine. Instead of hanging up, Steele would often preach to the callers over the phone, telling them about nonviolence, redemptive love, and the life of Christ, even inviting them to call back after he finished his meal. Lois Steele recalled that her husband felt no animosity toward his persecutors but that she herself was bitter about the harassment of her family.[5]

Shocked by the violence that greeted the New Year in his hometown, Governor Collins decided to use his new emergency powers to suspend all bus services in the capital beginning 1 January 1957. Blaming both "irresponsible Negro Leadership" and "rabid pro-segregationists" for creating the disorder, the governor called upon both city officials and demonstrators to work toward a settlement. Disappointed, Steele accused the governor of bowing to the demands of the White Citizens Council. The ICC demanded that Collins restore bus service under "effective and forthright law enforcement."[6]

Collins insisted that his only goal was to maintain order in the capital city. "We in Tallahassee don't like the idea of having a Governor, even though he's one of us, stepping into a local dispute and closing down the bus system," wrote Malcolm Johnson, "but he acted for our best interests." The *Tampa Tribune* agreed with the ICC, however, noting that Collins's action unfortunately "gives to the [White Citizens] council an illusion of influence and power which it neither has nor deserves." The *St. Petersburg Times* asked why Collins decided to cancel the bus service rather than ordering Tallahassee police to maintain law and order. Whatever his motives, Collins's decision to cancel the buses rather than order the police to protect passengers seriously undermined the ICC's struggling desegregation campaign.[7]

On 2 January 1957, a cross was burned in front of Steele's home while the minister was attending an ICC meeting. Twelve-year-old Clifford Steele first saw the flames and helped his mother and a neighbor knock over the cross and extinguish the fire. Tallahassee race relations again received negative commentary throughout the state. Malcolm Johnson wrote that "we hold nothing but revulsion in our hearts" for the perpetrators of the crime, who might have been "a crude man with a coward's heart . . . or a youngster with a crude background." In the "current situation," Johnson added, "we might not even discount the possibility that a Negro seeking sensation might have done it to create another incident."[8]

Two weeks later, vandals found the right address for Dan Speed's store and blew out the front windows with shotgun blasts. Speed remembers that the pattern of destruction became so frequent that he and his family became resigned to it. When any of the family caught sight of a car full of whites heading for the store, they shouted to one another to take cover. Neither Speed nor any member of his family was ever hurt, but both whites and conservative blacks stopped buying from him.

Amid violence and intimidation, official resistance continued. During the suspension of the Tallahassee bus service in early January, city commissioners received word of another blow to their determination to preserve segregation. In Miami three months earlier (after rejecting a boycott as "untenable") the local NAACP had filed suit against that city for operating an illegally segregated transportation system. On 3 January, federal judge Emmett Choate ruled that Miami's bus segregation laws and those of the entire state were unconstitutional. In Tallahassee, shocked city commissioners announced that local laws would not be abandoned until a specific ruling was handed down in Tallahassee.

Four days later, on 7 January, commissioners announced the repeal of the segregation clause of the transit firm's franchise because of its "doubtful legality." In its place, they unanimously adopted a bus seating assignment plan

(Ordinance 741) to be implemented upon return of the buses. Under this plan, "obviously aimed at maintaining segregation," all seats on the bus would be reserved, and the drivers would assign seats to provide "maximum health and safety" for the passengers. Those who refused their seating assignments were subject to arrest and a maximum fine of $500 or sixty days in jail.[9]

Commissioners argued that this plan would give all citizens the right to sit where and by whom they wanted. If people, black or white, did not approve of the seat assigned, or did not like the person who sat down beside them, they could ask for their money back and get off the bus. Commissioner Mayo believed that this policy was analogous to the reserved seating policies of airlines. The ICC considered the policy to be a last-ditch effort to preserve segregation.

Indeed it appeared that once again the white community was closing ranks. On 8 January, attorneys for the bus company and the city announced that all suits and countersuits, including the charges against the nine bus drivers and the manager of the bus company, would be dropped. As in the past, whites had deftly prevented local segregation ordinances from being debated in federal court, where they might be overturned.

Steele was out of town when the city commission enacted its next strategy to preserve segregation. At the urging of activist Bayard Rustin, who had been in Montgomery during the boycott, Steele, King, and Fred Shuttlesworth of Birmingham had issued a call for a conference of southern black leaders to discuss the necessity of expanding bus boycotts and protests so as to mount a wider attack on segregation and political inequality. Meeting during the second week of January in Montgomery, the participants agreed to establish a "Southern Leadership Conference on Transportation and Nonviolent Integration" and to meet again in New Orleans in February.

Ninety-seven people met in New Orleans at the New Zion Baptist Church on 14 February. The group adopted the name Southern Leadership Conference and made plans to sponsor its first mass action event—a prayer pilgrimage to Washington, D.C.—in May. Montgomery's Martin Luther King Jr. was elected president of the conference, and Tallahassee's C. K. Steele, first vice president. Steele attended the prayer pilgrimage, which drew approximately 25,000 people to the Lincoln Memorial. Three months later the Southern Leadership Conference met in Montgomery, adopted the name Southern Christian Leadership Conference (SCLC), and announced plans to sponsor a "Crusade for Citizenship" throughout the South. Steele's stature as a civil rights leader outside of Tallahassee grew along with his role in the SCLC and the new nonviolent civil rights campaign.

people interpreted the governor's words as justifying their positions. In Tallahassee, Malcolm Johnson wrote, "There will be those who won't like his plain declaration that Supreme Court decisions are 'the law of the land' . . . , but they will be 'heartened' by his vow that 'segregation in the public schools can be expected to prevail for the foreseeable future.'" [14]

Legislative response to the governor's speech was generally cautious and noncommittal. Tallahassee city commissioners refused to comment on Collins's remarks about bus seating but told reporters that they took a "favorable" view of the overall speech. Several local blacks, who had listened in a roped-off area near the capitol, responded favorably, if not enthusiastically.

On 12 January 1957, four days after his inauguration, Collins lifted his suspension of the buses for a "good-will" test. The governor made clear that his decision was not to be seen "as an expression of approval of the action taken by the City of Tallahassee amending the franchise ordinance." Collins reiterated his view that the "attitudes of the people," regardless of any law, "will determine the ability of this community to overcome the situation which for so many months has provoked discord and disruption of normal community life." The governor announced that he would close down bus service if violence resumed. [15]

During the first week of bus service resumption, sporadic violence aimed at ICC leaders also resumed. Collins warned that he would intervene in Tallahassee if local authorities did not take "some effective action" to restore peace. Chief Stoutamire quickly announced that he was going to "put a stop" to the destruction of Negro property, adding, "I don't stand for that sort of thing. That's not my kind of law enforcement." Stoutamire added that he would meet his police officers shift by shift and tell them that he expected them to do something about the violence. [16]

Meanwhile, Malcolm Johnson noted that "all of Tallahassee will be happy if the warnings of Governor Collins and Police Chief Stoutamire are heeded" and if the violence against "bus integration leaders" is stopped. It was a particularly important time for all southern communities to prove they could enforce the law, Johnson noted, because Congress was debating civil rights laws "that would be an intolerable federal supervision over our local affairs." [17]

On 18 January, Stoutamire reported that he had rounded up eleven white youths who knew something about the violence and that he had given them a stern lecture on the seriousness of the crimes. The chief later told Steele that the destructive youths were just "pranksters" not bent on serious destruction. [18]

Although the bus boycott in Tallahassee was officially over, there had been no final resolution, no clear-cut court-based vindication of black demands as there had been in Montgomery. Consequently, many blacks would not ride the

While Steele was in Montgomery in early January, LeRoy Collins was sworn in for his second term as governor of Florida. Collins was unusually somber on that day, aware that his ambitious plans for business development, education reform, highway expansion, and legislative reapportionment were in danger of being overshadowed by a growing legislative preoccupation with maintaining segregation at any cost. At the same time, the governor was personally distressed by the recent events in his hometown and by the potential for greater racial violence throughout the state. Unlike so many of his friends and neighbors, Collins had experienced "a growing feeling that my attitudes were not correct and that there was much inherent in segregation which was unfair and wrong to black people." [10]

Yet Collins remained ambivalent about changes in race relations. He was sure that for "a large portion of people in the state, the abolition of segregation was just a bad dream." Collins devoted half of his inaugural address to race relations, specifically school desegregation and the Tallahassee bus boycott. On the one hand, he assured whites that there would be no integration of the public schools "in the foreseeable future." On the other hand, he dismissed as "demagoguery" and "anarchy" plans to nullify the high court's decision in Florida. If and when the time came to implement the desegregation ruling, Collins said, "it will do us no good whatever to defy the United States Supreme Court." [11]

Turning to the bus boycott, the governor was convinced "that the average white citizen does not object to non-segregated seating in buses anymore than he objects to riding the same elevators with Negroes or patronizing the same stores." But it was understandable, he added, that whites resented "some of the methods used to achieve certain ends." The state's race problems could be solved, Collins concluded, "if the white citizens will face up to the fact that the Negro is morally and legally entitled to progress more rapidly . . . and if the Negro will realize that he must merit and deserve whatever place he achieves in a community." [12]

Collins's remarks were at times contradictory, naive, and patronizing, but they set a tone of moderation on racial issues and made clear that his administration would seek compromises and would oppose "extremism" in solving Florida's race problems. More important, Collins undermined the moral and legal arguments for maintaining segregation while recognizing that blacks were entitled to a vague notion of "progress." The governor made clear that, while he sympathized with black demands, he did not condone "boycotts, ultimatums and peremptory demands." [13]

Reaction to Collins's speech varied throughout the state, but in general bus for fear of defying the new seating assignment policy. Others decided to continue to boycott the bus unofficially until the new policy was repealed. Without a suit pending in federal court, blacks were forced to challenge cleverly disguised local segregation ordinances and expose themselves to local justice—including jail. In late January, with the buses running half empty, the ICC decided to challenge the city's new seat assignment policy. But according to Dan Speed, there were few people in the black community ready to face possible arrest and jail sentences for violating the seating policy.

Once again, young people came forward. Three Florida A&M students (including Speed's son Leonard) and, to the horror of most Tallahasseeans, three white FSU students, volunteered at an ICC meeting to test the seating arrangements. On 19 January, the six students boarded a city bus and were assigned their seats by the driver. The three white youths were given seats at the front of the bus, and the three black students seats near the rear. All initially took their seats, but during the ride, Speed, Spagna (who was white), and Johnny Herndon changed seats so that all six were riding as interracial pairs. The driver ordered them back to their assigned seats, and when they refused, they were arrested and charged with violating Ordinance 741.

The three students petitioned the federal district court in Tallahassee to block their trial in municipal court and to declare the bus seating assignment unconstitutional. The petitioners referred to the ordinance as a "subterfuge" to preserve segregation and cited the recent Miami ruling as evidence that Florida's bus segregation laws were unconstitutional.

At the hearing on 8 February federal judge Dozier DeVane denied the plaintiffs' petition for a change in venue, thereby guaranteeing that the students would be tried in Tallahassee's municipal court. DeVane also refused to rule on the constitutionality of the ordinance until after the first trial. This decision not only shifted the focus of the trial away from segregation but also virtually ensured that the students would be convicted of violating the law. The judge further refused to enjoin the city and the bus company from enforcing the seating assignment ordinance.

DeVane, who had earlier stated that "segregation was deader than a doornail," insisted that recent Supreme Court rulings did not mean that "integration is the right of anybody." The judge asked attorney Francisco Rodriguez whether the defendants were attempting to destroy the bus company. "On the contrary," Rodriguez said, the petitioners "more than anyone else need the buses." But DeVane accused Rodriguez of being "hot under the collar" and defended the bus company for doing its best to operate. He instructed the opposing attorneys to work out their problems in a "Christian spirit." [19]

While legal counsel contemplated the judge's directive, Speed, Herndon, and

Spagna were subpoenaed to appear before the Florida Legislative Investigation Committee. Police Chief Stoutamire opened police records and files to the committee and provided the services of his vice squad detective, R. J. Strickland, as chief investigator for the committee.

On the third floor of the state capitol, the young men were interrogated by committee counsel Mark Hawes (appointed to this post shortly after his successful prosecution of the ICC in 1956). Hawes tried repeatedly to make the three admit that their ride had been prearranged by the ICC. Spagna insisted that the integrated ride was a spur-of-the-moment sightseeing diversion and refused to admit that he or the other riders had been given money for fare or had been promised legal counsel. Spagna so infuriated committee members with his one-syllable answers to their rambling questions that Representative J. B. Hopkins admonished him to show "some proper respect to counsel and to this Committee" and to refrain from using so many "yeps and nopes" as answers to questions.[20]

Unable to coax information from the recalcitrant witness, Senator Dewey Johnson told Spagna, "I would like to acquaint you with the fact that you can be called before the Legislature under contempt proceedings for failure to answer questions as called upon." After Spagna's dismissal the committee recalled the other riders (all of whom had been subpoenaed but not questioned the week before), who reluctantly acknowledged that they had ridden the bus with the ultimate goal of being arrested. Leonard Speed testified that he had given each rider a dollar for fare but refused under intense examination by Hawes to incriminate his father or the ICC.[21]

On 27 February 1957, Speed, Herndon, and Spagna faced Judge Rudd in municipal court. During testimony, the city claimed that the seating ordinance was necessary to protect the safety, health, and welfare of the community and had nothing to do with race. Under Rodriguez's cross-examination, however, the bus driver who had assigned the students their seats was unable to defend the assignments on the basis of any safety consideration, including the weight distribution of the passengers. Rodriguez charged that the ordinance was "patently and clumsily designed to evade recent high court rulings on the question of segregation in intrastate travel" and that it violated both the state and the federal constitutions.[22]

As was expected, the students were pronounced guilty by Judge Rudd, were sentenced one week later to sixty days in jail, and were fined $500. Rudd told the young men that he considered their actions a "deliberate overt act to violate the peace and tranquility of our city in a time of great crisis." He urged the defendants to consider their obligations as citizens of the community rather than attempt to be "modern fly-by-night martyrs."[23]

At the same time, Rudd ordered cameramen representing various Florida television stations to destroy any film shot in the corridor outside the courtroom during the trial. Jack Murphy of WTVT Tampa ignored the request and sent the film to his station, which showed it on the air. Rudd maintained that he had to protect the integrity of the court. He then found Murphy in contempt of court and ordered him to pay $100 and to serve thirty days in jail. Murphy's attorneys, who believed that their client had exercised his right of free speech, obtained a writ of habeas corpus from a Leon County circuit court. The charges were later dropped.

Rudd was not the only white official who wanted to limit the publicity surrounding the trial and the bus seating ordinance. At a 29 January meeting of Governor Collins's newly appointed Advisory Commission on Bi-Racial Problems, members discussed the ongoing turmoil over the buses in Tallahassee and agreed that the whole situation "would straighten itself out" if they "could just get it quieted down and off the front pages for a few days." It was generally agreed that if the city buses "gradually and quietly stopped assignment of seats everything would settle back down to normal." Judge L. L. Fabisinski, the commission chairman, told the commission on 5 March that while he felt that the Tallahassee seating ordinance was constitutional, he agreed with commission attorney Lewis Hall that the drivers should be told to assign seats only where they felt it to be necessary. The commission's advice appeared to have filtered down to local officials and to owners of the bus company as well as to the staff of the *Tallahassee Democrat*, which greatly reduced coverage of the case and the year-long appeals.[24]

On 11 March federal judge Dozier DeVane refused to rule on the constitutionality of Tallahassee's bus seat assignment ordinance until a review of the law had been completed in state court. On 15 November 1957, one year after a federal district court had declared Alabama's segregated bus ordinances unconstitutional, the students' convictions were upheld in circuit court. Judge W. May Walker ruled that there had been no denial of any constitutional or statutory right of the appellants.

Bypassing the Florida Supreme Court, Speed, Spagna, and Herndon appealed their case to the U.S. Supreme Court. Their attorneys charged that the city ordinance violated the Fourteenth Amendment, as it had been applied solely to segregate patrons because of race or color, and that their conviction for an orderly refusal to return to segregated seats arbitrarily assigned to them by the driver violated due process. The city countered that the ordinance was a reasonable exercise of state police power and that no facts of racial motivation had been admitted by the driver.

Despite the superficiality of the city's argument, the Supreme Court denied certiorari on the ground (as the city had argued) that there was no jurisdiction unless or until the decision had been reviewed by the federal district court (which had refused to rule) and the Florida Supreme Court. Although the denial did not speak to the constitutional claims of the defendants, it was a severe setback for civil rights protest in Tallahassee. The ordinance was obviously a subterfuge, and the Court's refusal to hear the case temporarily weakened its condemnation of race segregation in local transit.

Both Speed and Herndon began to serve their prison sentences. Meanwhile, Spagna, who had graduated from Florida State University, eluded local police. Attorney Rodriguez appealed the case to the Florida Supreme Court, which on 9 April 1958 ironically refused to review the lower court's decision. Finally, Rodriguez announced that he would file a motion to dismiss the injunction against the city, which was still pending in federal court, and would petition the city commission for clemency for the incarcerated youths.

On 10 April, Judge Rudd recommended suspending the sentences of Herndon and Speed, who had already served fifteen days in jail. At an emergency meeting, Rudd told commissioners that the young men "were not the real culprits, but were the victims of circumstances and acted under the influence of persons and organizations who gave little or no consideration to the public interest or the interest of the defendants." Acting as a clemency board, the commission voted unanimously to accept the judge's recommendation.[25]

Rudd then ordered Speed and Herndon released from jail, an action that pleased Malcolm Johnson, who noted that the "ends of justice and racial harmony were well served." But by depicting the young men as pawns who had been "exploited and used for unlawful purposes," Rudd not only failed to acknowledge the men's courage and serious intent but also blamed the ICC and the NAACP, both of which were being investigated by the FLIC for abusing the legal system by "stirring up lawsuits."[26]

Throughout February 1957, the FLIC continued its investigation of the state and local chapters of the NAACP. According to one committee member, the purpose of the investigation was "to prove that the NAACP was promoting and financing lawsuits in violation of state law." To help the committee gather evidence against the organization, investigator Strickland presented members with "a fairly complete record of the names and addresses of the various officers of the NAACP in Florida who are potential witnesses which the committee may want to examine." The chief investigator assured the committee that their hearings were justified because "ample evidence" existed "that . . . the NAACP has formulated plans for the complete integration of Negroes into all phases of American life by the year 1968."[27]

After interrogating the students who were arrested for violating the seating ordinance, the committee turned its attention to the Florida A&M faculty and administrators who had participated in the boycott or who had been perceived as sympathetic to it. Among those questioned was President George W. Gore Jr. The president was asked whether he had forbidden faculty to participate in the boycott. Gore said that he had advised faculty members not to participate "actively" in the boycott and that he had warned individual faculty members that he would not be able to defend them or protect them from possible retribution. He admitted that some FAMU employees had made it clear to him that they would continue to participate in the boycott because they thought it was "right." [28]

Under questioning, Gore testified that "maybe half" of his faculty members belonged to the NAACP. Although Gore himself was not a member, committee counsel Hawes established that Gore belonged to the American Teachers Association, which donated 10 percent of its income to the NAACP on an annual basis. The president was asked how his faculty salaries compared with those at other "state-owned Negro institutions." When Gore responded that they were "among the top group, in the first five or ten," Hawes asked him whether he knew of any condition "that would give the faculty members at this university any cause to become dissatisfied above those faculty members at other southern universities?" Gore artfully answered, "I would say the situation is the same or better." [29]

Later in the same day, Professor Emmett Bashful told committee members that he had never interpreted Gore's actions or words as a direct order not to attend ICC meetings or to participate in the boycott. "I thought he meant to be as careful as possible and not to involve the school too much," he said. Hawes questioned Bashful about his appearance at an ICC meeting on 4 July 1956. "I was asked to read on that program certain excerpts from the Declaration of Independence and the Bill of Rights," Bashful said. "It was a celebration on the Declaration of Independence. . . . I was happy to, and I am always happy to read from the Declaration of Independence for any organization, and the Bill of Rights of the Constitution of the United States." [30]

Clearly angry over Hawes's insinuations that he was not a loyal state employee, Bashful said, "I am a human being in this community and a citizen, and I am teaching students to be citizens and to take part in the activities of their government. I tell students that this is a democracy; then to be told that I can't take part in a movement with which I might identify my interests—you see, to me that is a violation of my constitutional rights." [31]

After grilling Bashful, the committee interrogated several local NAACP members and was incensed to find that the organization had sent most of its records to another Florida location. Even though Hawes's own background investigation proved that the ICC, and not the NAACP, was the organization behind the Tallahassee bus boycott, the attorney labored hard to establish that the NAACP had sponsored or had been directly involved in the bus boycott in Tallahassee. When NAACP attorney Francisco Rodriguez admitted under questioning that as an NAACP representative he had a direct interest in all civil rights cases brought by blacks in the South, the committee saw no need to call further witnesses.

Committee member Senator John Rawls of Marianna accused the NAACP of "going out and actively soliciting litigants and money to develop lawsuits." Rawls said the committee would make definite recommendations aimed at correcting "abuses of Florida's judicial system by the NAACP."[32]

The FLIC wielded intimidating power in Tallahassee, but it could not destroy the city's nascent protest movement. Emboldened by the boycott and the spirit of protest, Reverend K. S. Dupont became the first black candidate to run for a seat on the Tallahassee city commission. With help from the ICC, Dupont ran a highly visible and well-organized campaign. At night men from his church kept watch over his home as cars full of whites drove slowly by, yelling insults and threats at the minister and his family. By day, the women from Dupont's church walked the streets of Tallahassee's black neighborhoods, encouraging people to get out the vote.

Dupont's candidacy forced the white community into a traditional yet contradictory position. Even though white leaders refused to take the minister or his campaign seriously, they warned voters that the election of a black Tallahasseean posed a threat to the stability of the community and the effectiveness of city government. Dupont's opponent, segregationist candidate Davis Atkinson, refused to debate the minister on any issue, and constantly referred to Dupont as "that Negro Candidate." Atkinson contended that Dupont was owned "lock, stock, and barrel by the ICC and the NAACP," which were trying to force total integration on the citizens of Tallahassee.[33]

Malcolm Johnson stated the obvious when he wrote that the race was "strictly a case of a Negro running against a white man." In an editorial several days before the election, Johnson told blacks that because of recent civil rights disturbances, the day was long gone "when the Negro population could expect or receive some considerable white acceptance of the fairness of having representation on the Tallahassee city commission." At the same time, Johnson expressed the fear that "if the minority race should at this moment—through some dereliction by voters of the majority race—obtain a seat on the commission, we sincerely believe a racial strain would be applied to nearly every decision and every action by the board." It would be best, he concluded, "if the white man wins."[34]

Two weeks before the election some 13,443 Tallahasseeans were registered to vote, a 46 percent increase from the previous year. Black voters grew from 20 percent of the total electorate in 1956 to 24 percent, "a block of significant size," as Johnson noted. On election day, 26 February 1957, 76 percent of Tallahassee's registered voters came to the polls, more than doubling the figure in 1956, a presidential year. The *Democrat* reported the voting results by precinct and by race. The official results revealed that Dupont had received 2,405 votes, but only 2,318 blacks had cast ballots. Apparently 87 whites in Tallahassee had voted for the city's first black candidate since Reconstruction. No blacks voted for Atkinson.[35]

Although black voters turned out in unprecedented numbers, they were no match for the turnout among white Tallahassee voters. Atkinson beat Dupont by a three-to-one margin. Malcolm Johnson wrote that the "overwhelming defeat of the Negro candidate must demonstrate to his people that whenever they bring their case to the greatest of all democratic forums, the ballot booth, on a strict issue of race vs. race they are going to lose." But Johnson had laudatory words for his adopted town. He noted that "Negroes in unprecedented numbers went to the polls unmolested, voting shoulder to shoulder with white people." Apparently impressed, he added, "White precinct inspectors and clerks, some of them citizens of the oldest Southern backgrounds and traditions, seemed to go out of their way to help ignorant first voters master the machines and cast their ballots."[36]

Johnson's arrogance aside, the election revealed that white solidarity in Tallahassee had once again been breached. During the campaign, it became front page news that a small number of FSU students were attending ICC meetings and that two students had actually spoken at one meeting to endorse Dupont's candidacy. Although students were not considered local residents and were therefore readily identified as "outside agitators," their actions were cause for alarm throughout the state. The Florida board of control, the body governing the state's universities, acted decisively to quell student support for Dupont or for the ongoing bus boycott.

In late January 1957, the board issued a stern warning to students at FSU and FAMU that they would be subject to the strictest disciplinary actions if "they stir up trouble in Tallahassee's race dispute." Shortly after the academic warning, the White Citizens Council of Leon County met and urged fraternities at FSU to organize a campuswide campaign against integrationists. The council demanded the expulsion from school of any students, white or black, who supported Dupont's candidacy.[37]

Tensions at Florida State had been brewing since December 1956 when one of the campus activists, twenty-six-year-old John Boardman, a doctoral candidate, had been expelled from the university for inviting three black foreign exchange students from Florida A&M to a Christmas party for international students that was sponsored by Florida State. Boardman told reporters that he had repeatedly asked officials at Florida State whether the invitation violated an existing policy of the board of control forbidding the mixing of the races on either campus. When he received no official statement on the matter, Boardman contacted Dean B. L. Perry at Florida A&M, who told him to issue the invitation and assured him that the students would attend the party.

Most Tallahasseeans were unaware that the three students had quietly attended the party until news of the affair was reported in the paper. What shocked the community was Boardman's disclosure that during the course of the evening, FSU President Doak Campbell had told him that he did not object to the black students' presence and declared that "there would be Negroes at FSU eventually." Campbell immediately and emphatically denied Boardman's remarks, adding that he could never make such a statement because he did not believe that blacks would ever attend the university. The president insisted that he had gone briefly to the gathering and solely to address those in attendance on the "spirit of Christmas." [38]

University policies often reflected the attitudes and customs of the community, and Campbell expected his faculty to adhere to community standards. Students, who were not protected by tenure, were in a more perilous position. Boardman, along with two other FSU students, attended several ICC meetings in January, publicly endorsed Dupont's candidacy, and called for an end to segregation. He was later questioned by the FLIC, whose members clearly regarded his activities and beliefs as both subversive and dangerous.

At a meeting of Governor Collins's Advisory Commission on Bi-Racial Problems in early 1957, President Campbell told fellow members that Boardman was part of "a little group of ten FSU students who regarded themselves as the saviors of the world." The president added that although Boardman was a "very brilliant scholar as far as mathematics is concerned," he was "unstable otherwise." He insisted that Boardman had been dismissed from the university for "insubordination," although Campbell had known, he said, that the dismissal would be blamed "on the race question. The boy is sick and needs help," Campbell insisted, noting that Boardman had joined three different churches, the last one being the Jewish synagogue. [39]

When other members expressed the fear that Boardman might be turned into a martyr figure, Campbell assured them that the suspension had "waked the students up to the fact that the University has broad authority, and that it [the suspension] might scare some of the more rabid ones into quieting down." When former A&M President J. R. E. Lee told the other commission members that black students considered Boardman something of a hero, they expressed the hope that the "Negro students did not think that the solution to their problems lay with a man like that." Campbell then added that, on the basis of profile reports on the students sympathetic to integration, he found them, like Boardman, somewhat "erratic" or somehow lacking in their backgrounds. Commission attorney Lewis Hall told Lee that the "right kind of white leadership would be developed to help in cementing the right kind of racial relations between the universities."[40]

But despite the concerted efforts of Hall, the commission, Tallahassee officials, the board of control, the newspaper, and the FLIC, a new system of "racial relations" was in the making, belying the superficial tranquillity that had returned to the weary city by the spring of 1957. In the aftermath of the boycott, an uneasy truce existed between the races. The bus company's strategy to phase out the seating policy without fanfare successfully brought many blacks back to the buses. On the mainly black bus routes the seating policy was never enforced, and it was only rarely used on other routes.

Because of the initial refusal of federal judge DeVane to rule on the constitutionality of the seating ordinance, blacks did not have the satisfaction of seeing the ordinance declared unconstitutional; instead it was quietly ignored. Because some issues remained unresolved after the bus boycott, many blacks never returned to the buses, and a lingering feeling of ill will and distrust permeated race relations in the community. Twenty-five years after the protest, former city commissioner William Mayo noted that the bus company did not recover from the effects of the boycott; patronage, he said, never returned to its pre-1956 level.

Beginning on 26 May 1957, the ICC celebrated the first boycott anniversary by hosting a four-day meeting of the Institute on Non-Violence and Social Change. Guest speakers included Martin Luther King Jr., Ralph Abernathy, F. L. Shuttlesworth, T. J. Jemison, and pacifist Glen Smiley from the Fellowship of Reconciliation. Workshops and seminars were held to underscore the institute's theme: "Dignity with Humility, Love with Courage and Justice Without Violence." The twenty-page program, which found its way into the hands of the Florida Legislative Investigation Committee, contained the names and pictures of the "ICC Official Family," the advisory board, and various committees. Missing were the names of those men once considered spokesmen for Tallahassee's black community.[41]

C. K. Steele, chairman of the institute, ICC president, and vice president of the Southern Christian Leadership Conference, was a nationally known civil rights activist, and Florida's capital city had secured a place in the annals of civil rights history. But the bus boycott had produced few palpable changes in race relations in Tallahassee. Blacks remained second-class citizens, disproportion-ally poor, denied equal access to the law, to education, to employment, and to the rights and privileges of free citizens.

Yet change had come to Tallahassee though not as dramatically as some blacks had hoped it would in the exhilarating days of May 1956. Still, notice had been served: there would be no more resigned acceptance of the ways of the past, no more quiet acquiescence to white authority. In one year's time, blacks, against overwhelming odds, with the constant and powerful opposition of every major political, legal, and business entity in Tallahassee, had quickly closed down the city's transportation system; had forced powerful whites to take their demands seriously; had won concessions from elected officials; had helped to sway the political ideology of the governor of the state; had significantly in-creased the number of black voters; had challenged a white candidate for po-litical office; and, most important, had dispelled the myth that blacks were content within the confines of the old race relations. Most whites remained opposed to changes in traditional race etiquette, yet they had been forced, re-luctantly, to view blacks from a different perspective. In short, race relations in Tallahassee could never be the same. The bus boycott and protest would con-tinue to have ramifications for racial politics in Tallahassee and throughout Florida for the rest of the decade.

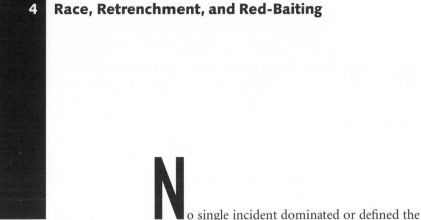

4 Race, Retrenchment, and Red-Baiting

No single incident dominated or defined the city's race relations like the bus boycott, but a series of incidents contributed to a growing consensus that the "southern way of life" was in jeopardy in Tallahassee. As black hopes and aspirations became more public, so did official efforts to thwart racial progress, making it more and more difficult for superficial congeniality to obscure race problems. In Tallahassee many legal and political battles were fought to preserve segregation throughout Florida. None was more inflammatory than those emanating from the Florida Legislative Investigation Committee.

On 7 February 1958, former governor Charley Johns, then a powerful senator from the small North Florida community of Starke, announced that the newly reauthorized FLIC would launch an extensive inquiry into "Communistic activities" in Florida that would uncover "the general aims, methods, and means of operating adopted by the Communist party." The racial agenda of the inquiry became clear when Johns noted that the investigation would "pay particular attention to efforts of the Communist Party in Florida to agitate racial conflict and unrest."[1]

The original Florida Legislative Investigation Committee, established in 1956 and known statewide as the "NAACP Investigation Committee," had seen its initial concern as the Tallahassee bus boycott. The committee spent a year and a half investigating, interrogating, and intimidating professors at Florida A&M, students, and community activists who supported the boycott. Almost nothing was uncovered to suggest that the boycott was part of an NAACP plot to disrupt Tallahassee's "good race relations."[2]

Determined nevertheless to link the NAACP to any kind of racial incident, the committee (which held hearings throughout the state) subpoenaed some sixty blacks who either had filed suit against a segregated school system or had merely signed a petition supporting integration. Virgil Hawkins, a black realtor suing for admission into the University of Florida Law School, endured hours of grilling from the committee's counsel on the NAACP's contribution to his eight-year battle to attend the institution. Attorneys for litigants seeking to overturn segregation ordinances faced similar scrutiny. After months of public hearings the committee persuaded many Floridians of the NAACP's role in fostering racial conflict and unrest.

During the 1957 legislative session, the committee introduced a package of five bills designed to make the NAACP's activities illegal in Florida. The package was defeated by legislators concerned that language curbing the NAACP's activities would affect other organizations and would seriously undermine personal liberties. Its main objective thwarted, the committee faced an uncertain future until Johns, with the aid of other conservative North Florida lawmakers (known euphemistically as the "pork choppers") persuaded the legislature to extend the life of the committee for two years and to expand its powers to include an investigation of other subversive organizations in the state. Two years after the boycott and four years after the school desegregation decision in *Brown v. Board of Education*, the committee was given legislative approval to initiate a process that could effectively stymie desegregation and permanently discredit its proponents.

Three days before the 1958 hearings of the legislative investigation committee began in Tallahassee, Senator Johns told reporters that he had "information regarding Communist activities in several vital phases of life in Florida and other states." The committee—now known as the Johns committee—released the names of thirty-nine Floridians who had been subpoenaed for questioning. Four of the witnesses were scheduled to appear before the committee in Tallahassee, and the remaining thirty-five would be questioned in Miami where, according to Johns, the committee planned to "dig into detail" concerning "the facts in regard to who these Florida Communists are, what their aims are, and what their activities are and have been." [3]

On 10 February, Johns introduced Joseph Brown Matthews, the committee's chief witness, whom he had earlier described as "the leading authority on the subject of Communism in the country." The former staff director of the House Committee on Un-American Activities from 1940 through 1944, Matthews was known in political circles as the "spiritual leader of the Far Right in America." He worked briefly for Senator Joseph McCarthy as staff director of the Permanent Senate Subcommittee on Investigations but was forced to resign in 1953 after his article "Reds and Our Churches" appeared in the *American Mercury*. In his article, Matthews accused Protestant clergymen of being the largest single group supporting communism in the United States. That shocking, unproven allegation not only was his undoing but also undermined both McCarthy's reputation and the subcommittee hearings. [4]

During his Tallahassee testimony, Matthews, who had kept in his personal possession materials suppressed by the old House Committee on Un-American Activities, told the committee that Communist influence had been "involved directly in all major race incidents since the U.S. Supreme Court decision prohibiting racial segregation in public schools" and that Communists had penetrated the South through organizations such as the NAACP and the Southern Conference Education Fund (SCEF), an organization sponsoring interracial educational projects. Matthews charged that the letterhead of the NAACP carried "236 names of national officers of various degrees and that 'public records show that 145 of these 236 individuals, or sixty-one percent, have records of affiliation with Communist organizations.'" Organizations included in Matthews's sweeping indictment included the National Negro Congress, the Alabama Sharecroppers' Union, the North Carolina Textile Workers' Union, and various other human relations and labor organizations. [5]

Most Floridians subpoenaed by the Johns committee in the winter of 1958 were members of the NAACP or the Florida Council on Human Relations. The four witnesses ordered to appear before the committee in Tallahassee were the secretary of the Florida Council for Human Relations, a reporter from Naples, Florida, FAMU Professor Emmett Bashful (who had previously testified before the committee in 1957), and James S. Shaw, treasurer of the Tallahassee Council on Human Relations and a respected white businessman. Shaw, who had taken over the position of treasurer from banker George Lewis only two days before, was instructed to appear with the financial records of the council.

A native of the rural northwest Florida community of Quincy, Shaw's liberal social and political views were at variance with those of the majority of his friends and neighbors. Until now, these views had remained generally private.

Concerned that his wife, Lillian, a Quincy native with similar opinions, would be upset over the subpoena, Shaw kept his upcoming appearance before the committee a secret.

On 11 February, Shaw appeared before the committee, records in hand, and was told that he could not make a statement regarding the nature of the committee's inquiry. When he attempted to explain the philosophy and activities of the Tallahassee council, he was interrupted by the committee's attorney, Mark Hawes, who demanded that he present the records and leave the hearing.

Indignant, Shaw said he would turn the records over under protest and began to criticize the committee's motives for issuing a subpoena for records he would gladly have provided voluntarily. Hawes immediately interrupted Shaw, saying that as a matter of policy the committee did not allow voluntary statements from witnesses. "You mean a person can't say what they want to?" Shaw asked incredulously. "Well," Hawes replied, "you can make all the statements you please, except, before this Committee, you just simply cannot make a statement." Undeterred, Shaw pressed on: "It seems to me that there's something bad wrong with the situation. . . . I mean that the Committee, in calling me, cast certain aspersions on me, as well as the organization, and if I don't have a right to say anything, why, it seems to me like there's something bad wrong."[6]

When Representative Cliff Herrell announced that he would like to hear what Shaw had to say, the committee instructed its attorney to confer with Shaw to work out a compromise. Counsel Hawes told Shaw that he would be allowed to speak if he would refrain from saying anything derogatory about the committee's action. Shaw refused, but the committee decided to let him make a statement and reserved the right to cut him off if he "got out of line." Back in the stand, Shaw told the committee, "this organization [the TCHR] is not a secret organization. Most of our meetings have been held in the Court House; they've been open to anybody. Anyone could come and see exactly what the organization was doing, which is just to more or less create a line of communication with Negroes and whites, and there has been little or nothing actually accomplished. There's nothing that anyone in the organization wants to hide."[7]

As he started to hand the records over to Hawes, Shaw hesitated. "I do give these records under protest because I don't feel that it was necessary." At this point Representative J. B. Hopkins and Chairman Johns objected to Shaw's "going beyond his scope," and the feisty witness was asked to leave the stand.[8]

Waiting to testify, Bashful complained to one of the committee members that he had been under suspicion since he had been called as a witness in a Communist investigation. "You're an intelligent man, Bashful," snapped Hopkins, "and you can see no aspersions or insinuations are cast upon you." The committee decided not to call Bashful (also a member of the council) to the stand but allowed him to read a short statement in which he said that the council believed that the "peaceful evolution of better race conditions in the South can be brought about by the interracial conscience of the South and that southerners of both races can take the lead in solving their own problems." The other two witnesses were dismissed.[9]

After leaving the capitol, Shaw issued a scathing statement to the press in which he accused the committee of smearing his reputation with unfounded allegations and misrepresentations. Shaw demanded that the committee make a public report on all of its investigations and defended his council as "an above board organization." In response, Representative Hopkins said that the committee had information that the Tallahassee Council on Human Relations might be a "Communist-front organization" and that it was on the U.S. attorney general's list of subversive organizations. U.S. attorney Harrold Carswell told reporters that the council was not on a list of subversive organizations, a statement that the U.S. assistant attorney general later verified in a letter to Shaw. Malcolm Johnson accused the committee of harassing Shaw for information that could easily have been obtained from the council's public record, and he hinted that the legislature was wasting the taxpayers' money. The editors of the *Tampa Tribune* added that while allegations that Communists were infiltrating the NAACP and stirring up racial unrest were unquestionably true, this news was "very stale."[10]

Undaunted by the lack of evidence that either the Tallahassee or the Florida Council on Human Relations were subversive organizations, the Johns committee continued to investigate both the local chapters and the statewide organization for the next seven years. The committee hired informants, including a detective agency, to infiltrate the membership and to spy on council meetings across the state.

Exasperated by years of harassment, the president of the Florida Council on Human Relations in 1961 asked the chairman of the committee to present a report of the state council's annual activities to the legislature to clarify the purpose of the council, which was to "promote unity and understanding between the races, and to gain insight into the problems of each." The committee ignored this request, preferring to gather information about each local council chapter as well as about the state organization.[11]

In Tallahassee, the local chapter continued to meet, its small membership composed of professors from both Florida State and Florida A&M and a sprinkling of townspeople. An informant to the Johns committee reported that the organization discussed such subversive topics as equal rights in job opportunities and writing the newspaper in support of efforts to improve race relations. (The latter, he noted, brought "a chuckle from all present.")

The Tallahassee Council on Human Relations remained important to the Johns committee (and evidently also to the Tallahassee police department) after Shaw's testimony. At one of the organization's meetings shortly after his interrogation, Shaw noticed that for the first time the wife of a Tallahassee police officer was present. The woman asked Shaw for a ride home and proceeded to tell him about "how she knew and liked Communists." When she invited him into her home (it was after 10:00 P.M.) Shaw declined. It later came to light that she was a paid informant for the Johns committee.[12]

Despite its brief notoriety, the Tallahassee Council on Human Relations remained an enigma to most Tallahasseeans, who associated it with the two universities, with outsiders, and with views that they did not hold. Members, including the Shaws, who "drifted apart" from many of their old friends after the committee's interrogation, found it more and more difficult to reconcile their views with the norms of the community. The Shaws resigned from the Trinity Methodist Church when the board of directors voted not to allow blacks to be seated during services. Eventually they spent more of their time participating in civil rights organizations and activities and less on the community's social functions.

The Johns committee's primary target in its ongoing investigation of civil rights organizations was and continued to be the NAACP. Shortly after James Shaw's interrogation, the committee subpoenaed Tobias Simon, who had defended several participants in the Tallahassee bus boycott. Simon was grilled about his affiliation with the NAACP and the organization's role in the Tallahassee bus boycott. Simon's testimony exasperated committee members, who were looking to link the boycott with a master plan of racial foment designed by the NAACP. Finally, it became clear that the ICC, while receiving aid from the NAACP (including Simon's services), had directed an autonomous local boycott.

A separate report to the committee conducted by the counsel and chief investigator stated that although "the integration movement in the South could not be progressing at the alarmingly rapid rate of speed with which it is without the organized legal machine of the NAACP . . . , the boycott movement [in Tallahassee] appears to have been spontaneously started and does not appear to have been either carefully planned or executed. The Inter-Civic Council has unquestionably been the dominant factor in its life, with the NAACP having relatively little to do with it, although they backed the Montgomery boycott to the very hilt."[13]

Stymied in its efforts to link the Tallahassee bus boycott, the ICC, the Tallahassee Council on Human Relations, and the NAACP with a Communist plot to infiltrate the South, the Johns committee moved its hearings to South Florida, where it promised to "name names, places and dates of a Communist conspiracy to start a racial revolution in the South." The focus of the committee's probe was the Miami NAACP, the organization's largest affiliate in Florida. To determine the extent of Communist penetration into the organization, the committee would match the names of "card-carrying members of the Communist party" against NAACP membership lists. Officials of the Miami branch were then subpoenaed and ordered by the committee to produce membership lists and to answer specific questions about fourteen suspected Communist members in their organization.[14]

On the first day of public hearings the committee ran into stiff resistance from witnesses, particularly NAACP president Father Theodore Gibson. Citing the protection of the First and Fourteenth Amendments, Gibson refused to relinquish the NAACP's membership list and refused to answer questions about the organization's alleged affiliation with the Communist Party. Before he angrily denounced the committee and stormed out of the hearing, Gibson produced copies of resolutions passed by the NAACP's national office in 1951 and 1952 that restricted NAACP membership to those who supported the "principles and program of the NAACP [which] include opposition to Communist infiltration and control."[15]

Outraged by Gibson's refusal to provide the NAACP's membership list, the committee initiated contempt proceedings against him and other recalcitrant witnesses. The state's circuit and supreme courts both ordered Gibson to provide the membership list to the FLIC, which he refused to do. When called to testify before the committee on 22 July 1960, Gibson told the committee that he knew "of no person in the branch who is a member of the Communist party or of any other subversive group at present. I have advised the committee that if they knew of any subversives who are NAACP members, if they bring that to my attention, steps will be taken immediately to sever their relationship with the NAACP. So much for the Communist issue."[16]

On 31 July 1960, circuit court judge W. May Walker found Gibson guilty of contempt, ordered him to pay a fine, and sentenced the minister to jail. While out on appeal, Gibson continued to refuse to provide the NAACP membership list to the FLIC. Meanwhile, the Florida courts upheld Gibson's contempt conviction, maintaining that there was no evidence that the FLIC "has in any fashion abused its power or undertaken to embarrass the appellants merely for the sake of arbitrary disclosure."[17]

Finally, in 1963, the U.S. Supreme Court reversed Gibson's contempt conviction, ruling that the state could not maintain that the information it sought (the membership list) was of overriding and compelling state interest because it had not proven that the Miami branch of the NAACP was a subversive organization or that it was Communist dominated or influenced. Consequently, the Court ruled, Gibson's conviction of contempt violated his rights of association, protected by the First and Fourteenth Amendments to the Constitution.

Although the Johns committee had failed to link the NAACP in Florida with communism or its members with the Communist Party, it continued to assert that "the NAACP has been the prime target of Communist penetration for the past thirty years. The record shows conclusively that the Communist apparatus has registered a degree of success in penetrating the NAACP which is not paralleled in the case of any other non-Communist organization of comparable size. . . . whether the NAACP has been infiltrated and influenced by Communists on the National level or in the State of Florida is not open to question. It definitely has been. The only question is the extent of such penetration and influence."[18]

In 1961 and again in 1963, the Florida legislature extended the life of the Johns committee, expanding its powers to include a "general investigation of all organizations whose principles or activities included a course of conduct on the part of any person or group which would constitute violence, or a violation of the laws of the state, or would be inimical to the well-being and orderly pursuit of their personal and business activities by the majority of the citizens of the state."[19]

The Johns committee continued to focus much of its attention on civil rights organizations. In 1961 after a public hearing in Tallahassee, the committee branded the SCEF a "Communist-controlled-front organization" and in a published report named the organization's board of directors, national officers, and Florida members. C. K. Steele was the only member from Tallahassee mentioned, but both the Florida and Tallahassee NAACP and the Council on Human Relations were listed as organizations whose "top officials" had been closely associated with and had closely cooperated with the "subversive SCEF." "Top officials" from Tallahassee included James Hudson, C. K. Steele, and David H. Brooks. Robert Saunders, field secretary of the Florida NAACP, was among those named, as were other NAACP officers throughout the state. Committee counsel Hawes criticized the NAACP for not breaking ties with the SCEF and demanded that the legislature bar both the SCEF and the NAACP from the state.[20]

The Johns committee investigated numerous groups suspected of violence and subversive activities and even took a cursory look at the Ku Klux Klan, but its main target continued to be the NAACP. After four years of investigations, interrogations, allegations, and threats, however, the legislature refused to ban the organization from Florida. With the popularity of the committee fading, Johns embraced an issue that would preoccupy the committee until its demise: homosexuality in Florida's public schools and universities.

From 1959 to 1964, the Johns committee harassed school superintendents and college presidents, demanding that the officials turn over the files of any teachers or professors suspected of homosexuality. By 1963, at least seventy-one teachers had lost their teaching certificates, and thirty-nine deans and professors had been removed from universities. The state's newest university, the University of South Florida, was almost destroyed by accusations that the institution was "soft on Communism," was harboring professors accused of homosexuality, and had hired teachers who used "anti-Christian" teaching theories.[21]

Finally, in 1964, the committee's obsession with homosexuality reached an apex with the publication of a report entitled "Homosexuality and Citizenship in Florida." The publication, which became known as the "purple pamphlet" because of the color of its cover, contained photos of nude men kissing and engaging in various sex acts. The pamphlet's photographs and narrative were so explicit that it was banned by Dade County state attorney Dick Gerstein and was considered pornographic by many Floridians.

Increasingly, members of the Johns committee found themselves fending off accusations that they were conducting a witch hunt and were unnecessarily tarnishing the reputation of many Floridians. The committee's high-handed, invasive tactics eventually led to its demise. The early work of the Johns committee, however—the effort to link communism and racial unrest—would be its legacy to the civil rights movement. This link became cemented in the minds of many Floridians and would taint civil rights organizations and activities for at least the next decade. In Tallahassee (as in most southern locales) virtually every organization concerned with the advancement of human relations had to face the charge that it was Communist inspired or Communist controlled.

The Johns committee was, in many ways, a barometer of the times, reflecting not only the anxiety undergirding race relations but also the fears of many native whites that Florida was changing in ways that they could not control. These fears were strongest in the state's rural northern area, where resentment of the population boom in Central and South Florida and of the relatively moderate politics of newcomers to the state led to widespread acceptance of conspiracy theories and of the dire predictions advanced by the Johns committee.

While the fears of domestic upheaval and social and political change were real, most Tallahasseeans cared less about the Communist infiltration of civil rights organizations, which they had long suspected, and more about preserving racial segregation and white hegemony. Oblivious to even the most blatant inequities in the capital city, whites looked back to the days before *Brown v. Board of Education*, the bus boycott, and the Johns committee as an era of "good feelings between the races in the South."[22]

But good feelings between the races did not entail any kind of real relationship between black and white in North Florida. In rural Madison (sixty-four miles east of Tallahassee), a white public health officer caused a scandal in October 1956 by having lunch in the back of a drugstore with a black nurse whom the public health officer supervised. As a result, Deborah Coggins was fired "without cause" by Jefferson and Taylor Counties, two of the three counties that she had served.

When Governor Collins heard that the Madison County Commission was considering a similar action, he pleaded with each commissioner not to dismiss the young physician. When they unanimously voted to fire Coggins, Collins called a press conference and denounced their decision. "I am sick about it," the governor said. "The action cannot be squared with right and justice and conscience." Meanwhile, Mrs. Flo Way, a fifth grade schoolteacher who came to Dr. Coggins's defense, was asked by the Madison County school board to resign; she refused. "The trouble with bigotry and intolerance," wrote Malcolm Johnson shortly after the two women's ordeals, "is that it feeds on itself, and grows bolder, more senseless and more arrogant with every success. There's no question of a stand on segregation here. . . . it makes no sense." [23]

In the fall of 1957, Collins was still so troubled by the Coggins incident that he mentioned it in his address to the Southern Presbyterian Men's Convention in Miami Beach. "Where in that situation," the governor asked, "were our Presbyterians . . . , our Methodists . . . , our Episcopalians . . . , all our churchmen?" Like Pontius Pilate, the governor charged, they "washed their hands" of the blood of an innocent person. [24]

But even as he was characteristically appalled by such individual acts of racism, Collins could not yet make the connection between such acts and the broader social atmosphere of hatred and intolerance breeding them. The governor, who by 1958 was known as a progressive and leader of the "Southern Moderates," told a reporter for *Look* in May of that year that before segregation could be abolished, blacks needed better health, education, moral and housing standards in order to improve their talents and gain the respect of whites. Little wonder that most Tallahasseeans were able to justify existing race relations and label any deviation from the status quo as subversive. [25]

Not all incidents and events that helped to shape race relations in Tallahassee before the onset of the 1960s activism and protests were as inflammatory as the Johns committee hearings. Few in fact were as newsworthy as the ongoing attempts by the Florida legislature to preserve segregation at any cost. But in reality, several less noted incidents played important roles in keeping tension high between the races in the community.

On 6 August 1957, the corporate charter for the nonprofit Capital City Country Club was approved by the circuit court of Leon County. The board of directors included some of the most prominent men in Tallahassee business and political circles. What distinguished this country club from countless private clubs around the country was that the property—all 205 lush, rolling acres— was being leased from the city for one dollar a year for ninety-nine years.

The original property, consisting of a nine-hole golf course, was developed in 1924 by private investors. The club flourished until the Depression, when hard times caused a drop in both membership and club use. In 1935, with funds provided by the Works Progress Administration, the course was expanded to eighteen holes, and the city took over the ownership and operation of the facility. An agreement signed by the original board of directors provided that if the city ever desired to be relieved of the operation, the now defunct Tallahassee Country Club would have the first option to repurchase the property.

By the early 1950s, Tallahassee blacks had begun to petition the city commission for recreational facilities such as playgrounds, tennis courts, and a golf course. On 3 June 1952, the commission authorized the city manager to determine whether the black Civic League would be willing to pay "reasonable fees" for a golf course, "the thought being that the present golf course is sustained through a collection of fees." Three months later, the stockholders of the old Tallahassee Country Club held a reorganizational meeting to discuss the possibility of leasing the city-operated golf course because of "dissatisfaction with the way the club is now being operated." Mayor W. H. Cates, who was opposed to turning over the property to the private investors, said he had never heard of any dissatisfaction with the way the club was being operated and noted that it would be foolhardy to relinquish such a valuable piece of public property for private use.[26]

Other commissioners expressed an interest in the offer upon learning that the city annually spent several thousand dollars more to operate the facility than it took in. But the commission, having little real interest in disposing of the course, dropped the matter for almost four years.

On 10 January 1956, the same Tallahassee Country Club stockholders presented a similar lease request to the city commission. This time, county commissioner H. G. Easterwood, who as a city commissioner had opposed the transfer of the city-owned property, charged that the private group was using a "whisper-campaign" to inject the segregation issue into a deal with the city.

Appearing at the city commission meeting, Easterwood reaffirmed his opposition to the lease and declared that "Tallahassee had no racial problem" but that the private group was using the issue as a basis for obtaining control of the golf course. Easterwood charged that the move to take over the city property had been made in secret meetings, without public consent. He reiterated his earlier contention that the land was too large a piece of public property to be in the hands of private citizens. He also worried that the private owners wanted the country club in part so that "they could maintain liquors at the clubhouse." Easterwood suggested that the city raise the green fees and other fees of the country club operation to help put the golf course back "into the black." [27]

Easterwood declared that, despite statements to the contrary being made by the private group, blacks would not be using the public course anytime soon, because "Negroes did not want to play golf with the white people and . . . there was no danger of any Negroes in Tallahassee attempting to play golf on the country club course." As proof, the commissioner pointed out that a Negro golf course had been set up near Florida A&M University. City commission members were not convinced. Although the battle to desegregate public facilities had not yet reached Florida, the recent decision in *Brown v. Board of Education* had persuaded many politicians and officials that integration could be avoided by removing existing facilities and institutions from the public domain. [28]

On 14 February 1956, the city commission voted to lease the golf course and property to Tallahassee Country Club investors for a sum of one dollar a year for a period of ninety-nine years. Mayor J. T. Williams, who protested that the terms of the financial agreement were far too generous, given the property's value, cast the only dissenting vote. Commissioners agreed that the city would consider giving the same deal on the brand new Negro golf course to "any reasonable group" that wanted to take it over. When asked whether the newly transferred course would be open to the public, Robert Parker, spokesman for the Tallahassee Country Club, said that "any acceptable person" would be allowed to play. [29]

Two months after receiving the lease agreement, the directors and subscribers of the Tallahassee Country Club, including U.S. attorney Harrold Carswell, state senator (and future senate president) Wilson Carraway, and attorney and former mayor Charles S. Ausley received a certificate of incorporation from the secretary of state's office recognizing a for-profit organization known as Capital City Country Club. Over the next few years the club was changed to a not-for-profit organization with a membership list that read like a who's who of Tallahassee's business and political elite and included Governor LeRoy Collins, who resigned in 1961. Although blacks in 1957 made several requests to lease the new nine-hole Jake Gaither Golf Course, the property remained under city control.

The decision of the city commission to transfer the public golf course into private hands was not only a telling commentary on the attitudes and atmosphere in Tallahassee in the late 1950s but had long-lasting political repercussions as well. The Supreme Court nomination of Carswell was derailed in 1970 in part because of the controversy over his membership in the private club. The black community from time to time asked that the club be returned to the city, but its demands were largely ignored. The issue remained a sore point in community race relations.[30]

On 2 May 1959, four armed Tallahassee white men surrounded a parked car near the Florida A&M campus and ordered the occupants, all students at the university, out of the car. The two black men were forced to kneel on the ground while the whites chose which of the two young women each pair would take. The women's dates were ordered to drive away. Taking advantage of a moment of confusion, the younger of the women broke free and ran. The other woman was forced into the car, was taken to the outskirts of town, and was raped by each of the four men.

Meanwhile, the male students returned to the scene and found the young woman who had run away hiding nearby. They immediately reported the incident to the police, who along with the sheriff's department and the highway patrol, began searching for the car described by the students.

A part-time deputy, riding a beat by himself for the first time, spotted the car, gave chase, and finally forced it off the road. Officer John Cooke, who had no police radio in his car, threatened to shoot anyone moving and held the car's occupants at gunpoint until another police car drove by. The young woman was found on the floor of the car, gagged with a baby diaper, her hands tied behind her. She was rushed to the hospital at Florida A&M University, where she was examined by a black physician who confirmed that she had been raped. By the next morning, the *Democrat* reported that she had also been examined by a white doctor who also determined that there was "evidence of intercourse."[31]

On 3 May, formal charges of rape were filed against the white men by Sheriff Bill Joyce. The oldest of the accused was twenty-four, the youngest, sixteen. On 4 May at a mass meeting and rally at Florida A&M, students voted to boycott classes the following day to demonstrate their anger over the rape and to show solidarity with their classmates. The students raised $500 in one day for a fund for the young woman, who remained in the hospital.

On 6 May, a specially called grand jury (consisting of eighteen white men) was instructed by circuit judge W. May Walker to "function without regard to race, color or creed, according to the law applicable to the case." The jury heard the evidence in the case behind closed doors. Photographers were prohibited from taking pictures of any of the witnesses. Following the grand jury's deliberation, the four men were indicted and a trial date was set for 9 June.[32]

In the days leading up to the trial, reporters from all over the country poured into Tallahassee. Governor Collins was besieged with letters and telegrams from across the nation, including one from Roy Wilkins, the NAACP executive secretary, demanding that for once "even-handed, color-blind justice" be served in a southern courtroom. The governor issued a statement deploring the crime, but because of his position on the probation and parole commission, he refused further comment on the case. (Unlike most of his constituents, Collins was opposed to the death penalty.) [33]

In December 1955, the governor had angered many Floridians when he commuted the death sentence of a black man accused of raping a white woman in the small Central Florida town of Groveland. The Groveland rape case of 1949 was so blatant an example of racially motivated injustice that three Florida historians later called it "Florida's little Scottsboro," after the more widely known but similar Alabama case. Despite overwhelming evidence that the four Groveland men had been railroaded (two of the accused died in the custody of local justice officials, while one, a sixteen-year-old boy, was given life in prison), Collins was accused of being a dupe of the NAACP and was even accosted by the alleged victim during a 1956 campaign stop. Groveland was certainly not the only example of legally sanctioned vigilante justice in Florida, though it was one of the worst. Many blacks were hoping that the trial in Tallahassee would be the exception to the existing rule of separate and unequal justice. [34]

On the first day of the rape trial, Tallahassee blacks poured into the balcony of the courtroom. An all-white, male jury was selected to try the defendants, who pleaded not guilty. The Leon County sheriff's department doubled security in the downtown area.

For four days the jurors heard testimony that clearly established the guilt of the accused, who did not take the stand in their own defense. On 14 June the jury returned a verdict of guilty but with a recommendation of mercy. That recommendation ensured that the men would not receive the death penalty but left open several possible sentences ranging from life in prison to probation. For eight days there was intense speculation over the severity of the sentence that the four men would receive. Interviewed about the Tallahassee case in Montgomery, Martin Luther King Jr. announced that although he did not believe in capital punishment, he believed in punishment "suiting the crime. If the court does this," King added, "it will be a great day for the South." [35]

On 22 June, Judge W. May Walker called the convicted men back into his courtroom and sentenced them to life in prison. During the sentencing Walker told the men that they had committed a horrible crime and were lucky to escape the electric chair. He asked the four if they had ever heard of the Supreme Ruler of the Universe. When they replied no in unison, Walker said, "He is the one to whom you should direct your appeal. He may offer you some comfort." Later Walker told a reporter that in his nineteen years as a circuit judge, he had tried a dozen rape cases but that this was the first time the accused had been white. [36]

Reaction to the sentencing among the black community was positive, although there was some grumbling about the recommendation of mercy, which had occurred in only half of the rape cases involving black men in Leon County. On the day Walker sentenced the four men in Tallahassee, a circuit judge in the nearby rural town of Marianna commuted the death sentence of a sixteen-year-old black boy convicted of rape to life imprisonment. The judge said he erred in not warning the jury that the boy's confession should be viewed "with extreme caution." The two events led Father David Brooks, the ICC activist and Tallahassee NAACP president, to declare that "we are on our way to eliminating the double standard of justice."[37]

Newspapers throughout Florida praised the results of the trial in Tallahassee and decried the critics of southern justice. The *Tallahassee Democrat* received an award from the Florida Bar Association for its "fair and impartial coverage of the trial." The Tallahassee branch of the United Daughters of the Confederacy praised the capital city for handling the trial with "true southern honor and justice . . . in the tradition of Robert E. Lee." Praise for Judge Walker, who remained characteristically modest, elevated him almost to the stature of a folk hero.[38]

Almost immediately after the sentencing, Tallahassee returned to its normal concerns. The outcome of the trial had little effect on race relations in the city. On 30 May the Civic League sponsored "the biggest and most ambitious program ever sponsored by the Negroes of Tallahassee." Designated Community Day, the program was designed to "make citizens community conscious and reward those who have during the past years made contributions over and above the duties usually expected of a citizen." A one-day workshop included sessions entitled "Responsibility of the Tallahassee Citizen" and "Know Your City Government." None of the organizers was a member of the ICC.[39]

Meanwhile at Tallahassee's all-white Leon High School, students in the American democracy classes held a one-day joint session to debate the important political and social issues of the day. The *Democrat* reported that the students objected to integration in high school on "moral grounds." The students felt that it would be more acceptable to have integration at the college level but only if the sexes were segregated. The students based their opposition to integration on "social" considerations rather than on "racial prejudice."[40]

Down the street from Leon High, the Florida House of Representatives mirrored the views of the students. As soon as it was announced that the Dade County school board had ordered four black children admitted to a white elementary school for the fall of 1959, the house approved a bill allowing county school boards to set up separate schools for girls and boys and a constitutional amendment plan under which the state could help pay for private educations for children withdrawn from integrated schools. The senate passed a measure (successfully vetoed by Collins and upheld by urban legislators) to abolish all of

Florida's public schools the day the first one was officially integrated. Tallahassee's brief moment of racial harmony was over. Agreeing with the conviction of four working-class white men guilty of a brutal rape was one thing; actually stepping beyond the rigid confines of racial separatism was another.

The 1950s ended on a contradictory note in Tallahassee. Events of the immediately preceding years—the bus boycott, the Johns committee hearings, local and state political races, school desegregation suits, and the rape trial—had affected the psyche of the community and had ensured that more changes in race relations, however unwelcome, loomed ahead. Yet as the new decade opened, few Tallahasseeans, indeed few Americans, foresaw the profound challenges such changes would present.

5 | The Sit-Ins Begin

In the summer of 1959, two Florida A&M students, nineteen-year-old Patricia Stephens and her older sister Priscilla, were in Miami visiting relatives. When a friend asked them to attend an "Interracial Action Institute" sponsored by the Congress of Racial Equality (CORE), they hesitated. Like most southerners in 1959, they knew little about CORE. Though Pat and Priscilla had been raised in a politically active family, they were reluctant to attend until their friend proposed dinner in Miami Beach after the workshop. The Stephens sisters never again needed any inducement to participate in CORE activities. The two women were instrumental in making CORE a household word in Tallahassee by 1960, and they were catalysts for many of the early civil rights activities throughout North Florida.

CORE, which had been founded in Columbus, Ohio, in 1942, was an outgrowth of the Christian-pacifist peace organization the Fellowship of Reconciliation. Based on the Gandhian philosophy of noncooperation with evil, CORE used direct action strategies such as sit-ins, standing lines, and economic boycotts to attack de facto segregation in the North. In 1947 after the Supreme

Court ruled that racially segregated seating on interstate buses was unconstitutional, CORE sponsored the interracial "Journey of Reconciliation" to see whether the decision would be implemented in the upper South. The small group of riders were arrested in several areas. Six riders were given jail terms, and one was beaten. This experience ended CORE's desegregation activities in the South for almost a decade.

CORE chapters and activities in the North and Northwest expanded throughout the 1950s, however. After the 1955 Montgomery bus boycott had introduced nonviolent protest to the South, CORE began to organize chapters below the Mason-Dixon Line. The first was organized in Nashville, Tennessee, and by the late 1950s a few CORE chapters had appeared in Kentucky, Louisiana, and South Carolina.

CORE grew slowly in the South because of the requirement that all chapters had to be interracial. Also it was not considered feasible for members to employ in the South the sit-in and other forms of direct action confrontation that CORE used in the North. Southern chapters therefore concentrated on voter registration drives and economic boycotts.

Florida proved to be the exception to CORE's southern rule. Miami CORE was organized in the late winter of 1959 during a southern organization trip made by field directors Gordon R. Carey and James T. McCain. Miami, Florida's biggest southern city, suffered from many of the racial problems of the Deep South, yet its large populations of northern immigrants and ethnic groups ensured at least some support for the fledgling interracial organization. Although membership in Miami CORE remained limited—in part because of the specter of the Communist-hunting Johns committee—the group staged the first and only southern sit-in during spring 1959 in a futile effort to desegregate local lunch counters.

Although national CORE officials realized that Miami CORE was a southern anomaly, Executive Secretary James Robinson chose the city as the site for CORE's first interracial institute. It was important to CORE officials that institute participants stay in a southern city where desegregated housing was at least minimally available and where they could learn firsthand how to organize and participate in direct action community programs.

Miami's Action Institute had two main goals. One was to train people from various parts of the country in the use of peaceful direct action as a weapon to advance integration. The second was to speed up the attack on segregation in Miami that CORE had already begun. Over 600 people from across the United States attended the institute's first session on nonviolent direct action that summer.

Participants at the institute read, discussed, and debated the works of Gandhi and his philosophy of nonviolent resistance to injustice and racism. National CORE officials explained how nonviolent protest could be used to attack and destroy racial segregation in America by revealing to the public the "moral injustice" of the segregation system and the "moral right of Americans to protest against this system." If individual or collective consciousness were not sufficiently moved by these demonstrations, then CORE would use local and national economic boycotts to force the business community to respond.

Many of the interracial workshop members participated in the first step of CORE's action program: "tests" of local lunch counters and theaters to document the extent of segregation practices in Miami's public facilities. Later, the institute took as its major project the desegregation of the lunch counter of the Byrons-Jackson department store. On 25 September 1959, after days of continuous sit-ins, a series of unsuccessful negotiations with department store management, and at least three incidents of unprovoked violence, the department store lunch counter was permanently closed.

Although CORE's activities in Miami failed to yield a desegregation victory, one of the city's largest department stores had been forced to close its lunch counters. This step in itself was encouragement enough for many of the "testers" to take the experience and the ideas of CORE and direct action protest back to their own communities. For Pat and Priscilla Stephens, CORE provided a way to convert personal dissatisfaction with second-class citizenship into an active campaign against racial injustice. The young women left Miami determined to bring CORE's message to Florida A&M and to Tallahassee.

Pat and Priscilla had been born in Quincy, a "shade tobacco town" twenty miles west of Tallahassee, and grew up in Palm Beach County, where their stepfather was a high school civics teacher in the working-class community of Belle Glade. The girls' parents were both involved in civic activities and concerns in Palm Beach County. Lottie Hamilton stressed the importance of self-reliance and personal responsibility and encouraged her young daughters to help her in voter registration drives and other community improvement projects.

When Pat was in the eighth grade, her stepfather spoke before her civics class about the use of the petition to effect change within a democratic society. The resourceful thirteen-year-old drew up a petition to have the principal of her high school dismissed on grounds of intellectual incompetence. After hundreds of students signed the petition, a rumor spread throughout the school that anyone whose name appeared on the petition could be arrested. That afternoon, Patricia was chased home by scores of frightened classmates who wanted to remove their names. Undaunted, she gave the petition to sympathetic adults, who took it to the Palm Beach County school board. For reasons never made public, the principal did not return to his position the following school year.

Although Pat did well in high school, and served in various elected positions in student government, she was overjoyed when she heard of the school desegregation decision in *Brown v. Board of Education* in May 1954. Both she and her sister believed that they would attend the modern, better equipped "white" school in Belle Glade in the fall. Then it became clear that Palm Beach County, like the rest of Florida, would not willingly comply with *Brown*. In June 1957, Patricia, like Priscilla before her, graduated from an all-black high school. The younger Stephens entered Florida A&M University as a music major in September 1957.

Things were quiet in Tallahassee when Patricia joined her older sister for the fall semester of 1957 at FAMU. The ICC, the student and local chapters of the NAACP, and the Tallahassee Council on Human Relations were active but served primarily as discussion groups. The student chapter of the NAACP, once one of the largest in the country, had twenty-nine members.

Under attack by the relentless Johns committee, the state NAACP had been drained by the ongoing charges and investigations leveled against its officers and attorneys. C. K. Steele cochaired the organization's "Fighting Fund for Freedom Campaign," designed to increase membership and raise $50,000. It was a tough battle. In 1957, many Floridians considered the NAACP radical and subversive and its members unruly troublemakers. In Tallahassee, the local chapter relied on letters and petitions to pressure the school board to adopt a desegregation plan for the Leon County public school system. Such demands were summarily ignored.

Although the NAACP, the ICC, and the Tallahassee Council on Human Relations all strongly supported the ideals of desegregation and black equality, they had no specific program or plan to attack segregation or discrimination in Tallahassee. A small group of black and white graduate students and faculty met surreptitiously during 1957 and 1958 to discuss ways to "get desegregation going" but made no real headway. Fliers that urged students not to "support segregation by silence" were circulated at FSU and FAMU but received scant attention (except from the Johns committee). What the Stephens sisters brought with CORE was a consistent strategy for pursuing the goal of desegregation aggressively.[1]

By the time they returned to Florida A&M in September 1959, both Pat and Priscilla had become civil rights veterans. Their first goal was to explain CORE to other students and to interest them in attending an orientation meeting. The atmosphere on campus was more conducive to civil rights activism than it had been two years earlier. The rape trial the previous spring had galvanized the black community, particularly at Florida A&M, where membership in the student chapter of the NAACP had risen to seventy-six members. Communication between faculty at the two universities had increased, as had discussions on race relations at Florida State University.

During the first weeks of the fall semester, the Stephens sisters canvased the women's dorms at Florida A&M, explaining the philosophy of CORE and its methods to anyone who would listen. They also contacted C. K. Steele, James Hudson, Daisy Young, and other Tallahasseeans who were identified as activists and spokespeople for the black community. The individuals with whom the sisters spoke were generally interested in learning more about the organization and its philosophy.

In early October 1959, approximately thirty students attended the first CORE orientation meeting. Pat and Priscilla explained the philosophy of CORE and the methods used by the organization to attack racial segregation. Some students lost interest when they discovered that the basic foundation of CORE was nonviolence. Those who knew that they could not "turn the other cheek" when taunted or attacked declined to join the new group. Before February 1960, when the lunch counter sit-ins in Greensboro, North Carolina, inaugurated a new era of student activism, it was difficult for many blacks to appreciate nonviolent direct action as an effective tactic.

As a concession to what one early CORE member described as the "poisonous sociological climate" of the capital city, the first organizational meeting of Tallahassee CORE met in late October 1959 in "semi-secrecy" at the home of Daisy Young, now the assistant admissions director at Florida A&M. Present were Young, three FAMU students, including the Stephens sisters, C. K. Steele, Florida A&M music professor Richard Haley, and CORE field secretary Gordon Carey. Carey had come to Tallahassee at the request of Pat Stephens to advise and guide the new affiliate.

Carey explained the history and importance of CORE's strategy of nonviolence to the small group. He emphasized that local members should try to solve local racial problems with minimal interference from the national office. Above all, Carey stressed, CORE must maintain an ongoing action program to avoid becoming "another human relations group." The group debated which of Tallahassee's myriad racial problems might best be attacked by CORE's direct action tactics.

The next CORE meeting was held at the NAACP-ICC office, still located in the back of the grocery store owned by Dan Speed. The two organizations had continued to share space since the boycott yet managed to maintain separate organizational structures and activities. Not all blacks who belonged to the NAACP were ICC members, but the leadership of both organizations was essentially the same. In 1959, for instance, Steele was president of both the ICC and the NAACP.

CORE's first "official" meeting was noteworthy for the presence of three young white people, Florida State University graduate student Robert White, his wife, Rosemary "Posey" White, and Susan Shuck, another FSU student. The Whites, who had moved to Tallahassee in 1957, knew a few Florida A&M students and professors through their friendship with Joe Spagna, the FSU student who had become notorious for his support of the bus boycott and ICC activities. The organization was unknown to members of the white community apart from a few sociology majors and faculty at Florida State. Gordon Carey was delighted to see the three young whites, but he warned Stephens that as with other interracial groups in the South, there was a danger that the organization would deteriorate into a "talking" group.

By early November 1959, CORE had grown to eighteen dues-paying members. They included Speed, who had become a Baptist minister after the bus boycott, and Florida A&M chaplain James Hudson. Richard Haley and Daisy Young served as informal "advisers" to the group, which consisted mainly of students. The fledgling group had so interested national CORE that both field directors, James McCain and Gordon Carey, made several trips back to Tallahassee before the end of 1959.

On 7 November, Tallahassee CORE chose its first project: a test of the seating policy on city buses. Two years after the bus boycott, it was compelling testimony to the strength of segregation sentiment that CORE members still felt it necessary to see whether Tallahassee blacks could ride unchallenged at the front of the buses. Haley told participants to sit in the front row or "near front row seats." Except for one incident, when a driver on a predominantly white route asked them to move to the rear (which they refused to do), the testers met with no resistance. Black and white CORE members did not try to sit together on the buses. Whites went along only as "observers," fearing that interracial seating was "too bold" a move for Tallahassee to handle.[2]

At the next meeting CORE members evaluated their test rides. They noted that some Tallahassee blacks continued to observe the old segregation customs and remained in the rear of the bus. Haley commented that it would be necessary "to combat the excellent indoctrination in second-class patterns of living which the Negro has received."

For their next project, CORE members, under Carey's tutelage, attempted to buy interstate bus tickets in the whites-only waiting rooms of the Greyhound and Trailways bus stations. The students assumed, as had members of the Journey of Reconciliation twelve years earlier, that federal laws prohibiting segregation of interstate travelers were being ignored in Tallahassee.

On 11 November, several black CORE members approached the ticket window of both companies while whites waited as observers in the crowd. In neither bus depot did the testers attempt to sit in the restaurant or use the restroom facilities. At the Greyhound station, the blacks were able to purchase their tickets, but at the Trailways station, they were curtly turned away and were told to leave the station. Pat Stephens reminded the Trailways employees that the law guaranteed blacks the right to travel on and use integrated interstate facilities. But it was as if she were "speaking to persons from another planet. They had no idea what the law was then, and more than that, they could have cared less. We knew what their response would be, but we had to find out first hand."[3]

CORE policy mandated that members attempt to negotiate a settlement with store owners or city officials before resorting to sit-ins or other demonstrations. Consequently, Tallahassee CORE spent several months "documenting" the extent of segregation in the city's public and private facilities. At Sears department store they were served food but were told to eat it outside. At the local dime stores they were served at stand-up counters reserved for blacks.

CORE members found segregation as thoroughly entrenched in public facilities, such as the airport and bus restaurants, as in private businesses. The group wrote to the Interstate Commerce Commission and the Department of Justice and complained about the lack of enforcement of laws pertaining to interstate travel. But such legal procedures, Richard Haley wrote Gordon Carey, were "slow, slow, slow." Furthermore, he added, "the Negro community must be reminded of its obligation to use existing laws."[4]

After four months of limited activity, Tallahassee CORE was not yet the prototype of a direct action civil rights organization. Nor had it yet exerted any effect on the city's segregation policies or customs. As Haley wrote to Gordon Carey in the summer of 1960: "No one [then] dreamed of the imminence, or even the idea of the subsequent sit-ins."[5]

While CORE members in Tallahassee debated their next move, four young black men in Greensboro, North Carolina, walked into the local Woolworth's, sat down at the lunch counter, and ordered coffee. When the students were denied service, they remained seated at the counter for several hours. The next day, they returned with a larger group. On the third day, hundreds of demonstrators, most from North Carolina Agricultural and Technical College, filled the store. Within a week, the activities in Greensboro had captured national headlines, had inaugurated a southern sit-in movement, and had turned nonviolent direct action into the dominant strategy in the struggle for racial equality for the next half decade.

There was no CORE chapter in Greensboro, but the four protestors had been encouraged to conduct the sit-in by a local Greensboro businessman who served on the executive board of the city's NAACP and who learned of CORE's methods from his reading of the organization's pamphlet, Erasing the Color Line.

As the sit-ins rapidly spread across the state, CORE sent Gordon Carey and James McCain to North Carolina to advise and assist the student activists. McCain was actually in Tallahassee when the North Carolina demonstrations began. A week after he left, he contacted a number of Tallahassee CORE members to encourage them to conduct their own "sympathy sit-ins" as part of a regional strategy.[6]

After a hastily called meeting, Tallahassee CORE members agreed to participate in the regional event scheduled for 13 February. On that day, eight Florida A&M students and two black high school students entered the department store, sat down at the Woolworth lunch counter, and requested service. When they were refused, they remained at the counter.

At first, white customers continued to eat, but they quickly left when it became clear that the students were not going to move. One white patron remained until he had finished his lunch and was thanked by the waitress for staying through all of the "indecency." Other patrons in various parts of the store began to gather around the counter. A few made threatening and insulting remarks to the demonstrators. Fearing a confrontation, the store manager closed the counter. As the students were leaving their stations, one waitress told the crowd of onlookers that the students weren't "doing anything" and should be left alone. A white man approached FAMU student William Larkins and told him that he was doing a fine job and to keep up the good work. The students remained seated for two hours, reading their schoolbooks and quietly ignoring the insults of a small group of white hecklers. Although the press arrived quickly, the police did not come until after the protesters had left.[7]

Pleased with their first public effort to protest segregation in their community, CORE resolved to return to Woolworth's on the next weekend with a larger and better trained group of protestors. Tallahassee demonstrations were always planned for Saturdays, as the leaders and a majority of demonstrators were busy with classwork and other activities. And as in many southern communities, large numbers of blacks and whites came downtown on Saturday afternoons to do their shopping and socializing.

During the week before the next sit-in, Haley and Pat Stephens thoroughly briefed volunteers on how to react to hecklers and possible violence. CORE members even acted out what Stephens called a "sociodrama" of what might happen on their return to the Woolworth lunch counter. It was agreed that two white "witnesses" would sit at the counter, would order food, and would remain to document what happened. Priscilla Stephens was chosen as spokesperson for the group.[8]

Seventeen black CORE members arrived at Woolworth's at about 2:00 P.M. on 20 February. They ordered food, but the waitresses ignored their requests.

The manager closed the counter. The other white patrons (except for the witnesses) quickly left. A few white onlookers gathered in small groups in the store. The CORE members began to read the books that they had brought with them. After forty-five minutes the two witnesses left. Within minutes the police arrived, accompanied by Mayor Hugh Williams and other members of the city commission. Williams personally asked the demonstrators to leave. Six got up and left. The eleven students who remained seated were arrested and were charged with "disturbing the peace by engaging in riotous conduct and assembly to the disturbance of the public tranquility."

Arrested along with the Stephens sisters were Henry and Charles Steele, two sons of C. K. Steele; six Florida A&M students; and forty-three-year-old Mary Ola Gaines, an ICC member and former boycott activist. Those arrested were led out of the store near a crowd of white onlookers, many of whom jeered loudly as the demonstrators were marched to the nearby jail.

Confusion reigned at the small city jail that generally served as a processing point or holding pen for prisoners on their way to the county facility. Officers barred reporters from entering the building while city manager Arvah Hopkins and city commission members met to discuss the arrests. Finally, Williams read a prepared statement defending the arrests as necessary to protect the peace of the community. Inside the jail, the arrested demonstrators were taunted by police officers, who reluctantly allowed them to call Steele and finally Dan Speed, who provided the money for their bail bonds.

The sit-ins caught most of Tallahassee by surprise, including blacks who had supported the bus boycott, worked in voter registration drives, and belonged to the NAACP. As historian Adam Fairclough notes in his book on the SCLC, many blacks, even those who were willing to boycott public services or facilities, were hesitant to sit in or physically to intrude on the premises of privately owned businesses, particularly in the South, where property rights and states' rights were sacrosanct, linked, and emotionally charged issues. Furthermore, few blacks in Tallahassee, particularly teachers and government employees, could rationalize or risk breaking the law deliberately and risking imprisonment.

Some black citizens were obvious exceptions to the rule, however. One was C. K. Steele. Unlike his contemporaries in the NACCP, the ICC, or the Ministerial Alliance, Steele had a connection to the nascent civil rights movement outside Tallahassee. The Tallahassee minister was vice president of the SCLC, counted Martin Luther King Jr. as a personal friend, and had traveled outside the South to raise funds to pay off fines associated with the earlier bus boycott. Like King, Steele had a commitment to social justice that deepened in the years after the Montgomery and Tallahassee boycotts.

When the sit-ins began, Steele became a convert to direct action protest, something the SCLC did not yet support and the NAACP continued to resist. Years later, Steele remembered that when he had urged members of the ICC to endorse the sit-ins and later the "jail, no bail" tactics adopted by CORE activists, he received a lukewarm response. Although he usually endorsed CORE's strategy, Steele never participated in a sit-in but supported the student protesters as did other black adults. "They [students] leaned on me a lot," Steele recalled in 1978, but "without the students, there would have been no protest, there would have been no movement. They were the militants, they were the soldiers."[9]

Steele was not the only adult black Tallahasseean who provided moral, financial, and emotional backing for the sit-in demonstrators. Not only was Gaines arrested with the students, but once again, as during the bus boycott, both Young and Hudson risked their positions at Florida A&M to encourage and stand by the protesters. Young became one of the most outspoken, uncompromising leaders of CORE's executive council. As Robert White remembered, "she always argued to keep up the pressure" when others sought a more conciliatory approach. Dan Speed provided bail money for those arrested and, according to Richard Haley, never asked to be reimbursed for his expenditures.[10]

Within a week of Tallahassee's first sit-in, lunch counter demonstrations had spread like wildfire across Florida and the South. By 1 March 1960, seven other Florida cities had experienced the sit-in phenomenon. But there were differences. In Daytona Beach, Dunedin, Jacksonville, Tampa, St. Petersburg, St. Augustine, and Sarasota, sit-in demonstrators were primarily students from *private* black colleges. Only in Tallahassee did the student protesters attend a publicly supported institution. Just as important, when the capital city sit-ins became interracial, Tallahassee achieved a notoriety that further distinguished it from many cities of the Deep South.

On Monday, 22 February, all eleven demonstrators in the Tallahassee sit-ins, represented by Howard Dixon and Tobias Simon, attorneys for the American Civil Liberties Union (ACLU), were arraigned in city court and pleaded not guilty to disturbing the peace. Word of their pending trial, set for 3 March, spread rapidly on Florida A&M's campus. A week before the trial date, the entire student body, galvanized by the sit-ins in Tallahassee, met and decided to skip classes on 3 March and to attend the trial. When news of their plan reached downtown, the trial was postponed for two weeks.

Local CORE members, fearing that another sit-in would hasten the trial date and would "harden the opposition," canceled a scheduled sit-in the week after the arrests. With this critical decision, CORE lost its momentum and press coverage just as the community was becoming aware and supportive of the organization's activities. As Richard Haley later noted, "we might have been more successful in court if we had never broken the rhythm of protest action."[11]

Despite their commitment to "moral suasion" as a tool to fight racism, CORE members knew that most whites in Tallahassee remained firmly committed to segregation and considered sit-in demonstrators criminal agitators. During his weekly news conference on 3 March, Governor Collins denounced sit-in demonstrations as illegal and dangerous and urged that they be discontinued. The "rights of private discrimination" were sacrosanct, said Collins, and superseded the "feeling of any citizen that he should be allowed the services of all phases of any business." More important, Collins added, demonstrations of any kind "lead to disorder and, of course disorder leads to danger to the general welfare. . . . I hope that we will not have any more of them in our state." But when asked if he would recommend that the Florida A&M students who had participated in the demonstration be expelled, Collins said that he saw "no basis for making any such recommendation."[12]

Collins's views on the sit-ins were amplified by Malcolm Johnson, who wrote that it was "the right of the business operator to deny service to anyone he feels will have an undesirable effect on his business." Johnson, who strongly agreed with the governor's dedication to the sanctity of private property, could not resist taking a swipe at those "false leaders" who were hurting the chances of blacks to win "reasonable privileges and concessions by sound democratic means."[13]

Collins and Johnson were on solid legal ground in 1960 in defending the right of private businesses to discriminate against potential patrons. But when they assumed that the goal of blacks was merely to be served in a private establishment, they missed the crucial point of CORE's early civil rights strategy. Demonstrators sitting at lunch counters wanted more than service; they sought to expose segregation as a moral issue relevant to all Americans and adversely affecting everyone. Pat Stephens often called civil rights agitation part of a "struggle for human dignity" and not just a campaign for black rights. Students such as Stephens believed that they could change segregation laws and customs by exposing the hypocrisy and immorality of segregation to white southerners, whose religious faith and patriotic commitment they had shared since childhood.[14]

On Saturday, 5 March, a small group of Florida A&M students sat down at the McCrory's lunch counter and ordered food. To keep the sit-ins going all day, volunteers were scheduled to replace each group that was arrested or left the store. It was agreed that only black students were to participate, but white CORE member Robert Armstrong decided at the last minute to join the demonstration.

The manager of McCrory's promptly closed the counter and called police as the first group of protesters sat down. Just as the police approached the store, the FAMU students left the counter. Only Armstrong was arrested, and he was later released. Despite CORE's disappointment that the sit-in had failed, the "abortive effort" received front page coverage in the *Democrat*. Over 200 people, including, for the first time, a "sizable number of whites," attended the organization's next meeting.[15]

How did a large group of white students become aware of, much less join, a civil rights organization dedicated to abolishing "America's color line" less than three years after an FSU graduate student had been expelled for inviting black students to visit the white campus? Despite the inhospitable atmosphere, the seeds for an interracial protest movement, first sown at Florida State University during the boycott, had begun to take root in 1958 at the Chapel of the Resurrection, "the Episcopal Church for Florida State University."

An Episcopal student center called Ruge Hall had first been established at FSU in 1931. In 1956, resident priest Harcourt Waller was able to persuade the Episcopal hierarchy of the need for another structure to house both a church and a new student center. The result was the Chapel of the Resurrection. Through his sermons and discussion groups at the Chapel, Waller emphasized the need to bridge the gap between the church and the world, to "live . . . Christianity" on a daily basis. Local Episcopalians, quietly ensconced in St. John's, were little aware of the effect of Waller's exhortations.[16]

In early 1958, Waller, with encouragement and financial support from several local townspeople, purchased an old and run-down house next to the Chapel of the Resurrection. Within a year it had become Canterbury House, a low-cost residence for fourteen male students. The residents had been chosen, Waller told them, with the expectation that they would be involved in "transforming the world, not hiding from it." Through study and discussion of contemporary moral and religious issues, the young men agreed to uncover "the meaning of Christian community" and carry the message to the university and to the city at large.[17]

Because the Canterbury House was located off campus and was separate from the downtown Episcopal Church, it was not subject to the same scrutiny as organizations connected with FSU or the larger community. Consequently, it was one of the few places where black and white students could meet together. At the Canterbury House black students from Florida A&M, encouraged by Waller to attend the Chapel of the Resurrection, first told white students about CORE. The word spread from the Canterbury House to other white students at FSU who, whether from religious convictions or personal ones, became interested in the new civil rights organization and the struggle for black equality.

After three weeks' planning and bolstered by large increases in both black and white membership, Tallahassee CORE held its largest and most dramatic sit-in. On 11 March 1960, CORE members talked with the managers of Woolworth's and McCrory's about changing their lunch counter policy. When the managers refused to negotiate, CORE members told them that there would be sit-ins at both counters on the next day, Saturday, 12 March.

During the week before those sit-ins, while support for direct action protest continued to swell at Florida A&M, CORE members and sympathizers met to decide who would take part in the demonstration. Because of the previous lunch counter arrests, the outcome appeared in little doubt. CORE leadership agreed that the sit-ins should be interracial, with an equal number of white and black participants. By the end of the meeting, six black male students had volunteered. Five white FSU male students agreed to join the sit-in at Woolworth's. Three white female students from FSU planned to arrive at that counter before the sit-in began to serve as witnesses.

Later that afternoon, Oscar (Bob) Brock, a junior at FSU who had never attended a CORE meeting or participated in any interracial discussion, was approached by Steve Poe, one of the white volunteers, and was asked to participate in "a test" of the segregated lunch counters. Brock had been identified as a "social liberal type person" in part by the way he came dressed to class—with his shirttail out, wearing flip-flops and bermuda shorts—and in part on the basis of a few conversations he had had with Poe. Brock agreed because he was "a rebellious person anyway" and wanted a chance to help "correct a wrong in society." His next contact with the sit-in participants occurred when the four other white students picked him up Saturday morning for the drive into town.[18]

At 9:30 A.M. fourteen students met in front of Woolworth's, walked in, and sat down at the lunch counter. The white students were waited on and the black students ignored. The manager closed the counter but did not ask the students to leave. Within minutes Mayor George Taff and the police had arrived. Taff instructed the students to leave. The three women students left immediately. Brock, who was at the end of the long counter, did not hear the mayor's order. Steve Poe and FAMU student Benjamin Cowins got up to leave. The other students turned to confer with each other. All eleven were immediately arrested and were told to line up against the wall. One officer, "a small Barney Fife kind of guy," grabbed Brock by the collar and told him to "get over there with your nigger buddies."[19]

The eleven demonstrators were led outside. As they appeared, FSU student Derek Lawler jumped in with them and was lined up with the interracial pairs and marched the short distance to the city jail. "Hold hands with your nigger buddies you love so much," the police taunted the group. Obediently, Brock took the hand of the black student next to him but then quickly dropped it "for fear we'd be beaten because of the homosexual thing."[20]

Once inside the jail, the young men were fingerprinted by Chief Stouta-mire. "You got this idea in church, didn't you boy?" the chief asked Robert Armstrong, a resident of Canterbury House. When the student answered yes, Stoutamire said, "Them preachers do a lotta talkin' about the brotherhood of men, but they ain't gonna help you white niggers now." Before being sent into his cell, Armstrong asked for two books, *Religious Drama* and the *Book of Common Prayer*. "You'll need them," an officer told him, and slammed shut the cell door.[21]

Meanwhile, at McCrory's, white demonstrators sat alone at the counter. The black CORE members had failed to appear in time to participate in the dem-onstration. Distraught by the failure of the McCrory's sit-in, Richard Haley re-turned to the CORE office, where he first learned of the arrests at Woolworth's.

Pat Stephens, who had been an observer at Woolworth's, rushed back to Flor-ida A&M and enlisted 200 waiting students to return to town with her to "fill the jails if necessary" to protest the arrest of fellow students. While the students formed a silent protest outside the jail, Stephens demanded to see the incarcer-ated demonstrators. When the police refused to let her in, Stephens sent fifty of the assembled students to Woolworth's to conduct a second sit-in and fifty more to McCrory's.

As soon as the first of the students entered McCrory's, they were arrested by waiting police. The students attempting to get into Woolworth's were stopped by a group of white men carrying baseball bats, knives, and ax handles. The leader of the group was Homer Barrs, president of the White Citizens Council, who brandished a club and dared the demonstrators to try to pass him. The students, most of whom had not been trained in nonviolent protest, hesitated and began chanting "no violence."[22]

Suddenly, several of the students moved toward the crowd of whites. The police, who were standing in front of Woolworth's, disappeared around the cor-ner when the situation approached a violent confrontation. Local newscaster Frank Pepper rushed up to a nearby officer who was directing traffic and im-plored him to "break this thing up before real trouble breaks out!" Pointing to the white crowd, Pepper said, "those men are armed!" The policeman replied, "it ain't none of my business—I can't do nothing!" The officer then turned and walked away.[23]

Pat Stephens, who saw the scene from across the street, rushed over and told the students to return with her to FAMU. Back on campus, they quickly orga-nized a group of 1,000 eager students to march to town to protest the arrests. Carrying signs that read "Give Us Back Our Students," "We're Americans Too," "No Violence," and "We Want Our Rights," the students, no longer on the sidelines of the sit-in movement, headed downtown together.[24]

As the students neared the volatile area, the twelve demonstrators were led out of the back door of the small city jail for transfer to the larger, segregated county facility. When they arrived at the Leon County jail, the protesters were led past a "bull pen," a large cell with prisoners who had not yet been processed and assigned a cell. "Put 'um in here, we know how to take care of those nigger lovers" several of the prisoners shouted. "For the first time I was really afraid," Brock remembered, "I decided that since I was a gymnast I would grab hold of the bars and kick them if they tried to attack me." Brock's physical prowess was not tested. The students were led away from the main jail population to the back of the building and were put in segregated cells.[25]

As he sped through town Saturday afternoon, city commissioner William T. Mayo was frustrated and angry. Now for the fourth weekend in a row he had been pulled away from his business because of a local law that required a member of the city commission to be present if citizens were arrested for inciting a riot. Expecting only a minor disturbance involving a few people, Mayo was stunned when he arrived downtown. Young white men were roaming throughout the city, many carrying bats, guns, and knives. Police told the commissioner that the mayor was busy at the rapidly filling jail and that 1,000 students from FAMU were preparing to march on the city.

Mayo quickly empowered every law enforcement official he could round up—city policemen, sheriff's deputies, and state troopers—and instructed Sheriff Bill Joyce to form a solid wall of armed men across Adams and Monroe Streets, blocking the main entrance into town from Florida A&M. As the commissioner positioned himself by the officers, he saw hundreds of students walking determinedly from the university toward a railroad track that served to divide black Tallahassee from white.

Taking a bullhorn, Mayo told the students to disperse immediately or face tear gas in exactly three minutes. Twenty-two years later, the former commissioner maintained that when the students refused to turn back, he was forced to order the firing of the tear gas to prevent them from reaching the armed whites waiting in town.

As the frightened students were forcibly turned away, Virginia Delavan, the editor of *Florida Flambeau*, who had come to town with three other reporters to observe the sit-ins, stared in disbelief from the corner of Duval and Monroe Streets. Some of the confused and frightened demonstrators were blocked by police as they tried to head back toward Florida A&M; others were arrested. Pat Stephens, who had been leading the marchers, stumbled blindly from the scene, a victim, she later contended, of tear gas that a policeman had aimed directly at her. Georgiana Fry, a reporter for the *Flambeau*, watched with horror as white men "armed" with nail-studded boards converged on the area and began swinging at the black protesters. "Why aren't you arresting these men?" a fellow reporter asked a nearby police officer. "Because there's no law against carrying boards," he replied, a now-standard response that shocked Frye more than the effects of the tear gas.[26]

Although Mayo contends that the police waited three minutes before throwing the tear gas, several eyewitnesses insist that the order and the tear gas were almost simultaneous. Richard Haley wrote Gordon Carey that the police action was nothing but "legalized hoodlumism." Many students were taken by FAMU faculty to the university hospital and were treated for burns and other related injuries.[27]

At the end of the day, thirty-five demonstrators had been arrested. When Chief Stoutamire was asked by a reporter whether any of the white men and boys who had threatened the students with sticks and clubs had been arrested, he replied, "Ain't no law against a man walking down the street with somethin' in his hands. It's what he does with it." Those "police blotter omissions" were wrong, argued Malcolm Johnson. "It would have put our community and our law enforcement in a more justifiable position if some of that bunch had been arrested and charged too."[28]

While the police chose to ignore armed white males roaming the city before and after the demonstrations, they were quick to notice any whites who appeared to support the protesters. Soon after the FAMU students had been forced back to their campus, editor Delavan and the reporters spoke with a few who had been at the rear of the march and had avoided most of the tear gas. The white students walked back to their car in silence. They had scarcely gotten into the vehicle when a police car drove up and six "sturdy" officers quickly surrounded them. "Your folks would be ashamed of you. Them niggers are better than you are," shouted the police. "You're worse than niggers. You sons of bitches." Reporter Nils Bateman tried to reason with the police—"a mistake," Delavan remembered. "If I wasn't in uniform, I'd kill you boy," an officer told him. "All those niggers live for is to produce bastards," they shouted at the young women. "And you want to help 'em." "You look like niggers turned inside out," they were told.[29]

Although they had not participated in the sit-ins or the march, the police took the FSU students to the county jail and placed them in a nine-by-fifteen-foot cell with six black students picked up during the march. The ten young people greeted one another "as friends," exchanging names and comparing majors. For the first time in her life Delavan had "met blacks who were my equals—an ironic outcome," she remembered years later, "when you realize that jail cells, like so much else then, were legally segregated."[30]

Every few minutes, a policeman came to the door of the cell and harassed the students. The tear gas on the FAMU marchers' clothing permeated the cell, causing everyone's eyes to water. Finally, the lights were turned out. Someone suggested that they all sing. In loud and clear tones, they sang "America the Beautiful" and "The Star-Spangled Banner." Suddenly, the cell door swung open.

The four white students were released Saturday night, without being charged, into the custody of FSU officials. Waiting for Katherine Warren, the dean of women, Delavan and reporters Georgiana Fry and Rosa Wilson saw their former cellmates brought out to be fingerprinted and booked; they exchanged smiles. As the white students were leaving the jail, the six black demonstrators were returned to their cell.

By the time the *Flambeau* staff had returned to Florida State University, Governor Collins had ordered the state highway patrol to confine Florida A&M students to the campus for the night. In an address to the people of Tallahassee, the governor declared, "Nobody has any right at any time anywhere regardless of his race or color or creed to persist in any demonstration which will likely result in violence and disorder impeding the peace and welfare of a community." The governor insisted that "other means must be found for the airing of grievances and the resolving of racial antagonisms." CORE leaders denounced the governor's order as "police terrorism." [31]

By the afternoon of Sunday, 13 March, the last of the six FSU sit-in demonstrators had been released from custody. Bail was provided by Harcourt Waller and three FSU professors. Plans were made for attorneys from the Florida Civil Liberties Union to defend the white students. Oscar Brock's father, a state official of the Young Men's Christian Association, arranged private counsel for his son. Shortly before trial, however, the Orlando attorney decided that it was not in his professional interests to represent the young demonstrator. The elder Brock then insisted that his son plead nolo contendere.

The other students from Florida State University were encouraged by Waller's assistant, Father George Steinhauser, to emphasize that their behavior was a result of religious commitment rather than part of an organized civil rights strategy. Two agreed to follow this advice. Each student promised to be on his best behavior until the trial.

CORE leaders encouraged the black students to call the national office for legal advice. This suggestion was prudent, considering that only $168.05 remained in the treasury of the local CORE at the time. Within one week national CORE had sent $500 to Tallahassee and announced that there was "a good chance" that a bail fund could be set up to help defray legal expenses. The local chapter raised an additional $775 in a five-day period following the students' arrest. Robert Saunders promised to send an NAACP attorney to Tallahassee immediately to represent the Florida A&M demonstrators. [32]

It had been an emotional weekend, and sentiment in favor of punishing the demonstrators and preventing future incidents grew quickly. On Monday, 14 March, all thirty-five were arraigned in city court. Judge John Rudd set the trial date for Friday, 19 March. Meanwhile, the Tallahassee chamber of commerce and members of the Leon County legislative delegation urged President Gore to meet with FSU President Robert Strozier to take strong disciplinary actions against student and faculty participants in the demonstrations. There was even support in the legislature for moving one or both of the universities to another location in the state.

After the two harried presidents had met to discuss the situation, Strozier announced that the universities were concerned about any student "who is arrested for violation of the law" but would not "prejudge a student" until the decision of the courts had been handed down. But no matter the outcome of the trial, Strozier said, the "disciplinary action of Florida State University and Florida A&M University will do little to solve the basic problem with which this community is faced." Strozier then called on the city commission to establish a "citizen committee to explore this serious problem." Strozier's idea was echoed by Governor Collins, who suggested that the commission appoint a biracial committee to "look into local racial disturbances."[33]

But as during the bus boycott, city commissioners were not interested in civic mediation. Nor were they interested in the progressive ideas of Robert Strozier, who had been at FSU for only two and half years. A native of McRae, Georgia, Strozier was widely known in academic circles as a "liberal" on race relations. His appointment by the board of control to replace conservative president Doak Campbell in 1957 had stunned many faculty and townspeople who were accustomed to regarding Florida State as an extension of the community's collective conscience and not as the "great university" that Strozier envisioned.

After meeting with Collins and officials at both universities, the city commission announced that "no unlawful demonstrations or gatherings will be tolerated at any time or place within our city limits." After denouncing "gang action and mob rule," the officials "rejected" the idea of a biracial committee because, as they wrote Collins, "we know from past experiences in dealing with racial problems that such committee action does not result in the inevitable positive decisions that must be eventually made by duly constituted authorities."[34]

Instead of appointing a biracial committee, the commission urged Collins "to use the authority of the Governor's office with the board of control and the presidents of these universities to force the students at Florida State and Florida

A&M to stop their downtown racial demonstrations." The commission also accused "some faculty members at both universities of participating in and encouraging students to take part in racial demonstrations." "Those faculty," the commissioners wrote Collins, "should be properly dealt with."[35]

On 15 March, after meeting with Florida A&M administrators, student government association president Ira Robinson announced that FAMU students would hold no further public demonstrations. Meanwhile R. R. Oglesby, the dean of students at Florida State, ordered students to "desist from participation in demonstrations, unauthorized parades, and acts of incitement." The student board of publications ordered the staff of the *Flambeau* to "tone down emphasis on the current sit-down incidents." To protest what she considered a violation of the First Amendment, Delavan ran the *Flambeau* on 18 March with empty white spaces where the lead editorial and the editorial cartoon had been. The deleted editorial criticized the proposal of Thomas Beasley, speaker of the Florida House, that college students who participated in sit-in demonstrations should be expelled. Three days later a publication entitled the *Free Flambeau* was distributed across campus. The paper warned that a social revolution was near and called upon students and faculty to "rise up in protest against this slavery [racism] and help usher in a kingdom beyond caste." The lead cartoon depicted the Tallahassee police as Nazi Gestapo. Delavan and others connected with the *Florida Flambeau* denied having any ties with the renegade newspaper.[36]

While Delavan's editorials at the *Florida Flambeau* were subject to university censorship, her critical analysis of Tallahassee race relations continued to reach other students. On 16 March the women's senate at Florida State University adopted a unanimous resolution charging Tallahassee police with "using profane and indecent language in the presence of ten white students" who later received "inhumane treatment" at the local jail. The resolution called on Governor Collins to investigate the allegations. Mayor Taff announced that an investigation of police conduct would take place but noted that "the account given by these students is entirely out of proportion to the facts of the matter." No results of any investigation were ever made public.[37]

Although racial demonstrations and protests in Tallahassee were locally led and nurtured, they were part of a nationwide civil rights movement. Many elected officials in the spring of 1960 agreed with Governor Collins's hypothesis that "racial discord in America is following a Communist script, whether or not it is written from the Kremlin." The specter of "white and colored Americans facing each other and glowering with hate, willing to set whole communities aflame," the governor said, "was destroying the image of the United States as a nation to be respected." Such efforts to "destroy American influence in the world," all over the "right to sit at the same lunch counters," had to come from foreign soil or to reflect foreign design.[38]

It was common in much of the South for any civil rights organization or activity to be suspected of being Communist inspired or controlled. First the NAACP and then CORE became the target of Communist witch hunters both nationally and in Florida. During the brief hiatus between the arrest and the trial of the eleven black students arrested at Woolworth's on 20 February, Tallahassee CORE worked to dissociate itself completely from any taint of Communist affiliation.

On 15 March, Carl Braden, the well-known civil rights activist indicted for contempt of Congress in 1958 after he refused to answer questions before the House Un-American Activities Committee, came to Tallahassee to cover the upcoming trial for the *Southern Patriot,* the newspaper of the Southern Conference Education Fund. Both Braden and his wife, Anne, worked for the SCEF, which by 1960 had been identified as an "integration organization" and was a favorite target of the Johns committee.[39]

The couple, notorious in Kentucky for their fearless civil rights activities, were so controversial that even national CORE leaders were wary of their public support. Letters between Anne Braden and CORE executive secretary James Robinson in the spring of 1960 reveal the extent of CORE's reluctance to be tied to any persons tainted with the Communist label.

In March 1960, the Bradens had offered to house a CORE field secretary who came to Louisville to meet with sit-in demonstrators. When their offer was declined by national staff, Anne Braden wrote Robinson of her dismay at finding that the executive secretary did not want "CORE's name associated with ours." Robinson wrote back that while CORE did not "exclude everyone who has ever been suspected of Communist sympathy . . . , we do exclude those whose basic loyalty is to a foreign power and those who would subvert the CORE organization for the purposes of other organizations." Without accusing them of such an affiliation, Robinson pleaded for the Bradens to understand the "principles of avoiding community divisions" and persons with "past political associations, known or suspected." Robinson's logic was lost on Anne Braden. "If you adopt a policy of refusing to work with people who have been called Communist," she wrote, "who in the South are you going to work with?" "Any white person in the South who acts for integration is going to be labelled a Communist."[40]

While in Tallahassee, Carl Braden was the guest of C. K. Steele, one of the few Floridians identified as a member of SCEF by the Johns committee. Steele asked Braden to attend a CORE meeting with him the evening of 16 March. The day of the meeting, Braden called Harcourt Waller at the Chapel of the Resurrection (now known as the "Chapel of the Insurrection" by some local towns-people) to discuss the recent sit-ins and Tallahassee race relations. Waller asked his friend Lew Killian to join him at the meeting. Killian, who respected Braden and his wife for their desegregation efforts, still had "reservations about some of their tactics." During a general conversation about race relations, Braden made continual references to the "enemy." Finally Waller asked, "Just what do you mean by 'the enemy'?" "The segregationists of course," Braden replied. But many of the people who opposed segregation were "good friends and fellow church members," said Waller. "We are thinking in terms of Christian love, not warfare."[41]

At the CORE meeting on the evening of 16 March, Braden, introduced as a "freedom fighter" by Steele, gave a brief talk on desegregation in the South and in the context offered $5,000 to Tallahassee CORE as an SCEF donation. A white student attending his first CORE meeting interrupted Braden and demanded that he explain his past political affiliations and prove his loyalty to the American government. After Braden defended himself, an angry debate over the wisdom of affiliating the local CORE chapter with the SCEF ensued. Haley remembered that he and CORE field secretary Len Holt attempted to prove that "a man is innocent until proven guilty" but to no avail. The meeting ended on an acrimonious note. Later that evening the CORE executive council voted to reject Braden's contribution.[42]

The next day, Killian was approached by the same student who had challenged Braden at the meeting. The young man confessed to the professor that he had just mailed a letter to right-wing radio personality Fulton Lewis Jr., a fervent critic of Braden, telling him that the civil rights activist had been in Tallahassee meeting with CORE. "That was all that Tallahassee needed," thought Killian, "Fulton Lewis getting into the situation and magnifying Braden's presence." Killian and the student raced to the post office, filled out some forms, and were able to retrieve what was perceived as a potentially explosive letter. In this tense and divisive atmosphere, CORE members met to debate their strategy for the next few months.[43]

While CORE members met in conference during the latter part of March 1960, Lewis Killian and fellow sociologist Charles Grigg from Florida State University were invited to meet with Governor Collins to discuss the sit-ins and race relations in Florida. The meeting was arranged at the behest of Collins's aide John Perry, a neighbor of Grigg and the "liberal" on the governor's staff. Killian and Grigg were both members of the Tallahassee Council on Human Relations and the Southern Regional Council, had written numerous articles on race relations, and were considered experts in the field. In 1956, they participated in a statewide lecture tour along with Florida A&M professor Charles U.

Smith to acquaint city and school board officials with the ramifications of *Brown v. Board of Education*. Killian had written a portion of Florida attorney general Richard Ervin's amicus curiae brief on the *Brown* decision and was often contacted by state officials to participate in surveys, studies, and practicums on race relations in Florida.

For much of one afternoon, Killian, Grigg, Collins's staff, and the governor discussed the sit-ins and the rationale behind the demonstrations. Killian and Grigg told Collins that his recent public statements had oversimplified the legal and moral complexities of the sit-in demonstrations and had erroneously blamed the resulting disorder on the protestors. The professors pointed out that Collins's views seemed to represent only those of the police and city officials. They urged the governor to look beyond the confines of the law and to judge the demonstrations within an ethical, moral framework. If the governor did not recognize the moral right of blacks to demonstrate against segregation, both Killian and Grigg believed that the sit-ins and the attending violence would continue.

Killian remembered that Collins acted somewhat like a "judge" during the afternoon debate. The governor listened closely to all the opinions presented. Perry encouraged the governor to consider the professors' advice and counsel. Other aides opposed the governor's changing his public stand against the demonstrators and urged him to "stay out" of the situation during his last year in office. But Collins could not avoid an issue that he believed was undermining a progressive plan for Florida's future. Not only did he sincerely deplore racial violence and disorder, but he had worked for years to lure new businesses to Florida to improve the state's economy. The recruitment of prospective business investors required an image of Florida as both harmonious and prosperous— an image undermined by racial disorder.[44]

To defuse the tense situation statewide, Collins mentioned to Killian and Grigg that he would soon publicly announce the formation of a statewide biracial committee whose members could "reason together" on the volatile issue of race relations. The governor said that he would ask local governments across the state to appoint their own committees to help ease racial tensions and problems.[45]

When they left the governor's mansion, both professors believed that Collins had seen their point of view and was considering making a public statement to acknowledge it. Collins, however, remembered the meeting as only one in a long series of events and personal experiences that helped shape his thinking on the race question. For over a month he had been considering sharing these views with the people of Florida. Now, he thought, the time was right.

Shortly after their meeting with Collins, Killian and Grigg met with Richard

Haley. They told the CORE adviser that Collins was preparing a major statewide speech on race relations, and they considered it expeditious for CORE to assure the governor in writing that demonstrations would cease until after the speech had been made and the biracial committee formed. If Collins received such a promise in writing, Killian and Grigg believed, CORE could expect a "reasonable tone" in his speech. Though no promise could be made concerning the governor's speech, Haley was asked to share this information with no one outside the membership of CORE's executive board. No one was to suspect that Collins was negotiating with the civil rights organization.[46]

Haley took news of the proposed compromise to the executive board that evening. A bitter debate ensued. Daisy Young, CORE vice chairperson, adamantly opposed establishing contact with the governor through this "back door" method. At last a compromise was reached. CORE would send a letter pledging that the organization would keep to the spirit of negotiation without promising to abstain from future sit-ins: "CORE must in good conscience decline to commit itself to abstention from further sit-ins. This does not necessarily mean we commit ourselves to the opposite, but rather that we look hopefully to the community for evidence that such procedures will no longer be necessary."[47]

CORE did not hear from the governor's office, and Tallahassee businesses remained segregated. Still, members chose not to resume the sit-ins. Meanwhile, a coalition of Tallahassee ministers led by Steele and Speed canceled plans to conduct a ministerial sit-in on Saturday, 19 March. But the clergymen announced that demonstrations would continue if the lunch counters were not desegregated after the governor's speech. In a statement to police chief Frank Stoutamire, the ministers pledged themselves to continue the fight for freedom in an orderly, nonviolent fashion. "We are ashamed that it was not us who first led the struggle," the statement read, and "we commend the young people for taking the leadership. They are far ahead of us but we are rushing to catch up."[48]

So that the protest would not completely lose continuity, the ministers, in conjunction with the student government at Florida A&M, instigated an economic boycott of the downtown area and urged all Tallahassee blacks to "Dry clean it for Easter" instead of purchasing clothing in stores that practiced discriminatory policies. To many local blacks, including Steele and Speed, it was hard not to believe in the effectiveness of an economic boycott only four years after its success against the city buses. But unlike the buses, whose patrons were approximately 80 percent black, department stores served the entire community in a city that was two-thirds white.

On 17 March, while the community anxiously awaited the governor's speech, Patricia Stephens and her ten codefendants from the February sit-in went on trial. They were charged with disturbing the peace, unlawful assembly, and six other related offenses. ACLU lawyers Tobias Simon and Howard Dixon knew that they would lose the case, but they hoped to show that their clients had been arrested for violating local racial customs and not for disturbing the peace or encouraging disorderly proceedings. The point proved impossible to make, however, because the city attorney announced in his opening remarks that the issue of race would not be introduced by the prosecution and would be brought up only if "defense counsel injects it." When Dixon and Simon sought to prove that, indeed, their clients were arrested on strictly racial grounds, city prosecutor Edward J. Hill appealed to Judge John Rudd to instruct the defense team "to get off that race question." The judge ruled that race had nothing to do with the case and could not be used in the proceedings.[49]

S. T. Davidson, the manager of Woolworth's, testified that he did not close the counter because the students were Negroes but because their presence "seemed to cause apprehension on the part of some of the people in the store." Mayor Williams said that he ordered the students' arrests not because of the students' color but because he "deemed their presence at the counter dangerous to the safety and welfare of the community."[50]

On 17 March, at the end of the one-day trial, Judge Rudd found the eleven demonstrators guilty of disturbing the peace and unlawful assembly and ordered them each to pay $300 in fines or to serve sixty days in jail. During the sentencing, Judge Rudd told the defendants that "if their acts had been a spontaneous student demonstration he could reconcile them as careless and immature, but that it had come to his attention that their conduct was fostered by the Congress of Racial Equality and the American Civil Liberties Union," which, he added, had been found by the House Un-American Activities Committee to be "closely affiliated with the Communist Party in the United States." Furthermore, Rudd stated, the issue in this case was not integration but property rights. "If a man wants to cater only to one-legged green Chinese, that is his business." With these words, the judge admonished the students to return to school to study the Constitution.[51]

After consulting with Dixon, Simon, and CORE attorney Len Holt, eight of the eleven defendants announced that they had chosen "jail over bail" and refused to pay their fines. Although they discussed the ramifications of their decisions with their attorneys and with CORE officials, the demonstrators had decided to go to jail before the discussions took place. Attorneys did advise three of the students to pay their fines so as to provide a case for an appeal to a higher court. Subsequently, the case, *Henry M. Steele et al. v. Tallahassee*, was appealed to the circuit court in Leon County, where the conviction was upheld. Bypassing the state appellate courts, attorneys filed a petition for certiorari with the U.S. Supreme Court.

Meanwhile, Patricia and Priscilla Stephens, Henry M. Steele, student government association president-elect William Larkins (also president of the local CORE chapter), and four other FAMU students became the first sit-in demonstrators in the country to accept a jail sentence rather than pay their fines. "We could be out on appeal," wrote Patricia Stephens in a statement widely circulated by CORE. "But we strongly believed that Martin Luther King was right when he said, 'We've got to fill the jails in order to win our equal rights.'"[52]

The night before they went to jail, the eight students attended a prayer service for "inspiration and strength." Then, in an attempt to prepare themselves for what they might face behind bars, they slapped each other, spat at one another, and called each other derogatory names. Even this tough conditioning, remembers Pat Stephens, "did not prepare us for life in jail."[53]

On 18 March, the demonstrators began to serve out their sentences. They were placed in two cells segregated by sex. Each cell had four bunk beds, one commode, and a leaking sink with cold water only. It was uncomfortable, Pat Stephens recalled, "but when you're doing something for a principle, you don't expect luxurious accommodations." Although it was a lonely and at times frightening experience, the students were soon the object of nationwide media attention—which national CORE used to advertise the jail-in as a civil rights protest tactic. "The faith shown in Tallahassee is a *major* factor in the growing pressure nationally to change Woolworth's policy," CORE executive secretary James Robinson wrote the worried parents of Pat and Priscilla. "The chances are good that we shall win. If so, much of the credit must go to the Stephens sisters."[54]

At first the students were allowed visitors every day, but after the first weekend, the police refused to let white visitors into the jail cells. The few FSU students who were allowed to see their incarcerated friends were followed by the police, stopped, and questioned concerning their activities in CORE. Robert Armstrong, arrested at the 12 March sit-in, wrote a letter to the governor to protest police policy but received no reply.

As the days went by, some of the jailers became aggressive and insulting. They berated the students, often waking them up at night to accuse them of being "troublemakers" and "bad niggers." The cells were cramped, cold, and dirty. By the second week, three of the eight demonstrators, including seventeen-year-old Henry Steele, who worked on the county chain gang during his incarceration, had paid their fines and left jail. The Stephens sisters, William Larkins, and brother and sister John and Barbara Broxton remained to serve out their terms.[55]

After she had been in jail for some time, Patricia Stephens was picked to be a "trusty" and was sent out to vacuum and clean up the police station. Everything went well until she refused to use the outside bathroom assigned to blacks.

When Stephens brazenly entered the "white ladies only" restroom inside the police station, she was sent back to her cell. That night, Priscilla, Patricia, and Barbara Broxton wrote freedom songs to the tunes of "Dixie" and "Old Black Joe." All through the evening, the young women sang the "Jailbirds' Protest Songs." The next day, several of the white women prisoners asked them for a copy of the words. That evening, the voices of both the black and white women could be heard singing in unison, their voices crossing the prison walls.

At first the students were surprised to receive a large quantity of mail. Soon the now-famous demonstrators found themselves spending much of their time answering letters from students, churches, labor unions, and activists around the world. Although each of the letters touched the students and helped stiffen their resolve, one letter in particular filled them with pride: "As you suffer the inconvenience of remaining in jail, please remember that unearned suffering is redemptive. Going to jail for a righteous cause is a badge of honor and a symbol of dignity. I assure you that your valiant witness is one of the glowing epics of our time and you are bringing all of America nearer the threshold of the world's bright tomorrows." These words had been penned by Martin Luther King Jr.[56]

National officials of CORE kept in close contact with the jailed students. Pat Stephens wrote often to Executive Secretary James Robinson, describing conditions in jail and speaking of her determination to "go to jail again if necessary" for the cause of freedom. Once she wrote Robinson that she was surprised to find that many of the people who wrote her did not understand the situation or race relations in the South. "I try and explain to them," wrote Stephens, "but my best in a letter is not enough. . . . there are so many things happening that people are completely unaware of."[57]

The correspondence between CORE officials and the Stephens sisters, the Broxtons, and William Larkins soon began to appear in the *CORE-LATOR* and in numerous black-owned newspapers in the North. The SCEF's *Southern Patriot* published a two-part series entitled "Jailhouse Notes" written by Barbara Broxton. "We do not consider going to jail a sacrifice but a privilege," the young woman wrote earnestly. "Every night we thank God we are able to help those who are denied equal rights."[58]

The national CORE office was soon besieged with requests from supporters who wanted to meet and hear the young "jailees." The next letter that Pat Stephens received from Robinson contained an invitation. Would the five students be willing to tour the country after their release to tell people about CORE and their experiences with southern justice? "My parents said Priscilla and I can go," Stephens wrote back, "but only if we have a chaperone."[59]

During the two months that the students were in jail, the city enjoyed a respite from the sit-ins and other demonstrations. But Governor Collins's televised speech on 20 March 1960 proved to Tallahassee whites that racial unrest would not go away simply because five black students had been locked up in the Leon County jail.

On the three-hour drive from Tallahassee to the Jacksonville television station where he would deliver his address, Collins made notes to himself but never wrote out a complete speech. He had been thinking for some time about what he wanted to say and had decided that it would be better to speak from his heart, without a script. Events of the last several weeks combined with the ongoing furor over school desegregation had persuaded Collins that it was time to make a break with the past.

His approach to race relations, rooted in his small hometown southern values, was no longer viable. He could no longer reconcile this view with the moral, religious framework that influenced his personal and public decisions. Just that morning at St. Johns Episcopal Church, the priest had woven these words from the gospel into his sermon: "every kingdom divided against itself is brought to desolation; and a house divided against a house falleth." To Collins, this statement described what was happening in Florida. For any governor worth his salt, the time had come to speak out.[60]

Collins began his address in a calm, reassuring manner. The people of the state had a right to expect their governor to have convictions, he said, and to "express those convictions directly to them." He had come into his listeners' living rooms to talk to them about a problem that affected every "man, woman and child" in the state. Collins provided a brief history of the "so-called demonstrations" and announced that first and foremost there would be "law and order in this state." He noted that while all citizens had the right to demonstrate, such public protests could lead to "public disorder," which was unlawful and damaging to the whole community. He reiterated that a merchant had the legal right to select the patrons he served and would be protected in the exercise of this legal right. "But actually friends," the governor said, "[we] are foolish if we just think about resolving this thing on a legal basis. And so far as I am personally concerned, I don't mind saying that if a man has a department store and he invites the public generally to come into his department store and trade, I think then it is unfair and morally wrong for him to single out one department and say he does not want or will not allow Negroes to patronize that one department. Now he has a legal right to do that, but I still don't think that he can square that right with moral, simple justice."[61]

"People have told me," Collins continued, "that our racial strife could be eliminated if the colored people would just stay in their place, but friends, we can never stop Americans from struggling to be free. We can never stop Americans from hoping and praying that some day in some way this ideal that is imbedded in our Declaration of Independence is one of these truths that is inevitable that all men are created equal, that that somehow will be a reality and not just an illusory distant goal." [62]

Collins's speech was more than an appeal to the better natures of his constituents. As promised to CORE, he announced that he had formed a biracial committee to work on solving the state's racial problems. The governor appealed to each community in the state to form a local biracial committee that "can take up and consider grievances of a racial character and . . . honestly and sincerely . . . try to find solutions to these difficulties. Florida needs you in this program," Collins pleaded. "We need more reason and less emotion. We need more love and less hate. We need more work and effort and less talk and less demonstrations. Citizens, please do not fail this great challenge." [63]

When the governor finished speaking, the television crew stood still, too stunned to move. There was complete silence until Collins left the station's tense atmosphere to fly to Miami. His aides remained behind to drive the governor's limousine back to Tallahassee through the long dark roads and small towns of North Florida.

6 The Attitudes of Yesterday

Reaction to Collins's speech varied widely. The governor received thousands of letters (many from other states) praising his courage and candor, but few of them came from his friends and neighbors in North Florida. The notable exceptions included a handwritten note from Robert Strozier: "Your speech was magnificent," Florida State University's president wrote, "a great humane appeal to reason. I shudder to think of Florida without you as governor." Strozier's words were echoed by University of Florida president Wayne Reitz and Florida A&M's chaplain, James Hudson.[1]

Blacks across the state were generally pleased with the address. In Tallahassee, at a mass meeting on the night of Collins's address, 500 blacks listened while speakers commended the governor. Then they voted to "start further demonstrations" and to extend civil rights activities into other fields, such as unemployment and school desegregation. CORE field secretary Len Holt, who was at the meeting, told a reporter that Collins "didn't go far enough" in his speech and that local blacks would continue to press for a variety of rights.[2]

But the impact of Collins's speech was undeniable. James Robinson, CORE's executive secretary, sent Collins a "congratulatory telegram" and later wrote Patricia Stephens that, in the view of the national organization, the students' "sacrifice in going to jail may very well have precipitated Governor Collins's remarks." Marvin Rich, CORE's community relations director, urged CORE members across the nation to write Governor Collins a letter supporting his speech and to contact Woolworth Company executives to protest the segregation of lunch counters in Florida and across the South.[3]

Meanwhile the news media in Florida mirrored the wide range of responses to the governor's speech. The editors of the *Miami Daily News* were delighted that Collins had introduced "courage and intelligence at a time when both of these human qualities are so badly needed to help solve this great moral issue." Collins's attempt to shift the argument over integration from constitutional grounds to moral ones won no favor with editors of Jacksonville's *Florida Times Union*. "The factor in this issue that must be weighed heavily is the culture of our region," they wrote. "Traditions crystallized by years of history change slowly."[4]

In Tallahassee, *Democrat* editor Malcolm Johnson was curiously silent, but the paper recorded the reactions of political leaders, many of whom disparaged the governor and his newly created state biracial commission. When the executive committee of the Tallahassee Council on Human Relations sent all Florida State University faculty members a letter urging them to support the formation of a biracial commission, it was circulated in offices and businesses downtown with a note attached that urged Tallahasseeans not to allow the faculty to "dictate the future of our way of life." Meanwhile, Tallahassee mayor George Taff announced that city commissioners saw no value in the state commission and would reject the governor's plea to establish a local one. Spencer Burress, president of the Tallahassee chamber of commerce, said that while he could not speak for the entire organization, "there was no indication of a change of attitude." Senate president Dewey Johnson declared that the governor's speech "substantiates what I thought all the time. He is a strict integrationist and will sell his soul to prove it for the benefit of his national political ambitions."[5]

Johnson's remarks revealed the paradoxical political position in which Collins found himself in the spring of 1960. The governor was a national figure because of his reputation as a "southern moderate," yet his progressive politics had seriously eroded his political strength and influence within his own state. The upcoming 1960 Democratic gubernatorial primary was considered a litmus test of Collins's leadership and stature within his deeply divided party and among his constituents.[6]

Three days after Collins's race relations speech, CORE members (who had already vowed to continue "integration efforts") met to adopt a "post-speech" protest strategy. Those in favor of resuming the sit-ins argued that they had produced the only significant progress in local race relations. Richard Haley argued that "it was highly unlikely" that CORE's activities had influenced official decisions or policy, but if they had, it was only because of the pressure generated by the sit-ins. Nevertheless, a majority of members voted to halt all sit-ins until after the Democratic primary. Haley wrote that the small group feared that more demonstrations would "throw the gubernatorial election to Farris Bryant the segregationist . . . , [would] embarrass Governor Collins," and would "place the governor's interracial committee in a weak position in its dealing with the Tallahassee City Commission."[7]

On 23 March, Johnson and house speaker Beasley announced a proposal that state legislators call themselves into special session to enact legislation making mandatory the expulsion of students from "tax supported colleges who participated in demonstrations and the dismissal of faculty members who encouraged such actions." As if to underscore the threat, the board of control announced that it "deplored the events which took place in Tallahassee on and prior to Saturday, March 12" and expected "the administration, the faculties, and the student bodies of each of the Universities to continue to maintain law and order."[8]

The same day that the official warnings were issued, CORE's James Robinson came to Tallahassee to address a joint meeting of the NAACP, the ICC, and CORE. During his speech, Robinson encouraged local civil rights activists not to abandon their coordinated protest movement. Some Tallahassee blacks interpreted his words as calling for a resumption of the sit-ins. But for the majority, many of them local ministers and NAACP members, it seemed prudent to replace the controversial sit-ins with a large-scale boycott of downtown merchants. In light of the tense, threatening atmosphere in Tallahassee, their arguments appeared valid. "While some of these reasons [for delay] seemed tenable to me at the time," Haley wrote Gordon Carey in June 1960, "they appear ridiculous now. It is to be hoped we've learned that compromise is usually best as a last expedient, not a first one."[9]

What Haley didn't write to Carey was the most obvious reason for abandoning the sit-ins. FAMU students, many frightened and discouraged over the recent arrests and incarceration of their leaders, were hesitant to risk a similar fate and were eager to boycott downtown stores and negotiate with city officials and lunch counter merchants. "The NAACP legalism is in control at present in the thinking of the majority," Len Holt wrote Robinson after the latter's visit to Tallahassee. "There will be no further direct action projects until the next school year."[10]

The tense atmosphere in Tallahassee continued to affect not just CORE strategy but events small and large throughout the community. On 25 March at a meeting of the board of control in Tallahassee, Florida A&M President Gore assured members that "he was following every lead to see that the students did not participate in demonstrations which would prove embarrassing to the Board, or to the community and State." Three days later the beleaguered president wrote Chaplain James Hudson that "in view of the present local situation, I do not think it would be wise if we took part in the Palm Sunday Program at the federal prison in Tallahassee." [11]

Later that week racial tensions in Tallahassee led to the cancellation of a long-awaited, first-ever recruitment program for black high school students in Florida, "Senior Day at Florida A&M." That such a drastic measure was deemed necessary in the capital city should provoke "civic concern ranging from uneasy conscience to outright shame in the mind of every Tallahasseean," wrote Malcolm Johnson. "We believe reason and responsibility has returned to our community." Johnson's optimistic assessment was not shared by the staff of the Governor's Commission on Race Relations, which presented a four-page analysis of the sit-ins and other racial disturbances in Florida to members at its 2 April meeting. "The most serious situation in Florida has developed in Tallahassee," the report noted, "where the city officials have failed to maintain the impartial attitude expected of law enforcement officers and have engaged in public demands for punitive action against the student demonstrators." [12]

With CORE's decision to suspend further sit-ins for the near future, it appeared that the city might have a respite from racial activism, but it was not to be. Two informal speeches made by Lewis Killian and a Florida State University religion professor precipitated an ugly controversy and revealed just how little most white Tallahasseeans were prepared to yield on race relations.

The Tallahassee Council on Human Relations, still active in the spring of 1960, held its weekly meetings in the Unitarian Student Center near Florida State University. Those "blessed Unitarians," Lillian Shaw recalled twenty-four years later, were the only ones who would take the small group in after they were denied use of the courthouse following James Shaw's testimony before the Johns committee. [13]

Most local residents ignored the council, but members of the Tallahassee Council on Human Relations began to notice new faces at their Tuesday night meetings as local and state officials began to show renewed interest in council proceedings and activities. Killian believed that senate president Dewey Johnson was one of a number of officials who sent "spies" to council meetings to monitor the small interracial organization.

One evening early in April, Killian, who had just returned from a lecture tour on desegregation sponsored by the Southern Regional Council, explained to the Tallahassee Council on Human Relations the role that the organization had played as mediator in the recent sit-ins in North Carolina. The next week, members of the city commission, the Tallahassee chamber of commerce, and the Leon County legislative delegation met secretly to discuss Killian's role as the mastermind behind the Tallahassee sit-ins. A delegation from the meeting demanded that President Robert Strozier fire the sociology professor for promoting racial unrest in Tallahassee.

A few days later, Strozier arranged for Wilson Carraway, a Tallahassee bank president and state senator, to meet with him and Killian in his office. In his deep Georgia accent, Killian reminded Carraway that the two had met before, "I've been banking with you for years," Killian said smoothly. "It's a pleasure to see you again, senator." Slightly startled, Carraway "sputtered a few words," and a brief but pleasant discussion ensued.[14]

Not even Lewis Killian's southern charm, however, could soften local outrage over what happened next. On 11 April 1960, an unusually large crowd of about fifty people listened while the Tallahassee Council on Human Relations debated the legality and morality of the sit-ins. Professor Jackson Ice of FSU's religion and philosophy department—who, unlike Killian, was not a native southerner and was a relative newcomer to the community—moderated the discussion that evening. Ice made a statement in which he said in part that "a people has a right under certain conditions to engage in civil disobedience." And furthermore, he added, "if you always obey the law and the law is no good, you get nowhere." Two days later, Ice was attacked in a speech by gubernatorial hopeful John McCarty, who added that if he became governor, instructors like Ice "had better stick to their business of teaching." A group of politicians led again by Senator Carraway visited Strozier to demand that something be done about Ice and other outspoken professors.[15]

Pressure on Strozier to fire Ice and to discipline outspoken professors and students continued to build during the first two weeks of April. A letter written by members of the Tallahassee Council on Human Relations to city commissioners urging them to appoint a biracial committee to solve the city's race relations problems circulated downtown with a heading that asked, "Do you know what Commie Professors are trying to do to your town?" Next, local businessmen read a "manifesto" in front of FSU's administration building demanding that the president fire professors involved in civil rights activities. Tallahassee residents called the president's office to insist that Strozier rein in those faculty members who did not adhere to "community standards." The president, however, held firm when he issued a statement concerning Ice's speech. The professor had voluntarily called him and had apologized for making "imprudent remarks," Strozier said on 15 April, but Ice had also insisted that he was quoted somewhat "out of context." Strozier concluded that although Ice's remarks were "at variance with the university's position on the present racial situation in Tallahassee," he had spoken "as a citizen of the community, in a church which is in no way connected with the Florida State University." [16]

When newspapers throughout the state called Ice's statement to the president "an apology," the professor quickly denied that he had apologized for his words. "I did not apologize for what I said," Ice told an editor for the *Flambeau*. "I deeply regret that my remarks were untimely, out of place, or misunderstood." There are taxpayers in this community who "seem to think that they own the university and constantly attempt to curtail academic freedom according to their own biases and prejudices," he added. "This places a university in an unfortunate situation." [17]

In the midst of the turmoil at FSU, the university hosted its annual "religious emphasis week," normally an occasion for speakers to debate ethical, moral, and spiritual issues of the day. Lewis Killian, a lay leader of the small faculty group that attended the Chapel of the Resurrection, invited one of the guest speakers to conduct a special service at the Chapel. The group also invited Father David Brooks, rector of St. Michael's Episcopal Church near FAMU, and members of his congregation to attend. A covered-dish supper was scheduled to follow the service. When the congregation of St. John's Episcopal Church learned that white and black faculty members were going to eat together, Robert Strozier was once again put in the position of defending his faculty. A friend who attended St. Johns told Killian that Strozier would not intervene but that "it would make life much easier for him" if they called off the dinner. In the absence of Harcourt Waller, who was out of town, the lay group decided to conduct the service but to cancel the dinner—a practical decision and one that thirty years later still troubled Killian. [18]

With townspeople, politicians, and even members of his faculty urging him to curb academic dissidents, Strozier found himself in an increasingly untenable situation. On Saturday, 16 April, Killian saw the president downtown. The professor remembered that Strozier looked unusually tired and drawn. "I've got to meet with the Board of Control to discuss you and Ice," Strozier told Killian. Associate Dean Milton Carothers had just told him that the board "had Killian cold and he'll be fired." "Don't worry," Killian told Strozier, "they don't have a chance of getting me." Four days later, the controversy at the university abruptly ended. Robert Strozier was dead of a heart attack at the age of fifty-three. [19]

Strozier's death stunned the university and left many people with a sense of personal loss and remorse. At his memorial service, faculty members praised the president for his "Christian stewardship" and goodwill in dealing with "town-gown relations." Those faculty and students whom Strozier had defended against attack felt somehow responsible for his death, although it seems unlikely that stress alone could have killed a healthy man in the prime of his life. Still, the perception that the president had died in part because of his role in protecting civil liberties persisted in the minds of many in the FSU community long after Strozier's death.

The search for a new university president gave CORE another reason to postpone further sit-ins. Although Haley and other CORE members argued against it, the group elected to delay further demonstrations until after the board of control had chosen a new president. It was a "natural reaction," Haley wrote despairingly to Gordon Carey, "of the non-criminal types to the imminence of jail."[20]

In lieu of demonstrations, local strategy turned to diplomatic—but fruitless—efforts to move city officials. The CORE executive council appointed a committee to meet with city manager Arvah Hopkins in the hope of establishing a foothold for interaction with the city. Members of the delegation asked Hopkins to push for a biracial committee to provide for negotiations between the black community and the white. Being "quite certain about the views of the city commission on this matter," he declined. "They are not going to allow integration and that is what such a meeting would be all about," Hopkins told the delegation. The most he would do was to invite CORE members to attend future city commission meetings as individuals.[21]

Meanwhile, on 10 May 1960, a delegation of blacks headed by Reverend G. W. Washington, chairman of the Ministerial Alliance, presented a statement to the city commission entitled "Toward a Solution." The statement was read by the city auditor at the meeting and was duly reported in the commission's minutes. According to the official minutes, the statement urged the commission to establish better race relations in the city by "using its influence to assure better accommodation of facilities downtown for Negroes including lunch counters, rest rooms, drinking fountains, libraries, and police protection." After hearing the statement, Mayor Taff noted that the relationship between the races in Tallahassee had been "most satisfactory until the last few years" and that the city had only recently provided "new and separate recreational facilities" for Negroes.[22]

By late spring much of the public's attention had turned to the upcoming Democratic gubernatorial primary. Concern over the race issue was foremost in the minds of the electorate. All six candidates for the nomination had reaffirmed their support for segregation and their opposition to sit-in demonstrations after Collins's race relations speech. Each man of course embraced the doctrine of racial separation to a different degree.

On 1 May, voters reduced the gubernatorial hopefuls to two men, Farris Bryant, the winner, and second-place finisher Doyle Carlton Jr., the state senator. Carlton, who supported many of Collins's policies and programs during his term in the senate, carried Leon County. Bryant carried the rest of North Florida. Florida voters were better acquainted with Bryant than with Carlton. Bryant had challenged Collins in the 1956 gubernatorial race and had been speaker of the house of representatives in 1957. That year, in a defiant reaction to the *Brown* decision, the conservative legislature had passed a rash of reactionary segregation bills, including an "interposition" resolution supported by Bryant and fiercely opposed by Collins. Now, with the other four gubernatorial hopefuls out of the way, Bryant became "the segregation candidate." Carlton, whom Bryant and the press had labeled as a "moderate integrationist," was increasingly seen as Collins's candidate.[23]

Bryant benefited not only from the electorate's slide toward a "massive resistance" approach to integration but from his alliance with the powerful conservative faction of the Democratic Party led by former governor Millard Caldwell. Carlton, on the other hand, was aligned philosophically with the Collins-led progressive faction of the splintered party. As the campaign wore on, more and more Floridians viewed the contest as pitting Collins against Caldwell and, more important, as a referendum on Collins's moderate racial stance.

Collins, despite his pledge to remain neutral in the race, under pressure from Carlton backers, and with the knowledge that his own reputation was on the line, at the last minute endorsed Carlton. In a statewide television speech on 23 May, the eve of the election, Collins urged Floridians to make Carlton his successor "to keep Florida on the road to progress." The governor charged that Bryant would lead "Florida down the road of reaction, retreat and regret." The next day voters turned out in record numbers and elected Farris Bryant governor. The Ocala senator received 55 percent of the vote, capturing all but eleven of the state's sixty-seven counties. Included in his sweep was Collins's Leon County and virtually all of North Florida. Carlton's support came from South Florida and from black voters throughout the state. Although Collins later insisted that Carlton's defeat was not a rejection of his administration or of his ideas, Bryant appeared to have been correct in his assessment that Collins was "out of step with Floridians on the racial issue."[24]

For Tallahassee blacks, Bryant's election was a low point in the dark spring of 1960. The one bright moment occurred on 5 May when the Stephens sisters, the Broxtons, and Bill Larkins were released from jail and returned to Florida A&M as local heroes and nationally recognized civil rights activists. Two days before their release, Marvin Rich, CORE's publicity director, advised Pat Stephens that "it would be well if in [her public remarks] you emphasized the purpose which you felt that you served by going to jail—that of reaching the conscience of the people of Tallahassee and, you hope, the rest of America." Rich added, "It would also be well if you could say that you bear no malice or ill will toward your jailers, to those who arrested you, or to the owners of the store. It is important that you state that your release from jail will mean a rededication to the fight and to our ideas—An America free of racial discrimination." Not wishing to imply that he had underestimated her commitment or capabilities, Rich added, "I know that you will say this kind of thing far better than I have."[25]

Rich never worried about Pat Stephens as spokesperson for CORE again. Interviewed as she was leaving the jail, the twenty-year-old student said, "Jail was an opportunity for us. We had time to think, to renew our faith in America and the power of nonviolence, to rededicate ourselves to the task of ending discrimination." Although the morale of the black community was low, the return of the students sparked an emotion-filled rally where all of the former "jailees" reaffirmed their determination to continue the "fight for freedom." Included in the crowd were those students who were scheduled to begin their trial in Judge Rudd's municipal court the next day.[26]

The trial of the twelve demonstrators who had participated in the Woolworth sit-in was briefly interrupted on the morning of 6 May by a bomb threat. Judge Rudd cleared the crowded courtroom for one hour while police searched the building. When nothing suspicious was found, the trial continued. The students, six of them black and six white, were charged with disorderly conduct and with disturbing the peace by engaging in riotous conduct and unlawful assembly. "Out of town lawyers" representing the ACLU and the NAACP appeared to defend the accused.[27]

The prosecution attempted to prove that the students had interfered with the legal right of Woolworth's manager "to refuse service to anyone he deemed undesirable." But the manager admitted that he had never asked the students to leave the store, because he "did not know there would be a disturbance." He had merely placed "closed" signs on the luncheon counter in four different spots. Therefore, defense attorneys argued, the students were not engaged in unlawful assembly, nor were they in violation of a Florida law that gave restaurant owners the right to ask unruly patrons to leave their establishment. By arresting the students, the police had violated the due process clause of the Fourteenth Amendment and were guilty of enforcing "private segregation." Just as important, defense attorneys added, the police were openly negligent in their duties when they failed to arrest members of the "menacing crowd" that had gathered outside the department store. This crowd, NAACP attorney G. E. Graves noted, was much more threatening than twelve well-dressed college students quietly sitting at a counter.[28]

City attorney James Messer countered defense arguments by drawing an analogy between the sit-ins in Tallahassee and the famous Haymarket riot of 1886, in which eight police officers had been killed and scores of people injured. Misreading history, Messer asserted that the Chicago tragedy had occurred because people refused to obey the mayor's orders to disperse. Mayor Taff, he contended, had reason to believe that "a disturbance was taking place which could lead to a riot." Prosecutors assured Judge Rudd that race was not a factor in the case and that the students would not have been arrested if they had obeyed the mayor's order to leave the store. As in the previous sit-in case, Rudd warned defense attorneys not to raise "the race issue," which was immaterial to the charges. After several hours of testimony, the judge found the students guilty. Robert Brock, the only student accompanied to court by his parents and the only one pleading nolo contendere, was put on probation for two years.[29]

In handing down his sentences, Judge Rudd scolded the demonstrators for "coming into our community and disturbing it as it has never been disturbed before. If you have to do these things," he said, "go into your own homes. You knew that you were not welcome at the Woolworth store under those conditions. You knew that situation would incite trouble. You can mask [it] under the guise of Christianity if you want to," Rudd sternly warned the convicted students, "but nowhere in the Bible is there sanction of intimidation."[30]

Rudd overlooked none of the scare tactics of civil rights opponents. If the students continued to indulge in protest activity, they would be following in the footsteps of Castro and Cuba, jeopardizing their families' reputations and happiness. Rudd implored the students to look clearly at "who and what you are following" and urged them to write the FBI and find out about the "organizations that are using you." When FSU student Jefferson Poland interrupted the judge to say that he had already carefully studied the civil rights organizations that he was involved with, Rudd angrily cut Poland short and told him that certain groups had recently "supplanted recognized Communist organizations." The judge also reminded Poland that students before him had been represented by attorneys "that you did not pay for."[31]

After advising the students to listen to their parents and not to some of their professors who had "read so many books they're out of touch with reality," the judge sentenced the eleven students to a fine of $300 or sixty days in jail. All eleven posted bond. Their attorneys appealed the conviction to the Second Judicial Circuit Court in Leon County, where their convictions were upheld by Judge Ben Willis. Bypassing the district court of appeal and the Florida Supreme

Court (as had been done earlier in the *Steele* and *Speed* cases), the students' attorneys asked the U.S. Supreme Court to hear the case. Meanwhile, the six students from Florida State were put on indefinite probation by Dean R. R. Oglesby.[32]

The Southern Scholarship and Research Foundation asked Jeff Poland to move out of a private scholarship house where he had been living; the board of directors feared the "bad public relations." Poland stayed briefly in the Canterbury House, but his lifestyle and agnosticism made him a poor choice for life at the Episcopalian residence. He moved to another off-campus location and remained at FSU for less than a year. Oscar Brock moved into Canterbury House in fall 1961 and lived there until he graduated the following year. Although he "was not particularly religious," Brock found that life at Canterbury House provided some "discipline, depth and added growth" to his college experience.[33]

Both President Gore and Dean Perry refused to say whether the institution would discipline the six Florida A&M students. Perry told reporters that the fate of the demonstrators was "being considered" in light of the punishment they had already received from the court. In the end, all of the demonstrators were put on academic probation (which meant that they had to maintain a certain grade point average) for the rest of their time at the university.[34]

As the spring semester drew to a close, FAMU and FSU students began final exams, and CORE planning and activity slowed down. Pat Stephens and the other students released from jail on 6 May were asked to withdraw voluntarily from Florida A&M because they had missed so many of their classes. Although some newspapers reported that they had been expelled from the university, all of the demonstrators were given the option of reapplying for classes in the fall. With their schoolwork over for the spring, Pat and Priscilla Stephens, along with Barbara and John Broxton and William Larkins, embarked on a whirlwind tour of the North and West to raise money for CORE and, the activists hoped, to awaken the consciences of liberal-minded whites.[35]

The tour was an extraordinary experience for the young demonstrators. In Watertown, New York, Barbara Broxton led a picket line around the building where Woolworth's stockholders were gathered for their annual meeting. Broxton's visit was preceded by a CORE press release noting that the company's sales had dropped 9 percent since the sit-ins began in February. In the meeting, Broxton described the movement to desegregate the Woolworth's lunch counter in Tallahassee. Several stockholders introduced a resolution in support of desegregating all Woolworth's counters, including stores in the North that had not yet integrated their facilities.

While Broxton and her brother John continued to meet with civic and business groups in upstate New York, Bill Larkins, at twenty-four the oldest of the group, was sent to the Midwest, where he appeared on television in Chicago and spoke before numerous civic groups. After one month he returned to Florida A&M to attend summer school. To register, Larkins had to get clearance from the dean of students and sign an affidavit acknowledging "probation and pledging not to engage in any activity that will tend to incite students." But, he wrote to Marvin Rich, "the dean says that the affidavit is a mere formality and is not intended to affect my relationship with CORE." [36]

Although a month of travel was enough for Bill Larkins, Pat and Priscilla Stephens continued to crisscross the country and appeared to thrive on the grueling schedule of interviews, lectures, public appearances, fund-raising luncheons, and cocktail parties. One of the highlights of their tour was a meeting with Eleanor Roosevelt, who sponsored a luncheon to raise money for CORE's summer program. The Stephens sisters, who had been joined during the tour by FSU student Robert Armstrong, recounted their trial in Tallahassee and told Mrs. Roosevelt's guests about segregation in the Deep South. While still in New York, Pat and Priscilla spoke to the members of Adam Clayton Powell's church and exchanged stories with Daisy Bates, the civil rights activist, at a cocktail party sponsored by Jackie Robinson. They then flew on to Pennsylvania, California, and Ohio, continuing the exhausting pace for three months.

While each of the five students was an asset to CORE's lecture tour, the Stephens sisters—with their boundless energy and remarkable poise—attracted the most publicity. CORE capitalized on the sisters' charisma, often scheduling them to appear in three different states on the same day. After accompanying Pat and Priscilla for the first few weeks, their mother returned to Belle Glade exhausted. At the end of the tour, when the five demonstrators received CORE's distinguished Gandhi Award for outstanding service in human rights during 1960, only the Stephens sisters remained in St. Louis to accept the group award.

It is unclear whether the students' tour strengthened northern and western support for the nascent civil rights movement. But the five young people brought to their northern listeners a keener understanding of segregation in the South before Bull Connor's dogs in Birmingham brought the sickening message of violence and racial hatred into the living rooms of millions of Americans. Although their audiences were often members of liberal organizations, such as the Americans for Democratic Action and the ACLU, and were consequently already sympathetic to the black struggle throughout the country, the students' message also reached hundreds of whites and blacks who had been uninformed or apathetic about the plight of southern blacks. Contributions from these audiences helped fill CORE's coffers.

Yet William Larkins, back in Tallahassee that summer, found a rather dispirited CORE group, some of whom resented the publicity accorded the Stephens sisters. To Robert White, the Stephens sisters seemed to have "forgotten about Tallahassee CORE." According to Len Holt, some of the students, particularly Larkins, believed that the young women had become too "publicity conscious," forgetting the many who had made similar sacrifices and had been left behind to keep the movement afloat. The situation was not helped by newspaper articles that misquoted the young women or embellished their own accounts of their experiences. One article, which appeared in the Oklahoma City *Black Dispatch,* quoted Patricia as saying that the girls had been expelled from Florida A&M and were planning to continue their studies in Africa. Carey wrote Larkins that the Stephens sisters knew they had not been expelled and were as surprised to hear about the trip to Africa as were the members of Tallahassee CORE.[37]

Meanwhile, the small nucleus of CORE members struggled to make plans for the upcoming year and voted to resume lunch counter sit-ins during the summer. But the organization's precarious financial situation concerned local and national leaders because of the ever-present need for supplies, bail money, and other necessities. Furthermore, factions within Tallahassee CORE and the local black community limited their options for challenging segregation effectively. At a CORE meeting on 25 May, C. K. Steele objected to CORE's conducting demonstrations without the approval of the "adult leaders," since they were the ones who "must answer for the consequences anyway." Although the students had clearly answered quite severely for their actions already, Steele's remarks went largely unchallenged. Later that month, after one postponement, a group of black Tallahassee ministers led a kneel-in on the steps of the capitol to pray for an end to segregation. Still, student leaders complained to Gordon Carey that the majority of adult blacks in Tallahassee were not committed to CORE or to the sit-ins and that their lack of support was "not conducive to a coordinated [protest] effort."[38]

Unfortunately, Tallahassee CORE lost one of its most effective and energetic spokespersons when Richard Haley lost his job only one month after being elected teacher of the year by the FAMU student congress. (The choice had been criticized by the group's adviser, Moses G. Miles.) Haley charged that he had been fired because of his CORE-related activities. President Gore countered that the professor's contract simply had not been renewed. Gore's only response to his many critics, including the American Association of University Professors, was that the action "was in keeping with the university policy dealing with nontenured members of the instructional staff."[39]

John Riley, the president's longtime adviser, remembered the incident a little differently. "Haley became a nut," Riley said. "He neglected his work, and raised a lot of trouble." Steele attributed Haley's dismissal to "more of a personality clash" than to his CORE activities. For whatever reasons, the decision to fire Haley infuriated CORE members and most of FAMU's student body. But Tallahassee had not seen the last of Richard Haley. After a summer at the Highlander Folk School in Nashville, Tennessee, the former professor became a CORE field secretary and then executive assistant to CORE's national director, James Farmer. Haley served in a variety of positions at the national office, including associate national director and director of the southern voter education project. Until his resignation from CORE's national staff in 1964, he acted as an important adviser to Tallahassee CORE and a personal friend of its members.[40]

With only a skeletal crew, Tallahassee CORE tried to expand the organization's membership during the summer months of 1960. Through its newsletter, the *Core of the Matter,* members tried to acquaint the community with the organization. "CORE is not a political group and no CORE group is allowed to affiliate or cooperate with such subversive groups as the Communist Party, or fascist parties. . . . CORE has a clear and respectable record according to the FBI." CORE members were constantly offering such assurances in part because of information emanating from the Johns committee. In the fall of 1960 Robert Saunders heatedly denied rumors that statewide NAACP leaders had told their local members that CORE was on the attorney general's subversive list.[41]

A new slate of officers was elected to guide Tallahassee CORE for the 1960–1961 school year. Of the three students elected, two were white and one was black. Bill Larkins, Jeff Poland, and Bob Armstrong had all been arrested during one of the recent sit-ins. It was imperative, Haley wrote to the new officers, that FAMU and FSU students protest the long-standing restriction against visiting each other's campuses without their parents' or the administrations' consent. "You can begin," he suggested, "by approaching the president, student governing body, school newspaper and others" to protest the restrictions and to demand that they be lifted. "Remember," he added, "real strength lies in firmness of purpose rather than in numbers."[42]

Adding continuity to the new slate of CORE officers was Daisy Young, who continued her important role as strategist and adviser to the organization. Young was one of the few adult blacks active in Tallahassee CORE. With help from Dan Speed, the local group tried to negotiate with the managers at Sears, Neisner's, and Howard Johnson. Members thought a breakthrough had occurred in June when Henry Steele was served lunch with a small group of white Florida State University students at Neisner's department store. But when another interracial group approached the counter, blacks were refused service. A spokesperson for the store told CORE's Robert White that local custom and the "enforced policies of the city commission" prohibited an open lunch counter. When Dan Speed attempted to eat at Sears, he was told that the only Negroes who would be served there were store employees.[43]

Despite segregation's iron grip on Tallahassee, the ongoing "test" of the lunch counters was "very significant," Gordon Carey wrote Young in June 1960. "It is almost fatal if an action group delays some kind of overt action over a period of months."[44]

Across the city, CORE members were told repeatedly that store managers' "hands were tied" by city policies. Some merchants went so far as to tell CORE members that they would open their counters to blacks if the city commission would provide police protection for the first few weeks. Incredibly, CORE members felt optimistic that the city commission would agree to do so, even though by the fall of 1960, Tallahassee still lacked an official biracial committee. Through its newsletter CORE members urged the black community to write and petition city commissioners to establish a biracial committee.[45]

The Tallahassee city commission refused to consider the formation of a biracial committee despite the boycott of local stores and the efforts of the Governor's Commission on Race Relations and the personal exhortations of its chairman, Tampa attorney Cody Fowler. "We insist that each community has the responsibility of reasserting its conscience, its intelligence and its capacity for good will in a long range approach," Fowler pleaded with city officials. "The more we study our racial problems, the more we realize that changes are in the making. The idea that the problems do not exist is just not so. These problems must be faced now."[46]

After six months of "studying the problems at length," the commission issued a memorandum to Florida business, civic, and religious leaders to explain further the need for the establishment of official local biracial committees. "There are strong indications that many factors and forces operating in the field of race relations in our State are increasing tensions between the races," wrote Chairman Fowler. "They are operating to a greater or lesser extent in all Florida communities, and are particularly strong in metropolitan communities as well as communities with large concentrations of college-educated Negro youngsters." Those factors and forces included:

1) The change from an "agricultural economy" to an "agricultural and industrial economy," and more recently to a "service economy" as well; 2) The change in Africa from a continent of stable colonialism to a crucial part of the free world in the throes of new nationhood; 3) The change in the number of Florida Negroes who are educated; and 4) The fact that so many major religious bodies or their leaders have seen fit to reassert the Judaic Christian understanding "that before God all men are created equal, and are entitled to equal opportunities."[47]

Fed up with the stonewalling of the Tallahassee city commission, a group of local ministers decided to form their own biracial committee to negotiate with local merchants. First Presbyterian Minister Davis Thomas was among the small number of white members who attempted to negotiate with the local managers. Thomas found that the managers, who were feeling the effects of the black boycott of their stores, were ready to desegregate their facilities if the police would provide protection for the first few weeks of integrated service. When they could get no assurances from Stoutamire, the managers retreated behind their policies of following "local custom." [48]

Although no member of any civil rights organization in Tallahassee participated in the negotiations, Larkins wrote Gordon Carey that the biracial committee was "a magnificent step forward for Tallahassee. The white men who serve on it have risked community ostracism by manifesting their belief in dignity for the individual." To Carey, such committees were "usually a bunch of hot air." He was stunned to hear that Tallahassee CORE had decided to let the biracial committee "flex its muscles" before sit-in demonstrations were resumed. Richard Haley agreed that the committee should be given "a chance to work out its own salvation" but admitted to Carey that its chairman "speaks gruffly but carries a small stick." Besides, he wrote, "it is already established unofficially that four out of five affected merchants are ready to integrate. But I greatly fear that the city commission will not only discourage it, but forbid it." [49]

With the fall quarter underway, Tallahassee CORE struggled to regain the momentum of the spring demonstrations, but white officials moved swiftly to crush any resurgence of overt civil rights activities. Richard Parker, a student who had been brutally beaten and then jailed in Jacksonville during the summertime racial crisis, was refused readmission to FSU. Students who had earlier been placed on academic probation were forced to sign affidavits promising that they would not participate in any further acts of civil disobedience. Black morale seemed particularly low in the fall when Pat Stephens, suffering from nervous exhaustion, moved in with the Steele family in an attempt to continue her studies at Florida A&M.

Meanwhile, FSU's new president, Gordon Blackwell, was preparing for his first semester at the university. Blackwell had been chancellor of the Woman's College of the University of North Carolina at Greensboro and was a veteran of civil rights protests when he accepted the job to replace Strozier. Blackwell had spearheaded the effort to contain student demonstrations after four white students from the prestigious women's college joined black students in the city's first sit-ins in February 1960. Blackwell not only persuaded his students not to return to the lunch counters but also helped negotiate a "cooling off period" with the black students from North Carolina A&T College that lasted six weeks. Historian William Chafe contends that Blackwell's remarks to the students at the women's college became the basis for criticism of the sit-ins in North Carolina that were voiced by Luther Hodges, the governor of that state. Blackwell's role in temporarily halting the Greensboro demonstrations no doubt made him an attractive candidate in the eyes of the presidential search committee in Tallahassee.

But like Collins, who had also disdained public protests, Blackwell believed in the rightness of the students' demands. With members of the city's biracial committee, the president tried to persuade the local Woolworth's management to integrate the lunch counters peaceably. When the company refused, picketing resumed. According to Blackwell, signs for the picketers were made by students from the art department at the women's college. By the summer of 1960, several local lunch counters had been desegregated.

Blackwell had met Bob Strozier before the latter's death and was "aware of the pressures and problems he had been under." Before Blackwell accepted the position at Florida State, he asked his former student Lewis Killian to "evaluate the civil rights problems which the next president of FSU would face." Convinced that he could handle the racial situation, and expecting to rely on Killian for advice, Blackwell agreed to come to the university. He told Killian "that if he ever saw me becoming too conservative, to tell me." One of the first things that the new president did after moving to Tallahassee was to request a meeting with the city commissioners. "I told them how much the University meant to Tallahassee economically and in many other ways. I told them that I was sure I would make some decisions which they would not like, but I asked them to remember that I would never make a decision which I was not convinced was in the best interest of the university and therefore of Tallahassee." [50]

Blackwell became convinced that his early overture to the commission "helped to defuse most of the kinds of criticism and pressure which I understood they had placed on President Strozier." But as he recalled twenty-five years later, "the shock of the civil rights movement was greater during Strozier's last year because then it was all so new to southerners. By 1961 forward movement on these issues had been made in a number of places in the South. It therefore became easier to gain acceptance of the inevitability of social change." [51]

Social change seemed eons away when Gordon Carey, distraught over the lack of civil rights activity in Tallahassee, wrote to CORE members in November 1960 that it was "rather disturbing to hear that Tallahassee has changed so drastically from last school year. "Frankly," he wrote, "I feel that if CORE would become really active again this picture would probably change." It was crucial for the national movement that Tallahassee be "reactivated," Carey wrote Richard Haley, now a CORE field director, if desegregation in the Deep South was to succeed. Haley later wrote Pat Stephens, urging her to work in organizing a "professional" sit-in group composed of the city's leading adult blacks in an attempt to enliven "talking support" from the Negro community. Such a protest never materialized. "CORE's influence may be fading more rapidly than we think," Haley wrote Carey, but "my own belief in the goodness of human nature is not so fickle that I conclude the Tallahassee student has changed his belief, like a shirt or a blouse. I believe the dual pressure of active, potentially violent hostility from the city government plus restrictions and lack of sympathy from the school administrations, has discouraged our youth to the point of near-paralysis of social action."[52]

CORE was not the only civil rights organization in Tallahassee, and many of its members continued to participate in other projects and groups designed to increase black participation in the community. A political watchdog group, "The Florida Legislative Project," was organized in Tallahassee on 30 September 1960. Members of the project pledged to alert the community to "bills pending in the state legislature which could affect integration, civil rights and civil liberties." The group would also be used to protest cases of injustice on the local and state level. Guest speaker at the project's inception was Carl Braden. This time no one questioned the civil rights activist's loyalty or motives. He noted that the coming years in Florida would require much commitment and courage from all those dedicated to the black struggle for equality.[53]

Finally, on 6 December, after months of testing local lunch counters and the city buses (four years after the bus boycott), a small group of Tallahassee blacks began to picket Woolworth's under CORE's auspices. Bill Larkins, president of Florida A&M's student body, distributed a memorandum on campus that asked students to help avoid violence by staying out of the downtown area when picketing was underway. Larkins, also CORE's president, hoped to keep attention focused on the segregated lunch counters without engaging in "illegal activities" or risking arrest.

For three days four or five picketers walked in single file up Monroe Street in front of the store. On all three days, a group of whites jostled the picketers, blocked the sidewalks, and eventually tore up the signs. Saul Silverman, a professor at Florida State University and a staff person for the Governor's Commission on Race Relations, and Frank Trippet, a veteran reporter for the *St. Petersburg Times,* both wrote that the peaceful picketers had been physically and verbally accosted by white "hoodlums." The police either did not come to the scene or rode away when the whites approached the black protesters. Trippet reported that city commissioners Joe Cordell and Hugh Williams and city manager Arvah Hopkins drove by the scene without stopping. On the third day of the picketing, white youths grabbed the picketers' signs, ripped them up, and threw them in the street. The blacks, including Pat Stephens, continued the protest. As soon as the whites left the scene, the police appeared along with a convoy of city officials. The police asked reporters to move on. When Martin

Waldron, a reporter for the *Tampa Tribune*, asked why, a policeman told him it was "because you had a mean look on your face." Another policeman agreed with this statement. "The Capital City could sleep easier knowing the police weren't going to let anybody go around frowning at everybody," Trippet wrote, "not without investigating the matter at least."[54]

On 9 December, the same group of whites returned to the front of Woolworth's, but no blacks came to picket, nor did they the next day. Meanwhile, Farris Bryant moved to Tallahassee to prepare for his inauguration as Florida's next governor. As the year drew to a close, it was relatively quiet in the capital city, with no more outward demonstrations of racial tension.

In January 1961, the federal Commission on Civil Rights published its annual summary of reports submitted from each state. The Florida Advisory Committee, which had not held one meeting in 1960, submitted the shortest report of all the southern states. "There was relative calm in Florida in 1960," the report read. "No complaints or charges have been filed with the Commission either verbally or written. . . . Florida has progressed in a sound and equitable manner on the state and local levels in the areas of public education, voting, housing, employment, administration of justice and the use of public facilities."[55]

7 Beyond Tokenism

Farris Bryant eased the minds of many Floridians when he pledged in his 1961 inaugural address to "confine the activities of state government to the conduct of the state's business—not to the settlement of local issues best left in the hands of local officials." Similarly, Bryant added, "we will oppose with vigor any efforts by the federal government to usurp the proper and lawful prerogatives of the state." Florida had "its roots in the South," the new governor said, "but its spirit [was] fixed on Cape Canaveral."[1]

Floridians might have been committed to a new future in space exploration, but they were hardly interested in pursuing new frontiers in race relations. Neither was Bryant. It quickly became clear that civil rights activists would have little support from the new governor. Despite its earlier mediative efforts, and the personal plea of chairman Cody Fowler, Bryant never convened the statewide race relations commission, nor did he encourage local communities to establish their own biracial commissions. The governor announced that "because of the very successful manner in which problems are being faced and met at local levels," he would rely on his own staff for advice on civil rights matters.[2]

Back in Tallahassee, William Larkins dispiritedly wrote CORE's Gordon Carey that he had returned to the city to attend a meeting of the city's ad hoc Bi-Racial Committee. His mission, he noted, was to "relate the story of the willful dereliction of duty on the part of the Tallahassee Police Department in protecting our right to picket peacefully." He asked committee members to "approach city officials with a request that police protection be given to us, [while we] engage in legal, peaceful picketing." The committee finally agreed to do so, he wrote, "after much vacillation and hesitation." Larkins had doubts that the police would honor such a request and feared that "any advances in integration in Tallahassee will be made only through the courts." "Our opponents are ready to fight us 'tooth and nail,'" he added, "and they have the legal machinery to aid them."[3]

Larkins complained to Carey that Tallahassee city officials "collude with the hoodlums to break up our picket lines, then order [protesters] to disperse because of imminent violence." The police chief had refused to protect the students during their most recent picket, he wrote, "on the grounds that the number of policemen was limited." Larkins believed that if CORE "had the large number of people willing to go to jail we could force the police to protect us." But primarily because the students' parents wanted their children not to risk jail or expulsion, "these people who would willingly go to jail are not present in our student body." To make matters worse he added, "we do not have the minimum support from the Negro community."[4]

While civil rights activity seemed at a virtual standstill in Tallahassee during the early months of the Bryant administration, an important U.S. Supreme Court decision and a change of national leadership in CORE brought renewed vigor to the campaign for racial equality in the South. The Court had ruled in 1944 that it was unconstitutional to maintain segregation in interstate buses and trains. But not until December 1960 did the Court extend the prohibition against segregation to include terminal accommodations as well. The Court's decision coincided with CORE's search for a major campaign that would propel both the organization and James Farmer, its new director, into prominence.

By early 1961, CORE's new strategy was set: a proposed freedom ride across the Deep South to test the effects of the court's new ruling. The campaign was modeled after CORE's successful 1947 Journey of Reconciliation, a test of integrated interstate travel in the upper South. This time, however, the freedom riders would penetrate the Deep South, would integrate terminal facilities, and would refuse to accept bail or pay fines if they were arrested by local officials.

While a small group of potential riders began training in Washington, D.C., blacks in Tallahassee—unaware of the proposed freedom ride—confronted the same merchants and city officials who continued to block efforts to desegregate public and private facilities. On 4 March 1961, Pat Stephens, Benjamin Cowins, and three other CORE members sought counter service at McCrory's, Sears, and Neisner's department stores. When police asked the young people to leave McCrory's, they complied. But at Sears, store managers locked the racially mixed group inside the restaurant and turned up the heat to near suffocating levels. After several hours, the demonstrators were led from the building by police and were briefly detained.

At that point, Stephens and Cowins went to Neisner's, where they sat down at the empty lunch counter and were refused service. Minutes after they arrived, two Tallahassee police officers, Lieutenant Harry Smith and Sergeant H. L. Coleman, were called to the location to investigate a "sit-in demonstration." The two officers arrived at the crowded department store, approached the two seated students, and stood behind them for five to ten minutes. "There's no city ordinance being violated here at this time," Smith said to Coleman, "let's go." As soon as the officers left the store, Stephens and Cowins got up to leave the lunch counter. Stephens was several feet ahead of Cowins. A white man approached Cowins and asked him to "step outside." Almost immediately Cowins was thrown to the ground by two whites, who proceeded to beat him. As Stephens turned and ran toward her friend, a glass shattered on the floor near Cowins. Customers crowded around the scene. Someone ran outside to tell the officers that a fight had broken out. The two policemen reappeared as Cowins struggled with his assailants on the floor. Smith led both Stephens and Cowins, who did not resist, outside, where a crowd of 150 to 200 whites had gathered. He told them that they were under arrest and had to stay in the patrol car. Meanwhile, Sergeant Coleman was attacked, not only by one of the white assailants, but also by the man's two sisters. The other white assailant escaped from the crowd and was never identified. Cowins and Stephens were charged with fighting and engaging in disorderly proceedings. The two spent the night in jail.[5]

On 7 March, Cowins and Stephens were tried in municipal court. Although both arresting police officers testified that they did not know who had started the fight, nor had they seen Patricia Stephens actually throw a glass, the city charged that Cowins had thrown the first punch and that Stephens had thrown the glass that struck Cowins, thereby escalating the conflict. During testimony, three white witnesses, including one who said he had seen "this nigger hit this white fellow," swore that they saw Cowins start the fight but could not be sure that Stephens had thrown the glass, which had cut him. Judge Rudd found Cowins guilty of fighting and disorderly conduct, and Stephens guilty only of disorderly conduct. Both students were sentenced to thirty days in jail and were fined $500.[6]

Stephens and Cowins appealed the case to the Leon County Circuit Court, where it was heard on 18 October 1961. Citing the "rather weak circumstantial evidence," Judge Ben Willis dismissed all the charges against Stephens but let Cowins's conviction stand. When he was ordered to begin his jail sentence, Cowins was suspended by FAMU officials.[7]

Distressed by Cowins's plight, Richard Haley wrote FAMU President Gore, calling upon his former employer to reverse Cowins's "punishment" and take a stand against his arrest and confinement. "We are Negroes with long and unhappy experiences in surrendering to racial discrimination," Haley wrote the president. "Tallahassee has a poor record of progress in human relations when compared with some of the rest of Florida. We cannot escape that the oppressive measures directed toward students by both its colleges have been prime factors in that record." Gore did not answer Haley's letter and refused to reconsider the suspension.[8]

Cowins's suspension was enough to put the "quietus on any general liberal action on the campus for perhaps the rest of the year," Haley told Marvin Rich. He asked Rich to write about Cowins in the *CORE-LATOR* to make the public aware of the "repressive atmosphere" in Tallahassee. In addition, Haley sent copies of his letters to Gore and Carey along with a brief summary of the events that had occurred before and after Cowins's arrest to Samuel Adams, a reporter for the *St. Petersburg Times*. "Ben Cowins' compulsory withdrawal was a quiet move that caused scarcely a ripple on the campus, it is practically unknown elsewhere. But it is a gross, unnecessary injustice; it should be known." An article about Cowins's plight appeared in the *Times* on 16 December 1961.[9]

Haley was all too familiar with the tremendous pressure on black students to remain in school and not to drain their families' meager financial resources by forfeiting tuition payments and fees. Consequently, he believed that CORE's direct action protest would not succeed "if the action would seem to lead to arrest." According to John Riley, one of Gore's advisers, the administration received hundreds of calls from parents of FAMU students who expected the administration to keep their children from participating in demonstrations that might lead to their incarceration and expulsion.[10]

Cowins's conviction left many adult blacks with a sense of guilt that once again young people had taken a costly stand on behalf of the whole community. On 12 November, a special "Ben Cowins' Day" was celebrated at St. Mary's Primitive Baptist Church as a fund raiser to pay the young man's fines and tuition losses.

Later in the week, copies of a letter written by several black ministers circulated in the community. Entitled "Sour Grapes," the letter admonished the adult black community to "come out of the audience and get into the act" and to send contributions to CORE to pay for Cowins's financial debts. The letter urged blacks to "give the lie to the liars who say, 'most Negroes prefer segregation,'" and warned them that if the community failed to rally around Ben, it would be cause for the "lasting shame of this city."[11]

To further strengthen the call for support, CORE, the ICC, the NAACP, and the newly created Non-Partisan Voter's Crusade distributed an open letter entitled "Rights and Teachers" in which they called upon black instructors to shake off the epithet of "gutless invertebrates" and join the struggle for civil rights. The joint appeal asked teachers to examine their consciences and do more "to win all human rights for all human beings. Contribute," the letter implored. "Don't stop at a token figure or a convenient one; support by sacrifice. It's worth repeating. Don't stop at a token figure or a convenient one."[12]

Teachers were not the only blacks who seemed reluctant to become personally or financially involved in the movement, yet their obvious economic and social status within the community elevated them to positions of potential leadership. Many middle-class blacks employed in both the public sector and the private experienced various forms of intimidation and retaliation for civil rights activities. Some ignored these threats and continued their civil rights work visibly or behind the scene; others did not.

Although not an instructor, Assistant Admissions Director Daisy Young was subject to the same pressures that were brought to bear on Florida A&M faculty. During the sit-ins, Young had received indirect messages from President Gore to tone down her involvement in civil rights activities. Finally, exasperated with these secondhand admonitions, Young spoke to Gore directly. "I know I just have a B.S. degree from A&M and not an M.A. or a Ph.D.," Young told the president. "But I'll tell you one thing, I think I speak good English, so instead of getting messages from everyone else, I want you to tell me what you want to say to me." Gore then told Young that he would like to work out a scholarship for her so that she could go off to another university and get her M.A. Surprised, Young told Gore that "it was too late for that." From that day on, she felt that the president respected her more, and he never again challenged her about civil rights activities on or off the campus.[13]

Despite the appeals for aid and the support of people like Young, only half of Cowins's $500 fine was raised in the local community. National CORE paid the remaining balance, although Haley cautioned Tallahassee CORE to consider the money a "loan," not a "gift." After serving thirty days in jail, Cowins was released on 25 November 1961 and resumed his civil rights activities. In 1962 he became president of the local CORE chapter.[14]

Meanwhile, Pat Stephens left Tallahassee to attend Howard University in Washington on a full scholarship. In September 1961 she moved to the Lower

East Side of New York to work in a neighborhood association that provided for local residents with legal and social problems. In Patricia's year-and-a-half absence, Priscilla worked with Cowins and a faithful few to keep CORE alive in the capital city.

Throughout the spring of 1961, Tallahassee CORE, the ICC, and the local NAACP urged blacks to boycott stores that refused to desegregate their lunch counters. The boycott proved difficult not only because all of the lunch counters remained segregated but also because without the sit-ins there was no dramatic rallying point for the black community. In a widely circulated letter, C. K. Steele urged blacks to "buy [only] the things that we must have, and [asked] that we not trade where we can't work and where we are not treated as equals. I have faith in you. . . . I have faith in the power of love over hatred and prejudice . . . of the power of right to prevail over wrong and evil. If what I believe is not true, then life has no meaning and is not worth living." [15]

Steele's faith was aggressively shared by two young people in Tallahassee, Derek Lawler and Jefferson Poland. In the spring of 1961, both white students returned to the Leon County jail to serve out their sentences after the U.S. Supreme Court refused to hear an appeal of their 1960 sit-in conviction. Poland had been suspended from Florida State University in January 1961 for "insubordination to an administrative officer of the University" after he accompanied a black law student to a play produced by the Florida State University Speech Department without first obtaining the permission of the department chairman. In addition, after applying to take a course at Florida A&M, he was questioned and detained by city police as he walked across the FAMU campus. When Poland attempted to bring a black friend to a panel discussion on segregation at FSU, the discussion was canceled. To make matters worse, Poland's landlady complained to FSU administrators that he entertained blacks at his apartment, and as a result he was evicted in the summer of 1960.

After his suspension, Poland left Florida to attend San Jose State College in California. He voluntarily returned to Tallahassee to serve out his jail sentence in late April 1961. Derek Lawler, still a student at Florida State University, refused to pay his fine and joined Poland in jail to protest segregation in Tallahassee. Henry Steele also refused to pay his fine and joined the two white youths in the Leon County Jail. While incarcerated, Poland began a hunger strike to bring attention to racial conditions in the capital city. From 7 May to 1 June 1961, Poland refused to eat but did drink "coffee, fruit juices, and a little milk . . . , even some beer and gin," he wrote Gordon Carey. "Gandhi would not approve, I fear," he added.[16]

Poland's hunger strike led C. K. Steele to organize a "fast for equality" that included seventy-five blacks and five whites who pledged to fast every Friday until lunch counters were desegregated. Finally, after losing over twenty pounds, Poland ended his hunger strike. He left jail but elected to spend the summer in Tallahassee before returning to California. The young man's fast did not generate the kind of publicity that CORE would normally have given it, because the national office was preoccupied with the upcoming Freedom Ride. It is not clear whether local sympathizers continued their fast, but lunch counters in Tallahassee remained totally segregated.

Meanwhile, a thousand miles away in Washington, D.C., thirteen volunteers—seven black and six white—embarked on CORE's historic Freedom Ride. "We will travel through the South and enter New Orleans on May 17," Gordon Carey wrote to Poland in jail, "that is if we squeak through Alabama and Mississippi without arrest." Of the interracial group, four were CORE staff members, including Executive Director James Farmer and James Peck, editor of the *CORE-LATOR,* the only rider who had participated in the 1947 Journey of Reconciliation. Most young blacks on the ride were already veterans of sit-in demonstrations in the Deep South, including twenty-one-year-old John Lewis, who would later become national chairman of the Student Nonviolent Coordinating Committee.[17]

Although the riders met with some resistance in the terminal lunch counters of the upper South, violence first erupted at the Greyhound station in Rock Hill, South Carolina, on 9 May when a mob beat two of the riders as they attempted to enter the white waiting room. But in Georgia, passengers on the Freedom Ride were unmolested. In Atlanta, they ate at the Trailways terminal and prepared for their journey into Alabama.

After crossing the border into Alabama, the protesters encountered a violent racist fury that permanently injured several of their group and left their bus a charred wreck. On 20 May, the riders were savagely attacked at the Montgomery Greyhound bus station. Martin Luther King Jr., accompanied by C. K. Steele and other SCLC officers, came to the city to offer support to the survivors and spent a terrifying night trapped in a church encircled by a mob of screaming whites. Finally at midnight the mob was dispersed by the National Guard.

The next day the riders continued their journey with fresh recruits from other CORE chapters and the Nashville, Tennessee, chapter of the Student Nonviolent Coordinating Committee. This time they rode on a bus provided by U.S. Attorney General Robert Kennedy. Alabama National Guardsmen rode on the bus as far as the Mississippi state line.

There was no mob violence in Mississippi, thanks to the work done in advance by the U.S. Justice Department. But when the riders arrived in Jackson, they were all arrested, charged with breach of the peace, and sentenced to sixty-seven days in jail. With James Farmer in "a dreary Mississippi dungeon," a new phase of the freedom rides began. Representatives from CORE, SCLC, and the Student Nonviolent Coordinating Committee set up the Freedom Riders Coordinating Committee to continue the momentum generated by the first riders. From across the country, independent of the committee, volunteers began their own freedom rides through the South. In early June, eighteen members of a CORE-sponsored, interfaith, interracial group left Washington, D.C., for the long ride to Tallahassee.[18]

Before the second wave of freedom rides began, Attorney General Robert Kennedy asked the Interstate Commerce Commission for an order officially abolishing segregation in interstate transportation. The administration sent pleas for the protection of travelers to governors in the South. Governor Farris Bryant received a call from Attorney General Robert Kennedy, informing him that the freedom riders were planning an extensive trip across North Florida to test buses and terminal facilities.

Bryant, anxious to avoid unfavorable publicity and violence, sent an aide in advance of the travelers to each targeted community to tell bus company personnel and local leaders that "the easiest way out was to leave these people alone." Furthermore, Bryant encouraged people to leave who did not want to be in the terminals when the riders were there. Otherwise, Bryant feared, "there will be a big news story and trouble."[19]

With Bryant's advice and the memory of Montgomery still fresh in the minds of many, the freedom riders met with little resistance in North Florida, though they did encounter dirty looks and exorbitant prices for meals. When the riders arrived in Tallahassee, they met with traveling NAACP "fact-finders" and ate an expensive lunch at the Trailways bus station that prompted one NAACP rider to ask how anyone could think that "people who would literally risk their lives to integrate the bus stations would be bothered by having to pay an extra quarter for a sandwich?"[20]

In Tallahassee, at the Greyhound bus station, a crowd of antagonistic whites gathered, and two of the black riders were pushed out of the white restroom. Police moved in and dispersed the crowd. Meanwhile, Greyhound management agreed to serve the riders but used black waiters to serve the blacks and white waiters to serve the whites. A small group of local blacks arrived to support the riders and later escorted them to the airport for the return flight home. At Tallahassee's new municipal airport, the thin veneer of compliance with the desegregation ruling finally cracked.

Before leaving office, LeRoy Collins had been approached by city leaders who wanted his support for a plan to subvert anticipated federal desegregation regulations by building a dining room at the new airport entirely with private funds. Collins was stunned by the request. He told the contingent of business and political leaders that it "was intolerable and it looks to me like if there is any place that people ought to be able to eat together it is at the airport," adding, "besides, the court would never uphold that type of devious activity."[21]

Undaunted, the city built the airport with the aid of federal funds but leased the restaurant to a private firm owned by Union News Company. C. K. Steele wrote to the Interstate Commerce Commission and complained of the terminal's segregated facilities—to no avail. On 23 April 1961, Gordon Carey received a letter from a CORE staff member who had flown into Tallahassee and had been refused service at the airport restaurant. Though Carey made a note on the letter to contact the executive secretary of Union News, it is not clear whether correspondence reached the company before the freedom riders got to the airport two months later.

When they arrived at the airport on the morning of 15 June, the members of the interfaith freedom ride found that the restaurant was closed. Eight of the members flew home. The other ten decided to stay in the airport until the restaurant was declared open to them. By nightfall, an "unruly" crowd of whites had gathered outside the airport, and police took some whites to the station for questioning. Plainclothesmen patrolled the area. By 10:00 P.M., the protestors had decided to leave the airport and to spend the night at a local black church. Dan Speed, assistant minister of the church, remembered that a group of local blacks sat up with the freedom riders and discussed Tallahassee's racial situation throughout the night.

The next morning, the ten clergymen returned to the airport, where they were met by local supporters, including Priscilla Stephens and Jefferson Poland, who had just been released from jail. Governor Bryant called Robert Kennedy and told the attorney general that he could not protect the freedom riders anymore. "You've got to get these people out of here," Bryant told Kennedy. "I've done all I can do." Alarmed, Kennedy asked Bryant to give him two hours to persuade the riders to leave peacefully. But just as Kennedy reached the group's spokesman, Reverend J. S. Collier, city attorney James Messer gave the group fifteen seconds to leave the airport. Collier, who was still on the phone, and the other nine riders refused to move. Immediately, the police arrested the protesters, including Poland, Stephens, and another black protester. All thirteen were accused of unlawful assembly. Stephens was also charged with resisting arrest and interfering with a police officer.[22]

When Bryant heard that local police had arrested the freedom riders, he was furious with the Tallahassee city commissioners. The governor had worked for weeks to guarantee that the riders were quickly served in North Florida and were sent on their way without violence, arrest, or unwanted publicity. "Eighteen cups of coffee and a half-hour of integration would have freed Florida of the first contingent of Freedom Riders," commented the *St. Petersburg Times*.

But to Tallahassee officials, such a trivial concession to desegregation protesters was apparently out of the question.[23]

After spending the evening in jail, all thirteen protesters were arraigned at a special session of city court where, represented by Tobias Simon, they pleaded innocent. During the trial, city attorney Messer stated that he knew nothing about any orders to close the restaurant. Restaurant manager Hubert Isbell told Simon, however, that he had planned to close for repairs sometime in the future but after meeting with city manager Arvah Hopkins had decided to do so on the day the riders came to town. Hopkins, who had met behind closed doors with city commissioners while the defendants were at the airport, testified that the presence of the group in town was only a "minor part" of the decision to close the restaurant.

When Simon asked police chief Stoutamire whether he considered the riders really guilty of unlawful assembly, Stoutamire replied that his experience in law enforcement led him to believe that public disorder and violence would have resulted from the continued presence of the group at the airport. When Simon persisted in asking police officers to state exactly which of the group's activities seemed likely to incite violence, Rudd intervened and told the attorney, "You know as well as I do that lawful assembly can become an unlawful assembly when certain conditions exist." More damaging to the defense case was Messer's contention that after the riders canceled their reservations, they were no longer bona fide interstate passengers and were not protected by federal law. Therefore, the city attorney testified, the riders were guilty of unlawful assembly.[24]

During a full day of testimony, the defense established that a vending machine operator had been called and had been asked to install his equipment in the airport "around the time the mixed group came to the city" and also that prices for the food had been inflated beyond normal levels. Afterward Judge Rudd pronounced all of the riders guilty of violating a city ordinance that made it unlawful to disobey a police official's order to disperse when there was a threat of violence. Each rider was sentenced to thirty days in jail or a fine of $500. Stephens, Poland, and Stephen Hunter were acquitted of unlawful assembly, after Simon proved that the three had moved to disperse when the police gave the order. But Rudd sentenced Stephens to a mandatory five-day jail sentence for resisting arrest and ordered her to spend thirty additional days in jail for violating probation stemming from her 1960 arrest.[25]

During sentencing, Rudd told the group that if they had come to Tallahassee for a "noble Christian purpose," he would have dismissed the charges against them. But, he said, "you came here for the whole purpose of forcing your views on the community." The judge reminded the riders that Tallahassee had a much lower crime rate than the cities from which they came and told them to go back and "clean up your own back yard before you go around trying to impose your views on someone else." [26]

Almost twenty years later, Rudd maintained that he was eager to get the riders out of town because the temper of the community was such that a "bad situation" would have developed if they had remained in town much longer. "In those days you would have to have lived in my position to understand and appreciate the delicate path I was trying to follow," he said. "I was trying to adhere strictly to the law, which was harsh enough at the time to keep down white tempers." [27]

Four months after the riders had been convicted, federal district court judge Harrold Carswell ordered the city of Tallahassee to remove all signs at the airport that were designed to enforce segregation of the races in the waiting and restrooms. The judge also issued a permanent injunction against the city commissioners, ordering them to refrain from making "any distinction based upon color in regard to the service of patrons at the leased airport restaurant." Priscilla Stephens's conviction of resisting arrest was overturned in circuit court in 1962 by Judge Ben Willis, who ruled that "a person has the right to resist an unlawful arrest." But Willis's ruling did not affect the conviction of the freedom riders. On appeal, the judge upheld their unlawful assembly conviction, ruling that "when citizens press their demonstrations in behalf of a cause (however worthy they deem their objectives to be) beyond the bounds of delivering their message, and reach the stage that they materially and harmfully interfere with the orderly business and lawful activities of others, then the conduct is disorderly assembly." [28]

Three years later the U.S. Supreme Court sent the case back to the Florida Supreme Court, which ruled (as it had earlier) that it lacked jurisdiction and ordered the appeal transferred to the circuit court. There the convictions were again upheld. In 1964, several of the riders who had refused to pay their fines returned to Tallahassee and served a brief jail sentence until they were released by Judge Rudd.

The Tallahassee freedom riders' experiences with the criminal justice system show that the civil rights demonstrators and their organizations bore a crushing financial burden especially as a result of the lengthy appeals process. Southern judges routinely used the courts to stymie protests. And as Farris Bryant knew, the power and effect of civil rights protest could be largely muted if police were able to contain violence, resist mass arrests, and thereby avoid a sympathetic backlash from white voters. In short, to be most effective, nonviolent direct action had either to elicit brutality, as in Alabama, or to evolve into a mass protest as in the Tallahassee bus boycott.

On 1 November 1961, largely as a result of the original freedom rides, the

Interstate Commerce Commission issued regulations prohibiting all forms of segregation in terminals and travel. Richard Haley came back to Tallahassee to help the local CORE chapter organize its "Big Bend Travel Tests." The purpose of the tests was to see how well nearby communities in North Florida, Georgia, and Alabama were complying with the new regulations.

The local riders, who included Priscilla Stephens, Ben Cowins, and John Due, were FAMU students except for Haley and FSU's Robert Armstrong. Their travel tests revealed that neighboring towns and communities grudgingly adhered to the new regulations. Groups of whites taunted and insulted the small group of riders when they entered the bus terminals, but they remained unmolested and paid the expected inflated meal prices with some relief. Richard Haley wrote Gordon Carey that before leaving Tallahassee, he revisited a bus station lunch counter where "a lady whose ancestry is tainted by Negro blood was summoned from the kitchen to minister to my wants." Such was the "compliance" with the new law.[29]

In Albany, Georgia, on 5 November, the Tallahassee group was barred from entering the station by police. Two weeks later, five local blacks were arrested at the same terminal. Their arrest and conviction precipitated a series of demonstrations that brought the SCLC, King, and Steele to the city in support of the newly formed "Albany Movement." Both men were arrested and jailed during the protests, but by the summer of 1962, Albany remained a "monument to segregation," and nonviolent direct action was losing momentum across the South.[30]

In Tallahassee, CORE's efforts to resume picketing and direct action activities were stymied by a lack of support within the black community. "The will to act is a rare, precious item in our great movement for human rights," Richard Haley wrote Father David Brooks in December 1961. "CORE needs action for its own organizational health, to stir the community here forcefully, and to remind white Tallahasseeans that they have not moved and we are not satisfied." Haley asked Brooks to reconsider his reservations about an upcoming picket line and "join us in this first direct action in many weeks."[31]

But Brooks, like most Tallahassee blacks in 1961, did not join CORE's protests at the city's segregated lunch counters. The black community's reluctance to embrace CORE's desegregation campaign seems an anomaly by comparison with its enthusiastic support of the ICC and to a large extent of the NAACP as well. But the resistance to CORE reflected not apathy or contentment on the part of Tallahassee blacks but a rejection of CORE's direct action tactics. And for good reason. CORE protesters went to places where they were not wanted, demanded service, refused to leave, and in most cases were arrested. Because of their confrontational style, CORE demonstrators attracted the attention of whites and elicited a hostile reponse from them. The protesters were physically threatened and were sent to jail. Furthermore, it seemed at best uncertain that such protests could ever defeat segregation. Unlike the intrusion method of the sit-ins, the bus boycott, which garnered the mass support of the black community, derived its effectiveness from patronage withdrawal, an effective tactic but one that permitted anonymity and entailed few of the dangers of direct action protests.

Although CORE's support in Tallahassee was dwindling, it continued to receive encouragement from the national office. "I can imagine the frustration you sometimes experience and the despair that comes from such frustration," Gordon Carey wrote to the local group in December 1961. "You are doing a wonderful job in the face of many obstacles. I hope you have the perseverance to keep up the good work." Carey wrote Haley that he was "especially anxious that Tallahassee be reactivated. Should this require more time than you can now spend there, you should feel perfectly free to return after visiting other areas." [32]

A small number of CORE members continued to picket Tallahassee lunch counters during the Christmas season of 1961, but neither direct action protest or a halfhearted selective buying campaign could compel department store owners—or, more important, the city commission—to open Tallahassee's lunch counters to black customers. Although segregation remained largely intact in Tallahassee as 1962 opened, the battle to desegregate interstate travel and facilities had been won there and across the South. Pockets of resistance remained, of course, but in the spring of that year the national office of CORE inaugurated a new project, "Freedom Highways," a campaign to desegregate restaurants in the South that were owned by large chains. The justification for the campaign was, most obviously, that "it is impossible for a Negro traveling by car to eat in any restaurant along the way without submitting to gross humiliation." Howard Johnson's restaurants were the focus of CORE's activities. In Florida, sixty-five of the sixty-seven restaurants were owned by the national company, which made the state the "most fruitful for project activity." [33]

Before the Freedom Highway project began, national Howard Johnson agreed to desegregate all of its Florida restaurants. CORE then turned to other southern states, particularly North Carolina, where many of the chain's stores were privately owned. By the end of the summer, half of North Carolina's Howard Johnsons were integrated, and a renewed interest in nonviolent direct action was spreading in many parts of the South.

By the fall of 1962, Florida was no longer a totally segregated state. Not only had most of the larger cities—including Miami, Tampa, St. Petersburg, and even Jacksonville—desegregated their lunch counters and public facilities, but many had official biracial committees that worked to ease racial tensions. Not so in Tallahassee, where local lunch counters refused to serve black patrons, where bus terminal managements still turned blacks away from "white" restrooms and waiting areas, and where the city commission remained firmly opposed to an official biracial commission.

Tallahassee civil rights supporters received a much-needed boost when Patricia Stephens returned to Florida A&M in the fall of 1962. She came back to school, she said, to prove that a black southerner could get an education in the South and work for racial equality. Another reason for her return was to rekindle her relationship with fellow activist and FAMU law student John Due. Once back at Florida A&M, Stephens joined the new CORE group that her sister had organized—as Richard Haley noted—with nothing more than "her will power and bare hands." Priscilla, who had graduated from FAMU, left Tallahassee to further her education in New York.[34]

Only weeks after her arrival, Pat and three other FAMU students were arrested at a privately owned restaurant inside the Trailways bus terminal. With their newfound determination and federal regulations behind them, the students filed a $1 million apartheid suit against the city of Tallahassee, the city commissioners, the police, and the owners of the Carrousel Restaurant. Three weeks after their arrest, the secretary of the Interstate Commerce Commission received a letter from the president of the restaurant chain, who insisted that while he knew nothing of the local affiliate's racial policy, he had warned its Tallahassee owners that segregation policies would not be tolerated in the future.

Although the law seemed clearly on the demonstrators' side, Judge Rudd convicted them of disturbing the peace by failing to obey a police officer. Rudd told the court that the Interstate Commerce Commission rulings were in the nature of "usurpation of legislative powers" and that a state law permitting the owner of a business to require any undesirable person to leave was the higher law.[35]

City Attorney Hill, in an obvious though unspoken reference to the 1961 airport sit-in, argued that because the four young people had not actually purchased bus tickets, they were not protected by the interstate law. Patricia Stephens was sentenced to sixty days in jail or a $400 fine. The other demonstrators received a slightly lower sentence.

The official tone of unrelenting opposition to racial progress in Tallahassee was mirrored across the state by the Bryant administration. In November 1962, the governor refused to appoint a civil rights advisory committee on state employment of Negroes, as requested by the U.S. Civil Rights Commission. The next month, Bryant announced plans to start a legal movement to "emphasize the Bill of Rights and probe the legality of the Fourteenth Amendment to the United States Constitution." At the Southern Governors' Conference that year, Bryant's support of segregation policies contrasted sharply with Collins's moderate stance at previous conferences.[36]

By the late fall of 1962, Tallahassee, the state capital, was the only major city in Florida that had not desegregated its downtown lunchroom facilities. In December 1962, blacks renewed the sit-ins at downtown eating facilities. This time there were no arrests, nor was there newspaper coverage. City officials had determined that the less publicity black protesters received, the less support they would garner. Yet the demonstrators were subjected to taunts and physical assault by whites who left before police arrived to disperse the crowds. Florida A&M student Reuben Kenon remembered that he was more frightened during that time than at any other point during the civil rights protests, because it seemed obvious that the demonstrators would not receive police protection. Kenon was spat upon, knocked off his stool, and repeatedly threatened with abuse or death by whites. He often felt that he would not return to Florida A&M alive after a Saturday demonstration at Woolworth's.

Many blacks chose to boycott segregated stores entirely. Others shopped but refused to patronize the segregated counters where black customers were forced to stand and eat their lunch. Yet to the consternation of many, a few prominent black educators continued to eat at the stand-up counters. White officials pointed to them and encouraged blacks to follow their "leaders" and accept the segregated counters, but most blacks ignored such behavior and advice. "We knew who the Uncle Toms were," remembered Daisy Young, "and their names were mud."[37]

If the white community in Tallahassee was not totally united in opposition to black equality, neither was the black community united in the ongoing civil rights struggle. Some conservative blacks were labeled "Uncle Toms" in their community. Others, like C. K. Steele, drew criticism for adopting a more activist, confrontational style.

As first vice president of the SCLC, Steele traveled widely throughout the South in the early 1960s. His position led him to Albany, Birmingham, St. Augustine, and later Selma during some of the most pivotal, dangerous moments in the movement's early history. In addition, Steele was often called upon by King to participate in SCLC strategy meetings that took the minister away from Tallahassee. Though Steele's supporters were proud of his stature in the nation's civil rights movement, many of the deacons of the Bethel Baptist Church were not pleased with their minister's activities out of town. On several occasions after 1960, they attempted to limit Steele to full-time "church sponsored activities." The deacon board also sought to restrict the right of "any outside group" to hold meetings at the church and to limit the number of times a guest minister could fill in for the absent Steele.[38]

On more than one occasion, Steele took the board's recommendations directly to his congregation, which continued to give him a vote of confidence. In retaliation, the deacons refused to grant the minister a salary increase for several years or to provide money to repair the parsonage.

Because of his many absences from Tallahassee, Steele was criticized by some blacks for failing to provide continuous leadership in the capital city's civil rights struggle. At crucial times, for example in the waning days of 1962, it was not Steele but Richard Haley, Pat Stephens, Daisy Young, and Dan Speed who led the struggle to break the color barrier at the city's lunch counters.

By December 1962, local store managers—who, as Haley noted, were not "dedicated integrationists," began to resent the financial pinch caused by the loss of lunchtime revenue as well as black patronage. Still, little pressure was put on the city to change its racial policies. As Saul Silverman, an aide to Collins, had earlier observed, it was "an understandable circumstance because the chamber of commerce budget comes in large part from the city commission."[39]

At last the loss of black patronage was sufficiently serious to motivate downtown merchants to action. The manager of McCrory's told Pat Stephens that he and other businessmen were meeting with Minister Davis Thomas of the First Presbyterian Church in an effort to reach a compromise with the city commissioners. "They saw what had happened in Albany and in some other towns and they were afraid," Thomas recalled.[40]

City commissioners told merchants that if they began to serve blacks, they would do so without police protection. But finally, as had happened during the bus boycott, the threat of continued lost revenue outweighed any fear of racial discord. When the chamber of commerce began to pressure the city commission to give in, a breakthrough occurred.

Without official city participation, several downtown store managers met with Thomas, a small CORE delegation, and the remains of the ad hoc biracial committee and agreed to integrate lunchroom facilities in January 1963, almost three years after CORE began its campaign to desegregate the capital city's lunch counters. What appeared to be a watershed in Tallahassee race relations was only a minor victory. The same month that Tallahassee's lunch counters opened, blacks began the largest, most constant demonstration in the city's history to desegregate the downtown movie theaters. The year 1963 marked the beginning of two years of civil rights activism that swept away the last vestiges of legal segregation, but it was by no means the end of the long, bitter struggle for racial equality.

8 Struggle Without End

On 23 January 1963, C. K. Steele met with Martin Luther King Jr. and other members of the SCLC's executive staff in Birmingham, Alabama, to finalize plans for a major desegregation campaign in that city. On the same day in Tallahassee, two black students, newly married Patricia Stephens Due and fellow CORE member Julius Hamilton, were arrested at the Florida Theater after entering the lobby with tickets purchased for them by a white supporter. The two were charged with criminal trespass.

Due and Hamilton were taken to the Leon County jail, where they spent the night. The next day they were arraigned and a trial date was set. Later that week, with no explanation, the city announced that it was dropping the case. City attorney James Messer told defense lawyer Tobias Simon that city officials were "tired of suits and litigations." [1]

Suspicious that Tallahassee officials were trying to avoid further desegregation in the wake of the lunch counter integration, Due and four other FAMU students again filed suit. They charged the city with racial apartheid. But at Steele's urging, they agreed to drop the action if the city would desegregate the courtroom, a particularly offensive symbol of racial inequality for Tallahassee blacks. Judge Harrold Carswell and Judge John Rudd assured Simon that the courtroom would be desegregated immediately if they would promise not to publish news of the agreement. The next day, however, when John and Pat Due, Julius Hamilton, and Reuben Kenon went to city court, they were all removed from the "white side" of the courtroom on orders from Judge Rudd.

Outraged by the duplicity of city officials, Due announced that she and other members of CORE would resume protests at the city's two downtown theaters. On 29 May, a large group of Florida A&M students marched in front of the State Theater on College Avenue. Across the street, Malcolm Johnson observed "a good many toughies and a few rough little hussies egging them on to a fight," but he found the demonstration "very much like a football pep rally, or an old fashioned camp meeting, or a college sing." Denouncing recent reports about "racial tension" in Tallahassee, Johnson reported that there was no "tension" in front of the theater, "only college kids with broad smiles, with bodies swaying with all the joyful spirit and rhythm their wonderful music possesses."[2]

A few blocks from where Johnson stood, FSU Methodist chaplain Austin Hollady was on his way downtown to Bennett's Drug Store when he saw the marchers in front of the State Theater. As he drove past Adams Street he noticed a group of white students leaving Lively Vocational School dressed completely in white with chains wrapped around their ribs or their belts. Assuming that they were enrolled in the school's bakery program, Hollady watched as the men made their way toward the State Theater. After parking his car on College Avenue, the minister told his three young daughters to stay in the car "no matter what" and dashed into the store. As he came out he saw the "bakery students" fighting with some black students on the corner. Hollady ran over to two of the men and tried to break up their fight. Instead he was punched in the face and knocked to the ground. He arose and quickly made his way back to the car and his terrified children.

The next day Hollady was meeting with six other campus ministers, including James Hudson and Harcourt Waller, when a call came from Mayor Sam Teague. He told the ministers that a large group of Florida A&M students was planning a march to the Florida Theater on Monroe Street. Despite Malcolm Johnson's optimistic prophecy, violence seemed a very real possibility. Teague asked whether the ministers would go downtown and try to prevent a confrontation between whites and blacks. Accordingly, the men piled into Father Lex Matthews's van and headed downtown.

Teague's call to the ministers was part of the young mayor's strategy to gain control of the racial situation in Tallahassee and to avoid a recurrence of events in 1960. Teague, who had served as a commissioner only one year before becoming mayor in 1963, was a thirty-four-year-old banker and neither a member of an "old" Tallahassee family nor part of the conservative business group first elected to the commission in the 1950s. Teague did, however, strongly share the prevailing white attitude toward public demonstrations and the "outsider" conspiracy theory held by many.

Teague recalled later that during his term as mayor he received "blueprints" from the FBI warning that three students who had "very elaborate plans" to create civil rights disturbances were going to enroll at Florida A&M. These students, Teague said, "armed with plans printed in Cuba," planned to get "mobs of people to block intersections, the firefighting equipment, and provoke police into confrontations." There were groups of people who used "civil rights demonstrations for their own selfish purposes," Teague recalled, "but I realized as Mayor that ninety-nine-point-nine percent of the students out here were well meaning American citizens trying to improve their lot in life."[3]

Faced with the first civil rights confrontation in his tenure, Teague made his primary objective the preservation of public safety. He was also determined to preserve Tallahassee's reputation as a "peaceful" city. Against the advice of city attorney James Messer, Teague invoked a provision in the city charter that gave him the power to take over the police department in a state of emergency. Teague instructed Chief Stoutamire to call all of Tallahassee's sixty-eight policemen to a meeting at 5:00 A.M. on 30 May.

Teague told the assembled officers that the eyes of the world were on the city and that he wanted them to conduct themselves with dignity, decorum, and goodwill. "The first thing I want you to do," Teague told the policemen, "is get rid of those night sticks and those electric cattle prods. I want you to uphold the law, I want you to be dignified, but I don't want anybody getting rapped on the head with a night stick. I don't even want those cattle prods taken out of this room." Teague then turned to Stoutamire, who told his officers, many of whom "were just furious," that anyone who could not do what the mayor had ordered "should hand in their resignation before leaving the room."[4]

That afternoon, between 200 and 300 students picketed the Florida Theater, where *The Ugly American* was playing. They carried signs reading, "Are You an Ugly American?" "Segregation Is Wrong," "We Are All Brothers in Christ." A larger crowd of angry whites watched from across the street. Police struggled to keep the two groups apart. Standing next to the ticket window, Austin Hollady watched as four young men on motorcycles parked near the theater and walked toward the window. After his earlier experience, the minister had already decided that he would not intervene physically to break up violence. One of the motorcycle riders edged closer and closer to the window where demonstrators were attempting to purchase tickets. As a black woman turned toward the ticket window, the motorcyclist reached forward to burn her with his cigarette. Hollady grabbed the man's arm and said, "You do that and you will undo in one second what it took [astronaut] John Glenn four and one half hours to do for our country." The startled man stared at Hollady and then melted back into the crowd.[5]

For several hours the uneasy standoff between demonstrators and white observers continued. Finally, after consulting with theater owners and Mayor Teague, circuit court judge Ben Willis issued an injunction to break up the demonstration. Specifically, the order forbade the protesters from blocking theater entrances and exits, from attempting to enter the premises of the theaters, from displaying derogatory or defamatory signs or posters pertaining to the policy of the theater, and from otherwise interfering with the right of the businesses to make money.

Shortly after Willis issued the injunction, the police read it to the picketers. It was summarily ignored. Two hours later, the police arrested 221 students, all but one of whom were black, and marched them to jail.

Teague breathed a short-lived sigh of relief. Even though people had been arrested, violence had been averted. Later that afternoon, however, when word came that over 100 Florida A&M students had begun walking toward town in a sympathy march—a sight that recalled the 1960 lunch counter demonstration—Teague ordered the use of tear gas, if necessary, to turn them back. Once again, as in 1960, police fired tear gas into the crowd. Thirty-seven students were arrested and taken to jail. Mayor Teague issued a statement denouncing the students who had defied the restraining order, noting that their "failure to honor the injunction could have resulted in a catastrophe." He assured the town that law and order would prevail.[6]

In a surprise move during the students' trial on 31 May, Judge Willis (perhaps aware that an injunction barring all forms of peaceful protest would be overturned in a higher court) dismissed the charges against the students and amended the restraining order. As of 1 June, a maximum of eighteen demonstrators walking single file eight feet apart was to be allowed at the Florida Theater. A maximum of ten persons at a time would be allowed at the State Theater. All protesters were to "stand or slowly walk in the area near to the curb, carrying signs which [were] not defamatory toward the theater or its personnel."[7]

Although Tobias Simon told a large crowd of cheering FAMU students that "this is the first time in a southern state that the right of Negroes to picket has been defined and put into an order," Richard Haley noted that "the restricted type of demonstration presently permitted extracts the teeth of effectiveness of the demonstration." As Haley predicted, the small, orderly demonstrations did little to arouse official ire and nothing, of course, to change the theaters' segregation policies. By the end of the spring semester, student interest in the demonstration had waned.[8]

Early in the summer of 1963, Patricia Due and Reuben Kenon left for Ocala, Florida, to visit demonstrators serving time in jail for civil rights activities. After they had been arrested for disorderly conduct and for interfering with prisoners at the county jail, a Marion County judge convicted them and sentenced them to two years in prison. The judge called Due a "jailbird" during the trial. While the convictions in Ocala were being appealed (Due and Kenon were released on bail), Tallahassee CORE canceled further picketing at the theaters.

In Due's absence, direct action protest in Tallahassee came almost to a halt. As CORE worker Zev Aelony later noted, demonstrations had stopped "largely because of the combination of the students being gone for the summer, and fatigue on the part of Pat Due. The situation reminds me of the bible story of the battle in which the People of Israel would win as long as Moses held his arms high, but as he became fatigued, the people lost heart and fell back. So it is in Tallahassee with Pat."[9]

Determined to keep the momentum of protest alive without her sister, Priscilla Stephens, along with Reuben Kenon, organized a small demonstration against the city's segregated swimming pools. For three straight days in June, Stephens and Kenon sought admission to the Meyers Park swimming pool. On the third day, Stephens slipped in through the gate but was kicked in the stomach by a policeman as she attempted to enter the water. She was then arrested. Finally the city closed the pool for the remainder of the summer.

Priscilla, Kenon, and Pat later attended a city commission meeting to register a complaint against segregated recreational facilities and police brutality. They were prevented from testifying, however, when Commissioners Joe Cordell and George Taff left the meeting in protest. Mayor Teague then praised the police department of Tallahassee for doing a "splendid job in protecting the rights of all of its citizens."[10]

One month later, two white students from FSU appeared before the commission to complain about the police department's "handling of civil rights matters." The commission voted to go on record "as being well pleased with the Chief of Police and his personnel in the conduct of all law enforcement activities of the City."[11]

Unable to swim in city pools, prohibited from using most of the community's recreational facilities or from launching boats in the county's most beautiful public waterways, Tallahassee blacks sweltered in the summer heat of 1963. In late August, however, all eyes turned toward the nation's capital, where the historic March on Washington for one momentous afternoon embodied the frustrations, hopes, and dreams of millions of black Americans.

Pat and John Due were among the tens of thousands who marched in Washington and found themselves both "moved and inspired" by the experience. For Florida's congressional delegation, however, the march was just another day. The state's fourteen reserved seats remained empty at the Lincoln Memorial, including those of Florida's two senators, George Smathers and Spessard Holland. "It is unthinkable that I would participate in any demonstration," Smathers told a reporter. "I did my marching in the Marines."[12]

Back in Tallahassee, the harsh contours of American race relations quickly brought Due back to reality. Before she could register for the fall semester, she was ordered to Ocala for a new trial on charges stemming from her participation in that city's racial protest.

Across town in Tallahassee, Clifton Lewis, who was anxious for firsthand news of the march, called her friends in Washington, LeRoy and Mary Call Collins. "Oh, Clifton," Mary Call said, as she described the events she had observed, "where are the hearts of the American people?" The next Sunday, at St. John's Episcopal Church in Tallahassee, congregants were surprised to find that the altar flowers, provided by Lewis, were dedicated "to the Glory of God, and in thanksgiving, for Roy and Mary Call Collins."[13]

The March on Washington had scarcely ended when Tallahassee was stunned by the publication of the *Report of the Florida Advisory Committee to the United States Commission on Civil Rights*. The reorganized committee, chaired by Clifton's husband, George Lewis II, had conducted meetings throughout the state to gather information. Unlike the 1961 report, which had denied the existence of racial problems in Florida, the 1963 report laid bare the hypocrisy behind the state's progressive facade.

In the introduction, the Advisory Committee lambasted state officials (with the exception of Attorney General Ervin and Secretary of State Tom Adams) for failure to comply with its requests for testimony and information. Committee members had anticipated, according to the report,

some form of official participation and assistance from state officials and had expected to report a climate of equal opportunity for the Negro citizens of Florida. It based this hope on the state's relative freedom from racial violence and on the quiet dignity with which some progress toward integration has been made. But in probing beneath this atmosphere of apparent racial calm, the committee discovered many gaps between constitutional principles and community practices, which are not always exposed to the bright sunlight of this southern climate. Specifically, the committee has found that the Constitution is not a guideline for state practices, and that there are still Floridians in positions of leadership who fail to understand that all citizens, regardless of color, are entitled to the full protection of the Constitution.[14]

Although the Negro population of Florida was small by southern standards, the report continued, it was an

indisputable fact that social taboos exist for the Negro in Florida, particularly in the northern part of the State, as solidly as in Mississippi or Alabama. Consequently, under the facade of relative racial calm, this remains a tight-white state. Florida's white "power group," which might be called the White Establishment, controls the economic and political life of the state. Supported by an education superior to that provided for the Negro in predominantly or totally segregated schools, the White Establishment supplies the state's industrial and business executives as well as its labor leaders and politicians. This group, moreover, holds the key to opportunities for advancement in Florida, but keeps the door generally locked to the Negro, even though in some instances, he may possess an equal ability to further the community's interest.[15]

After condemning the state for impeding the integration of public schools and for denying equal protection for its black citizens, the committee lamented a "void in leadership at the higher levels of business and industry as well as among members of the state's officialdom. So, too, white lawyers and ministers have failed to insist that discrimination cease. . . . it is not surprising, therefore, that the degree of desegregation that has been achieved in Florida bears the increasingly familiar title of tokenism."[16]

A separate section of the report, "The Tallahassee Story," contained some of the committee's most severe criticism. "The atmosphere in Tallahassee does not promote the expression of any opinions that vary, however slightly, from established orthodoxy." Members blamed the Johns committee's investigation of the NAACP and the cooperation of the police department with the committee's activities for stifling much of the civil rights movement in the city. "Generally," the report concluded, "Tallahassee Negroes are afraid to participate in civil rights demonstrations because so many of them are dependent on the state for their livelihood."[17]

The report noted that blacks in Tallahassee were constantly beset by segregation problems that do not "make the big courts." It gave as an example the lack of urban renewal programs to clean out the worst Negro slums in the area, the denial of city recreation areas to blacks, and other day-to-day indignities that seldom made front page news.[18]

The explosive situation in the state's capital, the report warned, "is clearly depicted by a Daytona Beach man in the following excerpts from a letter he wrote to a member of the Advisory Committee." "I spent four days recently in Tallahassee, which is truly sitting on a powder keg. The State, Leon County and the city ought to move rapidly to blow out the fuse and dampen the powder before there is a disastrous blow up." [19]

The publication of the fifty-one-page report prompted quick and vigorous rebuttals from Tallahassee political leaders, who criticized the committee's work. Mayor Sam Teague, for example, stated, "It is my opinion that reports of this nature may well do more harm than good. Due to the fact that many members of the Civil Rights Committee, including the chairman who is a Tallahasseean, are well known for their pro-integration views and due to the fact that by far the majority of the witnesses who appeared before the committee are pro-integrationists, this report can hardly be considered to represent the impartial testimony of a cross section of the people of Florida." [20]

In response, Chairman Lewis sent Teague a letter reminding the mayor that when the committee met in Tallahassee the previous May, only one state and three federal officials out of the twenty-four invited had testified. "On the other hand," Lewis wrote, "many official representatives of minority group organizations as well as private citizens attended and provided information regarding the denial of rights in many areas on the basis of race." Lewis acknowledged that "much progress has been made in Tallahassee since we met here May 10 in both the public and private sector." But, he added, "much remains to be done, and the Florida Advisory Committee continues to welcome evidence of improvement, as well as information on work still to be accomplished, from every willing source." [21]

On 24 September 1963, in a unanimous vote, members of the city commission requested that Leon County's congressional representatives oppose the reauthorization of the U.S. Commission on Civil Rights. Teague sent a telegram to Senator Spessard Holland personally asking him to vote against reauthorization of the commission. Malcolm Johnson, who attempted to refute many of the committee's findings in the *Democrat,* called on the advisory committee to "file an amendment to straighten out the distorted record reflected in 'The Tallahassee Story.'" [22]

Although George Lewis was accustomed to public and private criticism of his views on race relations, his work on the Florida Advisory Committee had very serious repercussions. Lewis's father, "Papa George" Lewis Sr., was upset that his son had not consulted with him before accepting a very public position on the Advisory Committee. In fact, when Lewis accepted chairmanship of the committee, the board of directors of the Lewis State Bank demanded his resignation. When he refused, the board members voted to oust him as bank president. Lewis was subsequently "kicked upstairs" as chairman of the board. His brother Cheever became president, and Lewis became a nonvoting officer of the bank that his great-grandfather had started before the Civil War.

The publication of the Florida Advisory Committee's report, along with the March on Washington, the SCLC's desegregation campaign in Birmingham, the murder of civil rights activist Medgar Evers in Jackson, Mississippi, and the defiant stand against integration taken by Governor George Wallace at the University of Alabama increased the resolve and activism among blacks in Tallahassee and across the South. Their tolerance for "gradualism" at an end, blacks took to the streets to launch direct action protests in thousands of southern communities. By the end of the volatile summer of 1963, the Kennedy administration was committed to the need for comprehensive civil rights legislation that would "strike at racial segregation and discrimination." The race issue was now at the front of the American political agenda.[23]

When Florida A&M students returned to Tallahassee in the fall of 1963, they found the city's two theaters still segregated and a permanent court-ordered injunction against mass picketing and demonstrations in place. On 14 September, Patricia Stephens Due, in direct defiance of the injunction, led over 200 students, many carrying "Freedom Now" signs, in a demonstration against the Florida Theater. Among the protesters were seven white students, five from Florida State University and two from the University of Florida. Leon County sheriff Bill Joyce warned the students that they must reduce their number to eighteen—the court-ordered size—and when 157 refused, they were hauled away by a contingent of city police, highway patrolmen, and state conservation agents. So many were arrested that temporary detention facilities had to be established at the Leon County fairgrounds.

In the evening of the same day, 100 more FAMU students marched to the jail in protest. When they were ordered to leave the property, 91 refused and were arrested for trespassing and disturbing the peace. When the students disregarded police orders, they were charged with resisting arrest and were forcibly carried into the jail. Bail was raised from the usual $250 to $500.

The next day, Sunday, 15 September, brought the sickening news that four black children had died when a church was bombed in Birmingham, Alabama. That evening hundreds of students at FAMU, their anger and frustration barely contained, were led by ministers C. K. Steele, David Brooks, and E. G. Evans to the front of the jail, where approximately 250 students were now behind bars. They were met there by Sheriff Joyce.

Joyce told the ministers that all of the demonstrators would be arrested for trespassing if they did not immediately disperse. At that point, the ministers advised the students to return to the campus. Outraged, the students demanded to speak with "our CORE leader," which caused Father Brooks to ask, "You mean you're not going to listen to us?" C. K. Steele addressed the increasingly angry students and told them that he had preached civil disobedience when necessary, but he felt that it was now best to leave. Steele's arguments were greeted with boos and shouts of disapproval. When a Florida A&M dean urged the crowd to "wait until tomorrow" for further negotiation, a student shouted, "I've been waiting for tomorrow for nineteen years." [24]

Joyce then gave the students five minutes to decide whether they would disperse or be arrested. FAMU student Roosevelt Holloman was then chosen to speak with the university's deans and the sheriff. Holloman told the men that the students had been taught in class to demonstrate against injustice and that they fully expected to go to jail for their principles. "I hope you have also been taught in class to obey the law," Joyce replied. Finally Holloman agreed to leave the scene. When he told the other students of his decision, they angrily denounced him and accused student leaders of breaking their earlier agreement to go en masse to jail. After further exhortations by the ministers and student leaders, the crowd finally dispersed. [25]

The next morning, however, 250 students from FAMU were back at the jail to continue the protest. When Joyce gave the order to disperse, 104, including Holloman, refused to leave and were arrested. There were now close to 350 students in jail. With the detention facilities bursting with jailed demonstrators, Judge Willis agreed on Tuesday, 17 September, to "release and restrict to campus" 107 of the original 157 students arrested on Saturday afternoon. Left in jail were the 50 students previously arrested in the May theater demonstrations— those who were presumed to have knowingly violated the court's injunction against mass picketing. Also detained, though charged with less serious crimes, were 191 students who had marched to the jail in protest on either Saturday evening or Monday morning. [26]

On the day that Willis released the students, the board of control announced that President Gore was meeting with student leaders to urge a return to studying instead of picketing, which was "a waste of time." Three days later Gore emphatically denied that he had ever asked students to end their demonstrations. The board of control was forced to issue a statement that it had "misunderstood" Dr. Gore's comments. Although Dean Moses Miles of Florida A&M officially asked students to work within the confines of "law and order," the university refused to rush into disciplinary proceedings. [27]

Over the next three weeks, the trials and sentencing of the demonstrators continued in both the city and circuit courts, depending on the charges. On 21 September, Judge Rudd suspended the jail sentences of eighty-six of the students arrested for trespassing and disturbing the peace on the evening of

14 September. Rudd then put them on permanent probation, explaining that if they broke the terms of the injunction again, they would be incarcerated. The judge warned the students that his decision was "not a show of weakness but an act of fairness and firmness. In the future," he said, "when you have something to protest, you should talk to a lawyer first and find out what is legal and within the law."[28]

In early October, 32 of the 107 students charged with disobeying an officer and resisting arrest following the 16 September demonstration were convicted by a jury in county court, fined fifty dollars each, and sentenced to thirty days in jail. Their jail sentences were suspended. The remaining students, who waived their right to a jury trial, were not fined and were spared a jail sentence.

On 5 October, Judge Willis found the 156 original theater demonstrators guilty of contempt for defying the court-ordered injunction. Twenty-two of the students who had been part of the May demonstrations were classified as second offenders and were sentenced to three months in jail or $500 fines. Thirteen of the accused, including the five students at Florida State University and two at the University of Florida, were sentenced to forty-five days in jail or $250 fines. The largest group of first offenders (119 students) got suspended sentences. The judge assessed them $250 fines. Patricia Stephens Due and Reuben Kenon, "the leaders" of the demonstrators, were sentenced to six months in jail and were fined $1,000 each. Total fines for the demonstrators amounted to $16,000.

During the trial, attorney Tobias Simon argued that the students who had been standing in line to buy tickets were not picketers and were therefore not aware that they had broken the law. Simon added that the students' right to protest was guaranteed in the Constitution and was as old as the American Revolution. The judge disagreed. On appeal (*Due v. Tallahassee Theatres*), federal district judge Harrold Carswell dismissed without a hearing the students' charge that local officials and theater owners had conspired to perpetuate segregation in public facilities. Carswell dismissed the complaint in a decision that was later overturned by the Fifth Circuit Court of Appeals. The case was remanded to the federal district court, and the original judgment was reversed.[29]

The thirty-two students whom the county court had convicted of willful trespass for refusing to leave the jail grounds were not as lucky. Having appealed without success to the state appellate courts, the plaintiffs turned to the U.S. Supreme Court, which granted certiorari. In *Adderley v. Florida*, a landmark decision, the majority of justices upheld the conviction of the demonstrators. Voting five to four, the Court ruled that the state had the power, "just as a private property owner has, to preserve its property for the use to which it is lawfully dedicated." This marked the first time since the sit-ins began that the high court had upheld the convictions of civil rights demonstrators. But to

Justice William O. Douglas, who dissented in a vigorously worded opinion and was joined by Earl Warren, William Brennan, and Abe Fortas, the majority view represented "a great break with the traditions of the Court" and allowed states to use trespass laws to "suppress civil rights." [30]

Official efforts to thwart civil rights protest in Tallahassee were hardly confined to the courts. On 8 October 1963, city commissioners voted to request the Second Judicial Circuit Court to investigate the "activities" of the students at FAMU and FSU who had participated in the theater demonstrations to determine whether "any further laws have been violated by the action of such students." The commissioners asked the court to make any "recommendations . . . it may deem advisable" to ensure "the peace and tranquility of this community." [31]

A letter from student government president Prince J. McIntosh circulated at the same meeting. It urged Florida A&M students to "join the ranks of those who are fighting for equality, of those who will not let misjustices and bigotry keep them from taking their rightful places in American society." The letter, which was entered in commission minutes, urged FAMU students to "show our brother[s] in Birmingham and Jackson, Mississippi that we will continue to uphold the banner of Justice, Equality, and Freedom for *ALL AMERICANS*. . . . if you are not willing to make sacrifices and to fight for your human rights, then stop complaining about segregation and join the Uncle Tom Society." [32]

McIntosh issued another statement denouncing the city commission for requesting an official investigation of the student demonstrators. The investigation that was needed, he wrote, was one that would expose "racial discrimination and prejudice in the city of Tallahassee." Far from apologizing for his earlier statement, which had been characterized as a "little inflammatory" by the *Democrat,* McIntosh noted, "This is a new day which has witnessed the evolution of a 'New Negro' who will not bow down his head in the face of bigotry and threats." [33]

Meanwhile, Florida A&M faculty and staff passed a resolution demanding that the city withdraw its request and denouncing the proposed investigation as a violation of the students' "rights of citizenship." Less than a week later the four circuit judges postponed the investigation until a new grand jury convened on 2 December 1963. The stated reason for delay was "heavy trial schedules in the six counties of the circuit." In the intervening months, the Florida A&M resolution was submitted to the state attorney for his "study and investigation." [34]

Scarcely had the furor over the theater demonstrations receded when FSU students began to picket four restaurants near the campus that were refusing to serve the twelve black students attending the university. The university had been integrated in 1962, and the owners of the Mecca, the Corner, the University Inn, and the Sweet Shop had repeatedly refused to meet with members of the University Religious Council, who, with President Blackwell's approval, had been trying since early 1963 to discuss the issue with the owners. Council members had asked the Tallahassee Chamber of Commerce to use its influence to persuade the reluctant owners to integrate their restaurants—but to no avail.

On 10 October the council presented the owners with a petition signed by 700 students at Florida State University pledging to patronize the restaurants if they were integrated. A survey conducted by the student government at FSU revealed that 68 percent of the student body approved of integrating the off-campus restaurants. When the owners refused to change their policy, another group, the Social Action Committee of the Liberal Forum, announced that it would picket the restaurants. According to spokesman Tony Sciff, the failure of the restaurants to desegregate was "an affront to the character and integrity of our University, its students and faculty, and its administration." Sciff announced that picketing was "not just for FSU Negro students to be allowed in these eating establishments, but A&M students as well." The University Religious Council issued a statement in support of the picket and encouraged students not to patronize the four restaurants.[35]

On the evenings of 14 and 15 October, violence was barely averted when 300 to 500 counterdemonstrators descended upon the scene, where twenty-five to thirty picketers and their supporters had gathered. The next day, Dean of Students Ross Oglesby announced that he was "forced to invoke the [board of control] rule which gives the University the power to prohibit student participation in mass demonstrations." Florida State University students were prohibited from congregating "on and around the corners of West Jefferson and Copeland Streets except for the limited number [earlier established by Judge Willis] engaged in lawful picketing." Students who violated the order, Oglesby said, would be subject to "University discipline."[36]

While the "lawful" picketing of the restaurants continued, it lost much of its moral intensity. It was briefly revived when famed black band leader Count Basie performed at FSU in early December. After the show, when Basie and FSU sociologist James Geschwender tried to eat at the Mecca restaurant, they were refused service. Basie briefly joined the picketers, and the moment was captured in articles that the press circulated throughout the country. The ensuing negative publicity was an embarrassment to the university, to Blackwell, and to many in Tallahassee. But the Mecca and the other three restaurants remained segregated until after the Civil Rights Act passed in 1964.

If any students at FSU had been tempted to break the university's injunction against "unlawful" picketing at the off-campus restaurants, they were quickly reminded of the consequences of such action when the university disciplinary committee placed the five students arrested at the September theater demonstration on "administrative probation" until they graduated. Under the probationary terms, the students were not allowed to "represent the university officially" or to receive any scholarship or financial aid. "Any violation of major Florida State University regulations or any violation of law or court order will result in their immediate suspension." In addition, the students were restricted to the campus for the remainder of the trimester.[37]

On 22 October, ten professors at FSU began a fund-raising campaign to pay the fines levied against the students. An appeal circulated among FSU faculty was obtained by the *Democrat* and was published on 3 November 1963. State representative C. E. Russell subsequently called upon the state legislature and the board of control to express strongly their "disapproval" of the fund-raising efforts. No official action was taken against the faculty members. President Blackwell noted that they had acted as "private citizens" and expressed his "own feeling that they were motivated by humane considerations." The students' fines were paid in large measure by the NAACP and CORE.[38]

Florida A&M was the last of the three universities to announce that the student demonstrators would be placed on probation—all of them, that is, except Patricia Stephens Due and Reuben Kenon, who on 28 October were suspended indefinitely from Florida A&M. Due, who had just begun student teaching in Jacksonville, was ordered out of the classroom. Prince McIntosh, president of the FAMU student government association, withdrew from the university in protest. Angry students from Florida A&M, determined to meet with President Gore, demonstrated at his home. For three nights the students conducted a "sleep-in" on the president's front lawn to protest the suspensions. Gore refused to meet with the students, although he did not insist that they leave his property. By the fourth day the students had all drifted away.

On 24 October, the Florida Civil Liberties Union announced that it was filing suit against Florida A&M for suspending the two students before their appeals had been exhausted. The organization charged that the university's action "creates an ironic paradox wherein one segment of the Negro community in a shortsighted, irresponsible and dangerous retreat, effectively undermines another segment in the fight to eliminate racial discrimination." Meanwhile, the board of control unanimously upheld the university's decision to suspend the two civil rights activists. ACLU attorneys then filed in U.S. district court for a temporary restraining order to prevent the board and the university from enforcing the suspensions. Judge Carswell denied the application. Attorneys for the two students filed a lawsuit against the university.[39]

While Due and Kenon continued to fight their suspension in the courts, Judy Benninger and Dan Harmley, the two white students who had been convicted along with them, were suspended from the University of Florida. Benninger, a graduate teaching assistant, also lost her Ford Fellowship. Her father, a professor at the University of Florida, later managed to get his daughter reinstated at the university on permanent probation. Seven years earlier, Benninger had lost his job at the University of Alabama for supporting the admission of Autherine Lucy, the institution's first black applicant.

Judy Benninger, a member of Gainesville's Students for Equal Rights, had come to Tallahassee in September to meet Pat Due, of whom she had heard from activists in Gainesville and Ocala. She was staying at Due's home when Due and Harmley were arrested on 15 September. It was her first mass demonstration and her first arrest.

Benninger and three other demonstrators shared a single cell for almost a week. "Coming from a middle class background with all my needs met, I was appalled by jail conditions," Benninger remembered twenty years later. "They didn't have enough to feed us because they were not prepared to have so many people in jail. FAMU students would bring their lunches and share with all the prisoners."[40]

What frightened Benninger most was the attitudes of the guards, who told other women prisoners that if they beat up the white civil rights demonstrators, they would be given favors. At night, two of the women who were waiting to be transferred to the state prison got broomsticks, attached razor blades to them with string, and stuck the weapons through the bars in an effort to cut the terrified girls. Benninger and her cellmates were able to avoid harm by crowding together at the very edge of their bunks for most of the night.

Benninger and her friends came to realize that their obvious contempt for the regular prisoners exacerbated the situation. One night, a rat ran into the common area where the prisoners were housed, causing all the women to scream for the guard, who ignored their calls for help. After this incident, Benninger remembers, "the jailer became our common enemy." The prisoners subsequently began to bring the demonstrators their dinners instead of hoarding the food.[41]

When the two groups of women were both finally able to leave their cells and walk around, they became friends. "They began to regard us as rebels, which they identified with," Benninger recalled. "I think it was a class interest that overcame the racial hostility. As prisoners, our interests were the same." When the demonstrators were finally released on bail, the other women prisoners cried. Benninger returned to Gainesville but not for long. Less than a year later, she and Pat Due led CORE's voter registration campaign for North Florida.[42]

Even before the 1964 civil rights bill was passed, CORE announced that it would launch a major voter education project in North Florida. On 22 March

1964, Executive Director James Farmer visited Tallahassee to meet with Patricia Stephens Due, CORE's new field secretary for the Voter Education Project. At a mass meeting, Farmer announced that CORE would not rest until "100 percent of eligible Negroes are registered." In addition, he said, the organization planned to "speed up its activities in Florida including a campaign for complete desegregation of public accommodations and more jobs for Negroes."[43]

Before leaving town, Farmer told reporters that CORE would work in "co-ordination" with the NAACP for the upcoming civil rights march slated for 27 March in Tallahassee. In reality, plans for the ill-fated march were already in substantial disarray and revealed the strain and distrust that had developed between CORE and the NAACP since the first student sit-ins in 1960.

The NAACP had consistently supported civil rights activists in Tallahassee since before the bus boycott in 1956. Over the years the organization enjoyed cooperative working relations with the ICC, the ACLU, and later CORE. Indeed, many local activists were members of all of these organizations and managed to maintain cordial relations. Even when its leadership role was usurped by other civil rights organizations, as happened during the bus boycott, the sit-ins, and the theater demonstrations, the NAACP continued to provide attorneys or bail money.

As with the national organizations and officers, friction between the state NAACP and the various civil rights groups in Florida increased as more blacks and whites became involved in the struggle for black equality. Debates over tactics to achieve that goal, not to mention competition for contributions and publicity, placed a strain on the delicate relationship between individual leaders and their followers.

Still, all things considered, there remained cooperation and friendly competition among civil rights groups in Florida. In October 1963, Florida NAACP field secretary Robert Saunders filed a written protest with the board of control over its directive ordering that disciplinary action be taken against students arrested in the theater demonstrations led by CORE. Saunders also wrote letters to Florida A&M alumni and various black organizations soliciting money to help pay the fines of the students who had protested "in the interests of all Negro Citizens of the State of Florida."[44]

But Saunders's support of the jailed students in Tallahassee (as elsewhere across the state) did not keep him or other NAACP officials from criticizing CORE for "conducting irresponsible and ineffective demonstrations and then calling on us to pay the resulting fines." In February 1964, the NAACP's growing concern about CORE's presence in Florida was revealed in a staff member's letter to Saunders about CORE activity in Florida. "Tallahassee was the first place I have found CORE activity anywhere in the state," wrote a staff member.

"But they will be in Gainesville too, if we don't make a change in the branch leadership there."[45]

By the early spring of 1964, the state NAACP was looking for a way both to reassert its priority among civil rights organizations in Florida and to exert pressure on Florida's congressional delegation, which solidly opposed passage of the civil rights bill of 1964. The idea for a march on Tallahassee "to show that Negroes are in agreement on the passage of the civil rights bill," was first publicly discussed at the November 1963 meeting of the Florida State Conference of NAACP Branches. On 27 February 1964, the organization's Church Committee for Florida (comprised of black ministers) set the date for Good Friday, 27 March. The ministers agreed that "other organizations, fraternal, civic, and civil rights operations in the State of Florida would be invited to take part in the March."[46]

Reverend C. K. Steele, president of the Tallahassee branch, was appointed state chairman of the committee to plan the march, even though he was not present at the meeting. Steele, also first vice president of the SCLC, not only had been involved in the organization's widely publicized and controversial desegregation campaign in St. Augustine but was also working as an informal advisor to CORE, was a member of the Tallahassee Ministerial Alliance, and was serving as full-time pastor of Bethel Baptist. His appointment as chairman of the march did not please everyone, including the NAACP's outspoken Ruby Hurley, who worried that Steele "wore too many faces" to do an effective job as chairman.[47]

Once plans for the march became public, misunderstanding and miscommunication between Saunders and Steele and local march chairman Father David Brooks threatened to undermine the unity and success of the event. Brooks, with Steele's approval, appointed several local activists including Due, Benninger, Dan Speed, Daisy Young, and two local CORE members, Frank O'Neal and FSU student activist Rosemary Dudley, to a march planning subcommittee.

At the first statewide planning meeting, O'Neal, unknown by most of the participants, was told by an unsuspecting NAACP member that since "CORE has been getting all the publicity in the state lately, we have orders to make this a successful NAACP march." This sentiment was underscored repeatedly over the next few weeks even though Saunders continued to welcome the support and participation of various groups and individuals.[48]

Meanwhile, it became obvious to the Tallahassee committee and other participants across the state that there was simply not enough time and money to plan and carry out a large, successful protest march. Richard Haley's earlier prediction that without "at least one full time coordinator" any march of "state-wide significance" would "degenerate into a mass of confusion well before the appointed date of action" was on the verge of coming true.[49]

As the date for the march grew near, disagreements intensified over numerous details, including the route marchers would follow, the guests who would speak, and even the tone of the event. It was not uncommon for Due, Steele, and Brooks to hold one view and for Saunders to hold another. Finally, on 22 March, one week before the scheduled event, Saunders announced that all local committees were being relieved of their duties and that they should discontinue any plans made and "cease to function."[50]

When Saunders met with Governor Bryant's staff (without Steele, Brooks, or Due) and approved a march route that would bypass the state capitol, the Tallahassee planning group sent a telegram to the governor telling him that there would be a change in the march route to include the capitol grounds. Confused, gubernatorial aides contacted Brooks, who told them to consider the route "changed." Meanwhile, Saunders received a telegram from city manager Arvah Hopkins, who refused to grant a permit for the march along the new route. Saunders then met with Bryant's aides, told them that Brooks's telegram was "out of order," and, according to Due, insisted "that any persons who deviated from the march route and who tried to go to the capitol should be arrested."[51]

One day before the march, Due sent James Farmer a telegram announcing that CORE "has no alternative but to withdraw its support from the March." There were, she explained, several reasons for the decision. Chief among them was the choice of route "through a negro neighborhood to a segregated baseball field and not to the capitol itself" and a scheduled program that "is not representative of CORE or the current leadership of the civil rights movement in Florida." The selection of speakers for the event, she later wrote, excluded "all persons connected with direct action" and included three people "whom nobody has heard of" and one man "who has been termed a thorough 'Uncle Tom' here."[52]

By 27 March, CORE was not the only organization that had withdrawn its support and participants from the march. Both Steele and Brooks refused to participate, as did several hundred members of various chapters of the ACLU, CORE, and the Council on Human Relations from around the state. Although early NAACP press releases had predicted that 10,000 people would participate, approximately 2,000 were on hand at noon when the announcement was made that "All NAACP groups should line up." Several hundred marchers withdrew when they discovered that the route had been changed and would not take them by the capitol. A large group waiting at the capitol also dispersed when maps of the route were distributed. Finally, about 1,600 strong, the march began, led by

Saunders and Hurley, who, Due contemptuously reported, rode ahead "in a police car."[53]

"Negroes' Protest Fizzles to 1,100," the *Tallahassee Democrat* reported on the day of the march, "after a leadership split developed and members of the Congress of Racial Equality pulled out." Although Saunders provided a positive report of the march to the national director of NAACP branches, as well as a larger estimate (approximately 2,400) of attendance, the march did little to garner support for the pending civil rights bill and did much to exacerbate tension and division among the state's civil rights groups.

On 3 July, Congress passed and President Lyndon Johnson signed the civil rights bill of 1964. This historic legislation outlawed segregation in most public and private facilities, barred stricter voter qualifications for blacks, authorized the U.S. attorney general to file suit to desegregate public schools, and outlawed employment discrimination. "The gallant battle of those opposing [the bill] is now a matter for the history books," Senator George Smathers wrote his Florida constituents, "but I can report with a genuine sense of pride that we made the House-passed version a little more reasonable and a little more democratic during the eighty-three days of debate." Smathers's assessment that the new legislation "violates and destroys the basic concept of our Federal-State dual system of government and the principles of individual choice and freedom" played well back home but was essentially empty rhetoric.[54]

As Smathers railed against the new civil rights legislation, President Johnson appointed another Floridian, former governor LeRoy Collins, to lead the agency that had been charged with assuring voluntary and peaceful compliance with the new law. Collins told reporters that the Community Relations Service would serve as a bridge for encouraging compliance with the civil rights bill "without lawsuits, and without disorder."[55]

Meanwhile, back in Tallahassee, Malcolm Johnson waxed philosophical about the new law. "Most of us in this part of the country have opposed it," he wrote on 3 July, but, "good or bad, wise or foolish, this is now the law of our land. Whether we like it or not, it is our obligation as citizens to observe it until we can, by due process of law, get it changed or repealed."[56]

Rev. C. K. Steele with
the four-foot cross
that was burned at
Bethel Missionary
Baptist Church
Parsonage on
January 2, 1957.

White resistance to front row bus seating demonstration planned by Inter-Civic Council and advertised in *Tallahassee Democrat,* December 1956.

Black-occupied homes on Meridian Boulevard, within sight of the State Capitol, 1958.

Reverend C. K. Steele with John Boardman, who was expelled from Florida State University for supporting Inter-Civic Council activities, and Rev. J. Raymond Henderson, of California, at Bethel Baptist Church, January 1957.

Picketers protest segregation of downtown Tallahassee lunch counters, December 1960.

Three 1960 sit-in demonstrators during a court recess called due to bomb threat. *(Left to right)* Vecient Moore, Florida A&M University, John Jefferson Poland, Florida State University, and Robert F. Kemp, Florida A&M University.

Patricia Stephens Due leads demonstration in front of State Theater, May 1963.

Demonstrators protesting in front of Florida Theater following May 1963 circuit court decision restricting number of picketers.

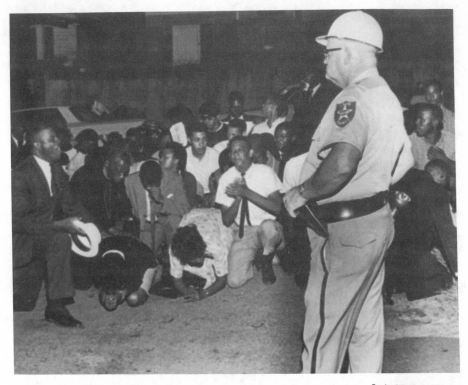

Protesters kneel in
prayer before mass
arrest during theater
demonstrations,
September 1963.

Governor LeRoy Collins receives a pen after President Johnson signs 1964 Civil Rights Act.

Editor Malcolm Johnson at work at the *Tallahassee Democrat,* 1966.

LeRoy Collins as mediator during 1965 Selma, Alabama, protest march. *(Left to right)* John Lewis, Rev. Andrew Young, LeRoy Collins, Rev. Martin Luther King Jr., Coretta Scott King, and Rev. Ralph Abernathy. This photo, circulated by Collins's opponent in Florida's 1968 U.S. Senate race, helped to doom his candidacy.

Blacks register to vote in Tallahassee City Hall, 1964.

Judge G. Harrold Carswell.

Leon High School, 1960.

Students at Raney
Junior High School,
Leon County, Florida,
1965.

9 Ballots and Backlash

In Florida, following the passage of the 1964 Civil Rights Act, Governor Farris Bryant announced that he did not anticipate calling in the federal Community Relations Service, headed by LeRoy Collins, to help the state with its "racial desegregation problems." The government's job, he said, "is to maintain a climate in which law-abiding citizens can operate, and not to enforce the new federal act." Bryant compared the enforcement of the civil rights law with the collection of federal income taxes. "The state doesn't collect the federal income tax," he noted, and "neither will it enforce provisions of the civil rights law." In a written reply to a concerned constituent, Bryant declared, "I would be trespassing on the rights of every Floridian if I tried to enforce [federal laws]." Before meeting with a biracial group of clergymen on 6 July, the governor issued a statement maintaining that "segregation has always been my policy" and expressing his belief that people should be free "to establish those relationships among themselves consistent with their own freedoms."[1]

Meanwhile, "race incidents" persisted across the state as more segregation barriers fell. The NAACP announced that it would file suit against public and private facilities that were not in compliance with the new law. As they tested the desegregation provisions of the new law in Tallahassee and in communities across the South, civil rights organizations stepped up campaigns to secure the ballot for thousands of disenfranchised southern blacks. Unlike the previous civil rights acts of 1957 and 1960, Title I of the 1964 law barred states from enacting tougher examinations or qualifications for black voters and allowed the attorney general (after a black litigant filed suit) to ask for an injunction and to ask a federal court to hear the case. The 1964 act did not have the sweeping provisions that would have been needed to abolish all barriers to black voting, but it became an effective weapon against mass disenfranchisement in certain areas of the South.

Unlike many of their southern neighbors, Florida legislators never enacted a literacy test as a means to keep blacks from voting. They did not need to. In 1889, twelve years after the state's white Democrats had returned to political power, lawmakers had enacted a capitation tax (poll tax) to be paid annually by all males age twenty-one or older as a prerequisite for voting. The same legislation required that counties provide separate polling places for state and national elections and that voters cast separate ballots in separate boxes for each elective office—a device designed to confuse, intimidate, and frighten away many potential voters. Both the poll tax and the multiple ballot box law effectively kept numerous blacks and many whites from voting. Therefore, the poll tax was outlawed by the Florida legislature in 1937. The multiple ballot box law was replaced by the Australian ballot in 1895.[2]

Still, obstacles to blacks voting remained. Like the rest of the South, Florida was a one-party state. Consequently, the Democratic primaries were the contests that really elected candidates and decided issues. The Constitution prohibited states from denying blacks the right to vote, but the Democratic Party as a "private" organization could ban black participation in the primary. Even if blacks were able to register and vote, there was no effective opposition to the white Democratic candidate. The exclusionary white primary became the most effective impediment to black suffrage throughout the South.

In 1944, the U.S. Supreme Court ruled in *Smith v. Allwright* that the all-white primary in Texas was unconstitutional. This decision paved the way for black political participation in Florida. After World War II, the NAACP initiated voter registration drives in some parts of Florida. But most blacks refused to risk their lives or livelihood to register or to vote for white candidates pledged to a white-controlled party dedicated to preserving segregation. In 1946, 6 percent of registered voters in Florida were black.

In Leon County, on 1 May 1944, only three weeks after the *Allwright* decision, Carrie Bentley, a twenty-four-year-old black schoolteacher, tried to vote in a

Leon County Democratic primary. When she arrived at the courthouse, Bentley was turned away by precinct officials, who told her that she would have to wait for a "legal ruling on her status." When she refused to leave the courthouse, the Leon County superintendent of public schools threatened to fire her. Bentley proceeded to Lincoln High School, where Principal Gilbert Porter assured her that she would not be fired if she returned to the courthouse. Later that day, Bentley and eight other Tallahassee blacks voted unchallenged.[3]

In the years following World War II, black registration increased steadily in Leon County. In 1946, only 508 blacks had been registered to vote. Two years later, there were 2,266 black registrants. Although black voters increased at a steady pace over the next fifteen years, they were outpaced by a larger increase among white voters. In 1954, the year of *Brown,* fewer than one-fourth of Leon County voters were black, although there was a black population of 40 percent.

Even as the state's population grew substantially in the postwar years (it increased by 79 percent between 1950 and 1960), twelve North Florida counties actually lost residents, as many blacks left for other parts of the country. Tallahassee and Leon County were among the few areas in North Florida that exemplified the state's rapid growth and shifting demographics. In 1940, Tallahassee's population was 16,240. Twenty years later the number had almost tripled, to 48,174. Leon County more than doubled in size (31,646 to 74,225) during those years. The black population of Tallahassee increased in the postwar years but at a much slower rate than the white. As a result, where blacks accounted for 41 percent of Tallahassee's population in 1930, this percentage had decreased to 40 percent in 1940, 34 percent in 1950, and 33 percent in 1960.

Among Florida's sixty-seven counties in 1960, five had an eligible nonwhite voting population of at least 40 percent. Four of these were in North Florida. The percentage of eligible black voters who were registered in the area (which was commonly known as the "Black Belt," or the "Old South" region) ranged from 3 percent (Gadsden County) to 36 percent (Madison County). The U.S. Civil Rights Commission reported in 1961 that "substantial numbers of Negro citizens are, or recently have been, denied the right to vote" in eight southern states. Although Florida was not considered a Deep South state, it contained five of the 100 counties where denials of voter registration had been documented by the commission's investigative staff since 1957. In two of these counties, no blacks had ever registered to vote. Blacks in rural Gadsden County, twenty miles west of Tallahassee, provided nine sworn complaints to the commission that threats of physical and economic reprisals had prevented them from voting.[4]

Because of Florida's antiquated apportionment system (the antithesis of the one man, one vote concept), less populous counties of North Florida were disproportionately represented in the state legislature. The five largest counties in the state had over 50 percent of the population but elected only 14 percent of the senators. In 1960, for example, Dade County, with a population of 935,047, had one senator, as did tiny Jefferson County, with a population of 9,543. Broward and Leon Counties both had two representatives in the 1960 legislature, although the former had four times as many people that year. Prior to legislative reapportionment in 1967, as few as 12 percent of Florida voters could elect a majority of the Senate and 15 percent a majority in the House. Thus conservative lawmakers—the aptly named "Pork Choppers" from Florida's northern tier—were keenly aware of the potential significance of a large black electorate.

From 1950 to 1960, Leon County's black electorate shrank by 6 percent as a percentage of all eligible voters. Still, Leon was among twelve counties, all but two located in the northern part of the state, where in the aggregate blacks accounted for roughly a third of potential voters. But by the spring of 1964, despite years of NAACP and ICC voter education drives, fewer than half of Leon County's 14,000 eligible black voters were registered.

When CORE inaugurated the voter education project in the waning days of 1963, the organization chose twenty-three-year-old Patricia Stephens Due as field secretary for North Florida. At her request, Judy Benninger, a white activist, became the project's assistant secretary. Initially, the two young women decided to focus their efforts (and meager funds) on two counties, Leon and Gadsden. Their first task was to find office space for the Big Bend Voter Education Project. The phrase "Big Bend," like "Panhandle," referred to Leon and thirteen surrounding counties. Due and Benninger finally found a ramshackle old building in Frenchtown, but the owner, fearful of white retribution, refused at first to give them a lease. Due later persuaded him to change his mind. When she had trouble getting a city permit to rewire the building, Due turned for help to Susan Ausley, the wife of the prominent attorney John Ausley.

Ausley met Due and Benninger at the building and agreed that electrical work was needed before the lights could be turned on. Ausley called the city and asked that an electrician meet them at the building. When he arrived, the electrician asked Ausley what she wanted done. "You should ask Mrs. Due," she replied. Within a half hour, Arvah Hopkins had called her brother-in-law at the family law firm. "Charles," the exasperated city manager said, "Susan's downtown calling a nigger Mrs. Due."[5]

Although she was connected with one of the city's oldest families, Susan Ausley was a maverick with social and political views that distinguished her from many of her relatives. Susan Mitchell had been born in Thomasville, Georgia, in 1921. She saw social issues differently from most of her friends, in part because she "read and traveled more." When she and husband John had lived in New

York City in the 1940s, Ausley read the *Daily Worker* and absorbed its views on southern race relations. Back in Tallahassee in the late 1940s, she continued educating herself about race relations by reading all of the available literature on the subject, and she took a sociology course at FSU, where she wrote a term paper on race relations.[6]

During the 1950s Ausley, along with Clifton and George Lewis, Lillian and James Shaw, and a few whites, belonged to the Liberal Forum and the Tallahassee Council on Human Relations. When she began actively supporting some civil rights organizations and projects, her husband (who shared her ideas "theoretically," she remembered) told her that "nothing's going to happen for the next fifty years. All you're going to succeed in doing is antagonizing people and interfering with my law practice and our income."[7]

But Ausley continued to risk social and family opprobrium. In the early 1960s, she and her husband hosted a glittering dinner party for international students at their home in the fashionable Betton Hills neighborhood. It was the city's first large interracial social event. In early 1964 she was at the Lewis's home when the community's first interracial political organization, the Tallahassee Good Government Association, was formed.

The Tallahassee Good Government Association was one of the organizations that Due contacted in her initial effort to make the voter education project a community-based effort. As in 1959, Due asked the NAACP, the ICC, and the Tallahassee Council on Human Relations for support and volunteers. An interracial steering committee consisting of James Hudson from Florida A&M, Samuel Hunter, the black principal of an elementary school, Clifton Lewis, and Lillian Shaw coordinated registration activities. In late January 1964, Due reported to CORE's James McCain that the Leon County campaign was operating with more than thirty volunteers canvasing neighborhoods for potential black voters. Student volunteers from FSU and from the Florida A&M chapter of the NAACP made up the largest contingent of volunteers.

With the voter education project proceeding smoothly in Tallahassee, Due informed McCain that she would soon turn her full attention to a voter registration project in Gadsden County. She would look for a place to establish headquarters in her old hometown of Quincy, leaving Judy Benninger in charge of the day-to-day operations of Leon County.

The Big Bend Voter Education Project was run on a shoestring budget out of a small building in the middle of Frenchtown. But as with so many civil rights activities, it caught the attention of the ever vigilant Johns committee. The committee's investigative staff met at the project office on 9 March 1964 and began interrogating Benninger. The committee asked her about the project, its goals, and its funding sources. In addition she fielded several personal questions about her background and personal ideology. Chief investigator John Evans noted that Benninger was living rent free in a room provided by the Lewises. The Johns committee compiled additional information on the project and its staff from various informants and investigators. The governor's staff located a letter complaining of Benninger's harassment by the police and other city officials in Leon and Gadsden Counties that Patricia Due had sent to the Florida attorney general. A copy was forwarded to the investigative committee. Police reports of civil rights activities in the same areas were also passed on to the committee.

Shortly after her encounter with the Johns committee, Benninger was served a summons by the Leon County Health Department. According to the summons, Benninger had "slept with many black men, was a venereal disease carrier, and a health threat to the community." Consequently, she was ordered to submit to a blood test or be arrested. Convinced that the results of her blood test in Tallahassee would be forged, Benninger went to a local black doctor and requested that he send the sample under another name to a laboratory in Gainesville. After the results came back negative, Benninger informed her parents, who were told by the health officer in Gainesville that the health department doctor in Tallahassee was a "real quack." The Gainesville doctor declared that he would call the authorities in Tallahassee and tell them to "lay off." [8]

Despite the fact that Benninger's blood test was negative, officials of the county health department continued to accuse her of being "a transmitter of a communicable disease." Pat Due wrote the state attorney general to complain. Meanwhile Benninger's car and health insurance were canceled, but there were no more official threats from the health department.[9]

By February 1964, Due was traveling daily the twenty-one miles between Quincy, the "shade tobacco capitol of the world," and Tallahassee. It was imperative to step up registration activities in Tallahassee, she wrote James McCain, because of the upcoming race for two city commission seats. In the Group I race, incumbent commissioner Joe Cordell, a strong proponent of segregation, was considered a shoo-in. In the four-man Group II race, incumbent Hugh Williams faced a serious challenge from only one candidate, attorney John Ausley. A black candidate, Curtis Corbin, was also in the race. Corbin never mounted a serious, organized campaign, and there was little enthusiasm for his candidacy in the black community or the Big Bend Voter Education Project, some members of whom suspected that Corbin had been "put up" by conservative whites to shift black votes away from Ausley, who emerged as the progressive candidate.

Unlike his brother Charles, John Ausley had never served on the commission or in any elective office. Early in the campaign he voiced strong opposition to salaries for city commissioners and supported a more open, accountable city government and additional public parks and recreational facilities. His political debut was supported by the Tallahassee Good Government Association. Ausley never campaigned in the black community or actively sought black support, but Williams later successfully used the moderate and reasoned answers that he gave to questions raised at a public voter forum on 7 February and later posed by the *Democrat* to undermine his candidacy among white voters.

The forum, sponsored by the League of Women Voters, was an opportunity for the candidates to comment on a variety of problems facing city government. The most pressing concerns, such as personnel problems at the municipal hospital, property taxes, and the cost of utilities, elicited similar responses from the candidates. Ausley was the first candidate to be asked about his stand on segregation. "I am asking all the people to vote for me," he said, "and all are entitled to be treated as citizens." Further pressed for specifics, he tried to strike a moderate tone. "I won't promise that I will attempt to desegregate the hospital or swimming pools tomorrow. But I will work with the aim that all public facilities will be made available to all citizens." When asked about job opportunities for blacks, Ausley said, "The city should hire people with the best brains available for the job-trends have been changing rapidly the past few years." [10]

Williams's answers to questions differed strikingly from Ausley's. The commissioner said that he supported "separate but equal facilities for blacks" and that his stand conformed to the "wishes of the people we represent." Furthermore, he noted, "the city commission gets undue criticism because Negroes can't eat at a certain place or see a certain movie. Business places are privately operated and operated as the owners see fit within the law." He noted once again that he was opposed to appointing a biracial committee "because it was tried once and failed." [11]

After the forum, members of the Tallahassee Good Government Association asked Due whether the Big Bend Voter Project would actively support Ausley's campaign. She was unable to offer such support and maintain the nonpartisan nature of the voter education project, she told McCain, but "we do believe that Mr. Ausley can offer the most to Negro citizens, and the entire community as well." Due agreed to distribute leaflets containing excerpts from Williams's and Ausley's speeches, and she encouraged black voters to attend all debates and public forums. Meanwhile, many of Ausley's supporters, including his brother and other whites, wanted the candidate publicly to deny the support of any civil rights or voter education groups. Ausley was "furious" at their suggestion, his wife remembered, and told her he would rather return campaign contributions to all of his white supporters than be told from whom he should accept money. After the general election, Ausley publicly stated that "every thin dime" he spent on the campaign had come from his own pocket. [12]

During the week following the forum, editors of the *Democrat* asked each candidate to express his views on five separate issues, one of which was integration of public facilities. The candidates' written responses appeared in the *Democrat* on 16 February 1964. Ausley was glad, he said, that all candidates had been asked to express their views on the integration of public facilities. "Honest answers to this question should stop candidates from talking one way in private and another way in public," he said. "It is not a question of how a candidate might personally feel, but one of the legal rights of citizens. As an attorney I will not, and certainly no public official should, willfully disobey the law, whether in favor of it or not. All citizens of all races, as well as all groups, have the same responsibility." Williams reiterated that he had always favored equal but separate public facilities and affirmed his belief in the sanctity of private property.[13]

On 18 February, election day, the *Democrat* reported that there was "heavy voting, particularly among Negroes" in all four of the city's precincts. The paper made clear which precincts were heavily black. Blacks accounted for nearly half the voters in Precinct A, "the northwest quadrant of the city," and for more than half the voters in Precinct D, the "southwest quadrant of the city." Precincts B and C had "few Negro registrants." By the time the polls closed, Williams had garnered 48 percent of the vote, less than was needed to avoid a runoff with Ausley, who came in second with 28 percent of the vote. Corbin received 6 percent of the vote, and the third white candidate, C. W. Brandt, got 17 percent.[14]

The turnout was the heaviest in Tallahassee city elections "in many years," the *Democrat* reported, as 67 percent of registered voters went to the polls. But as a percentage, white registrants outnumbered the black registrants who voted, which hurt both Ausley and Corbin. Only 60 percent of registered voters in precincts A and D, where Ausley received his largest support, went to the polls on election day. In the overwhelmingly white precincts (B and C), 73 percent of the voters went to the polls. Williams received almost 60 percent of the vote in these two precincts, Ausley approximately 25 percent. It was clear that Ausley needed a large strong black vote and a strong contingent of white voters to win the runoff.

Despite a week of heavy campaigning by the Tallahassee Good Government Association, Williams beat Ausley by a two-to-one margin. Less than 60 percent of registered voters went to the polls for the runoff election. Ausley received 45 percent of the vote in precinct A and 46 percent in precinct D. He received approximately one-quarter of the votes in the two predominantly white precincts. Ausley's "margin of loss could have been taken up by the registered Negro voters who were not reached by [his] basically middle class campaign plus those Negroes who were not registered at the time of the election," Due wrote

McCain on 29 February. But Ausley's defeat clearly reflected a white backlash against his moderate stance on civil rights.

The Big Bend Voter Education Project stepped up its campaign to register more black voters before the gubernatorial primary in May. Front-runners in the governor's race included Jacksonville's "strong segregationist" mayor, Haydon Burns, who had twice used force to put down serious race riots and had subsequently refused to appoint a biracial committee to discuss racial problems. While he was mayor, Burns agreed to sell the city-owned golf course to private investors and to close the public swimming pools rather than integrate them. In its opposition to civil rights his platform was exceeded only by that of his rival, state senator Scott Kelly. Miami mayor Robert King High, who refused to accept large campaign contributions and ran against special interests and back room politics, was the voice of moderation among the key contenders. As mayor of Florida's largest city, High had skillfully steered Miami through racial crises and a myriad of urban development problems. Unlike his key rivals, he announced during his campaign that as governor he would fully enforce any federal civil rights legislation. "That was enough to brand him a radical liberal," Due wrote McCain. Indeed, Burns described High as an "ultra liberal" and the "NAACP candidate" once civil rights emerged as a key campaign issue.[15]

Although it did not generate as much interest as the governor's race, the 1964 race for seats in the U.S. Senate revolved around the civil rights bill. Spessard Holland, Florida's popular senior senator, campaigned vigorously against the pending legislation. His opponent, Brailey Odham of Orlando, supported it. Odham's challenge was never taken seriously by the major newspapers or the political pundits. "All the signs are that [Holland] will be perfectly safe to stay in Washington and vote on the pending 'Civil rights' bill," wrote Malcolm Johnson, "instead of coming home to cast one of the thousands of ballots which will favor him over his AFL-CIO NAACP sponsored challenger, Brailey Odham." Odham "embraces nearly all the social theories that Holland has fought against for years," Johnson continued, including "forced integration of the races in private business . . . , fewer restrictions on labor unions, medical care for the aged regardless of need, required minimum wages so high that they discourage employment of men most subject to replacement by machines—the whole gamut of New Deal, Fair Deal, Johnson Deal governmental encroachments." But the central issue in the campaign was, as Johnson knew, "the pending civil rights bill." The editor wrote, "Spessard L. Holland is the only man running for public office who can directly reflect a citizen's objections to that bill. Those who have objections, or even conscientious reservations to the bill should place their votes against it by casting a ballot for Holland next Tuesday."[16]

Against such strong anti–civil rights sentiment, Due and Benninger continued their efforts to expand the voter registration project. Although the Big Bend Project was "having difficulty breaking through the apathy of Leon County," she complained to McCain, Due's small group of workers and volunteers succeeded in reaching an increasing number of blacks through their canvasing drives. In March 1964, the project targeted Florida A&M after it was discovered that 24 percent of the faculty and staff were not registered to vote. Letters were sent to each faculty member urging them to register and to persuade their colleagues to do so. Similar letters were sent to blacks employed by the county school board.[17]

Due also targeted black churches as crucial components of the voter education project. In March she reported that "Negro ministers who belong to a faltering group in Tallahassee dedicated to registration, have expressed their desire to revitalize the old registration campaign by supplying us with canvassers, transportation and financial aid." One week before the registration books closed for the upcoming gubernatorial primary, Due reported, "The county has been divided into the thirteen precincts having Negroes. A precinct leader has been assigned to each precinct. City buses have been hired, and people have been carried to the registration office in large numbers." After years of pressure from local blacks and more recently from the voter education project, the county registrar agreed to open the office one night a week and on Saturday mornings. On the first evening session, Due proudly noted, 179 persons registered in a two-hour period.[18]

On primary election day, 5 May 1964, Holland beat Odham by more than a two-to-one majority. He received over 70 percent of the vote in Leon County. As expected, Haydon Burns was the winner in the four-man gubernatorial race, but it was the second-place finish of Robert King High that stunned observers who had expected "arch segregationist" candidate Scott Kelly to emerge as Burns's runoff opponent. Indeed, High squeaked out a second-place finish primarily because of his strong showing in heavily populated Dade County and in much of South Florida. Kelly took most of North Florida, although he came in a strong second in Leon County behind well-known conservative state senator John Matthews. High received 14 percent (2,893) of the vote in Leon County. There were 6,145 eligible black voters. "Only about half of the registered blacks in Leon County voted for High," Due wrote McCain after the first primary, because of "a last minute sell-out of certain Negro leaders who capitulated to more conservative candidates and confused many voters. As a result, a conservative gubernatorial candidate got many Leon Negro votes, as well as [incumbent] Sheriff [Bill] Joyce."[19]

On 26 May 1964, riding "an anti–civil rights tide," Haydon Burns swept to victory in Florida, winning in all but three of the state's sixty-seven counties.

Leon went for Burns almost two to one, although this time High received nearly 7,000 votes. Although Burns's victory was testimony to racist politics in Florida, High's strong showing in voter-rich South Florida (he captured 42 percent of the popular vote) proved that the Pork Choppers risked losing control of the state.[20]

Although recent elections in Leon County had been disappointing, the voter education project could point to some positive results. In six months, an additional 771 blacks had registered, a grassroots voter education campaign had been reactivated, registration hours had been expanded, interest in voting had been rekindled, and the county's first interracial political organization, the Tallahassee Good Government Association, had been established. Confident that local volunteers could keep up the momentum in voter registration, Due asked Benninger to join her full time in Gadsden County.

In June 1964, CORE expanded its voter education projects in four states that included areas of South Carolina, Louisiana, Mississippi, and North Florida. The projects were actually part of a larger multiorganizational "Freedom Summer" coordinated by the Southern Regional Council in Atlanta, but in North Florida, CORE was principally responsible, as it was in Louisiana. The sixteen targeted counties in North Florida fell into two geographic areas separated by Leon County, which was not included in the new project. The per capita income in each of the sixteen county regions fell well below the state average. Most of them remained totally segregated.

By the time additional funds and personnel were available, Due had organized volunteers and staff to take on the Ninth Congressional District, comprising eight North Florida counties in which blacks represented the largest potential voting bloc but lived in conditions "approaching slavery."[21] In two of these areas, Liberty and Lafayette Counties, no black had ever registered to vote.

Headquarters for the new North Florida Citizenship Education Project were in Quincy, where Due had been working since January to establish a permanent voter registration drive. Gadsden was one of only two counties in Florida where blacks, at 59 percent, were a majority of the population. When Due first arrived in January 1964, only 469 out of 12,261 eligible black voters were registered. Race relations were "medieval," she wrote McCain, but despite "great fear, much of it justified," blacks were "willing and interested in direct action and voter registration." With volunteers from FAMU and Florida State University, Due began "a concentrated canvass effort in Gadsden County." They spoke at churches, at schools, and went house to house, farm to farm, "fish hole" to "fish hole," encouraging blacks to register and vote. Many blacks lived on tobacco plantations, isolated from the rest of the community and dependent on landlords for their very existence. Workers for the voter education project canvased these plantations with the help of some courageous local blacks.[22]

Despite the atmosphere of intimidation, voter education project workers were received with enthusiasm within the black community. Due was literally chased down by a group of local teenagers who wanted to help with the project and form a CORE chapter. After initial hesitation, the black Business and Civic League of Quincy supported the registration drive. Reflecting tensions from the past, the state NAACP was initially wary of CORE's premier role in the project. NAACP field secretary Robert Saunders told Due he wanted to see two or three NAACP members arrested in Quincy, because "'the NAACP has laid the groundwork for voter registration in Gadsden County.'" She was happy to see other groups interested in this field, Due wrote McCain, "but this does indicate the necessity for building up a strong CORE program in the area as soon as possible." Some local NAACP leaders refused to cooperate with her staff on orders from the state office, Due reported, but these were minor impediments to the work of the voter education project.[23]

Local ministers allowed Due to address their congregations, and Reverend J. T. Crutcher allowed the voter education project to use his church for its temporary headquarters. "Registration of Negroes in Gadsden County has been amazing," Due wrote McCain in early February 1964. "A reliable source informed us that on Monday the registrar said to him, 'what's getting into these Negroes? Over two hundred have registered today.' But it will take many more registered voters to begin the process of straightening out this area," she added.[24]

By early summer, a dozen project workers lived and worked in the Freedom House, a small, modest home owned by a black religious organization in Quincy called the Good Shepherd's Group. "No matter how hot things got," Due recalled, "this group never asked us to leave." The leader of the Good Shepherd was Whit Campbell, the principal of one of Gadsden County's black schools and later president of the Gadsden County NAACP.[25]

The small staff of the voter education project worked long and exhausting hours. Everywhere staff members went they were followed by local police. On occasion, whites shot at the Freedom House at night and threatened and harassed the workers during the day. Working in the county was like "going into a lion's cage without a weapon," Due recalled. "It was quite an accomplishment to persuade people that it was important enough to face whatever repercussions they might have to face to register and vote."[26]

The official place for Quincy residents to register was in the newspaper office. The editor was the part-time registrar. Blacks who came on the one day a week when registration was allowed often waited outside in the blazing sun for hours, as only one person at a time was allowed inside. Meanwhile, employers rode by and wrote down the names of their maids and handymen and farmers. Many were fired as soon as they returned to work. Those who were finally allowed into the building registered to vote underneath a huge presidential campaign poster for Barry Goldwater.

At some point during 1964, every single one of the white civil rights workers was arrested on fabricated charges, but Patricia Due was never arrested by the Gadsden County police. "Pat was fearless," Judy Benninger remembers. "Her family had been one of the educated, black bourgeoisie of that community. If they had ever arrested her, blacks would have burned that town down. And they [the police] knew it." Once, Benninger recalls, she was arrested by a Gadsden County policeman after she and Pat had shared a cola together in a black restaurant. When the officer put Benninger in the back of the squad car and drove off, Due followed them in her own car. "She was amazing; she called him a cracker and a racist and told him that the arrest would never stick because the owner of the restaurant was a friend of hers so I was obviously not trespassing." Finally, the policeman told Due to "go ahead and let her out if you want to!" The two young women then drove off, leaving the stunned policeman standing in the middle of the dusty road.[27]

As the summer wore on, more workers were recruited, and the voter education project fanned out into neighboring counties. Workers went through lengthy training seminars and were counseled on what to do if they were arrested. "We cannot guarantee that CORE will be able to pay for your bail if you are arrested," Due told the young workers. "The standard for the summer is no bail for jail. No guarantee will be made that participants will be out of jail [although each was] by the end of the summer." By 7 July, only five days after President Johnson had signed the Civil Rights Act of 1964, black registration in Gadsden County had tripled, bringing the total number of black registrants from 469 to 1,427.[28]

By midsummer 1964, Due was supervising workers in eight North Florida counties. As more male volunteers and workers joined the staff, some criticism over Pat's and Judy's "authoritarian" leadership style found its way back to CORE headquarters. Due chose to ignore such criticisms as irrelevant to the project's goals, but Benninger chafed under what she considered the "constant insults" to Due's leadership. "But if they questioned her authority or hassled her, she fired them," Benninger recalled. "She signed their paychecks."[29]

Due's concerns that summer were too great to tolerate petty infighting. "I was constantly worried about the safety of the people working with me," Due recalled. "We had some rigid rules. If workers were leaving for a place, they were expected to take thirty minutes to get there; after forty-five minutes or an hour, they had to call in and tell us they had gotten to their destination. We did not allow a lot of time to lapse because state troopers and others followed us and sometimes there were interracial pairs riding along in these counties and we were concerned about their safety." Occasionally, Due would call or write the Federal Bureau of Investigation to investigate a civil rights violation but the federal government offered little protection or assistance in North Florida during the summer of 1964.[30]

Hostility was "patent throughout the area," agreed ACLU attorney Ernst Rosenberger, who lived in the Freedom House for several weeks in August 1964. "Voter registration workers were assaulted. Firebombs were placed under automobiles. Shots were fired through the window of a house where volunteers were staying." Just as frightening to Rosenberger and other civil rights attorneys were the complicity of the local police in these acts of violence and the antagonistic attitude of the courts toward the workers and their counsel.[31]

As black registration soared, threats and individual acts of violence against civil rights workers increased. In nearby Madison County, harassed workers felt as if they were "going into another time and world." In Gadsden County, crosses were burned in front of black homes, Due and Reverend Crutcher received life-threatening phone calls at home, and workers—who lived totally segregated by sex at the Freedom House—were accused of indulging in mixed racial orgies. In some areas of North Florida, Due reported to McCain, staff have "lost all support of the so-called Negro leadership," who "have apparently been so intimidated that they are afraid to help." The people themselves, however, were reported to be "rallying around the project." In one county, she noted, "the [registration] books have been literally closed." Police intimidation of workers and local black residents was constant in each of the sixteen counties, yet despite "gross intimidations by the registrars" in Gadsden, Madison, and Suwannee Counties, "general community support has been increasing in every county."[32]

By September 1964, the percentage of blacks registered in the three counties with the largest proportion of black residents had increased dramatically in one year. In Gadsden County, for example, the percentage of blacks registered grew from 4 percent to 25 percent, in Madison County from 37 percent to 67 percent, and in Jefferson County from 17 percent to 31 percent. "The line Saturday in Quincy, last day of registration, stretched around the police station and back around to the post office parking lot," Judy Benninger reported. "At seven that morning over a hundred people were standing in line." As registration increased in all North Florida counties, physical violence against the interracial civil rights workers increased.[33]

In Gadsden County, Stuart Wechsler, a black volunteer with the voter education project, narrowly escaped with his life when he and several other male workers ventured onto a county commissioner's property to discuss voting with blacks working in the tobacco fields. The vicious beating that Wechsler received, his arrest (on charges of criminal trespass), and his subsequent incarceration became the subject of habeas corpus proceedings. The case came back to haunt Judge Harrold Carswell during the confirmation hearings when he was nominated for a seat on the U.S. Supreme Court in 1970.[34]

Although male workers were the more likely targets for physical beatings, the voter education project's women workers, both black and white, were vulnerable to equally dangerous situations. One summer evening, after delivering a voter registration speech at a Quincy night club, Benninger and Rosemary Dudley, a student at Florida State University, were arrested and were charged with disturbing the peace. Benninger later recalled that the women were taken to a "classic 'To Kill a Mockingbird' type of jail."[35]

> There was no full time jailer, so at night they would leave a trustee in charge. There was no government employee in the jail. One night there were two white women arrested for something not related to civil rights, so we were taken out of our cell block and put into a cell with eight white men. What the jailer expected was that those men would rape us. But it was very interesting: they were terrified that they would be charged with rape. They said don't worry, we know they want us to rape you but we won't. They beat on the window to attract the attention of people on the outside, and finally raised so much commotion that we were taken out and put back in our cell.[36]

Julius Hamilton, a student at Florida A&M, went to the jail to protest the women's arrest but was himself jailed, charged with using "open profanity." Finally, Pat Due, with the aid of her attorney husband, was able to arrange for the students' release from jail. A formal complaint was filed with the Justice Department. All charges were dropped before the trial.[37]

On 3 November 1964, over 3,500 Gadsden County blacks voted in the presidential election. Barry Goldwater, who was seen as the only "white man's candidate," carried the conservative county by just 150 votes. A last-minute black write-in candidate for sheriff received an unprecedented 1,529 votes. After the election, the voter education project expanded its work into other areas of civil, economic, and political rights.

But for twenty-four-year-old Patricia Stephens Due the work of the voter education project was over. An ectopic pregnancy left the fiery activist seriously ill, and she was forced to leave the project and join her husband in Atlanta. Her extraordinary and largely unheralded work with CORE—begun when she was a nineteen-year-old college junior—had ended, but her civil rights work in Florida, and her legacy to the movement, would continue. Due's indefatigable spirit, often the catalyst for and the force behind civil rights strategy and activities in Tallahassee, was not easily replaced. She was succeeded as North

Florida field director by Spiver Gordon, a Louisiana veteran of the civil rights movement.

Soon after Due's departure, Judy Benninger returned to Gainesville, organized a CORE chapter, and later joined the local chapter of Students for a Democratic Society (SDS) at the University of Florida. She became an attorney and a pioneering feminist author and is credited with having formed the first radical women's liberation organization, Gainesville Women's Liberation, in the South.

The voter registration project continued in rural North Florida without Due and Benninger. By January 1965, despite continuing acts of intimidation and violence, blacks had registered to vote in every county in the state, including—for the first time—Lafayette and Liberty Counties. The voter education project's operations in all areas of civil rights were greatly hampered by a lack of funds and by internal division in national CORE during the last two years of operation. But at the end of the project, more blacks had been registered in North Florida than in any other area of the South. Black voting power was a decisive factor in Lyndon Johnson's slim victory in Florida in 1964. Although Goldwater carried both Gadsden and Leon Counties (by only 190 votes in the former), Johnson beat his Republican rival in part because of heavy black voting in South Florida. It was the first time since 1948 that a Democrat had carried the state.[38]

By the beginning of 1965, over 50 percent of eligible black Floridians had registered to vote. In other areas of the South, particularly Alabama, Georgia, Louisiana, and Mississippi, literacy tests, poll taxes, hostile registrars, and threats of violence still kept thousands of blacks disenfranchised. To garner national support for a federal voting rights bill, the SCLC, aided by the Student Nonviolent Coordinating Committee, mounted an intensive voter registration campaign in Selma, Alabama, where only 300 blacks were registered. The campaign resulted in the famous Selma-to-Montgomery march, which was brutally curtailed by a contingent of baton-wielding Alabama state troopers at the Pettus Bridge outside Selma on Sunday, 7 March 1965. The assault stunned the nation. King announced that the march would be completed on 9 March, and more bloodshed seemed imminent. President Johnson sent LeRoy Collins, director of the Community Relations Service, to Selma in an effort to avoid the seemingly inevitable confrontation. After a harrowing twenty-four hours, Collins succeeded in working out a compromise that allowed the marchers to achieve a symbolic victory without further violence. On 15 March, capitalizing on nationwide support for federal action, President Johnson introduced his promised voting rights bill. Five months later, after considerable debate and revisions in Congress, the Voting Rights Act was signed into law.

Two years after the Voting Rights Act became law, voter registration among eligible blacks in Alabama had grown from 19 percent to 52 percent, in Georgia from 27 percent to 53 percent, in Louisiana from 32 percent to 59 percent, and in Mississippi from 7 to 60 percent. In Florida, one of five southern states not subject to federal intervention, black registration went from 51 percent to 64 percent.[39]

In 1966, two years after the voter education project first organized in Leon County, black voters had increased in number but were still only 22 percent of the electorate. In that year, however, they succeeded in breaking the color barrier to elective office. Charles U. Smith, George W. Conoly, Edwin Norwood, and Arnett C. Greene became the first blacks since Reconstruction to be elected to the executive committee of the Leon County Democratic Party. But it was easier for blacks to get elected on the precinct level, as Russell Anderson discovered in his unsuccessful bid for the school board that same year. Anderson, a medical doctor with a Ph.D., was defeated by the white incumbent endorsed by the *Democrat*.

White progressives fared no better in Leon County politics that year. George Lewis, backed by the Tallahassee Good Government Association, challenged Mallory Horne, the speaker of the Florida House, for the Democrat nomination in the District 8 state senate race. Horne had shocked his constituents in 1964 when he endorsed Barry Goldwater for president and actively worked on his campaign. Goldwater carried Leon County in the election, and so it was obvious that many registered Democrats voted for the Arizona conservative. But the rules of the Florida Democratic Party required each candidate for elective office to sign an oath that he had supported 90 percent of the candidates of his party in the last general election. When Horne signed the oath on 18 February 1966, Lewis decided to run against him.

Lewis ran a spirited campaign, but it was clearly a protest effort. On election day, 4 May 1966, the *Democrat* reported, "Negroes appeared to be voting heavily throughout the day, possibly more than other voters in proportion to their numbers." But it was not just the Lewis race that brought black voters out. John Due, who with Pat had moved back to Quincy, was also running for the Florida Senate from nearby District 4. Due ran on the need to improve employment opportunities for his largely poor, rural neighbors. Lewis called for reapportionment, increases in teachers' salaries, and reducing the voting age to eighteen. Both men were soundly defeated at the polls.[40]

By far the most interesting local race of the 1966 election year was the contest between Judge John Rudd and Davis Atkinson for a seat on the city commission. Atkinson was elected in 1957, defeating Reverend K. S. Dupont, the first black to run for the city commission. Atkinson ran his 1957 campaign on a segregationist platform and had never moderated his views. At the same time, Rudd, who had resigned from the bench the year before, had—in the eyes of many blacks—long represented the epitome of an unjust southern judicial system. But to others, Atkinson, and not Rudd, stood for the "never surrender" philosophy of the Deep South. In addition, Rudd was considered by many in Tallahassee (including himself) to be the "outsider" candidate challenging the "benevolent oligarchy" that had ruled city hall for so long.[41] ·

Rudd first ran unsuccessfully for the city commission in the late 1940s, when the three-seat commission was reserved for "the old timers" and "a certain group of families." In 1950, the year the commission was expanded to five seats, William Mayo and H. G. Easterwood ("young upstarts" like Rudd) were elected to the city commission. Shortly afterward, Rudd was appointed to the city bench, where he remained for twelve years.[42]

The race between Rudd and Atkinson didn't heat up until after the primary election on 15 February. Atkinson, who had come within twenty-eight votes of victory, was forced into a runoff with Rudd. The former judge immediately charged that Atkinson had obtained city-owned computer tapes to address campaign literature to registered voters and had pressured city employees, including policemen, to work on his campaign. Atkinson countered with the startling charge that Rudd had been asked by the commission to resign as city judge in 1965 following his arrest on charges of drunkenness and prowling. In a remarkable few days of political crossfire, Rudd countered with the information that the woman who charged him with the offenses was now his wife and that it had simply been a domestic misunderstanding.

As the details of the incident became public, Rudd, whose advertising had emphasized his good character, continued to insist that Atkinson's charges were "full of half truths and innuendoes." But the police report released to the *Democrat* on 17 February confirmed that Rudd had been apprehended by police at the home of his "fiancée," who accused him of creating a "disturbance in general" and of striking her son. According to the report, Rudd "cursed and abused the officers and refused to cooperate generally." In addition, a "drunkometer test" administered to the judge yielded results above the minimum reading under the law. "The Tallahassee City Commission contest has turned into a two-fisted fight, probably the first in our long history of genteel, patronizing municipal politics," Malcolm Johnson wrote on 17 February. "There will be dissent from our elders . . . , but to newer residents of a growing city, popular government requires candid truth to guide electoral judgment."[43]

On Friday, 18 February, Associate City Judge Steve Watkins resigned in protest against the release of "questionable confidential police reports and information" in the campaign. Then, on the day before the election, Mayor George Taff confirmed that the commission had asked Rudd to resign as city judge. Taff said that since the matter had come up for public discussion he felt obligated to set the record straight. He confirmed that "all members of the Commission at that time [1965] after long and conscientious consideration felt it was in the best interest of the court and the city to ask this man not to sit on the bench for the remainder of his term." Rudd responded by accusing the mayor of "actively campaigning for my opponent" and insinuated that the whole matter was part of a grand scheme to prevent the election of "a new voice in city government that would speak for all the people." [44]

On election day Tallahassee voters "were surging to the polls" in numbers that far exceeded those in the previous week's primary. By midday all four precinct clerks were predicting a record turnout in their areas. When the votes were tallied, Rudd was declared the winner by 304 votes. Rudd's largest margin of victory (860 to 58) was in Precinct A, the *Democrat* noted, "which has the largest number of Negro voters." Rudd also scored big in Precinct D, "which has a sizeable Negro population." Atkinson carried Precinct B, where he and Rudd lived along with most of Tallahassee's prominent white families. Rudd narrowly defeated Atkinson in Precinct C, the other primarily white neighborhood. Twelve years later Rudd acknowledged his debt to the black voters who had helped carry him into office. He attributed his success in part to his "friendship" with C. K. Steele. [45]

Not until 1969 did a black candidate, Democratic Party committeeman Edwin Norwood, reach the runoffs for a seat on the Tallahassee city commission; not until 1971 was a black candidate, James Ford, actually elected to office. But 1966 marked the beginning of a new political era in Leon County and Tallahassee politics. No candidate for elective office ever again ran a campaign based on overt racial antagonisms or divisions. The same was true for Democratic candidates for statewide office in Florida. Nonetheless, powerful resentment and anger aroused by the social upheaval and political changes of recent years fueled a backlash in Florida that blocked further progress in race relations—even before the gains of the civil rights movement had been fully realized.

The upheavals of the 1960s wreaked havoc on state politics, particularly in the Democratic Party. The Republican Party, however, benefited from statewide dissatisfaction with Johnson's Great Society and from the influx of thousands of retirees and Latin immigrants with no historical ties to the Democratic Party. For the first time since Reconstruction, Florida Republicans presented a serious challenge to Democratic hegemony.

In 1964, to help counter the growing strength of a Republican electorate, Florida Democrats succeeded in changing the governor's race to off-year elections to avoid the possibility that a Republican governor might ride into office on the coattails of a popular presidential candidate. Thus, Haydon Burns, who had swept into office in 1964, was up for reelection in 1966. Burns, who was neither a popular governor nor a skillful one, faced another election battle with Mayor Robert King High and State Senator Scott Kelly. Burns won the first primary but was forced into a runoff with High. Although the race had an element of déjà vu, the political landscape had changed substantially in two years. Blacks now composed over 17 percent of the electorate. For the first time in Florida history, both gubernatorial candidates openly courted black voters. Blacks strongly supported High in Leon County and throughout the state. But the Miami mayor, who projected himself as the champion of underdogs fighting the special interests, also appealed to a large number of Floridians who distrusted Burns and his big monied backers. To the surprise of many conservative Democrats, High won the runoff. His election seemed certain.

High's Republican opposition, businessman Claude Kirk, proved to be a skilled, worthy adversary. He successfully attacked the mayor as an extreme liberal supported by labor, the Kennedy family, and the NAACP. Kirk's supporters even circulated literature that tried to link the Miami mayor with the black power movement. Defeated candidate Burns refused to endorse High, a move that led to even more factionalism within Democratic ranks.

In the final weeks of the campaign, the governor actively supported Kirk and publicly accused High of having pressured a Dade County grand jury to withhold evidence of a scandal in city hall (an accusation without basis that the governor was forced to withdraw). Fanning the fires of white discontent and fear, and capitalizing on High's disorganized campaign, Kirk became the first Republican governor in Florida since 1872. Burns told reporters that he was "extremely pleased" that Kirk had won the race. The financier Edward Ball, one of Florida's most powerful lobbyists, declared that Kirk would be a governor "who would be clear of the control of labor union bosses, civil rights agitators, and the undesirable riff-raff of our country." Kirk won by a decisive vote of 821,190 to 668,233. He carried all but eleven counties. His victory was seen as a triumph for conservatism, but it also revealed the strength of the black vote in North Florida. High carried seven of the Big Bend counties, including Leon and Gadsden. He won in Leon County by fewer than 100 votes.[46]

Kirk's victory notwithstanding, the winds of change, beginning slowly in 1956 and building for ten years, had permeated Florida and Tallahassee. Blacks, supported by the federal government, had finally won the right to American citizenship. In the next few years, both the possibilities and the limitations of this victory would be revealed.

10 The Limits of Change

The Civil Rights Act of 1964 and the Voting Rights Act of 1965 marked the high points of the civil rights movement. Segregation and disenfranchisement were "pronounced dead," but many battles, often divisive and disheartening, lay still ahead. In the years immediately following the passage of the civil rights bills, virulent remnants of segregation and sanctioned inequality remained. In Tallahassee, four distinctive but related volatile issues—the integration of the public pools, the desegregation of the municipal hospital, the closing of the FAMU Law School, and the violence that rocked the city following the death of Martin Luther King Jr.—demonstrated the daunting challenge of dismantling the separate worlds of black and white.

The Tallahassee public pools were first closed following a series of demonstrations led by Priscilla Stephens in 1963. They were reopened in the summer of 1964, but on 5 July, after "a group of Negroes attempted to integrate Levy Park Pool," the city commission ordered the three pools (one was for blacks only) closed "for an indefinite time." On 6 July, four days after passage of the Civil Rights Act, Mayor Hugh Williams announced that the "Summer phase" of the city's recreation program was being curtailed for "financial reasons" and that the sale of the three municipal pools was under consideration. "Fees for the use of the pools do not nearly meet the cost of operation and maintenance," Williams announced.[1]

At the end of the summer, the commissioners announced that the city could no longer afford to open or maintain the pools because of needed repairs. This explanation seemed curious, since taxpayers were still paying $25,000 a year plus interest on a $250,000 bond the city had floated to finance their construction. During the summer of 1965, blacks, led by C. K. Steele, picketed outside city hall and demanded that the city reopen the pools to all Tallahasseeans. In July 1965, Steele, represented by attorney John Due, filed suit against the city in U.S. district court. Judge Harrold Carswell ruled that the city could not be forced to reopen the pools, though it could be compelled to desegregate them if they resumed operation.

In the summer of 1966, Steele, CORE field secretary Spiver Gordon, and other blacks were joined by a number of white Tallahasseeans who also demanded that the pools be reopened. Commissioners steadfastly refused to discuss the issue. Steele and Gordon became so vocal at city commission meetings that the mayor threatened on more than one occasion to have police escort them from the room. Finally, on 26 July, after a particularly heated exchange with commissioners, Gordon was forcibly removed.

Commissioners found it particularly difficult to deal with white protesters. FSU professor Robert Spivey, who represented the Tallahassee Council on Human Relations, testified in favor of reopening the pools, as did Tom Bates, chairman of the Boys and Girls Clubs of the Tallahassee Kiwanis Club. When the commission still refused to discuss the issue, blacks and whites began to picket city hall. This unprecedented action prompted Malcolm Johnson to encourage the city to reopen the pools. "We don't believe that racial integration required by court made laws could cause any great trouble," he wrote. If it did, "they [pools] would be closed again promptly."[2]

Nevertheless, the city commission held firm even after a scathing editorial in the *St. Petersburg Times* quoted Tallahassee Mayor Bob Cates as saying, "Everybody knows why they [pools] were closed. . . . I'm not going to make the city commission a sounding board for those people to rave about it." The day after it appeared, Clifton Lewis distributed copies of the editorial to commissioners and spectators at a city commission meeting. But Mayor Cates still refused to discuss the pool issue, accused the assembled dissenters of "trying to get their names in the paper," and announced that he would hear only "from legitimate citizens of Tallahassee." At that point, Lewis, identifying herself as "a citizen and an Episcopalian," said she was tired of helping to pay $20,000 a year for pool property that was depreciating every day. She added that swimming was not a recreation, but a life-and-death matter—a "life saving program." The meeting ended, once again, with the problem unresolved.[3]

By the next spring, the issue had generated enough heat that Spurgeon Camp, a newly elected city commissioner, had promised during his campaign that the city commission would initiate a straw ballot to find out whether Tallahassee citizens wanted the pools reopened. Commissioner Cates declared that the straw ballot was "unethical" and a waste of money, and he and fellow commissioner Taff voted against it. But Gene Berkowitz and Camp (who had replaced longtime commissioners Hugh Williams and J. W. Cordell) voted in favor of conducting the poll, as did John Rudd, the new mayor.[4]

On 1 August 1967, the results of the straw ballot showed that by a small majority, Tallahassee residents wanted their pools reopened. But the pools remained closed for the rest of the summer of 1967. On 9 April 1968, five days after the assassination of Martin Luther King Jr., when riots engulfed the city, Tallahassee commissioners, with one abstention, voted to open the city's three swimming pools.

The five-year battle over Tallahassee's pools paled in comparison to the one involving the city's municipal hospital. Tallahassee Memorial Hospital, the city's first modern permanent medical facility, had been built in 1949 with federal funds and had been subsidized with a combination of state, county, city, and private monies. The only medical facility that served blacks within a 150-mile radius of Tallahassee was located at Florida A&M University. The initial facility, built in 1911, had begun as a rudimentary clinic designed to serve the health needs of the college. At that time, a single nurse was in charge of all operations. Fifteen years later, the small structure had expanded into a community hospital that included a school of nursing and a full-time medical director.

Serious overcrowding and unsafe conditions at the two-story wooden facility made the need for a new modern hospital and nursing center of paramount importance to FAMU president J. R. E. Lee. In the late 1930s, the president began a serious campaign to secure funds to build and maintain a new multipurpose health facility. When it became public knowledge that the city had plans to build a municipal hospital, Lee, other Florida A&M officials, and members of the Civic League began to lobby the city commission for an appropriation to the college's hospital building fund. On 9 December 1941, the city approved a new wing for the existing A&M facility if it could be "worked out" with federal funds to "obviate any questions with reference to the Negroes of the community wishing to have space within the new [white] hospital." That same day, the city appropriated $100,000 for construction of a "municipally owned hospital."[5]

Efforts to secure funds for a new hospital for blacks continued into the administration of President William H. Gray. In 1945, the city authorized the payment of $50,000 toward the construction of a new A&M hospital with the stipulation that the facility would provide "a standby service" for local blacks. No operational funds were provided. Yet two years later, commissioners agreed to levy a 10 percent tax on utilities to support the white municipal hospital.[6]

In January 1948, the city commission approved a plan to provide another $100,000 to the FAMU hospital. Nine months later, commissioners agreed that "excess" state and federal monies coming to the city to help finance the construction of the municipal hospital could be "diverted" to the board of control to be used for construction of a hospital at Florida A&M to serve "the Negro population of this community." In other words, a hospital located on a college campus would be expected to provide services for area blacks at the same time that all Tallahassee residents were charged a utility tax for the operation of a segregated white hospital.[7]

In 1950, the new Florida A&M College Hospital, Health Center, and Nursing School was formally opened. The next year, the 105-bed hospital had ten departments and four black doctors, but the majority of the medical staff was white. Only months before the new facility opened, Russell Anderson, the director of student health, wrote President George Gore that "no beds have been assigned, as yet, specifically to students"—even though, as Anderson noted, "each student is now charged six dollars per semester for medical and dental care," three dollars of which sum was being "used to retire the debt on the new hospital." At a 1952 meeting of the A&M Hospital advisory board (chaired by then state senator LeRoy Collins), H. B. Foote "again raised the point that since Florida A&M College Hospital serves as the city and county facility, it should share in the mil. tax which is levied presently for the support of Tallahassee Memorial Hospital only." No action was taken. Foote noted in a follow-up report to the board that "approximately fifty percent of the patients that have been treated in the hospital have been charity cases." There was simply no way for the hospital to raise operating funds through patient billing.[8]

On 25 March 1953, Senator Collins wrote the Leon County Commission to request funds to take care of "at least a substantial part" of the cost of caring for indigent patients. The senator also requested "an allowance of $8,500 from the city commission from public funds raised for indigent and welfare purposes. At the time I was advised that it would be difficult to make any such contribution immediately because of lack of budgetary provisions," he wrote. "I urgently request that you take care of this in the most effective manner possible." Florida A&M students continued to subsidize a city and county hospital while funds appropriated to run the university were siphoned off to pay for the escalating cost of running the medical facility.[9]

On 26 January 1954, the Leon County Commission voted to provide the city with the proceeds derived from the levy of one mil. on all taxable property in Leon County to help pay for indigent care at Tallahassee Memorial Hospital. Three months later, the city approved another request from the board of control for $10,000 to help defray the cost of indigent care at the Florida A&M hospital. The county, so generous with funds for Tallahassee Memorial Hospital, did not approve a similar request from the board of control. By the end of the year, the county had amended its annual hospital contract with the city to read "pay the city $20,000.00 instead of the amount received from one mil. taxes."[10]

By 1960, the Florida A&M hospital had fifty practicing physicians and was providing health services to thousands of area blacks, still without receiving any portion of the city utility tax. Four years later, Tallahassee Memorial Hospital was admitting a minuscule number of black patients into segregated rooms. Despite the protests of Russell Anderson, Tallahassee Memorial Hospital had no black doctors on its staff. The Florida A&M hospital had virtually no white patients. It is highly probable that the two hospitals would have remained essentially segregated facilities had not the federal government determined that the two segregated institutions operated in violation of Title VI of the 1964 Civil Rights Act and were ineligible for Medicare and other federal funds.

When the threat to withdraw federal funds became public, Senator Mallory Horne, chairman of the board of Tallahassee Memorial Hospital, announced that without Medicare funds there would be "a half million a year loss" for the hospital, which "would bankrupt the institution and force its closing within a short time." In addition, the hospital would lose the $1.5 million in federal monies needed for a proposed hospital addition. "It is plain," Horne announced, "that the hospital and the hospital board has no choice but to comply with the Civil Rights Act." The board quickly ordered Tallahassee Memorial Hospital to admit black patients on a nonsegregated basis. At the specific insistence of federal investigators, the board agreed to review Anderson's application to join the staff of Tallahassee Memorial Hospital. His application was denied. That summer, Anderson's son-in-law, the gynecologist Alexander Brickler II, became the hospital's first black doctor.[11]

Meanwhile a bigger bombshell was waiting to explode. On 24 June 1966, Broward J. Culpepper, chancellor of the state university system, announced that $30 million in all forms of federal funds would be withdrawn from Florida's universities unless the Florida A&M hospital integrated its facilities. After a closed-door executive committee meeting (to which FAMU president George Gore was not invited) Chester Ferguson, chairman of the board of regents (formerly the board of control), announced that because of the deteriorating condition of the FAMU hospital and "the financial burden on the Board to subsidize the health needs of Leon County and the City of Tallahassee," the FAMU hospital would close. A phasing-out period of twelve to eighteen months would be necessary "to ease the burden of Tallahassee's only other hospital, Tallahassee Memorial Hospital." [12]

Unlike the desegregation of the lunch counters, buses, and recreational facilities, the desegregation of Tallahassee Memorial Hospital was a bittersweet victory for blacks. The Florida A&M hospital had struggled for over fifty years to survive and had become a symbol of black perseverance and accomplishment. It was a source of pride for many in the community. But it consumed a large share of the university's budget, and without a broader base of patients and adequate support from the city (or the state after 1967), it could never be a first-rate facility or compete with Tallahassee Memorial Hospital. Popular sentiment produced several halfhearted attempts to save the old hospital, but its doors closed for the last time in 1971.

The demise of Florida A&M's hospital, and the gradual integration of Tallahassee Memorial Hospital, revealed the strange dichotomy of desegregation. In order to right a wrong, to provide equal access to public facilities, black institutions were deemed inferior, beyond rehabilitation, and were destroyed along with the heritage and history that bound them to their community.

Nothing revealed the double-edged sword, the cruel irony of the costs as well as benefits inherent in dismantling the dual system of separate and unequal, more than the closing of the FAMU Law School. Established in 1950 to keep a black applicant out of the University of Florida Law School, the school had gradually emerged as a small but reputable facility for legal education. By 1959, Governor Collins had become genuinely convinced that segregated graduate or professional education was not only illegal but a waste of state revenue. He suggested that some university graduate programs should be integrated to save money. At the same time, a few lawmakers and newspaper editors from South Florida began to question the fiscal practicality of maintaining a separate law school at Florida A&M when blacks were supposedly entitled to attend the University of Florida's law school. "There comes a point at which the strongest emotion must yield to reality," wrote the editors of the *Tampa Tribune,* on their way to the conclusion that "the law school at A&M should be abolished." [13]

Legislators from North Florida, led by Senator Wilson Carraway of Tallahassee and speaker of the house Tom Beasley of northwest Walton County, suddenly discovered new legislative support and money for the nine-year-old black law school. Carraway said he wanted to see the school made into such a fine institution "that there will be no demand for integration." Equally adamant, Beasley said that "the people are willing to pay whatever is necessary to maintain segregation." [14]

Such sentiments appeared to prevail for the next four years. The FAMU Law School, which comprised seventeen students in 1962, continued to operate, and the University of Florida Law School remained a haven for whites who aspired to be attorneys. Then in early 1963, civil rights attorneys Tobias Simon and Howard Dixon filed a suit with two other attorneys to close the FAMU Law School. The suit charged that the University of Florida Law School had been integrated since 1958, and it was therefore a waste of taxpayers' money to continue to fund the small program at FAMU.

Suddenly white politicians, many of whom had castigated Simon and Dixon in the past, rushed to join them. The politicians and other critics charged that only thirty-two students had graduated from the school and that of this number only nine had been admitted to a state bar. Defenders of the school, led by law dean Thomas M. Jenkins and supported by local blacks, the Tallahassee Businessman's League, and the ICC, fought to mobilize statewide support for the embattled school. "You cannot erase the by-products of a dual system of education in twelve years," Jenkins wrote to President Gore. "Students should not be informed that an opportunity to complete [law school] will be denied them, largely, one suspects, because of inadequacies over which they had little or no control." Only twenty-one of the thirty-two law school graduates had even applied to take the Florida or any other bar exam, Jenkins protested, and nine of those had been admitted to the bar of Florida or some other jurisdiction. Of the twelve persons who had not been admitted to the bar, Jenkins noted, nine "have an unqualified right to re-seek admission to the Bar" by taking the examination two more times as "is automatically allowed." [15]

In August 1963, the suit was dismissed by circuit court judge W. May Walker, who ruled that the absence of white students at the Florida A&M Law School did not mean that the school was not integrated any more than the absence of black students at the University of Florida Law School meant that that school was not integrated and that it should be closed. Meanwhile, the board of control and the state's white politicians—once committed to keeping black students out of the University of Florida at any cost—were now committed to closing down the FAMU Law School and opening a new one at Florida State University. "You know that we do not want to do anything which would hurt your institution," Florida State University president Gordon W. Blackwell wrote Gore in 1964. "However, it has seemed to us that the State would probably not find it economically defensible to continue your Law School much longer." [16]

Continued talk about the possibilities of closing the black law school cut into its expected enrollment and outside contributions. Supporters of the law school charged that the board of control had pressured Florida A&M not to admit white applicants to support charges that the school was not integrated. Gore, already deeply involved in efforts to stymie a proposed move to merge all of FAMU's undergraduate programs with Florida State (a proposal that took more than a decade to defeat) did not mount an effective defense to save the law school.

A well-organized campaign to persuade the legislature and board of control to open a new law school at FSU (two miles from Florida A&M) captured political sentiment in Tallahassee. Suddenly everyone agreed that blacks were welcome and were qualified to enroll in the state's graduate programs. John Due argued vehemently that blacks in Florida would not immediately be capable of meeting the entrance requirements at either the University of Florida or Florida State and would effectively be denied any form of legal education. But Due's warning had little impact on FSU supporters. The 1965 legislature passed a bill submitted by recently converted senator Carraway that provided a lump sum to the board of regents to be used to plan the new law school. So that their intentions could not be mistaken, lawmakers appropriated a total of $100,000 for the biennium for operation of the FAMU Law School but authorized the board of regents to transfer the second year's money to Florida State if plans for the new law school proceeded. On 19 July 1965, after months of debate, the board of regents voted to release part of the legislative funds to FSU "in order to start planning for a new law school." A dean was hired, and classes began at FSU in the fall of 1966. Meanwhile, the fate of the FAMU Law School was sealed when the board of regents agreed in 1966 that no new students could be accepted. The last students graduated in 1968. Although the board of regents promised that Florida A&M law faculty would not be displaced, only two law professors from FAMU applied for positions at FSU Law School, and both were rejected. In 1970, the first black professor was hired by the Florida State University Law School.[17]

As the 1960s drew to a close, many blacks remained frustrated by the slow pace of change in an era that had promised so much. Second-class citizenship no longer meant a back seat on the bus or a segregated lunch counter or voting restrictions. But it still meant inequality. And despite changes in race relations that would have astounded an earlier generation of Tallahasseeans, blacks remained on the periphery of the community's life and institutions. Nowhere were the limits of the civil rights struggle felt more keenly than at Florida A&M University, where smoldering resentment over the demise of the FAMU hospital and law school was fueled by concern about the possibility that Florida A&M might be merged with Florida State University.

Student opinion about the merger was overwhelmingly negative. FAMU "Black Power leader" Roscoe Ellis told a reporter for the *Florida Flambeau* in early April 1968 that students would "burn down every building on this campus" before they would allow a merger with the white institution. Florida A&M students, who once marched to protests in dresses and coats and ties, began to embrace or discuss the meaning of Black Power and black separatism. They quoted Stokely Carmichael and H. Rap Brown and increasingly criticized not just whites but the "uncle toms who have a monopoly on administrative positions in black colleges."[18]

Embittered by the racism that still permeated Tallahassee and the nation, many FAMU students focused their anger on university administrators whom they perceived as remnants of second class citizenship. Particularly galling to students were the restrictions and rules that seemed to belong to another era or mindset. But President George Gore, personally or through his administrators, kept a tight rein on all aspects of the university, including curricula, faculty appointments, and student activities.

In November 1967, after refusing to approve Stokely Carmichael's speech at Florida A&M (the activist delivered it anyway), Gore declared that no speakers could be invited to appear on campus without his approval. Shortly thereafter, the editor of the student newspaper called for "real" changes to correct the "gross injustices which are done to the FAMU student body. . . . the administration is only willing to give in to those student proposals (dress regulations, curfews, compulsory class attendance) which have little if any significance," she wrote, but "real changes" such as revisions of the curriculum to include black history and literature, revisions in the rules governing speakers, and the abolition of mandatory Reserve Officers' Training Corps were needed if students were to "have some effect on the existing social order. Now is the time," she concluded, "for united Black Power."[19]

As was true with FSU's *Florida Flambeau*, the *FAMUAN* came increasingly to represent the views of the more progressive voices on campus. The newspaper defined Black Power as a "coming together of black people to obtain their freedom by any means necessary. . . . the possibility of rioting cannot be excluded, however, it is by no means the preferred method of exacting change." By the spring of 1968, the FAMU administration had granted several concessions and had lifted a few restrictions governing student behavior. But the more vexing problem, FAMU's second-class status within the state university system and its uncertain future, helped to foster an atmosphere of resentment and bitterness among students.[20]

On 31 March 1968, former congressman Adam Clayton Powell spoke to a large, enthusiastic audience in Florida A&M's Lee Hall with the approval of the administration. The flamboyant Powell told the audience that nonviolence was finished. He called for a "young people's revolution" against a sick society that was "topless from the neck up." Powell said the new Black Power movement was a victory not just over whites but over "our own Uncle Toms and Aunt Jemimas." The audience cheered wildly throughout his remarks. Four days later, Martin Luther King Jr. was assassinated in Memphis, Tennessee.[21]

News of King's murder spread quickly at Florida A&M. By early evening, groups of students who had gathered in peaceful protest began to throw rocks and bottles at cars passing near or through the campus. The first casualty was a white youth who was injured when bricks and bottles crashed through his windshield as he drove along South Monroe Street. City commissioner John Rudd was cut on the arm by a flying object as he rode in a police car through Florida A&M. "I felt that I had enough friends on campus that I could go and act as a peacemaker," he recalled, "but shucks they bombarded my car [driven by Captain George Dawes] and busted out the windows."[22]

As the night deepened, student rioters fanned out from the campus. They firebombed a downtown business and beat back firemen with a barrage of bottles and bricks until police arrived. After they pushed barrels onto South Adams Street and began attacking passing cars with an assortment of objects, police reserves were called in to join regular officers near the scene. Lawmen cordoned off the FAMU campus in an attempt to seal off students and keep out local blacks. Detective Larry Campbell of the Leon County sheriff's department was ordered to the volatile area and found policemen barricaded behind patrol cars and paddy wagons. Students began shooting at the officers with "light firearms," but not many of the bullets from the small caliber revolvers reached their intended destination. Finally, a number of students broke into the Florida A&M "armory" where physical education equipment was stored and armed themselves with bows and arrows. When the arrows began to rain down on their targets, the police were forced to search for trash can lids to protect themselves. Finally, Officer Burl Peacock, who twelve years earlier had arrested C. K. Steele when he led the bus boycott, shot out the streetlights.

For four and a half hours, police surrounded FAMU. They were ordered to hold the students there with tear gas and to "shoot only to protect life." President Gore and his family left their campus home and sought shelter with friends in the community. Without a campus police force, the university was basically unprotected. As the night progressed, violence spread away from the campus. Several businesses were attacked and burned. Word came down the hill to the police that the students had plans to destroy parts of town and to kill some white people. In the early hours of 5 April, Campbell and a number of officers were called to a blazing fire on Lake Bradford Road near Florida A&M. There firemen were trying vainly to rescue nineteen-year-old Travis Crowe, who was trapped inside his bedroom above the family-owned grocery store. The young white man was the only member of his family who had not been able to escape the inferno. Investigators determined that the fire had been started by a home-made Molotov cocktail thrown from a passing car. Crowe's death was deemed murder by arson.

The next day, Sheriff Joyce announced that there were no suspects in the Crowe murder and that police "did not definitely connect the death with a university student or students." Several persons were arrested for possession of illegal firearms and destruction of property. Although a measure of calm returned to the city on the morning of 5 April, many parents kept their children home from school. Governor Kirk ordered the National Guard to Tallahassee to preserve order.[23]

At 10:00 A.M. Friday, President Gore returned to campus and addressed over 2,000 Florida A&M students gathered for a memorial service for King. He praised King's leadership and vision and pleaded with the assembled students to "observe the passing of this great leader in a sober and respectable manner." Although some students booed Gore and shouted protests when the president spoke of King's philosophy of nonviolence, most of the audience remained quiet. Two white FSU students, the president and vice president of the student government association, went to FAMU to attend the memorial and noted the "conspicuous tension and hostility on the campus. We were very unwelcome there." Both left after a student at FAMU told them, "Don't come back on our campus. You guys have guts to come here."[24]

After the service, according to the *Democrat*, a "Negro leader" reported that "most of the administration of Florida A&M feared the Black Power militants on campus." President Gore, fearing more violence, asked Robert Mautz, the chancellor of the board of regents, for the authority to close Florida A&M until 15 April. Mautz announced that he had decided to "permit the students at FAMU in this moment of despair and frustration to return to the normalcy of family life." Most of the students at Florida A&M made plans to leave the city quickly, but others remained in town even though the dorms were closed.[25]

Meanwhile, Sheriff Joyce ordered all liquor stores closed until further notice. He asked businesses to restrict sales of gasoline and ammunition to known customers. Sporadic violence continued Friday and Saturday nights in the heavily guarded city. By Sunday morning, tension in the capital city had begun to dissipate. Tallahassee's turmoil, mild compared to that which engulfed Washington, Detroit, Chicago, and other metropolitan areas, had run its course. On 8 April, C. K. Steele, vice president at large of the SCLC, left with his wife to attend King's funeral. "Many young people have lost faith in America and in the church, and they are frustrated," Steele said. "If all the energy and ingenuity which was placed behind this violence had been put into non-violent objection to the injustices of our society it would have been a more appropriate expression of our love and appreciation for Martin."[26]

Shortly after Florida A&M had closed, Mautz met with Gore and faculty members to discuss the recent incidents. He announced that university authorities and local police would seek and punish those responsible for the violent acts. On 24 May, police issued arrest warrants for thirteen persons accused of participating in the 4 April "rioting." Charges included "conspiracy to make and throw firebombs, assault with a deadly weapon and rioting and inciting to riot." Nine were students from Florida A&M.[27]

Two days later, three black youths were charged with the murder by arson of Travis Crowe. One of the young men, Billy Ray Oliver, was already in jail on an unrelated charge and confessed to the crime after lengthy interrogation over a six-day period. Seventeen-year-old James Colbert, taken into custody without a warrant, also confessed and implicated Oliver and two other men. Although Oliver and Colbert were advised of their rights, neither had counsel present. More than one month lapsed before either of the accused was brought before a judicial officer. The third man arrested, Curtis Lee Wortham, refused to confess. He told Deputy Campbell that "he didn't think the sheriff's office could prove he did it." On 28 May, a fourth suspect, Rossie L. Howard, was arrested in Miami and was sent back to Tallahassee. None of the men arrested was connected with Florida A&M University.[28]

While the above-mentioned cases were pending, President Gore agreed to appoint a committee consisting of faculty, staff, and students to meet with a cross section of students and to make recommendations for solving long-standing problems and improving internal relations at FAMU. According to Leedell Neyland, the professor who chaired the panel, the early sessions were dominated by militant students, Black Power rhetoric, and "the denigration of all organized authority." In addition, Neyland and C. U. Smith, another professor, worried that there was still potential for "serious violence" on campus, including threats against Gore. Consequently the two men stationed themselves in a nearby building where, unseen, they could monitor student activity around the president's home.[29]

Ultimately the committee agreed that King's assassination had been a catalyst for the "frustrations and resentments of second-class citizenship long felt by FAMU students. If the increased tension among FAMU students over the past year can be attributed to any one problem, it is the fear that FAMU would be closed down or merged," members noted. But "the violence of April 4 must be traced beyond any possible tension and problems within the university to the human relations problems that exist throughout the state and nation."[30]

After submitting hundreds of recommendations and grievances to President Gore spanning a wide range of issues, the committee disbanded, to be replaced by the permanent Florida A&M Improvement Committee. As a result of the work of the initial committee, the university developed a separate black studies major and revised other curricula to highlight the achievements and contributions of black Americans. The administration revised disciplinary procedures to take student input into greater account, and many restrictions, particularly those affecting women students, were lifted.

At a meeting of the board of regents one month after King's assassination, Gore reported on "the various steps" that had been taken since FAMU's reopening to restore communications and to establish new procedures. He received approval from the board of regents to erect a memorial to King on campus that would be financed by private contributions. Chairman Chester Ferguson congratulated Gore and Chancellor Mautz for "the prompt and appropriate action" they had taken to preserve order, and he praised the majority of students for the "responsibility" they showed during the crisis. "The policy of this Board," Ferguson added, "is that Florida A&M shall exist in the same format and for the same purpose that it is now . . . until the circumstances so change that its function is no longer desired or required."[31]

Meanwhile, the trauma of the recent events, the problems associated with the threat of the merger of Florida A&M and Florida State University, the long years of civil rights protests, and student unrest had taken their toll on Gore. On 1 July 1968, the sixty-six-year-old president announced his resignation at a meeting of the board of regents. In his letter of resignation, Gore noted that his tenure in office had been "a most challenging and rewarding experience. . . . it is my fondest dream and sincerest hope," he wrote, "that [Florida A&M] will be continued for many years yet to come as a separate and autonomous state university."[32]

Mautz reluctantly accepted Gore's resignation. He declared it his belief that the president's "constructive efforts will . . . result in the continuation of Florida A&M University as a separate and autonomous unit of the State University System for the predictable future." Ferguson declared that Gore had "made major contributions to higher education in Florida and had been a leader in promoting racial harmony in the State." Praise for Gore poured in from leaders across Florida. There was much speculation as to why the president had chosen to leave when the future of Florida A&M remained uncertain. When questioned, Gore simply answered, "I think I've earned the right to do as I want to do."[33]

Before Gore left FAMU in September 1968, the board of regents established a new disciplinary policy. The regents granted the president of each university the "authority to expel any student who shall be found to have committed an act which disrupts or interferes with education or orderly processes or operation of the University." Charges against the students involved in the rioting were eventually dropped. The reaction to King's death began to recede.[34]

Then, in December 1968, James Colbert and Billy Ray Oliver were indicted by a grand jury. Both were subsequently convicted of first degree murder in Judge Ben Willis's circuit court and were sentenced to life in prison. Their conviction and sentence were upheld on appeal to the First District Court. The court on 23 October 1970 denied a request for rehearing.[35]

King's death and the violence it spawned did not unite the black community in a boycott or demonstration against racism as had the events of 1956. Things had changed. Many great legal and political battles had been won, but the struggle to expose and eradicate racism and its vestiges—poverty, inequality, and exclusion—would be a continuing struggle. The year 1968 ended with many complex racial issues smoldering just below the surface. These were issues with which future generations of Tallahasseeans would be obliged to deal.

Shortly after King's death, C. K. Steele, a veteran of the Poor People's Campaign in Washington, along with other members of the ICC, organized a "Vigil for Poverty" at the Florida capitol to draw attention to the plight of the poor. In his written statement to Governor Kirk, Steele asserted that the "basic needs of adequate food, shelter, clothing, education and employment should be basic rights for every individual regardless of his skin color or background." Steele and other activists began to picket local businesses that catered to blacks but would not hire them. They pressed both the city and state governments to hire blacks beyond the token appointment or traditional award of unskilled jobs. They found that in many ways, blacks faced problems that were different, and at times more difficult, than those that had just been overcome.[36]

Yet even as they struggled to face new challenges and opportunities, one old fight remained to be won, one that more than any other typified the era of inequality that stubbornly refused to recede. It began in 1954 and did not end until 1970. The public schools were to be Tallahassee's first, last, and most bitter civil rights battleground.

11 Justice Delayed

On 5 September 1963, three black teenagers and one black seven-year-old walked for the first time into the all-white public schools of Leon County. On that humid fall morning, nine years after the Supreme Court had unanimously concluded that the doctrine of "separate but equal" had no place in public education, the capital city took its first steps to integrate its schools. Yet the struggle was hardly over: seven additional years of protest, litigation, and strife passed before Leon County, under a federal court order, finally abolished its dual system of education.

As the capital of the state, Tallahassee was the place where Florida's official stance on desegregation had developed and where the policies to thwart integration had been initiated. The struggle for desegregation in Leon County was influenced, more than in any other county, by ongoing state and national events that played out again and again in its own backyard.

In addition, Governor LeRoy Collins and Attorney General Richard Ervin, the two people who shaped the state's initial response to desegregation, were both natives of North Florida (Collins had been born in Tallahassee; Ervin, in nearby Franklin County) and lived in the city. The political views of the two men had been forged in the same conservative milieu but increasingly diverged as the governor's personal beliefs and national political aspirations set him apart not only from Ervin but also from the massive resistance sentiment that swept across Florida in the late 1950s.

By the time Collins left office in 1961, Tallahassee, like most of Florida, remained committed to preserving a segregated school system. While other barriers against integration fell before new federal laws and changing race relations, segregated schools remained a stubborn reminder of the depths of racial fear and mistrust.

Separate schools for black and white children had first been mandated by the Florida Constitutional Convention in 1885. Ten years later, the state legislature made it a "penal offense" to educate black and white students together. The expense of maintaining a dual school system throughout Florida contributed to the wretched quality of public schools for both races and devastated education for blacks. In 1890, Florida's population was 44 percent black. In that year, per pupil expenditures for black students were $13.12, or less than half the $26.66 allocated for each white student.[1]

Despite the paucity of educational facilities for blacks in the late nineteenth century, Tallahassee was the site of one of the three black high schools in the state that had been established before the end of Reconstruction. Although it was in session just five months out of the year, the Lincoln Academy remained a source of pride for Tallahassee blacks for almost 100 years. The only institution of higher education for blacks in Florida, the State Normal College for Colored Students, was also located in Tallahassee. The college had been authorized in 1887 to train black teachers (it was illegal for white teachers to teach black students), and its curriculum was soon under attack by the state superintendent of public instruction, who insisted that the new college focus on mechanical and agricultural training rather than on liberal arts. The state's interest in maintaining a stable agricultural workforce far outweighed any official concern with giving blacks opportunities to receive higher education. Still, the very existence of the black "college" made future conflict over the course and role of black education inevitable.

The gap in educational appropriations for black and white schoolchildren in Florida reached a peak in 1910 just as race relations were at their worst. That year, the state spent $9.95 for every black student and $36.05 for every white student. The disparity persisted for the next four decades but was particularly glaring during the Depression. A report by the state superintendent of public instruction in 1932 found that teachers at black schools were underqualified and underpaid. Fully 24 percent lacked a high school education, and 98 percent earned less than $1,000 a year.[2]

Black education began to improve in Florida after World War II. In 1947, Governor Millard Caldwell, with the help of state Senator LeRoy Collins, prodded the legislature into creating the Minimum Foundation Program, a finance program jointly operated by the state and the county to ensure that educational expenditures did not fall below a certain minimum for any school district in the state. Counties that did not meet this level through local taxes received supplemental state funds. The program helped close the tremendous spending gap between the wealthiest school districts and the poorest, most of which had large black populations. The program also served, although it had not been intended to do so, as a sort of equalization program for black education.

In some Florida counties, as in others across the South, spending on black education increased as a result of the equalization suits brought against school boards by the NAACP during the 1940s and 1950s. In 1940–1941, state per pupil expenditures were $72.40 for whites and $28.80 for blacks. A decade after both the Minimum Foundation Program and the equalization suits took effect, per pupil dollar expenditure for blacks had risen almost tenfold, so that the percentage difference in 1952–1953 was only 19 percent. Just as important for black education in Leon County was the consolidation in the 1947–1948 school year of forty-five "one-teacher" elementary and junior high schools into ten schools with separate classrooms for each grade. In the same year, school buses were provided for the first time for black schoolchildren, who composed 53 percent of the county's school population.

The NAACP first challenged school segregation at the graduate and professional levels where opportunities for blacks were most limited. NAACP strategists correctly presumed that such an approach would elicit less white anger than a frontal assault on segregation at the primary or secondary level, where the effect on whites was far greater. Between 1938 and 1950, four major cases brought by the NAACP reached the Supreme Court. In each, a black plaintiff was suing for admission to a state-supported white university, and the affected state had offered (as a means of avoiding integration) either to pay so that the plaintiff could attend an out-of-state institution or to build a separate facility for him.

In 1945, the Florida board of control began to offer out-of-state graduate school scholarships to black students recommended by William Gray, who was then the president of FAMU. For the next four years, the board of control provided state funds so that approximately thirty to forty black students a year could study for varying lengths of time at institutions outside Florida. When a black applicant sued for the right to attend the University of Florida Law School in 1949, the board of control voted to build a separate law school for black students at Florida A&M. At the same time, it voted to establish separate schools of mechanical engineering, agriculture, and pharmacy. While these programs were being created, the board voted to continue providing out-of-state scholarships for qualified applicants. In conjunction with the Southern Regional Education Board, Florida also participated in a program to provide out-of-state professional training for blacks in medicine, dentistry, and veterinary science. By 1964, the state had paid out over half a million dollars for this purpose.[3]

The Supreme Court seemed no longer willing to tolerate separate graduate educational facilities by 1950. On 5 June of that year, the Court ruled in *Sweatt v. Painter* that Texas could not provide the black plaintiff with an equal educational opportunity in a separate law school. In this ground-breaking case, and in *McLaurin v. Oklahoma,* which immediately followed, the Court opened the door to the first direct assault on the constitutionality of "separate but equal" as it related to education.[4]

By 1950, school desegregation cases involving black elementary and secondary school students began to reach the Supreme Court. At the end of 1952, the Court announced that four similar cases, each challenging the constitutionality of mandatory school segregation laws, would be consolidated and heard as *Oliver Brown v. Board of Education of Topeka, Kansas.*

In all five cases, the lower courts had found that the education offered black students was substantially equal, or soon would be, to that offered to white students. Thus the question before the Court was whether public school segregation per se, and not unequal facilities, was unconstitutional. This determination, of course, was just what the southern states hoped to avoid. The vast improvements in the quality of black education throughout the region in part reflected anxious prescience among whites. In Florida, where the gap between total expenditures for black and white schoolchildren had continued to narrow, capital outlay per pupil (the measure of monies spent on construction costs) in 1952–1953 was $60.09 for blacks and $54.92 for whites. In Leon County two years later, per pupil instructional expenditures for white children were $150.92, and for blacks, $143.78.

On 17 May 1954, Chief Justice Earl Warren read the unanimous opinion of the Court in *Brown v. Board of Education.* The Court found that the segregation of children in public schools solely on the basis of race deprived the children in the minority group of equal educational opportunities "even though the physical facilities and other 'tangible' factors may be equal." Such segregated facilities were "inherently unequal," had a detrimental effect on black children, and deprived them "of the equal protection of the laws guaranteed by the Fourteenth Amendment." "Education," the Court concluded, was "perhaps the most important function of state and local government. . . . in these days, it is doubtful that any child may reasonably be expected to succeed in life if he is denied the opportunity of an education. Such an opportunity, where the state has undertaken to provide it, is a right which must be made available to all on equal terms."[5]

The Court's historic decision dealt the doctrine of "separate but equal" a fatal blow. It did not, however, end the South's commitment to segregation. At the time of the *Brown* decision, fewer than 1 percent of black southern schoolchildren attended schools with whites. For over a decade, every possible legal means, and sometimes illegal means, were used to keep the races separated in school. In almost every state of the former Confederacy, legislatures quickly passed bills to provide for private school funding, optional school closing, and—in the antebellum spirit of nullification—interposition laws that would pit the state's sovereignty against the power of the federal judiciary. In the beginning, many states, including Florida, were able to forestall integration by developing ingenious desegregation "plans" that appeared on the surface not to violate the intent of the Court. These so-called pupil placement or freedom-of-choice plans were meant to dissuade all but the most courageous and determined blacks from applying to white schools—and of course they did.

Although many Floridians viewed 17 May 1954 as a "day of catastrophe— a Black Monday—a day something like Pearl Harbor," the state's official reaction to *Brown* belied the intensity of the opposition that would later emerge. U.S. Senator Spessard Holland called the ruling "revolutionary" but expressed the hope that it would be met with "patience and moderation." Attorney General Richard Ervin assured Floridians that there would be "no immediate disruption of our school system" and that there would be opportunity to "present argument as to the time needed in which to make the adjustment to non-segregation." After initial consideration, Acting Governor Charley Johns announced that there was no need to call a special legislative session to deal with the problem of ending segregation (as several southern governors had done), and state senator LeRoy Collins suggested calling "the best brains in our state to study the situation and meet it calmly and properly."[6]

In contrast, in neighboring Georgia, Governor Herman Talmadge accused the Supreme Court of having "reduced our Constitution to a mere scrap of paper" and pledged that "Georgians will not tolerate the mixing of the races in the public schools." Eugene Cook, Georgia's attorney general, proposed that state attorneys general boycott the decision by refusing to attend or recognize the deliberations on segregation scheduled by the Court. Mississippi's Senator James Eastland, an arch conservative, warned that the "South will not abide by nor obey this legislative decision by a political court." After a few days of such defiant posturing, *Tallahassee Democrat* editor Malcolm Johnson decried the "wild and loose talk in some southern states." Optimistically but prematurely,

Johnson declared that "in Florida the issue of segregation in the public schools has been met in a spirit of thoughtful calm."[7]

One reason for Florida's rather mild reaction to *Brown I*, as the original decision came to be known, was the state's economic and demographic base. In 1954, after decades of black emigration and white immigration, only 20 percent of Florida's population was black. Slightly more, 22 percent, of the state's 645,000 school-age children were black. Overall, the population in Florida was more heterogeneous than that in other southern states and was growing at a phenomenal rate. The attitudes of recent northern transplants (many of them people with grown children) who lived in the southern region of the state imparted a more moderate tone to the rhetoric of race relations. Florida's dependence on tourism and the diversification of the state's economy both provided additional steadying influences that helped explain the mild response to the Court's decision. The parts of Florida that bordered on Georgia and Alabama, however, and had large black populations or economies with an agricultural base became the areas most resistant to the Court's decision.

In Leon County at the time of *Brown I*, 43 percent of the children enrolled in grades one through twelve were black. The county was one of only seven in the state with a black population of 40 percent or higher. In neighboring Gadsden County, 64 percent of the students enrolled in the public schools were black. In contrast, in south Florida's Dade County, only 17 percent of children in grades one through twelve were black, and in neighboring Monroe County, blacks were 13 percent of the school population.

Florida's subdued reaction to *Brown I* had as much to do with what had been omitted from the decision (the Court did not set a timetable for desegregation) as it did with the state's demographics. Because the words "integration" and "desegregation" did not appear in the Court's opinion (nor was there a definition of a "constitutional" school system), many Floridians agreed with federal judge John J. Parker's subsequent assessment that the *Brown* decision "does not require integration, it merely forbids discrimination."[8]

Although the Court had declared unequivocally that segregated education was unconstitutional, the justices decided that further arguments needed to be heard on how and when the controversial decision should be implemented. Consequently, the Court invited the attorneys general of the states that were party to the decision and those states with segregated schools to appear as amicus curiae to help formulate the decrees to abolish school segregation. The Court's reluctance to order the immediate dismantling of the dual system of education was based, in part, on the expected ramifications of such a prodigious undertaking. Racist attitudes and "cherished customs" aside, there were practical aspects to consider.

In May 1954, an extensive building program was underway at Florida A&M University, while $2.5 million had just been approved for the construction of black secondary schools in Leon County. When asked whether the county would, in the light of *Brown,* continue to build segregated schools and maintain a separate school system, Thomas D. Bailey, the superintendent of public instruction, and the Florida cabinet said yes. This business-as-usual attitude of politicians in Florida led many citizens to believe that integration of the public schools could be delayed for the indefinite future. Nevertheless, the Court's rejection of a "separate equality" for black schoolchildren, and the "wide applicability" of *Brown,* left no doubt that integrated classrooms, however unthinkable, were indeed inevitable.[9]

When the Court's decision was announced, the acrimonious Florida Democratic gubernatorial primary was underway between Acting Governor Charley Johns (who had been in office one year following the death of Governor Dan McCarty) and Senator LeRoy Collins, one of the late governor's closest allies. Although the Johns-Collins race was in full swing when *Brown* was announced, the ruling did not become a campaign issue. Johns's immediate response was to ask Attorney General Ervin to make a study of the decision and how it might apply to Florida. Johns directed Ervin to present the report to the Florida cabinet at its next meeting. Meanwhile, candidate Collins told the press that he favored any legal measure to keep Florida's schools segregated. He promised that as governor he would use all the lawful power of that office to preserve a dual school system.

On 18 May 1954, Ervin told fellow Florida cabinet members that, since Florida was not involved specifically in the cases before the Court, it would take "new suits dealing with the Florida situation to force compliance" with *Brown.* It would be at least a year, "perhaps more," the attorney general added, before the Court issued an order making the ruling effective. After approving the multi-million-dollar school construction program that contained "a greater proportionate share of improved school facilities for Negroes," the cabinet asked Ervin to prepare an amicus curiae brief for submission to the Court on the "practical problems involved [with desegregation] and recommendations for the time needed to put the rule into effect gradually."[10]

The Supreme Court during the deliberations in *Brown* had drawn on social science data in the form of studies showing that segregation had a detrimental effect on black children. Ervin shrewdly judged that it would be advantageous if Florida's brief used social science data as well. Consequently, the cabinet approved the attorney general's request for $10,000 to conduct a survey of opinion throughout the state to determine what problems Florida would face in attempting to desegregate its public schools.

To ensure that Florida's survey had as much credibility as possible, Ervin wanted a sociologist with "research credentials" to head the project. There was little time for planning; the brief had to be filed by 1 October 1954. Standing in his yard one evening shortly after the cabinet gave Ervin the go-ahead, FSU sociology professor Lewis Killian was approached by Robert Gates, his next door neighbor as well as a consultant to the Florida Department of Education and an adviser to Superintendent Bailey. "How would you like to direct a study of how Florida will respond to the desegregation decision?" Gates asked Killian. Flabbergasted at first—he had been in Tallahassee for only two years, knew neither Ervin nor Bailey, and held racial views that he felt were antithetical to theirs—Killian nevertheless accepted the offer to direct the research. He was assisted by a "research advisory committee" comprising educators, executives, and bureaucrats, but the actual research design was developed by Killian and his assistant, a psychology graduate student trained in statistics.[11]

Before accepting the task, Killian made it clear to the attorney general that he would not conduct a survey of attitudes and opinions among the general public, because the results were too predictable and the Court had not asked for public opinion polls as guides to implement its decision. Killian convinced the attorney general that a leadership survey, one that measured the attitudes and opinions of people in positions of power and prestige in their communities, would provide clues as to how and when Florida might adjust to desegregation. Pressed for time, Assistant Attorney General Ralph Odum directed Killian to forgo the "textbook approach to social science research" and get the survey in the mail.[12]

During the summer of 1954, Killian and his assistant sent nearly 8,000 questionnaires to a wide variety of groups including school principals (white and black), parent-teacher association officers (white and black), newspaper editors, legislators, ministers, county officials, and peace officers. In general, the questionnaires asked three basic questions: (1) How do you feel about the Supreme Court decision and what would you do in the event desegregation was ordered? (2) How do the members of your community feel about the decision and what would they do if desegregation was ordered? (3) How do the public officials of your county feel about desegregation and what would they do if desegregation was ordered? [13]

Even before the survey was in the mail, it was the object of much criticism. After attending a "segregation conference" of southern governors in early June, Governor Johns denounced the Court for its "coercive judicial mandates," reversed his earlier support for submission of an amicus curiae brief, and asked the cabinet to rescind the $10,000 allotted for the survey. Johns, like many southerners, had come to believe (erroneously) that an amicus brief would make Florida a party to the *Brown I* decision or at least would imply consent. When the cabinet refused to rescind the money, the survey moved forward.[14]

Killian and his staff, including Odum and Bailey, set out on a "kind of lecture circuit of speaking to public gatherings, to school boards, to various groups of people who wanted to know what the attorney general was up to." As public reaction to *Brown I* began to harden across much of the South, Ervin found himself under growing pressure to explain to his constituents why he was filing a brief and why he was not taking a stand against the Court's decision. Under increasing political constraints, Killian began to worry that Ervin, Odum, and Bailey fully expected the results to prove that Florida was not ready for school desegregation in the near future.[15]

Response to the surveys was 51 percent. The results were analyzed and turned over to the attorney general's office for incorporation into the brief. In general, Killian's findings and conclusions revealed that the majority of the white respondents (77 percent) disagreed with the decision, but there were some startling exceptions. Of the white principals and supervisors, 53 percent agreed (ranging from "firmly agree" to "agree with strong reservations") with *Brown*, as did 62 percent of white ministers and 50 percent of newspaper editors. (Almost no whites agreed that the decision should be implemented immediately.) Police officers (89 percent) were the group most opposed to the decision, followed by 71 percent of county officials. Respondents from white groups differed from one another in their willingness to comply with enforcement of *Brown* regardless of their personal feelings, yet only 30 percent indicated that they would refuse to cooperate with any move to end segregation or would actively oppose it.[16]

As expected, black respondents overwhelmingly supported the decision, but only 12 percent supported an immediate end to segregation. Whites who supported the decision favored a very gradual, indefinite period of transition to integrated schools. Most revealing of the survey results were the gaps between the whites' and the blacks' perceptions of each other's views. Only one-fourth of black respondents believed that most white people disagreed with *Brown*. Equally telling, of the white groups asked, from one-fourth to one-half of the respondents believed that most blacks disagreed with *Brown*. Apart from peace officers, no white groups in any substantial numbers predicted that mob or serious violence would occur if desegregation was enforced. Almost no blacks predicted violence of any kind. In Killian's opinion, although the survey demonstrated overwhelming resistance to the concept of immediate desegregation, the results did not support the theory that desegregation at any time would lead to violence or would have dire consequences in Florida.

While the attorney general's office worked feverishly to prepare Florida's brief, the gubernatorial race between Collins and Johns heated up. Although Johns's attitude toward *Brown* had hardened in the last weeks of the campaign, race—or desegregation as an issue—never became the focal point of the election in 1954. There was simply no clear distinction between the candidates on the matter in the minds of most voters. Collins continued to support lawful means of protecting segregation, while Johns voiced firmer opposition to the Supreme Court's power. Their differences, which would intensify in subsequent years, were not immediately clear in 1954. Collins defeated Johns and was inaugurated on 4 January 1955.

On 12 May 1955, four months after Collins's inauguration, Richard Ervin submitted Florida's amicus curiae brief to the Supreme Court. There was "some reason to believe that segregated schools can be ended in Florida in an equitable manner without destroying the school system itself," argued the attorney general, "but there is no reason to believe that this can be accomplished hurriedly or through the legal coercion of school officials." Furthermore, Ervin said, results of the opinion poll as well as other pertinent data proved that "any attempt to compel an immediate desegregation in Florida schools would constitute a shock treatment so drastic" that efforts to bring about gradual, peaceful integration of the public schools would be nullified.[17]

The attorney general voiced the usual concerns over the administrative and fiscal details related to desegregation, but he argued that the "widely divergent scholastic standards" and the "health and moral welfare" of blacks constituted legitimate impediments to desegregation and most clearly reflected the concerns of many whites opposed to integration. There were, he noted, differences in illegitimate births between whites and blacks (2 percent versus 24 percent). After mentioning a figure said to be the number of reported cases of gonorrhea among blacks in Florida, Ervin asked the Court, in deciding when and how to integrate the public schools, to consider the economic inequalities that led to "the wide cultural gap between Negro and white in the South."[18]

The overriding theme in Attorney General Ervin's brief was not the differences between the races, or the evidence that Florida, unlike other southern states, had "marked regional variations in the intensity of the feelings of the people," but was instead the need for time, patience, planning, and careful consideration before Florida was forced to desegregate. The attorney general argued that the Supreme Court should permit "consideration of local problems and attitudes in the desegregation method and . . . there should be no deadline for the beginning or the end of the process." In essence, Ervin's brief provided the definitive model for what became known as "gradualism." No politician in Florida would say just how long a gradual adjustment to integration would take. Thinking he was overestimating the time period for public acceptance, Assistant

Attorney General Odum told a federal judge that Florida would need ten years to desegregate its public schools.[19]

On 31 May 1955, the Supreme Court handed down what became known as *Brown II*. The ruling provided the guidelines for implementing the first *Brown* decision. The Court's decision stated once again that racial discrimination in public education was unconstitutional and that "all provisions of federal, state, or local law requiring or permitting such discrimination must yield to this principle." While the Court conceded that "full implementation of these constitutional principles may require solutions of varied local school problems," the chief justice made it clear that school authorities had the "primary responsibility for elucidating, assessing, and solving these problems" and the federal district courts had to decide whether the action of school authorities "constitutes a good faith implementation of the governing constitutional principles."[20]

The five defendant school districts were ordered to make a "prompt and reasonable start toward full compliance" with the decision. "At stake," the chief justice wrote, "is the personal interest of the plaintiffs in admission to public schools as soon as practicable on a nondiscriminatory basis." Once a suit was filed, the local school board would have to formulate a desegregation plan and the federal district court would have to review and rule on the adequacy of the plan to "effectuate a transition to a racially nondiscriminatory school system." In reviewing the plans, the district courts could take into account the "public interests and local and administrative problems" pertaining to desegregation. Under no circumstance should the courts allow school boards to postpone enacting a plan merely because of "hostile community feeling," the chief justice continued, because "the vitality of . . . constitutional principles cannot be allowed to yield simply because of disagreement with them." Warren then ordered the states that were party to the *Brown* decision to begin desegregation "with all deliberate speed."[21]

It seemed indisputable that the Court intended to eradicate school segregation, but what about the states (all but four and the District of Columbia) that were not plaintiffs in the *Brown* case and still required or permitted school segregation? If local and state governments continued to operate dual school systems, it would be up to black litigants to file suit to begin the desegregation process. In other words, the states that were not directly affected by *Brown*, places where no legal action to desegregate the public schools had been initiated, had no legal obligation to act, with or without deliberate speed. Although the moral directive to end segregated schools was implicit in *Brown II*, local officials and courts were left with a great deal of latitude in implementing the Court's directive.

On the whole, Florida officials were pleased with the Court's decision. It reflected, as Malcolm Johnson noted, the "well-reasoned" gradualism that lay at the heart of the attorney general's brief. Two decades later, Ervin, now retired from the Florida Supreme Court, recalled that although he considered the *Brown* decision "morally right" in 1954, he recognized a need to "ease the *Brown* decision along"—to implement the results of the decision carefully and subtly so as to avoid violence and discourage extremism either from the legislature or from proponents of the Court's desegregation order. While Ervin in his initial response to *Brown* was among the most moderate and conciliatory of southern attorneys general, his opposition to school desegregation became stronger in subsequent years. According to some observers, Ervin's resistance to the Court's decision came about because of a 1956 electoral challenge from Prentice Pruitt, an outspoken segregationist candidate. Despite his efforts to forestall school integration, Ervin maintained publicly throughout 1954 and 1955, and often in the face of derision, that the Supreme Court's decision, no matter how objectionable, was legally binding.[22]

The ambiguity of the Court's two desegregation rulings made misunderstanding and contention inevitable. On 24 February 1955, the Florida NAACP sent a letter to Attorney General Ervin threatening to "seek the intervention of a higher jurisdictional body" unless the state acted to ban the construction of separate schools for black children and white children. This threat was ignored. Four months later, when the organization demanded that state officials initiate immediate plans so that children of both races might attend desegregated schools, state school superintendent Bailey told the group that the problem of desegregation was now in the hands of local school officers and that there was nothing that he or the state could do about it. According to Bailey's interpretation of the Court's second ruling, the counties, and not the state, were responsible for implementing the judicial mandate. At the first meeting of the Leon County Board of Public Instruction after *Brown II,* there was no discussion of desegregation. Board chairman W. T. Moore Jr. told the *Tallahassee Democrat* that the measure would come before the board in "due course," but he preferred to say nothing on the issue. For its part, the Florida legislature in anticipation of *Brown II* had passed a pupil placement law that went into effect the day before the decision was handed down. Drafted in Ervin's office, introduced by newly elected senator Charley Johns, and signed by Governor Collins on 30 May, the law was the first of many pupil assignment laws passed in the South.[23]

In compliance with the Supreme Court's mandate, the new legislation omitted race as a criterion for the assignment of pupils, but it vested discretionary power in local school boards for making assignments on the basis of county boards' regulations. The regulations might take into account factors such as health, education, safety, and public welfare. The law authorized county school boards to appoint citizens' committees and local study groups to assist in formulating the regulations. The act also authorized the boards to employ special counsel to represent them in any litigation arising from their decisions under its provisions.

To comply with the Supreme Court's mandate that county schools use "good faith" in implementing *Brown II,* the Florida law provided an administrative procedure for a pupil requesting assignment to a different school. This provision, of course, put the burden of the desegregation efforts on black children and their families. It also allowed the local school board to reject a request on the basis of a myriad of "conditions." As long as the local board did not use race as a reason for rejecting a student's application, the county could, by all legal criteria, be in compliance with the Court's decision.[24]

Although the 1955–1956 school year in Florida opened with totally segregated classrooms, it appeared that Florida's seven-year battle to keep its university system segregated might be over. Virgil Hawkins, a black college administrator and native Floridian, had been waging an ongoing legal battle to gain admission to the University of Florida Law School since 1949.

Hawkins's initial application to attend the state's only law school had been turned down by the state board of control on the basis that Florida law required the separation of the races in education facilities. Despite the Supreme Court's 1938 decision in *Missouri ex rel. Gaines v. Canada,* the board offered Hawkins money to attend law school in another state, which he refused.

Hawkins appealed to the Florida Supreme Court, which in light of *Gaines* had no choice but to rule that the board's offer to send Hawkins to an out-of-state law school violated the equal protection guarantee of the Fourteenth Amendment. The Court did find, however, that the board's pledge to build a separate law school in the state for black students would be constitutional if Hawkins were allowed to take courses at the University of Florida until the law school at FAMU had opened its doors.

Accepting this partial victory, Hawkins prepared to enter the University of Florida in 1950. Still, the board of control refused to admit him to the all-white public university. Hawkins petitioned the Florida Supreme Court for a second time to intervene on his behalf. For two years the Florida court refused to order his admission, despite the 1950 *Sweatt* decision that should have ended the concept of separate and equal facilities in higher education forever. Ignoring the recent and directly applicable decisions of the U.S. Supreme Court, the Florida court ruled against Hawkins in 1952, asserting in its majority opinion that the Fourteenth Amendment merely required that "substantial equal opportunities and privileges . . . be afforded every citizen." In addition, the court ruled, "equality of treatment need not mean identity of treatment with respect to a tax-supported facility." With that decision, the Florida justices assured that the Hawkins case would reach the U.S. Supreme Court on appeal. In 1954, seven days after the *Brown* decision had been announced, the high court ordered the Hawkins case back to Florida for reconsideration.[25]

Apparently desperate to find a way to avoid admitting Hawkins while appearing to be in compliance with recent judicial mandates, the Florida Supreme Court ruled in 1955 that the *Brown II* implementation decision did not impose upon the state "a clear legal duty to admit Hawkins immediately." Citing the rights and powers ceded to the states by the Tenth Amendment, and the duty of such states to protect their citizenry, the court refused to admit Hawkins without first conducting a study to determine whether his entrance into the university system would present "grave and serious problems affecting the welfare of all students and the institutions themselves." Two justices, H. L. Sebring and Elwyn Thomas, dissented, arguing that the constitutional right of Hawkins to attend the school of his choice should not be denied because of any inconvenience that a state might suffer in eliminating the administrative obstacles that prevented him from attending. Sebring, who wrote the minority opinion, retired from the bench soon afterward to become dean of the newly established law school at Stetson University in Deland.[26]

When Assistant Attorney General Ralph Odum once again asked Lewis Killian to direct a research project on the effects of desegregation, Killian was astounded. He told Odum that it was ridiculous to do such a study, given the *Brown II* decision, and that state officials should allow Hawkins to enter the university before the federal courts took the task out of their hands. Still, Killian agreed to undertake the task if he could do it his own way. He wanted to conduct the survey properly, with scientific sampling and using good, pretested instruments, which he felt would show that university students and faculty were far more ready for change than the white leaders studied after *Brown I* had been. But Killian once again encountered disagreement over strategy with yet another "advisory committee" and with assistant attorney general Odum, and he withdrew from the project. The board of control, assisted by part-time student help, went ahead with the project.

Over 57,000 questionnaires were mailed to Florida faculty members, alumni, students, parents, and high school seniors. The overall rate of return was 59 percent (62 percent of whites and 44 percent of blacks). The results revealed that 73 percent of the white student respondents would either continue attending their school as if there had been no change in policy or would continue in school and try to make the new policy (desegregation) work well. Students were far less willing to live, socialize, or participate in sports or activities with blacks, but only a small minority indicated that they would leave school or would go out of their way to make black students feel uncomfortable. The students' parents, as a group, voiced the most strident opposition to integrating the state's university system. Of the white parents surveyed, 68 percent responded either that blacks should be denied admission as long as legally possible or that they should not be admitted under any circumstances. Fully 42 percent of parent respondents answered that they would withdraw or transfer their students to another university or college if their institution was integrated.

Faculty members at the two white state universities appeared more tolerant toward integration. Some 38 percent agreed that blacks should be admitted immediately to the universities, while 44 percent said they should be admitted after a reasonable time period. Only 12 percent of the faculty members believed that the state should delay admitting blacks for as long as possible, and over 92 percent were willing to start teaching black students in the classroom immediately.

On 12 March 1956, before the board of control's report had been compiled and disseminated, the U.S. Supreme Court ordered the governing body to admit Hawkins into the University of Florida at once. In denying the state's petition for certiorari, the Court ruled that, in institutions of higher education, unlike elementary or secondary schools, there was "no reason for delay" in permitting the "prompt admission" of qualified black candidates. In the wake of the Court's decision, the state cabinet met in emergency session and pledged to use all possible legal means to resist the edict.[27]

Although the Florida Supreme Court was under a direct mandate to order the board of control to admit Hawkins to the University of Florida, it refused to do so. In a majority opinion written by Justice B. K. Roberts (Justices Thomas and Drew dissented), the court cited the board of control's study as proof that Hawkins's entry to the University of Florida could cause violence and "a critical disruption of our universities." In addition, integration of the state university system "would seriously impair the financial support to be expected from our state legislature" and would "unquestionably result in the abandonment of substantially all of the graduate work now being offered at [FAMU] because it would be an unnecessary duplication of the same courses offered at the University of Florida or at Florida State University." But Justice Thomas identified a larger issue, namely the matter of obedience to the mandate of the higher court. "It seems to me," he wrote, "that if this court expects obedience to its mandates, it must be prepared immediately to obey mandates from a higher court. . . . I think this litigation has ended and that the matter is now one purely of administration." Justice E. Harris Drew was more succinct: "It is a fundamental truth that justice delayed is justice denied."[28]

Whether the majority of justices of the Florida Supreme Court really believed that Hawkins's entry into the law school would cause violence and disruption is not certain. It is certain, however, that the justices believed (contrary to any evidence in Florida) that the U.S. Supreme Court's desegregation decisions had, in the words of Chief Justice Terrell, "engendered more strife, tension, hatred, and disorder than can be compensated for in generations of attempt on the part of those who are forward looking and want to do so. They [the Supreme Court] have done more to break down progress and destroy good feeling among the races than anything that has taken place since emancipation. Social progress in any time is not measured by legislative acts and decree; it is measured by qualitative citizenship." [29]

The authority of the sovereign states to defy a "dangerous" or "offensive" order of the Supreme Court was central to Terrell's arguments. "The big question," he wrote, "is not one of defying constituted authority, it is one of finding a way of solving a serious problem recently thrust upon the states with segregated schools and at the same time preserve their traditions, their moral, social, cultural and educational standards." The Florida court's decision was determined by contemporary legal experts to be "one of the strongest assertions of the doctrine of states' rights to appear in a legal opinion." [30]

Hawkins's battle to enter the University of Florida Law School made him a favorite target of the Florida Legislative Investigation Committee. When the Communist-hunting committee met in Tallahassee during February 1957, Hawkins was grilled for three days by committee counsel Mark Hawes, who appeared determined to make the NAACP and not Hawkins the focus of the eight-year-old admissions case. Hawes repeatedly pressed Hawkins, who earned less than $4,000 a year, to admit that the NAACP had provided him with attorneys and attorneys' fees during his lengthy litigation against the best legal minds in the state. [31] The committee's obsession with the NAACP caused Hawes to overlook the fact that Hawkins's legal fees were being partially financed by the Florida State Teachers Association. The conservative segregated educational organization had been working behind the scenes since 1955 to desegregate the University of Florida Law School. Concerned to keep its support of integration at the University of Florida from becoming public knowledge, officers in the Florida State Teachers Association listed Hawkins's case as "Project X" in all official organizational records. [32]

Hawes was unable to make Hawkins admit to having received support from any outside group. Hawes finally asked, "Why were you so intent on going to the University of Florida Law School over the A&M Law School or over any other law school that the state would pay you a scholarship to?" Hawkins replied:

I am a citizen of the state of Florida, a native citizen. I think I am a citizen like any other human being born and reared in Florida, and I am a taxpayer. I have a family, I have loved ones. I'm a grown man. I can't accept the responsibility of going out of the state, away from my loved ones and away from my livelihood. . . . I felt that, first of all, the University of Florida was one of the finest law schools in the country. That was first. The next thing, I felt as a citizen of that state of Florida, that I had a perfect right to go there. You asked me why I didn't go to Florida A&M University Law School after they set it up. I can hardly see that the Florida A&M Law School, set up on one or two days' notice, could match, could equal, could give me the kind of education that a law school that was set up over a period of fifty years could do, and that was one of the main reasons that I wanted to go there.[33]

In January 1958, Hawkins appealed for the last time to the U.S. Supreme Court to order his admission to the University of Florida. The Court, bypassing the Florida Supreme Court, referred the case to the federal district court in Tallahassee, where the judge could, if he chose, hold the appropriate state official in contempt of court for refusing to obey its order. The federal district court refused to hear the case on "technical grounds."[34]

In the end, the board of control found an ingenious way of keeping Hawkins out while avoiding charges of racial discrimination and contempt of court. On 15 May 1958, the board issued a regulation, effective 3 September 1958, that required all applicants to the University of Florida Law School to score 250 on the law entry exam. Hawkins had scored 200 points when he took the exam in August 1956, seven years after first applying to the university and at a time when entry exams were not required. In June 1958, the district court ruled that Hawkins had failed to establish a right under the law "applicable to cases of this character" and would therefore be denied the right to enter the University of Florida Law School on the basis not of his race but of his lack of qualifications.[35]

Virgil Hawkins never attended the University of Florida Law School, but his long battle had not been fought in vain. On 18 June 1958, federal district judge Dozier DeVane ordered the board of control to accept all qualified applicants regardless of race into the "graduate schools and graduate professional programs of the University of Florida." Governor Collins said he knew of "no reason why Florida cannot expect to obey the court order without difficulty." Subsequently, the board reversed its discriminatory policy for graduate and professional programs at all three state universities. On 15 September 1958, George H. Starke, a black air force veteran and graduate of Morehouse College in Atlanta, entered the University of Florida Law School without incident. Over the next five years, the state's public universities quietly integrated their graduate and professional schools. In 1962, both Florida State and the University of Florida enrolled black undergraduates for the first time.[36]

Why did Hawkins's attempt to attend the University of Florida cause such a furor at a time when the state's secondary schools were firmly segregated and higher education remained beyond the reach of much of the populace? Hawkins's struggle became not only an early symbol of the state's determination to resist desegregation at any level but also a major factor during the 1956 gubernatorial campaign. The election pitted Collins against a field of tough gubernatorial hopefuls. Segregation became the explosive issue as the candidates vied with each other for the best way of maintaining the state's dual school system.

After Collins had won the bitterly fought primary, newspapers in the state and outside interpreted the election as a defeat of extremism and a victory for racial moderation. The results, however, showed something else. Collins carried South Florida by a landslide, yet in all of North Florida he carried only his home county. White supremacy advocate Sumter Lowry, a political novice, swept conservative North Florida and finished second in the race, beating out the well-known Farris Bryant and former governor Fuller Warren. Lowry's substantial showing revealed something of the strong undercurrent of extremism in the state, noted by observers both in Florida and elsewhere. Bryant's close third-place position was important too, as it hardened his conservative stance and put him in a good position for the next gubernatorial race. Lowry's showing also put pressure on Collins to call a special session of the legislature to implement new segregation laws. In the end, the 1956 legislature accentuated the differences between the state's conservative constituents and Collins's more moderate leadership.

Early in the summer, Collins received the report of a committee of well-known attorneys whom he had commissioned to recommend ways of maintaining segregation legally. In the preface, the Fabisinski committee (named for its chair, Judge L. L. Fabisinski) stated that its main objectives were "to maintain the public school system of Florida" and "to determine the best interests, from an educational standpoint, of all the children of our state." Its conclusion became known across the state as the "Four Point Program." It called on the legislature (1) to strengthen the existing Pupil Placement Act, which would place children in schools according to "their individual needs," (2) to pass a law to ensure that white and black teachers would teach only children of their own race, (3) to grant the governor the power to make and enforce rules relating to the use of public facilities needed to "maintain law and order and to prevent domestic violence," and (4) to clarify and expand the governor's emergency powers.[37]

By far the largest portion of the committee's report was devoted to a denunciation of the Supreme Court's desegregation rulings. "We as members," the committee asserted, "recommend that the invasion by the Supreme Court of the rights of the States of the Legislative and Executive Departments of the United States and of the people be denounced in clear and unmistakable language and every lawful means be adopted to restore these rights and curb this threat to our liberties." The Supreme Court, the report continued, "has assumed the power, by judicial decree, to change the meaning of the Constitution of the United States, and thus to amend the fundamental law of the land."[38]

In Tallahassee, editor Malcolm Johnson praised the committee for its "wise, well-reasoned" program. He particularly singled out the recommendation that the legislature "adopt a resolution denouncing the United States Supreme Court for its growing tendency to usurp the power reserved by the Constitution for the sovereign states; the Congress and the executive branch of the government."[39]

In contrast, Collins chose to comment only on the committee's four-point program. He called it a "plan I can live with." On 18 July 1956, the governor called the legislature into special session to enact a program that "effectively prevents race mixing and meets all legal tests." Collins warned lawmakers not to exceed the recommendations of the Fabisinski committee and thereby "weaken the legal efficacy of the program they have recommended."[40]

Less than one week into the special session, Malcolm Johnson expressed concern that legislators were being so cautious in dealing with the Fabisinski committee's program for maintaining segregation that "we're about to cover up the whole concept. It may be time for a bold declaration that the purpose of the legislation is to preserve segregation in Florida public schools just as long as the majority of the people in any county, acting through their elected officials, want to keep it."[41]

Johnson had little to fear. The legislature first passed a beefed-up pupil placement law that provided more elaborate criteria for the assignment of pupils and included detailed administrative remedies for pupils seeking reassignment. These so-called remedies, a confusing maze of reviews, appeals, and delays, were crafted deliberately to discourage all but the most determined black parents, who, if successful in challenging their child's "assignment," would then face the wrath of the white community. Conservative lawmakers presented bills that included a proposed amendment to the U.S. Constitution aimed at clarifying states' rights, a measure allowing local areas to set up state-supported private schools if threatened by integration, and a bill providing jail sentences and fines for anyone coercing any child to attend an integrated school. Most important was the interposition bill, which would match the will of the state of Florida against the actions of the U.S. Supreme Court.

Although Collins had repeatedly spoken against the last measure, other southern states—Alabama, Arkansas, Georgia, Louisiana, Mississippi, South Carolina, and Virginia—had already passed interposition bills. In Florida, political support for interposition grew. Attorney General Ervin told members of the Fort Pierce Rotary Club that, until tested, an interposition resolution represented "the only legal means to formally raise the question of usurpation of state sovereignty by action of the Supreme Court." Although Ervin later contended that he never supported an interposition resolution because it would obviously be ineffectual, the attorney general's office did support and call for the passage of an interposition resolution as a "legitimate and proper expression of opinion by the legislature." [42]

The attorney general also became involved in another emotional issue. On 30 July 1956, he told the House Committee on Education and Internal Affairs that the Florida "school system would not suffer from adoption of a proposed constitutional amendment under which public schools could be abolished in areas faced with integration." Ervin's support of such a reactionary measure typified the growing political chasm between him and Collins, one that would widen over the next four years. [43]

Adding to the growing tension within the halls of the Florida legislature in 1956 was the controversy brewing in Tallahassee over the two-month-old bus boycott. Legislators were in no mood to placate those who appeared soft on integration. On 25 July, after both houses had passed the Collins-supported legislation, Representative John Orr of Miami rose to his feet and told his stunned colleagues that he belonged to the NAACP and considered segregation to be "morally wrong." Orr, a onetime law partner of former U.S. senator Claude Pepper, told the house members that had the members of the legislature "devoted as much energy, time, and talent to discovering means to live under the law instead of in defiance of it," they could have found a way to do so. Angry representatives began a move to oust Orr from the legislature, and one irate colleague threatened to present a bill that would bar members of the NAACP from holding office. Orr's family received menacing phone calls, and Tallahassee representative Mallory Horne repudiated Orr's speech on the house floor the next day. [44]

As the mood of the legislature hardened and with several radical segregation bills waiting on the agenda, Governor Collins made a historic decision. On 1 August, while house members debated the interposition bill, Collins took advantage of a little-known provision in the state constitution and adjourned the legislature. Flabbergasted lawmakers were forced to abandon their proposals until 1957.

In January 1957, Governor Collins made his second inaugural address and attracted nationwide attention. Although he assured Floridians that "segregation in Florida schools can be expected to prevail for the foreseeable future," he became the first southern governor to affirm the validity of the Supreme Court's decision. The Court's decisions are "the law of the land," Collins said. "And this nation's strength and Florida's strength are bottomed on the premise that ours is a land of law." Collins told his audience that while Florida had found a way to prevent integration for the foreseeable future, it was "little short of rebellion and anarchy to suggest that the state can isolate and quarantine itself against the effect of a decision by the Supreme Court." Unlike some other states, Collins said, "Florida has provided legislation which best will enable it to live honestly, honorably, and peacefully with the two great realities facing us: the court decision, and the social and economic conditions existing in the South."[45]

To national observers, the governor had raised "the first firm official voice in the Deep South for moderation and gradual compliance." He was mentioned as a possible candidate for the Democratic presidential nomination. While Collins began to gain in stature nationally, he faced criticism from a substantial number of Floridians, particularly those from his own North Florida backyard who supported the massive resistance movement sweeping the South. Because the legislature provided a disproportionate amount of power to these smaller, rural counties, Collins faced growing opposition to his approach to integration.[46]

In his opening message to the 1957 legislature, Collins tried to set a moderate tone by telling the lawmakers that the state's existing pupil assignment law was the "best that any state has devised" and did not need to be changed. The governor warned that "competent counsel advise that going further might only destroy its integrity." Collins, on the advice of Ervin, asked the legislature to establish an advisory group to assist the governor in the areas of race relations. The legislature, still seething from the adjournment of the year before, created the commission but otherwise ignored Collins's request for moderation. Instead lawmakers passed a "last resort" school bill, backed by the attorney general, that would allow districts to close the public schools rather than to integrate them. The measure stunned the members of the Governor's Advisory Commission on Bi-Racial Problems (the Fabisinski committee), who condemned Ervin for introducing legislation that would give "people under emotional strain the right to hold an election to abolish the public school system." Commissioners agreed to oppose the bill as both public and private citizens.[47]

To the amazement of the commission (composed almost entirely of attorneys), the legislature enacted an interposition resolution declaring that the Supreme Court's decisions weakening state powers were "null, void and of no effect." Attorney General Ervin admitted that the resolution did not have the force of law but maintained that it was "a solemn and deliberate declaration of right." Before sending it to the governor's office, Ervin declared that the resolution "expressed the will of the majority of Floridians." The attorney general's opinion of the resolution was noted with "much derisive comment" by commission members, whose "regard for his ability," the secretary of the body noted on 30 April 1957, "is at about the lowest ebb possible."[48]

Collins, who had repeatedly denounced the idea of such a resolution and had adjourned the previous legislative session to forestall one, labeled it a lie and a "cruel hoax on the people." Although he lacked the power to veto the resolution (unlike a law) Collins wrote a scathing denunciation across the face of the resolution, which was then filed in the secretary of state's office. "This resolution of interposition is meaningless," he wrote. "It means nothing in that it has absolutely no legal efficacy. It means everything, for it is an expression before the nation, before the entire world, of the sense of the Florida Legislature which can only cause it to be held up to ridicule by men who know the law and in disrepute by all citizens who know better in their hearts." Most of the major newspapers in Florida agreed with Collins. Malcolm Johnson wrote that the resolution made Florida look foolish. Editors of the *St. Petersburg Times* and the *Tampa Tribune* agreed.[49]

Collins vetoed the "last resort bill," and to his immense relief, the Florida House of Representatives sustained his veto. Other attempts at legislation of the same genre were defeated in committee or on the floors of the chambers. Florida had managed, thanks in large measure to Collins, to avoid the most extreme segregation measures enacted by other states. But the governor, still trying to balance his own changing views with political reality, seemed destined to distance himself further from most Floridians. Not long after the session ended, Collins told reporters that "someday somewhere somehow we will have some integration in schools in Florida—but not in the near future. I don't think that will come until it comes in the minds and hearts of the people who must accept integration." No white hearts anywhere in Florida, certainly not in the capital city, appeared ready to accept integration.[50]

For Tallahassee and most of the South, school integration seemed a distant worry in the fall of 1957, a war of words that lay dormant among politicians between election cycles. Then came Little Rock. The sight of army troops stationed in Arkansas in front of Central High School to enforce the admission and safety of a few black students stunned the South and set off waves of anxiety among Floridians, who feared similar confrontations in their communities. Unfortunately, the Florida legislature was in special session to consider constitutional revision when events in Little Rock exploded. Support for the defunct last resort bill was revived. Massive resistance filled the corridors of the capitol.

Passage of the bill seemed imminent. Reluctantly, Collins agreed to a compromise. He would sign a bill that allowed the public schools to close only if federal troops were sent in to force integration. As on other occasions, the governor issued a statement declaring his distaste for the legislation.

At the height of the tumult over Little Rock, LeRoy Collins made a speech at the Southern Governors' Conference in which he exhorted southerners to accept change in their customs without defying the law outright. Returning to a favorite theme, Collins warned that if the South wrapped itself in a "confederate blanket," the whole region would bury itself politically and economically for decades. In 1958, Collins announced his plan to facilitate desegregation "when and where desegregation is feasible." The Collins plan was based on the premise that the Fourteenth Amendment charged Congress, and not the courts, with implementing the rights that it guaranteed. Consequently, Congress could create special educational adjustment commissions (comprising local citizens appointed by the president) that would assume original jurisdiction in school desegregation cases and would, in assuming this role, replace the federal district courts. The governor believed that state-level participation in determining the "whens and wheres" of desegregation would prevent the violence and discord that had occurred in Little Rock. Although Collins's idea, not long on concrete solutions, received some favorable press, it did not elicit widespread interest in Congress or among southern governors.[51]

While Collins distanced himself philosophically and politically from the more intransigent southern governors, Florida counties continued to resist integration by every means. This reality led a reporter to ask Collins on national television whether his "moderate" leadership had provided only "high standing principles" rather than concrete compliance with the Court's ruling. Collins admitted the existence of "legally coerced racial discrimination in Florida" but insisted that it was necessary to develop "a good climate of racial tolerance" before attempting integration. As is evident from his speeches, the governor continued to struggle with the social, economic, and moral gulfs that he saw between the races. As with most southerners, he believed that school integration should come only after black living standards had improved. How blacks could improve their lot in a racist environment, one that produced and sanctioned blatant inequality, was a question too difficult to contemplate much less solve.[52]

Despite appearances to the contrary, the governor was not all talk and no action when it came to school desegregation. Although he remained loyal to the duplicitous pupil placement law, Collins quietly urged a few school officials to take the first steps toward integration in their districts at a time when the federal government had adopted a hands-off policy in that area. Finally, in February

1959, after a year of planning, the Dade County school system announced that the Orchard Villa elementary school in Miami would be integrated that fall. In the wake of the announcement, Collins tried to persuade other Floridians that the pupil assignment law was the only vehicle for the state's gradual adjustment to peaceful integration. At a news conference on 19 February, Collins told reporters that if the assignment law was to be upheld by the courts as constitutional, then it must be "administered in good faith"; somewhere along the line some integration was bound to occur.

Collins's response to the Orchard Villa announcement coincided with the release of the first report of the Governor's Advisory Commission on Race Relations. The members announced that, not withstanding their "personal views" concerning desegregation, "no person or state can ignore or disregard with impunity the pronouncement of the Supreme Court of the United States." Despite the "hope and desire of many," the maintenance of complete segregation by race in a public school system was now impossible. The commission urged Floridians to stand by the existing pupil assignment law, which was in their opinion the only lawful means to "minimize the impact of the desegregation decisions." Florida was faced with the "choice of maintaining our public school system operated under the terms of the pupil assignment law, or abandoning the public school system." [53]

While the news of the state's first integrated school district pleased Collins and members of his race relations commission, it sparked a revolt among Florida lawmakers. Two months after the decision had been announced, twenty-four state legislators met in Daytona Beach (home of Virgil Hawkins) and signed a "manifesto" pledging "no surrender on completely segregated schools." The signers included the speaker-elect of the house, two representatives from Dade County, and the future chairman of the Johns committee, Leon County representative Richard Mitchell. [54]

Before the legislature convened that spring, Attorney General Ervin submitted to Collins several recommendations for new legislation to deal with "desegregation problems." The recommendations included a "parent-option plan" to provide public funds for private tuition to parents who objected to sending their children to an integrated school. A plan of this nature, Ervin wrote, would stand the "legal tests" prescribed by the Supreme Court "provided no strings were placed on the money other than that proof of attendance of the child in an accredited school be furnished." Ervin also recommended that the pupil assignment law be broadened to give school boards more discretion in assigning students to schools. These recommendations included consideration of "the possibility or threat of friction or disorder among pupils or others . . . or economic retaliation within the community." The attorney general's recommendations also included the possibility of establishing single-gender schools if integration took place. "A major fear which has been expressed, by those who oppose integration," Ervin wrote, "is the eventual intermarriage between the white and Negro races." Another option was to develop three classes of schools, one for all white children, one for all black, and one that "would be attended on a voluntary basis by both white and Negro children."[55]

Despite these and other plans to forestall integration, Collins managed to keep the lid on the most radical anti-integration measures that were proposed during the 1959 session. A "school closing bill" was rejected, but legislators did empower counties to separate the sexes if integration occurred. They passed a law to ensure that no child had to attend an integrated school if his parent or guardian filed a written objection.

By 1960, the battle over school desegregation in Florida (and throughout the South) had shifted from the legislature to the judiciary. As important as the legislative and executive roles were in shaping the states' response to desegregation, the district courts ultimately set the guidelines as to how and when desegregation would take place. This shift came in part when local desegregation suits finally made it to the federal courtroom. Many of the suits had been and would continue to be tied up in the appeals process for years. It did not take southern lawmakers long to realize that the lengthy process replaced the need for legislation to circumvent integration. More important, for a decade after *Brown*, the Supreme Court took an almost hands-off policy toward public school desegregation. There was little to motivate district judges to thwart the will of the populace.

Despite the obstacles facing black plaintiffs, lawsuits filed in federal court to force the desegregation of Florida's school districts became almost commonplace. *Gibson v. Dade County*, originally filed in 1956, led the way. Plaintiffs asked that the sections of the Florida constitution requiring racially segregated schools be declared in violation of the Fourteenth Amendment and that the Dade County school board be required to submit a desegregation plan. The case was dismissed by the federal district court in Miami on the grounds that the plaintiffs had not applied for admission to a particular school under the provisions of the state's new pupil assignment law.

During a three-year legal battle between the district and appellate courts, it was established that the pupil assignment law was a valid means to end segregation as long as it was not used to delay integration. But in late 1959, when it became clear that Florida's pupil assignment law was not leading to desegregation in Dade County, the Fifth Circuit Court of Appeals ruled that the pupil assignment law was merely the legal machinery for effectuating desegregation and did not meet the requirements for a plan of desegregation, nor did the law constitute a "reasonable start toward full compliance with the Supreme Court's May 17, 1954 ruling." While the court did not rule the pupil assignment law unconstitutional, it pointed out that there was nothing in the law that "was inconsistent with a continuing policy of compulsory segregation."[56]

The *Gibson* ruling worried school officials across the state. The Florida Education Association voted to support a "parent option" plan that would provide state funds so that parents could send their children to private schools. But this option would be needed only in a few places, Assistant Attorney General Odum assured the group, where "normal geographic districting" would fail to ensure segregated schools. In these rare places, Odum said, "the criteria provided by the school placement law, such as scholastic level, will result in a high degree of natural segregation." Odum's prophecy that residential segregation would in most cases act as a natural barrier to school desegregation proved correct throughout Florida for most of the next decade.[57]

By the end of the Collins administration in January 1961, the state's political leadership once again reflected the conservatism of the citizenry. The three governors who came after Collins, beginning with his successor, Farris Bryant, all took strong stands in their campaigns against integration, civil rights, and school busing. Bryant never reactivated Collins's statewide biracial commission after the chairman charged that Bryant wanted only men "whose opinions would be congenial with his own." Bryant and his successors neither took militant steps to block integration nor provided Florida with the kind of moderate forbearance that had distinguished Collins's administration. The Tallahasseean moved to Washington, D.C., in 1961 to accept a job with the National Broadcasters Association, and none of his successors consulted him during the state's desegregation battles. Before his first legislative session, Bryant urged lawmakers to fund an advertising campaign that would defend segregation to the rest of the country.[58]

For more than ten years after the initial *Brown* decision, blacks in Florida had both the law and the resources of their communities stacked against them in their struggle to desegregate the public schools. Until the U.S. government actively intervened on the side of racial equality, their efforts remained costly, discouraging, piecemeal attempts that pitted black plaintiffs (represented almost always by attorneys from the NAACP Legal Defense Fund) against a wall of impenetrable, limitless, state-sanctioned resistance. Each of the state's sixty-seven counties resisted desegregation; some fought longer and harder than others. Equal access to public education in Leon County was the longest and the most bitter chapter in the community's civil rights struggle.

12 The Plaintiff's Burden

The NAACP began to petition school boards in Florida as early as 1955, demanding that the county schools be desegregated. In Leon County, it was the Inter-Civic Council, not the NAACP, that submitted the first desegregation petition to the school board in the wake of *Brown*. On 29 April 1957, the executive committee of the ICC submitted a petition to Amos Godby, the superintendent of public instruction in Leon County. The resolution reiterated all the tenets of the two *Brown* decisions and noted that the school board had made no progress in implementing the Court's directives. Instead, it had continued to provide public schools for black children that were "tangibly and intangibly unequal and inferior in every respect to those furnished for white children." Therefore, the ICC was resolved to, "without malice or ill-will, but in the spirit of peace and good order, love of God and our fellow-men, and in an effort to create an atmosphere of faith, confidence and good will, petition the Board of Education of Leon County, to advise it and the community as to what plans have been made, or are being considered for a good faith implementation of the United States Supreme Court mandates."[1]

Two days after the resolution and petition had been mailed, Judge L. L. Fabisinski, chairman of the Governor's Advisory Commission on Race Relations, "took the liberty" of writing Godby and offering him the support of Leon County circuit judge J. Lewis Hall: "If you desire legal assistance in the drawing of the reply . . . , the response to the petition will be circulated in the press, and it will be helpful to the general state situation if the reply is carefully drawn." The response was drafted but was never sent to the ICC. It included a "few facts and figures concerning the rapid progress that we have made in the construction program" [of black schools,] "all located within the city, on beautiful sites, comparable in appearance and equal to any other schools in design and construction within the county." Personnel, finance, and transportation were (according to the board) also equal, which proved that the county was "operating our school system within the provisions of Federal, State and local laws for the best interests of all concerned." On 7 May 1957, the resolution was presented to the board at its regular meeting and was duly noted and filed.[2]

On 2 July ICC president C. K. Steele wrote to Godby to ask what steps the board had taken to integrate the schools in Leon County. A second petition was included. The organization received no reply. On 20 August the ICC sent a third letter to the superintendent to request a meeting with him and school board members to determine what plans the board had made to "carry out the mandate of the Supreme Court of the United States. We are trying in good conscience to prevent litigation in this area," Steele wrote, but "we are sincere in our efforts to see that the decision of our highest court be implemented with moderate dispatch."[3]

Three weeks later, Godby wrote Steele that he had presented the letter and petition to the school board at its last meeting. When it was clear that no member of the ICC would be invited to discuss integration plans with the school superintendent or board, Steele wrote Godby back that he was aware of "a stubborn disposition on the part of many in our county to keep Negroes in a place of second class citizenship. . . . therefore, we are neither asking for nor expecting a miracle from you nor the School Board." Steele called the superintendent "a friend of democracy and a man of fair minded Christian principles," a person whose suggestions and advice about how to proceed the ICC would heed. "If we can obtain the least glimmer of hope for a fair chance at education for our children," Steele wrote, "I think we can persuade our people to wait a reasonable length of time for complete compliance to the Supreme Court decision of May 17, 1954." Any positive response that Steele and the ICC may have awaited never materialized. The 1956–1957 school year in Leon County opened as usual, with segregation intact, and no plans or lawsuits challenged its hegemony.[4]

On 17 November 1961, six years after the first Florida desegregation suit had been filed in Dade County, the Tallahassee NAACP sent a petition to the Leon County school board "requesting that a plan be devised with all deliberate speed to the end that our children may be admitted to the school for which they are qualified at the next school enrollment date." The petition was signed by President C. K. Steele and twenty-two other black parents. The petition was received and noted four weeks later at a school board meeting. No official discussion or action was taken on the request. That fall, under court orders, four counties in Florida joined previously integrated Dade County and desegregated their public schools for the first time. Some 552 black students statewide (less than 1 percent of the total population of black students) attended seventeen previously all-white schools. No violence occurred.[5]

On 2 March 1962, five sets of black parents, including C. K. Steele, filed a class action suit in federal district court against the Leon County school board. The action accused the board of operating an illegal dual school system in Leon County and of using that system to "deny admission of Negro children to certain schools solely because of race and color." According to their suit, the parents had not "exhausted the administrative remedy provided by the Florida Pupil Assignment Law for the reason that the remedy there provided is inadequate to provide the relief sought."[6]

The black parents charged that the defendants (the school board and the superintendent) "have not employed the Pupil Assignment Law as a means of abolishing state imposed race distinctions nor have they offered to plaintiffs, by means of the Pupil Assignment Law, a genuine means of securing attendance at nonsegregated public schools." Attorney Charles Wilson of Pensacola (one of the few black attorneys in the area) asked the court to enter decrees to forbid the county from assigning students and teachers to schools on the basis of race and from subjecting black children seeking admission to the public schools to "criteria, requirements, and prerequisites not required of white children."[7]

Three months later, on 1 June 1962, depositions in the case were taken by Wilson, and W. A. O'Bryan of the firm of Ausley, Ausley, McMullen, O'Bryan, and McGehee, representing the school board. Board chairman W. T. Moore Jr. told Wilson that the county no longer operated a biracial school system, although all of the twenty-seven schools in Leon County were still segregated by race. Moore admitted that the board had not adopted any specific policy to desegregate the Leon County school system other than to operate under the pupil assignment law, "where any child is permitted to ask for assignment to any school." When asked whether the board had made "any announcement of the fact that all of the children in Leon County have a right to indicate a preference with reference to the school he attends," Moore replied that he was "sure there have been some public announcements on that, I don't recall the specific dates, nor if there are any."[8]

The chairman was not sure how black parents would obtain the forms necessary to request a new assignment for their children. Nonetheless, the racial composition of the schools would remain segregated until "some student applies under the Pupil Assignment Law for assignment to a school in which he could not have been previously admitted." Superintendent Godby told Wilson that students were assigned to schools on the basis of many factors, including "a general attendance area in the proximity of one's residence," but under further questioning he admitted that the two county high schools, the five junior high schools, and the nineteen elementary schools were all totally segregated by race regardless of where the students lived. When asked whether the board had done anything to change the racially segregated school system of Leon County since he had become superintendent, Godby replied only that the board had agreed "to abide by the law . . . , by the Pupil Assignment Law," and to "sit in readiness to apply the Pupil Assignment Law if necessary."[9]

During two pretrial conferences in the late fall of 1962, attorneys for the Leon County school board asked federal district judge Harrold Carswell to dismiss the *Steele* suit because the plaintiffs had not yet exhausted all the remedies for relief contained in the pupil assignment law. In addition, the board denied that it had "deprived the pupils and parents [of] any right, privilege or immunity guaranteed to them by [the] due process and equal protection clauses of the 14th amendment." Carswell refused to dismiss the suit, but as he had done a year earlier in an Escambia County desegregation case, the judge announced that he would not hear arguments concerning the mandatory segregation of the faculty. During the final pretrial conference, Carswell ruled that he knew "of no case that says there must be compulsory integration. The burden is upon the plaintiff to show discrimination because of race." The trial was set for early 1963.[10]

It would be impossible to overestimate the role of Judge Carswell in the desegregation suits that appeared before the U.S. District Court, Northern District of Florida in the 1960s. The Northern District comprised four divisions, each of which contained several counties. The divisions were Pensacola (to the west of Tallahassee), Marianna (arguably the most conservative), Tallahassee (Leon and six rural counties), and Gainesville (Alachua, home of the University of Florida, and four other counties). Carswell, a native of Georgia, had lived in Tallahassee for so many years that he was considered a local by city natives. Before establishing his own Tallahassee law firm in the early 1950s, Carswell was an associate in the law firm of Ausley, Collins, and Truett. His legal career soared when at the age of thirty-three he was appointed U.S. attorney by President Eisenhower.

Five years later, in 1958, Carswell was appointed to the Northern District court.[11]

Carswell's first big school desegregation case, *Augustus v. Board of Public Instruction of Escambia County,* filed in Pensacola in 1960, was one of the first court-ordered desegregation cases in Florida and had a tremendous effect on the *Steele* case in Leon County. As a result of *Augustus,* black schoolchildren in Escambia County (along with a few in nine other Florida counties) began attending school with whites in the fall of 1962. Leon County was the only county in Florida with a black population above 30 percent that had a desegregation suit pending in federal court. Only two of the integrated districts in Florida had a black population of over 20 percent.

By the time the *Steele* case came to trial in early 1963, plaintiffs in the ongoing *Augustus* case had won a significant round in the Fifth Circuit Court of Appeals. In July 1962 the appellate judges ruled that while the Escambia school board had shown good faith by submitting a desegregation plan, "we are forced to conclude that it had not gone far enough." Consequently, the board's plan had to be amended to provide for desegregation at the rate of one grade per year beginning in the fall of 1963. In the first year, both the first and the second grades were to be integrated; in 1964, the third grade would follow. The court decreed that new pupils entering the school system should be assigned to schools without discrimination as to race. In a blistering rebuke, the judges declared that Carswell had erred when he refused to consider the plaintiffs' charge that segregation of faculty could be injurious to black students and was central to the charges of unlawful racial discrimination. As a result, Carswell ordered the school board to answer the complaints dealing with the integration of teaching and administrative personnel and to comply with the court's instructions to eliminate the dual school districts.[12]

In light of recent developments in *Augustus* and other Florida desegregation cases, the outcome of the *Steele* case was a forgone conclusion. On 28 February 1963, school board attorney O'Bryan argued that the board had conscientiously followed the assignment law but that none of the plaintiffs had applied for transfer under its terms. That, he implied, was why the Leon County schools were totally segregated. Furthermore, if the pupil placement law was applied carefully, it was a sufficient means to desegregate the county schools. As she had successfully argued in *Augustus,* NAACP Attorney Constance Baker Motley argued that the board was deliberately operating a dual school system and that the pupil assignment law was a "built in scheme to preserve racial segregation." The lawyer called for a single school zone to replace the dual one now in operation.[13]

At the close of arguments, Carswell ruled that the school board had established that "segregation is not an official policy" in Leon County, and he refused to issue an injunction against the board as requested by the plaintiffs. "Although there may in fact be segregation," Carswell said, "there is no evidence of a single child in Leon County who has been denied assignment or transfer to a school because of race." While this leads to a "clear statement of no discrimination," the judge added, "the question is: How to insure that the requirements of the Constitution shall continue to be met." Carswell ordered the Leon County school board to submit a desegregation plan that would adhere to constitutional principles and the pupil assignment law. Remarkably, despite the appellate ruling in the *Augustus* case, Carswell refused to consider the issue of segregated faculty.[14]

On 1 April 1963, the Leon County school board submitted its desegregation plan to the federal court. The plan followed what had become known in Florida as the Escambia model, which called for grade-by-grade desegregation beginning with the first grade in the 1963–1964 school year. The plan also stipulated that students already enrolled in the school system would be assigned to their old schools but could apply for transfer or reassignment under the requirements of the pupil assignment law. Letters explaining the transfer policy would be mailed to each parent or guardian of school-age children in Leon County. Carswell accepted the Leon plan even though it had been over a year since the Fifth Circuit Court had ordered Escambia County to desegregate two grades a year beginning in the fall of 1963.

The judge again turned down the suggestion made by NAACP attorney Motley that the board adopt a single school zone in place of the dual zone currently in use, noting that he did not believe that "zone lines provide the magic answer to school desegregation." Carswell directed the school board to hold countywide registration for one week prior to the fall term for parents who wished, in person, to request a reassignment or transfer for their children.[15]

Steele and the other plaintiffs strongly opposed the new plan for the obvious reason that it placed the burden of desegregation on the black community by requiring its children to transfer to white schools. To blacks, this was a "naked open door" assignment policy that placed no burden on the school system itself to take any affirmative steps toward dismantling the dual system. Moreover, it was a policy that required black parents who wanted access to the best (white) schools to send their children into hostile environments where they were clearly not wanted. It led also to the unmistakable assumption that black schools, teachers, and students were inferior, and all white schools, teachers, and students, superior.[16]

At the end of the 1963 school year, Leon and six other Florida counties announced that they would "desegregate" their public schools in the fall. Seventeen of the state's sixty-seven school districts and 2 percent of Florida's black schoolchildren would then be "integrated." In Leon County, only four black pupils out of a total student population of 16,803 would attend a "white" school in Tallahassee, but plans for the first desegregated school year began months in advance.[17]

During the week in May set aside by Judge Carswell for parents to request a school reassignment for their children, the parents of Phillip Hadley, Marilyn Holifield, and Harold Knowles submitted applications for their children to be considered for enrollment at Leon High School, and the parents of Melodee Janice Thompson enrolled their child in the first grade (the only grade ordered desegregated by Carswell) at Kate Sullivan Elementary School. The three high school applications showed that Holifield and Knowles were at the top of their classes and had scored in the upper quartile of the tenth grade statewide achievement tests. Holifield attended the demonstration high school at Florida A&M University (commonly called FAMU High), and Knowles attended Lincoln High School. Hadley, who had recently transferred from an integrated school in Broward County, also attended Lincoln High and was a good student with average test scores, but as his file noted, the fifteen-year-old had a much higher "ability score." [18]

In a letter to school board members, Superintendent Godby suggested that the board approve the three requests, although he had some concerns that Hadley might not meet "all pupil assignment requirements." Nevertheless, "based on confidential information" he had received, the superintendent wrote, "it would be accepted and less agitation would be created in the Negro school and Negro community" if all three students were reassigned.[19]

The reassignment of the students, while of paramount importance to the school board, was also of major concern to city and county law enforcement. During the third week of August 1963, Chief of Police Stoutamire, Captain Robert Maige, Sheriff Bill Joyce, four officers of the county sheriff's department, a U.S. marshal, the chairman and superintendent of the school board, and the principal of Leon High School met in Joyce's office to discuss plans to protect the four black pupils, to prevent community disorder, and to work with the news media. It was decided that police officers would be stationed at the bus stop, along the route followed by the bus, and at the schools that the four students would attend. Godby recommended that officers remain indefinitely in the vicinity of the two schools but stay on the grounds for no more than three nights before and after school opened. It was agreed that the news media would be allowed to interview the three older black students only in the principal's office and after the first day of classes.[20]

Three days before school started, on 5 September 1963, the Florida Advisory Committee to the U.S. Commission on Civil Rights issued a highly critical report on Florida race relations. The five-member body called for an end to "token integration" in the state's public schools and criticized Floridians for "doing little to crack the well established segregated pattern for living."[21]

On 8 September 1963, three nervous black teenagers prepared to crack the pattern as they made their way to their first day of school at Tallahassee's Leon High, not on the school bus, as originally planned, but in private cars, an added safety precaution.

No one was more anxious for Tallahassee's first experiment with school desegregation to go smoothly than Leon High principal Robert Stevens. Throughout the summer of 1963 the former teacher and assistant principal had met first with Superintendent Godby and members of the school board, then with Leon faculty and students, and finally with the black parents and students. According to Stevens, the school board's primary concern was "to carry out integration with the least possible disturbance of normal school operation." In deference to community standards, there would be a "gradual approach to participation of black students in extra curricular activities, athletics and groups involved in out of town trips." Stevens's major concern was getting white students to accept the change and easing the way for the blacks "in the face of open rejection by many students."[22]

During the spring of 1963, Stevens met with every class at Leon, told the students about the school board's decision, asked for their cooperation, and implored them to "control their personal feelings" when their black classmates appeared. While he expressed total faith in his faculty and administration, Stevens worried about some of the white students and their parents who were "strongly opposed to integration." Tallahassee in 1963 was "a deep south community with a long standing and firmly imbedded feeling about blacks," Stevens recalled. It was an "atmosphere . . . not conducive to immediate change." On 8 September, the first day of classes, Stevens stationed teachers in the halls to maintain order. Members of the local and national press were on hand to record the moment. No ugly incidents marred the fifty-seven-year-old school's first experiment with desegregation. After two weeks of outward tranquillity, school integration at Leon was deemed a success by the newspaper, by the school board, and by community leaders. But to Harold Knowles, Phillip Hadley, and Marilyn Holifield, three blacks in a school of nearly 2,000 students, integration was a day-to-day, at times frightening, and often disheartening personal odyssey. To the 6,240 other black schoolchildren in Leon County, and to their parents, school integration remained a distant, elusive goal.[23]

Back in April of 1963, when Harold came into her business education classroom at Lincoln High School, Christene Knowles told her students to continue working and stepped outside with her son. "Mamma, have you changed your mind about letting me go to Leon?" Harold asked. "Well, if you want to go,"

Mrs. Knowles replied, "I'll go get the application papers today." As a teacher and a concerned parent, Mrs. Knowles had kept abreast of the *Steele* suit, the pupil assignment law, and other court cases concerning desegregation. She frequently attended school board meetings and often stopped by the superintendent's office to pick up additional information on the county's desegregation proposal.

After she received the court-ordered letter from the school board notifying black parents that their children were eligible for reassignment, Knowles knew that her son had a good chance of becoming one of Leon High School's first black students. A studious, conscientious young man, Harold hoped to be either a dentist or a lawyer, but his mother feared that with the "inadequacies" in black education, her only child would not "measure up" on state board examinations unless he was exposed to the best the county had to offer. At Lincoln, students and teachers alike struggled with scarce resources, secondhand books, decaying facilities, and—most troubling to Harold—one microscope for every thirty biology students. Although Knowles had never pressured Harold to go to Leon ("integration is something you can't force upon a child"), she was proud of her son's decision. Nevertheless, she was afraid of the dangers he might encounter.[24]

After talking to Harold, Mrs. Knowles went to Leon High School to pick up the necessary forms and then drove to the superintendent's office to apply for Harold's transfer to the white school. She was unaware that the parents of Marilyn Holifield and Phillip Hadley were going through the same process to enroll their children at Leon. When she arrived at the superintendent's office, Mrs. Knowles was given the papers to fill out and was told how to complete Harold's application.

Superintendent Godby asked Knowles why, as a teacher at Lincoln, she wanted to send her son to Leon. "Mr. Godby," Knowles said, "there are some things that common sense will tell you. And common sense tells me that you would take a white kid and stand him on the right of your desk and take my black kid and stand him on the left, and common sense tells me that you are going to give your kid on the right something that is better than my kid on the left. And that is what is happening in Leon County. All I want to do is expose my kid to what you have on the right." The superintendent sat back in his chair, stared at Knowles, and said nothing.[25]

Although Harold was anxious about attending a white high school, he saw Leon as a ticket to his future. He assumed that all of his classmates would feel the same way and would request reassignment to the white school, but only two others did so. Puzzled at first, Harold soon came to know what the white community already knew. Blacks, fearful of what their children might face in a white school, and concerned that their families or jobs would be threatened, hesitated to become the guinea pigs of social change. For many middle-class and professional blacks, FAMU's developmental high school served as an alternative to the county's only black public high school and provided a safe, nurturing environment for bright black children. Meanwhile, for those black parents who wanted to send their children to white schools, the county's pupil assignment forms and procedures remained a daunting barrier.

While whites in Leon County blocked desegregation in every conceivable way, blacks remained understandably ambivalent over the advantages and disadvantages of integrating the public schools. On the one hand simple justice dictated that black children should be allowed to attend the "best" schools in the county. But as black educator James Ford remembered, many parents resented the premise that their children had to attend white schools in order to receive a good education. "Blacks really weren't concerned about going to white schools, that wasn't the black dream. The black dream was to have a school with all the facilities and equipment, new books and the same things that anybody else had and that has never happened in this city."[26]

In this city, home to a strong black university and one of the first black high schools in the state, a large number of parents "didn't think that it would necessarily enhance their children just to be somewhere where a white child was. . . . [they thought] that they were somebody already." To Aquilina Howell, a teacher and administrator who had to attend graduate school on a board of control "out of town scholarship," it was important to be a strong proponent of desegregation while feeling proud of herself, her community, and the "long tradition" of black education in Tallahassee. "We didn't feel like we should beg to be admitted to white schools, that was humiliating," she remembered, but "someone had to be out front . . . like Reverend Steele."[27]

Just as with the battle to desegregate other public facilities, blacks who integrated the public schools had to go to places where they were not wanted and had to force whites to let them in. But this struggle differed from the battles over equal access to theaters, lunch counters, and public transportation in that blacks who went to white schools, were, in essence, turning their backs on their own schools, institutions that represented the very heart and soul of the black community, places removed from white control that had helped to define and sustain black life. In short, there were no easy answers to the problems and dichotomies created by years of separate and unequal schools. All black parents wanted the best educational opportunities for their children, yet there was no consensus as to how to achieve the dream, only a recognition that, as in the past, black people would have to take on the task of correcting entrenched evils.

Throughout the weeks leading up to Leon's integration, the parents of Harold, Marilyn, and Phillip met with Superintendent Godby and Principal Stevens. They were told that their children would not be allowed to take physical education classes or to participate in any physical contact sport with white students. The three black teenagers would be protected in the halls, but if they chose to go into the bathroom, they did so at their own risk. Christene Knowles was told that her son could not ride his small motorcycle to school because white students would blow it up. Harold, Phillip, and Marilyn were to ride the Lincoln High school bus, which would drop them off and pick them up at school.

When Stevens told Christene Knowles that all three black students had been assigned the same classes, lunch periods, and assembly periods, she balked. "I told him that the kids were not even friends and that they did not share all the same interests. I insisted that they be assigned classes just like the other students." Unfortunately for Harold, his mother's insistence made his life at Leon even tougher. While Phillip and Marilyn had the same schedule, Harold saw the two other black students only on the bus and after school.[28]

The first weeks of classes at Leon were quiet. An "eerie quiet," Harold remembers. "We thought, hey, this is a piece of cake." But after the novelty wore off and the press left the school, things changed. Every morning as they got off the bus, the three students would pass by a "committee" of whites who would hurl epithets and insults at them. In class, no one sat near Harold Knowles or spoke to him, but the teachers were fair and consistent in their grading. Faculty members patrolled the halls to protect the three black students, but they could not stop the dirty looks, name-calling, and occasional jostling. "It was the first time I faced real racial hatred," Holifield recalled of her two years at Leon. But even more troubling than the day-to-day intimidation was her feeling that the administration did not care. "Three black teen-agers faced incredible relentless hatred, and the principal was no help."[29]

While administrators did little to create a supportive atmosphere for the three students, they did refuse to condone or tolerate outright violence against the trio and tried to be fair when conflicts occurred—which they did most often between Hadley and white students. To Knowles, who was a more reserved young man, Phillip Hadley was "a little bit fearless," even careless, when dealing with white students. Once when Phillip started laughing at a white football player over an incident in the hall, Harold told his friend, "This guy is going to kill us. . . . I was scared to death . . . , but Phillip, he didn't let them bother him." But things were not always as they appeared for the affable, easygoing Hadley. Principal Stevens remembers that the young man came into his office in tears one day because while classes were changing he had been hit in the face by a white student who disappeared into the crowd. While he was talking to Phillip, a young white female student entered the office and left a note on his desk with the name of the boy who had hit Hadley. When Stevens called the assailant into his office, he defended his actions, saying, "He [Hadley] doesn't belong here."[30]

Stevens sternly admonished the boy, sent him home, and told him to return with his parents. Shortly thereafter, the boy's angry father called to say he would not come to the principal's office and that his son had been right. Furthermore, the father said, he would go to the school board and would have Stevens fired. The irate parent went to Superintendent Godby, who told him that his son would not be allowed back in Leon unless he could assure Stevens that such behavior would never occur again.

Assistant Principal Mike Conley remembered that one day Hadley retaliated against a white boy who had tormented him all year in the hall between classes. "Phillip had had about all he could handle of him and he turned around and popped him one day and he never had any more problems with that boy."[31] Conley and Stevens often talked to Phillip, as did a few white teachers, all of whom felt that he was able to bounce back rather easily from unpleasant, even frightening racial incidents. Equally determined to succeed at Leon, but more sensitive to their status as "interlopers," Marilyn and Harold struggled each day to overcome stomach "butterflies" before they left their homes for school.

Time spent out of the classroom during the school day was the most troubling aspect of all three students' experiences at Leon. The worst for Harold was lunch period. At first, he attempted to eat in the cafeteria, but when he sat down at the end of one of the long tables, everyone else would rise in unison and walk away. "I didn't need that," Knowles remembers, "so I quit eating lunch. I would just go to my next class and wait for it to begin. In the morning I never ate breakfast because my stomach was in knots. To this day I can't eat breakfast," he said twenty years later. "I never went to the bathroom at Leon, never. Not for two years . . . , for two years. But you find that you get used to anything, anything you have to. You just do what you have to do to survive."[32]

The experiences of the three pathbreaking students at Leon did not stop during school hours. Their parents were insistent that their children attend the school's social functions. "Mother told me that I could not be a token student," Knowles remembers. "She said that I had to be a part of the school whether the whites wanted me to be or not." Since the parents of Marilyn and Phillip felt the same way, the three children attended the school's social functions together. In 1965, they went as a threesome to the prom. Harold and Phillip would dance alternately with Marilyn.[33]

The event they all dreaded the most was the senior party. "I told mother again that I did not want to go" but to no avail, Knowles recalls. Off the three went to a white student's house for the party. The school had of course told the parents of the student that blacks would be attending, and so no incident occurred when they arrived. During the festivities, however, John Herz, one of the few white students who had been nice to the three blacks, asked Marilyn to dance. While they were dancing, the host's father stormed into the room, grabbed Herz by the collar, dragged him down the long front yard to his car, and literally threw him into the street. "Get off my property," he yelled, "and don't come back." Sickened and embarrassed, the three black students left the party.[34]

"There were some white students who were nice to us," Knowles remembers, "but they were usually the 'odd balls,' the kids who were considered strange anyway." Knowles also recalls being shocked when he realized that a rigid class system at Leon separated white students from each other in addition to separating white students from black. To some students and parents, class distinctions were as sacrosanct as racial distinctions.[35]

Although Harold, Marilyn, and Phillip faced a constant barrage at Leon High School, they found themselves alienated in a more painful way within the black community. Many of their former classmates showed resentment because the three had left their black high schools for Leon. "They thought that we thought that we were better than them," Knowles remembers. "It was a constant division." Marilyn and her date were turned away from the FAMU High School prom by a teacher who would not let her in because she attended Leon.[36]

The reaction extended as well to the adult community. Christene Knowles recalled, "I was ostracized, especially by the black educators. They felt that school integration was coming anyway and that you didn't need to get involved." Many of them felt that segregation would just "roll over in time. I figured they had been brainwashed." When her principal indicated that Mrs. Knowles, because she was a teacher, should not let Harold attend Leon or get involved in the integration battle, she told him that her child came first. "I told him that if he and the superintendent wanted my job, they would have to fight to get it."[37]

Sending Harold to Leon had many consequences, but worst, of course, was the constant harassment by whites. Because the Knowleses owned a laundry business, they had a business phone, and many times it seemed to ring off the hook with crank calls. Finally, Harold was forbidden to answer the phone. One day at school, a white girl shot Harold in the back with a water pistol, ruining the look of his starched brown and white shirt. "It was my pride and joy for Harold to look nice every day," Knowles recalls. When that happened, he lost his composure and "grabbed the girl." Fortunately, a teacher witnessed the incident, and the girl was suspended from school. That night, her father called Harold's step-father and threatened to kill the young man. "You come into this neighborhood and you won't drive out," yelled Erelson Knowles. Later, they considered calling the police but decided not to. "It wouldn't have done any good," said Christene Knowles. "Marilyn's mother and I often said we thought it was the police who were behind a lot of those calls."[38]

When it came time for graduation from Leon, Harold Knowles did not want to participate in the ceremony, but as usual, his mother insisted. "Both Marilyn's and Phillip's last names began with an H," Knowles recalls, "so naturally they walked together. No one would walk with me. The boy I was assigned to walk with stayed a few steps ahead of me in the procession. The two students directly behind me walked slowly. Consequently, I walked across the stage by myself." A few months later, Harold left for DePauw University. "I just wanted to get out of the South," he remembers, "just get away from Leon High School."[39]

By the time Harold, Phillip, and Marilyn graduated from Leon in 1965, only five black students were attending the school. Assistant Principal Conley remembered that many people in the community thought that 1963 was just an "experiment," that Leon High School would never be really integrated, that black students would find the climate too difficult to endure and would go back to separate schools. Principal Stevens remembers that the school administration expected more and more blacks to attend the school, and the administration planned accordingly. But given the attitudes of local whites, Stevens doubts that the county schools would ever have been fully integrated without the passage of the 1964 Civil Rights Act.

While Tallahassee schools integrated at a glacial pace, the *Steele* desegregation suit continued to inch its way through the court system. Progress remained slow despite the passage of the 1964 Civil Rights Act and some related decisions from the Fifth Circuit Court of Appeals and the U.S. Supreme Court. Throughout Florida and the South, it took not only a forceful nudge from the federal government but also clarification from the Supreme Court to indicate what exactly was expected and what would not be tolerated from local school boards and the lower courts.

In 1963 the Supreme Court began to express its growing impatience with the pace of school desegregation. In *Goss v. Knoxville*, the Court unanimously declared it "readily apparent" that the school board's plan would continue segregation and was therefore unconstitutional. One year later, the Court left no ambiguity about what it had meant a decade earlier in *Brown*. On 25 May 1964, the justices ruled in a Virginia case that "there has been entirely too much deliberation and not enough speed in enforcing the constitutional rights which we held in *Brown*." Notwithstanding the Court's new emphasis on increasing the speed with which schools desegregated and the federal government's willingness to intervene on behalf of black plaintiffs, most southern communities refused to budge without direct intervention.[40]

With desegregation barely begun in Tallahassee in the spring of 1964, the plaintiffs in the *Steele* case returned to court, seeking a unitary school system based on geographical attendance lines for grades one through six and requesting "further relief" in the acceleration of the existing plan and teacher assignment. NAACP attorney Leroy Clark argued that only 4 of the county's 6,244 black schoolchildren were attending desegregated schools and that in light of recent decisions by higher courts, Leon County's desegregation plan was woefully inadequate. On 26 May, Judge Carswell sustained the school board's objections to raising the teacher segregation issue and delayed further hearings on the merits of the desegregation plan until after school had opened for the 1964–1965 school year. Six weeks later, on 2 July 1964, Congress passed the long-awaited Civil Rights Act.[41]

13 Deliberate Speed

Unlike the 1954 *Brown* decision, the 1964 Civil Rights Act immediately exerted a clear effect on school desegregation throughout the South. Specifically, the new legislation authorized the U.S. attorney general to bring suit against a county charged with making racially biased school assignments and to intervene in cases already underway. Most important, Title VI of the act outlawed discrimination on the ground of race, color, or national origin in "any program or activity receiving federal financial assistance."[1]

When the act passed, state and local governments in seventeen southern and border states were receiving over $176 million in federal aid for school programs administered by the U.S. commissioner of education, and the amount of federal funding was increasing. In 1965, Congress passed the Elementary and Secondary Education Act authorizing some $590 million in additional federal aid to local school districts. In 1954, the year of the *Brown* decision, Florida public schools received $7 million in federal aid. During the 1963–1964 school year, at a time when fewer than 2 percent of black children attended school with whites, Florida's public schools received over $17 million in federal aid. When funds to the state university and community college systems were included, the state was scheduled to receive over $40 million in federal funds for the 1965–1966 school year.

In December 1964, the Department of Health, Education and Welfare (HEW) assumed a key role in the desegregation of the nation's elementary and secondary schools when it published a set of regulations designed to implement Title VI of the Civil Rights Act. Under these rules, to take effect in January 1965, school districts and colleges were required to sign "assurances" that they would no longer practice discrimination. Any that refused would forfeit all federal aid.

Four months later, the Office of Education (part of HEW) issued its first set of uniform standards establishing procedures by which a school district could prove that it had made "a good faith start toward desegregation." A school system could persuade the agency of its intent to cease discriminatory practices in three ways. The first applied only to districts that were fully desegregated by the fall of 1965; there was none in Florida. These districts would submit an "assurance of compliance" to the department, pledging no future discriminatory procedures in their jurisdictions. The second way applied to districts such as Leon County that were under a final court order to desegregate. These districts were to submit the orders to the U.S. commissioner of education and were to agree to comply with the orders and with any modifications. The final method, which applied to most other Florida school systems, ordered the districts to submit plans for desegregation to the commissioner for assessment as to their ability to accomplish the goals of the 1964 Civil Rights Act.[2]

As strongly and simply worded as it was, the Civil Rights Act, with its guidelines for implementation, did not eradicate segregated school systems in Florida. First, HEW was willing to accept local desegregation plans based on the old freedom-of-choice system that had proved inadequate across the state. The responsibility for initiating desegregation consequently remained with black citizens, not with school districts. And the civil rights bill provided only the legal apparatus for desegregation; it did nothing to foster a climate that would be conducive to racial change. Without strong leadership from school personnel and without the cooperation of teachers and parents, white students were under no obligation to treat black students as anything but interlopers. While violence was not tolerated, kindness, acceptance, and understanding were not encouraged or expected. Apart from the few black children who braved ostracism and antagonism from their white classmates, integration remained largely an illusion in Tallahassee.

In the fall of 1964, Anita Elaine Thorpe joined Harold Knowles, Phillip Hadley, and Marilyn Holifield at Leon High School. Thorpe, a sophomore, was the only black student in her class and endured the same coldness, jeers, and taunts that made the older black students' lives miserable at Leon. Mary Louise Ruff, who was a member of Thorpe's sophomore class, remembers that the administration did not try to encourage civility toward Thorpe or the other black students, voiced no expectations of courteous treatment, and made no set rules or suggestions on how white students were to behave. To Ruff, Leon's official position seemed to be that the fifteen-year-old Thorpe did not exist. The one place where this generalization did not apply was in Thorpe's geometry class, where teacher Mary Lois King had assigned seating so that classmates could not avoid sitting next to Thorpe. Ruff found herself sitting beside Thorpe in geometry, began to chat with her before class, and sometimes, along with a few other white students, joined her at lunch.

Ruff's decision to break with standard protocol at Leon earned her the kind of treatment typically reserved for those who defied the town's racial etiquette. One day while walking home from the bus stop, she overheard some white students walking behind her talking about the "nigger lover" who obviously couldn't help herself because her parents were Yankees. When she got to her family's driveway, Ruff, who had been afraid that she would be asked to get off the bus because she had been called a nigger lover, whirled around and shouted at her accusers, "We're from Mississippi!" It was a revelation so amazing that she was never taunted on the school bus again. Things did not improve at Leon for Thorpe, who after completing her sophomore year enrolled at FAMU High School.[3]

In Tallahassee, and across the South, only the bravest and most stubborn of black parents were willing to apply for their children to attend a white school. For one thing, white schools were almost always located, because of residential segregation, beyond the safety of black neighborhoods. Enough black parents did apply, however, to satisfy HEW initially that many local school districts were making a good faith effort to comply with the law. While the desegregation plans submitted to the U.S. commissioner of education were admittedly inadequate, they were invariably more stringent than those used by the school districts under existing court orders to desegregate. Such school districts, in counties that included Leon and Escambia, had plans that fell under the jurisdiction of the federal district court, not the U.S. commissioner of education.

On 20 January 1965, six months after the Civil Rights Act had passed and less than three weeks after the HEW compliance regulations had gone into effect, Judge Carswell ruled on the motions in the *Steele* case that had been postponed since May. Because of three recent decisions from the Fifth Circuit Court of Appeals, the clear precedent for speedier desegregation ordered by the Supreme Court, and the directives contained in the Civil Rights Act, those close to the case felt certain that Carswell would rule in the plaintiffs' favor and would order the Leon County school board to file a new plan. Instead, the judge ruled that the school district had acted upon transfer applications "consistently and uniformly without consideration of race" and that all applications for transfer had been "acted upon favorably wherein a pupil has applied to attend a previously segregated school."[4]

Carswell found the board to be in compliance with the 1963 court order and dismissed the plaintiffs' request that the local plan be brought into compliance with recent court decisions. The night before Carswell entered his decision, the Leon County school board voted unanimously to continue to comply with the county plan for administering the pupil assignment law and to send a copy of the court order to the Department of Education as assurance of compliance with Title VI of the Civil Rights Act.

Following three months of legal maneuvering, attorneys for the black plaintiffs were back in district court to seek "further relief" from the 1963 court order. Specifically, they sought a modified and accelerated version of the existing pupil assignment plan for Leon County.

Carswell again refused to reorganize the desegregation plan and ruled that evidence to support such a change "would just be an idle gesture regardless of the nature of the testimony." The judge confirmed his earlier ruling that the Leon County plan was intended to be the same as the revised *Escambia* plan approved after modifications by the Fifth Circuit Court in 1962. "Basic structural changes" in the Leon County desegregation plan were unnecessary, the judge ruled on 19 April 1965, "to guarantee the full Constitutional rights of plaintiffs and the class they represent." In effect, Carswell made it plain that he would ignore new developments in the law and would wait for each case to be reversed by a higher court. He did not have long to wait. Plantiffs' attorneys in the *Steele* case immediately appealed the judge's ruling to the Fifth Circuit Court of Appeals, which reversed Carswell's decision in 1967.[5]

Meanwhile, school districts across Florida found themselves obliged to implement HEW's guidelines by fall 1965. In general, counties were required to offer a free-choice desegregation plan under which parents could send their children to any school in the district unless the district had already established nonracial residential zoning. Full notice was to be provided to all parents.

As for the 1965–1966 school year, at least four grades had to be desegregated: the first grade, the first year of junior high school, and the first and last years of senior high school. Schools were to begin faculty desegregation as part of their compliance plan. Officials in all school districts were to file compliance reports showing, first, what they proposed to do and, second, that they had done it. As the new guidelines revealed, those counties required to submit desegregation plans were clearly subject to more stringent measures of compliance than those under federal court orders.

The effects of the new guidelines and the determination of the federal government to enforce them became clear on 14 May 1965, when HEW rejected the plans of thirty-seven Florida counties. The seventeen counties, including Leon, that were under a court order to desegregate were not affected by the new guidelines and received notice that they would continue to receive federal aid. Only Dade and Charlotte Counties in South Florida filed assurances that their schools were no longer segregated and were judged to be in compliance.

Superintendent Bailey accused the federal government of being more interested in "integration than education," but he and the impacted counties scrambled to revise and resubmit their desegregation plans to HEW. By the time school started in September 1965, three-fourths of Florida's forty-eight affected school districts had plans approved by the federal government.[6]

One month before school started in the fall of 1965, the *Tallahassee Democrat* reported that a total of thirty-two black students would be attending "white schools" during the 1965–1966 school year. Other school districts were desegregating at a similarly slow pace. In early 1966, the U.S. Commission on Civil Rights conducted a survey across the South and found that only 5 to 7 percent of black children in the South were attending integrated schools. The commission found that Florida had a better overall record (10 percent of black children were in desegregated schools) but that sixteen counties in the state (located primarily in the northwest section of the state) continued to operate totally segregated school systems even though their desegregation plans or court orders had been approved.[7]

The commission found that integration had been delayed because HEW had accepted lax freedom-of-choice plans, because federal court orders remained based on a "grade a year" integration, and because many black children were afraid to go to white schools. By the end of 1965, 25,000 black students (10 percent of the black student population) had attended schools with whites in Florida. Yet the state ranked fourth in black enrollment among the former states of the Confederacy, primarily because South Florida had a few large counties. Only Virginia, North Carolina, and Texas ranked higher.[8]

In Tallahassee, the struggle to desegregate the school system amounted to much more than formal court cases and implementation guidelines. Like all civil rights activities, it entailed compelling personal struggles. Fed up with the slow pace of desegregation in her hometown the year her son graduated from Leon High School, Christene Knowles decided to expand her family's battle against segregation into a community effort. In May 1965, Knowles walked into the school superintendent's office and demanded a large number of pupil placement forms. "You only have one child," superintendent Freeman Ashmore told her. "You don't need that many forms." "Superintendent Ashmore," Knowles replied, "are you denying me forms in this public office?" Embarrassed, the superintendent left his desk and returned with an armful of the documents. A black teacher who had witnessed the scene told her colleagues at Lincoln High School, "Christene has lost her mind."[9]

That same week, Knowles began her crusade. Armed with her typewriter and forms, and with the protection of her dog, she went from neighborhood to neighborhood, encouraging and helping parents to register their children for transfers to white schools. "I would call people that I knew in those areas, people were always congenial to me; if I were late to a meeting, they would wait because they knew I was coming. I just had my dog and I was frightened, but I always lived by the philosophy of Martin King. He said if you live on earth and you don't do anything, you're dead anyway. I did a lot of traveling at night. I took the time to explain to people what would happen. That is how we really began to integrate the schools of Leon County."[10]

Knowles extended her efforts to the legal battle over desegregation when she intervened as one of the thirty plaintiffs in the *Steele* case in the fall of 1966. Although the case was on appeal to the Fifth Circuit, the plaintiffs were back in district court on 15 September 1966 to request further changes in the county's desegregation plan. Judge Carswell ruled that he did not then have jurisdiction to make a basic change in the county's plan, but he ordered the school board to grant transfer applications to the thirty named students if the school to which they requested transfer was the one nearest their residence and if the transfer did not jeopardize the pupil-teacher ratio necessary to retain accreditation. The school board subsequently reviewed the thirty transfer requests and approved all but five.

NAACP leaders in Tallahassee charged that the thirty requests represented only a small number of the transfer applications filed. The fact that only 170 blacks (2 percent of black student population) were enrolled in white schools in Tallahassee in the fall of 1966 was testimony not only to white resistance but also to the weakness of HEW guidelines. "The legal system was the biggest impediment to integration; it was stacked against us. We had to fight the law with the law," Knowles later explained. "We never won on the state level, we won everything on appeal. That takes a long time. In Tallahassee, all the lawyers and judges got together and would wine and dine and decide what was what. A lot of times, I would hear what was going on from a black person who had heard them talking while serving the dinner. Leon County was a rotten system."[11]

While they waited for the Fifth Circuit Court of Appeals to rule on *Steele,* determined blacks kept up the pressure on the school board to explain why there was no student integration in over half of the county schools, why there was no faculty integration in any of the county schools, and why the quality of all-black schools was still substandard by comparison with that of all-white schools. In a petition to the school board in October 1965, a coalition of black parents demanded to know why certain transfers had been accepted and others had not, and they asked what criteria were being used to deny transfers. The parents accused the school board of "practicing discrimination in assigning pupils to the various Tallahassee schools" and charged that the school board understood "better than anyone" what effect its actions were having. Furthermore, the black parents concluded, if the board members were "bent on doing what is just and right with regard to ALL school age children, they would go beyond what a court ordered five years ago rather than wait until FORCED to do so." [12]

The school board made a standard and unacceptable reply to the angry black parents, many of whom began to picket the school board building and the homes of the superintendent and board chairman. At the same time, there continued to be demands for faster integration and relief from overcrowding in black schools. The board announced in the summer of 1966 that because of overcrowding, the entire sixth grade class at all-black Griffin Junior High School would be transferred to another all-black school, where portable classrooms would be set up. Angry parents asked HEW to determine why the school board, in light of recent federal regulations, would require the sixth graders to move to a school across town when a white elementary school was near Griffin.

During the fall of 1966, a group of black parents released a study on the "conditions in the Negro schools." Their investigation found that only 2 percent of Leon County's black students attended desegregated schools and that black schools were overcrowded, sometimes hazardous, and inadequately supplied. The school board refused to heed a subsequent petition signed by over 400 black parents that demanded remedial action. [13]

By November, blacks were fed up with the school board's apparent duplicity and the federal government's inaction. On 22 November 1966, Daisy Young, chairperson of the Educational Improvement Committee of the NAACP, announced that the organization, in conjunction with the ICC and the Tallahassee Ministerial Association, would cease picketing the home of W. T. Moore, chairman of the school board, and would instead prepare for a "school holiday." The three groups asked black parents to keep their children home from school on 28 and 29 November to protest the school board's refusal to integrate the public schools of Leon County and to improve conditions in the segregated black schools.[14]

Both FSU and FAMU students were encouraged by the *Flambeau* to come to one of the eleven "Freedom Schools" set up in black churches to teach those who would be going to school in church rather than in the Leon County schools. Kent Spriggs, a Harvard-trained white civil rights attorney who had only recently moved to the city, served as "superintendent" of the freedom schools.[15]

To get the word to all black families, the three sponsoring organizations sent out flyers announcing the boycott. Christene Knowles, a member of the NAACP's Educational Improvement Committee, rode through the black neighborhoods of Leon County proclaiming the importance of the boycott from a portable public address system attached to her car.

On 28 November, 73 percent of Leon County's black schoolchildren stayed home from school, costing the county some $20,000 in lost federal money. Only 88 students attended classes at Lincoln High School out of an enrollment of 867. Attendance among black students at some elementary schools was higher in part because of the difficulty of "getting the word out" in some of the rural areas of the county. On the second day of the boycott, despite the opposition of some black educators, 71 percent of the county's black students stayed away from school or attended one of the community's freedom schools.[16]

While the editors of the *Flambeau* praised the work of the black community and castigated the school board for its segregationist policies, the *Tallahassee Democrat* labeled the boycott "an exercise in truancy." Malcolm Johnson echoed the sentiments of many white Tallahasseeans: "We thought Leon County was doing pretty well at desegregation. But apparently for the sole sake of agitation, the NAACP succeeded in keeping several thousand Negro youngsters out of classrooms where they could be absorbing so much needed learning." On 29 November, the school board authorized its attorney to look into the possibility of bringing suit against the NAACP, its local president, Dan Speed, and Christene Knowles "for their conspiracy to decrease the amount of state funds to the Leon County schools." The board authorized the superintendent to prohibit Knowles from "harassing students and teachers in the various schools."[17]

Before any effects of the boycott could be measured, the Fifth Circuit Court of Appeals in December 1966 handed down one of the most important decisions affecting school desegregation in the South, *United States v. Jefferson County Board of Education.* In its opinion, the court specifically rejected the notion that the decision of the U.S. Supreme Court in *Brown* required not integration but only an end to enforced segregation. The court concluded that integration and desegregation meant one and the same thing under *Brown* and ruled that the nation's public school systems "had an absolute duty to integrate, to take affirmative action to reorganize school systems by integrating the students, faculty, facilities, and activities, wherever the effects of *de jure* segregation persist." [18]

The ruling ordered district courts to "give great weight" to the guidelines established by HEW when approving local school desegregation plans under their jurisdiction. The true test for any school desegregation plan, however, was to be whether it achieved substantial integration. "The clock has ticked the last tick for tokenism and delay in the name of 'deliberate speed,'" the court declared. The only school desegregation plan that meets constitutional standards "is one that works." If it did not meet such standards, the court ruled, "then it must be abandoned and a more effective plan adopted." [19]

In the course of its opinion, the court noted the obstacles presented by many freedom-of-choice, or pupil assignment, plans. It noted that "only Negroes of exceptional initiative and fortitude choose to attend white schools, and new construction and improvements at the Negro school plants attract no white students and yet diminish Negro motivation to transfer to white schools." In short, the court found that freedom-of-choice plans, while not unconstitutional, "must lead to a unitary, non-racial school system" or be replaced by another alternative such as a geographic attendance plan. School authorities were no longer charged with merely permitting token integration but had the "affirmative duty to break up historical patterns of segregated school facilities." Specifically, the judges ruled that overcrowding of schools (often cited in Leon County) was not a legitimate reason to avoid integration. [20]

The ramifications of the *Jefferson County* case were particularly significant in areas like Leon County that were operating under permissive court-ordered desegregation plans that did not meet the stricter HEW guidelines. The *Jefferson County* ruling established a uniform desegregation decree pertaining to all districts operating free-choice plans under court order in the Fifth Circuit. In other words, school districts in Alabama, Florida, Georgia, Louisiana, Mississippi, and Texas were now subject to the HEW guidelines. The decree spelled out how counties were to "disestablish all school segregation and to eliminate the effects of past racial discrimination in the operation of the school system." [21]

All grades were to be desegregated beginning with the 1967–1968 school year; faculty and staff were to be hired or reassigned without consideration of race; schools that were "heretofore maintained for Negro students" were to be "equalized" and were to be closed if equalization was not possible, with the students reassigned under a freedom-of-choice plan. Such plans were to be widely disseminated in the community, were to be available for all students, were to contain provisions for a first and second choice, and were to make provisions for transportation if necessary. Finally, all school services, activities, and programs were to be open to all students, with remedial programs provided to enable those "who have previously attended all-Negro schools to overcome past inadequacies in their education." District court judges were ordered to make few exceptions to the decree but were allowed in certain circumstances to "require something more, less or different." "However," the court warned, "that 'something different' should rarely, if ever, be less than what is contemplated by the HEW standards."[22]

On 18 January 1967, the Fifth Circuit Court of Appeals ruled that the Leon County pupil assignment plan failed "in a number of important respects to meet applicable standards" and was therefore constitutionally inadequate. The court remanded the case to the district court with orders that the county modify the existing plan to meet the *Jefferson County* standard. The court ruled that the school board should have the opportunity to demonstrate "the feasibility of a freedom of choice plan meeting the standards of *Jefferson*." But it also noted that the district court might find it desirable to hear arguments on the advantages of a "unitary plan based on zoning," or the kind of plan that had been requested from the district court since 1963.[23]

On 24 March 1967, the Leon County school board approved a freedom-of-choice plan to be administered by the district schools. The plan was almost identical to the one prescribed by the *Jefferson County* ruling. The plan was filed that day with the district court and was provided to the attorneys for the plaintiffs. One week later, Judge Carswell heard arguments relating to the plan, and on 19 April 1967, he approved the new freedom-of-choice plan with an additional requirement that students make both a first and a second choice of schools initially and a third choice if space was not available in the first two. Faculty and staff were to be assigned to Leon County schools without regard to race or color "except that race may be taken into account for the purpose of correcting the effect of the segregated assignment of teachers in the dual system."[24]

The 1967–1968 school year opened in Tallahassee and across Florida with more black children and white children attending school together than ever before. Statewide, 71 percent of all students (60 percent of elementary and 85 percent of junior and senior high school students) were attending integrated schools. The actual racial composition varied greatly, however, ranging from a token number of black pupils in some county schools to 40 or 50 percent in others.

Statistics also revealed a lingering pattern of segregation in some areas and schools, as well as the complexity of disestablishing the dual school system. For instance, 43 percent of Florida's black pupils in grades seven through twelve were still in totally segregated schools, while 93 percent of white pupils in grades seven through twelve were in "desegregated situations." The reason was that white students did not ask to be transferred to a "black" school, and many black students preferred to remain in the schools in their neighborhood where they had achieved a successful academic record.

Black parents were opposed, some vehemently, to the board's decision to close the traditional black schools and to scatter black children and faculty among the "white" schools. "When they closed all the small community schools," James Ford remembered, "they destroyed the infrastructure of that community. The school was the one and only cohesive force in the community that the people who lived in that community rallied around regardless of religion or anything. You took those kids and transported them twenty miles from home, you placed them in an environment alien to everything that they knew and stood for." When black schools closed, they got "rid of the principal at the school," who was the link between the larger community and the neighborhood, the person who kept parents, everybody, up to date on what was happening with voting and other matters of concern. After that when they came for help, Ford added, "no one was there." [25]

In January 1969, three recalcitrant counties in Florida were found ineligible to receive federal school funds, while six more were under investigation by HEW. The federal government recognized only five counties as fully desegregated. Still, James Campbell, Florida's associate commissioner of education, remarked that "in spite of some increased problems and difficulties—Florida may still be proud of its record of adjustment to the requirement of court decisions and the Civil Rights Act." [26]

14 Root and Branch

Leon County proceeded to desegregate its public schools under the freedom-of-choice plan approved by Carswell in 1967. The plan did not lead to substantial integration because the burden of compliance continued to fall on black children. Despite *Jefferson* and the complaints of black parents, the board still refused certain transfers because of "overcrowding."

A key problem with choice plans was residential segregation, particularly at the elementary and junior high levels, where it was considered most important for schools to be located in a child's or student's neighborhood. In some areas, black students clearly lived nearer a white school than a black one and should automatically have been assigned to it. But in other areas with a large concentration of black residents, children had to ask to leave their neighborhood and attend a more distant white school. No whites, of course, ever asked to attend a black school. But as long as school officials provided the means, however meager, for black students to attend the school of their choice, then according to the district court they were not preventing integration. Therein lies the problem with interpreting desegregation decisions of the higher courts before 1968.

Attorneys for the plaintiffs in the *Steele* case charged Carswell and the school board with token integration and accused them of deliberately trying to ignore the courts' directives. But to Graham Carothers of the Ausley law firm, who succeeded William O'Bryan as school board attorney in 1967, it would have been a "very dramatic, serious position" in regard to school desegregation to assume that "the Constitution of the United States requires anything more than the unrestricted right of a parent to choose where his or her child will attend school." If you assume that it does require more, Carothers said in 1993, "then what you are then compelled to substitute for that is that the Constitution of the United States requires the artificial forced mixing of racial or ethnic or national origin groups of students against the will of some of them."[1]

The school board had diligently followed the dictates of the district court, Carothers contended, and "there was never a circumstance in which Judge Carswell did not do what the Fifth Circuit told him to do." It was simply a matter of definition, he insisted; Carswell and the school board did not know what the court meant by "fully integrated."[2]

On 27 May 1968 the U.S. Supreme Court finally attempted to answer the question when it struck down a freedom-of-choice plan used to maintain segregated schools in a rural Virginia county (*Green v. County School Board of New Kent County, Virginia*). In an opinion that underscored and elaborated the Fifth Circuit's decision in *Jefferson County,* the Court ordered local school officials to "take whatever steps might be necessary to convert to a unitary system in which racial discrimination would be eliminated root and branch" from the public school system. "The burden on a school board today is to come forward with a desegregation plan that promises realistically to work and . . . to work now."[3]

To the dismay of many southerners, the highest Court had finally, and in no uncertain terms, taken the burden of initiating desegregation away from black parents and children and had placed it on local school boards. Although the Court did not say that freedom-of-choice plans would never work in *any case,* it insisted that school boards must provide positive, verifiable proof that their desegregation plans would ensure integration and not merely prevent segregation. The Court even provided alternatives to freedom-of-choice plans, such as geographical zoning, in areas where the plans were clearly not working.

For over ten years, southern judges, officials, politicians, and lawyers had interpreted *Brown II* to mean that school districts had only to make a "prompt and reasonable start" toward eliminating dual school systems. And without clear guidance from the Court as to what constituted "all deliberate speed" or "unequal education," or even as to what defined an integrated school system, they applied the most restrictive possible interpretation to the Court's opinions. The long years of delay, it seemed, were finally over.[4]

Shortly after the *Green* decision, litigants in the *Steele* case were back in district court to demand that the Leon County school board establish a unitary school system. Although it was not exactly clear what a unitary school system was, the plaintiffs had requested that the board shift to a system based on geographical attendance zones as early as 1965. In May 1969, despite the Court's directives in *Green,* the Leon County school board submitted a desegregation plan that retained freedom of choice at the county's elementary and junior high schools. Although black students by then accounted for only 35 percent of the total student enrollment, and despite the fact that four all-black elementary and junior high schools had closed in recent years, two elementary schools in Leon County were still 100 percent black, one was 98 percent black, and one was 95 percent black. One junior high was 95 percent black and one was 87 percent black.

According to the 1969 plan, the county's senior high schools were placed in geographical attendance zones. This step caused little consternation because there was no longer an all-black high school in the county. The board had voted two years earlier to convert Lincoln to an elementary school. Part of the reason for this decision was that despite renovations made after *Brown,* the black high school was not considered a facility modern enough for use with white students. Furthermore, school board members knew that white parents would resist sending their children to a school so closely identified with the black community. But for many blacks, Lincoln High School, despite its inequities, was the symbol of black education in Tallahassee, "an anchor to the community second only to the church." Now it was gone, and black students would be in the minority at Leon and in the county's two other new high schools. Consequently, white students would be spared much of the adjustment to integration.[5]

Pupil assignments aside, Leon County's new plan provided no quotas and no specifics as to how or when faculty integration would be achieved or how and when extracurricular activities and athletic programs would be further integrated, even though the ruling by the Fifth Circuit Court of Appeals in *Jefferson* had addressed both matters two years earlier and its mandates had later been reiterated by the Supreme Court. Nevertheless Judge Carswell approved the county's plan. One month later, on 27 June 1969, President Richard Nixon appointed him to the Fifth Circuit Court of Appeals.

Carswell's appointment incensed his detractors, including attorneys on the NAACP Legal Defense team, who accused the judge of "magnificent inaction" in his stewardship of school desegregation in the Northern District of Florida. Nevertheless, after a brief stint on the appellate court, Carswell was nominated by Nixon to the U.S. Supreme Court. At Carswell's nomination hearings in early 1970, Leroy Clark, NAACP senior attorney on the *Steele* case, testified that Carswell was the "most hostile Federal District Court judge I have ever appeared before with respect to civil rights matters." Clark accused Carswell of deliberately delaying litigation, of denying routine motions by plaintiffs' attorneys, and of being "insulting and hostile" to black lawyers.[6]

Charges such as Clark's that Carswell did everything he legally could to postpone integration in Tallahassee are "so ridiculous they make me laugh," said Graham Carothers in 1993. Carswell was "tougher on the defendant school board and more sensitive to what the plaintiffs asked him to do than you could ever imagine." In the end, Carswell was haunted by his past association with the Capital City Country Club as much as by his judicial record. The judge's membership in the "whites only" club proved to be a sore point in particular for several members of the Senate Judiciary Committee, despite the personal testimony of former governor LeRoy Collins and other distinguished Floridians in Carswell's defense. His nomination to the Supreme Court was defeated.[7]

Shortly after Carswell's appointment to the Fifth Circuit in 1969, this court upheld an appeal by school districts in Mississippi for a further delay in school desegregation to avoid "chaos, confusion and a catastrophic educational set back." Although the decision reflected the Nixon administration's new "southern strategy," it outraged the U.S. Supreme Court. In *Alexander v. Holmes County Board of Education*, the Court reversed the Fifth Circuit's order and issued this stern directive: "Under explicit holding of this Court, the obligation of every school district is to terminate dual school systems at once and to operate now and hereafter only unitary schools." *Alexander* was remanded to the Fifth Circuit, where integration had to be ordered for all school districts in litigation under its auspices.[8]

On 12 December 1969, after reversing three of Judge Carswell's previous desegregation rulings in the Northern District, the Fifth Circuit Court overturned Carswell's final decision in the *Steele* case and ordered Leon County to establish a "unitary school system . . . within which no person is to be effectively excluded from any school because of race or color." The school board was ordered to submit a plan for complete student and faculty desegregation by 1 February 1970. After some frantic last-minute negotiations and appeals by the governor, education associations, and parents of both races, the appellate court authorized a delay of pupil desegregation until September 1970 so as not to disrupt the school year further.[9]

As soon as the final order was entered by the district court, the school board did turn, as suggested by the court, to the Florida School Desegregation Center at the University of Miami to help prepare a new desegregation plan. The Miami Center, one of many federally funded regional desegregation centers across the South, was established to help school boards implement and adjust to the courts' directives and to help shift the responsibility of desegregation to an outside source. There is ample evidence to suggest that the center's recommendations, the board's willingness to follow them, and the court's decision to wait until the fall of 1970 rather than integrate in the middle of the school year helped defuse some of the hostility toward the final desegregation decision.

On 30 January 1970, the U.S. District Court for the Northern District of Florida ordered the Leon County school board to desegregate faculty, other staff, and transportation by 1 February and to follow the plan prepared by the Florida School Desegregation Center to complete student desegregation by September 1970. The board was to allow schools to follow a "minority transfer policy" so that students could transfer from a school where their race was a majority to any school within the system where students of their race were a minority. "It should be made abundantly clear to all that no longer shall any child be denied the right to attend a particular school simply on the basis of his race, color or creed," wrote U.S. district judge David Middlebrooks. "This court is of the opinion that implementation of a plan for a unitary system can be effected at this time without a mass transfer and shift of students." The next day Superintendent Ashmore, weary but relieved, told the board staff, "I don't want you to tell me why it can't be done, we have to make some plans to get it done."[10]

It took Leon County sixteen years after the *Brown* decision and eight years after the filing of *Steele* in district court to adopt a unitary school system. As with other civil rights issues, the desegregation of the county's schools was resisted, stalled, circumvented, and bitterly fought, but in the end, when there were no other options, the white community surrendered peacefully.

Because the final desegregation plan had been drawn up by the Florida School Desegregation Center in Miami and not by the school board, individual board members were spared some community opprobrium. Desegregation experts from the desegregation center and from both Florida State and Florida A&M Universities helped smooth the transition to an integrated school system, but the school board staff, in collaboration with parent advisory groups, redrew the county's attendance zones. It was a painstaking and at times acrimonious process, remembered Sterling Bryant, the former assistant superintendent of instruction, who after fifteen years as a Leon County teacher and principal was in charge of faculty desegregation for the district. For the most part, he noted, the community was finally ready to "make it work."[11]

Implementation of the plan eliminated the all-black schools, although five of the county's twenty-nine schools remained approximately 50 percent black two years later. In the spring of 1970, after years of debate over the cost of remodeling the forty-year-old structure, the school board voted to close Lincoln Elementary School. After an outcry from the black community, U.S. district court judge David Middlebrooks ordered an architectural review to appraise the condition of the school to determine whether it was safe for occupancy. On 31 July 1970, the court-appointed architects reported that one part of the facility was unsafe and another part required "prohibitively" expensive renovations. Consequently, Judge Middlebrooks ruled that the school should be shut down. Later, board chairman Ernest Menendez concluded that "the school should have been closed two years earlier, even though it is honest to say that integration required that such a decision be made now." Despite the architectural review, many blacks remained incensed over the architects' recommendation that Lincoln be converted into a community center with the help of federal funds. "If Lincoln is so unsafe that it can't be used for a school," exclaimed Reverend R. N. Gooden, "how can it be safe for a community center? They seem to think we're nothing but nuts over here." Despite black demands that a new school be built near or in the Lincoln area, black children were reassigned to two white schools. Because the distance from the farthest point in the old Lincoln zone to both schools was one-tenth of a mile less than two miles, the board determined that buses were not needed to take Lincoln's pupils to either Ruediger or Sullivan.[12]

Despite the inevitable conflicts over school assignments, zones, and bus routes, students and parents of both races adjusted to integration far more easily than state and local leaders had predicted in the tumultuous years after *Brown*. Of course Leon County had experienced some integration since 1963, and the community, state, and nation had weathered and accepted monumental changes in race relations in the years leading up to the final desegregation plan.

While students at Leon, Godby, and Rickards High Schools experienced various racial conflicts, usually at extracurricular events, the human relations councils and biracial committees at each school helped alleviate most disturbances. But they could not eradicate the alienation that many black high school students felt in the midst of the predominantly white culture at the city's three high schools, particularly at Leon, where 27 percent of the assigned student population was black in the fall of 1970. In contrast, at Rickards High School in southwest Leon County, where a greater number of black and poor white families lived, black students composed 41 percent of the student population. Attempts to redraw the zone lines between the two schools to provide for greater racial balance were met by fierce resistance from white parents in the Leon school district. Despite overwhelming pressure, criticism, and initial confusion, school board staff pursued a very hands-on approach to desegregation in all of the county schools and both encouraged and insisted that parents do the same. Before school started in the fall of 1970, open houses were held at all public schools so that parents could meet teachers and staff. School board headquarters remained open the night before school started so that last-minute questions about zones or transportation could be answered.

Some whites, believing that integration would undermine the quality of education in the county, enrolled their children in private schools, three of which were built in the late 1960s. In August 1970, one month before classes began in the county's first unitary school system, the *Democrat* reported that the public schools were losing approximately 1,800 students to the city's three major independent schools, "the loss of more than a whole school of pupils." But the withdrawal of these students only reduced overcrowding in the schools, Superintendent Freeman Ashmore recalled in 1972, and rid the system of "all the dyed-in-the-wool segregationists." At least some white parents became less hostile to the idea of sending their children to formerly black elementary and junior high schools once they visited the facilities, met teachers and staff, and became involved in the parent-teacher association.[13]

Yet it quickly became evident that the plan would never achieve racial balance in some areas, because it was based—except for the majority-to-minority transfer policy—on residential zoning. Elementary schools in the inner-city area remained heavily black, particularly after the bitterly fought decision to build low-income housing projects in the Frenchtown area. They were also the schools, even when the zones were redrawn, that were drained by "white flight" to private schools and to other neighborhoods. Because the overall black student population in Leon County was slightly more than one-third, and because so much of it was concentrated in particular neighborhoods, residential segregation impeded desegregation more than any other factor.

The court-ordered desegregation plan set faculty and staff desegregation at a ratio of about 70 percent white and 30 percent black. Although the school board had refused to address faculty and staff desegregation adequately in its earlier plans, some faculty integration occurred after several black schools had been shut down in the mid to late 1960s. While most displaced black teachers had been transferred to other black schools, some were sent to positions at the board office, and a small number were transferred to predominantly white schools. Once meaningful faculty desegregation began, teachers and administrators attended workshops designed to foster communication and cooperation between black educators and white educators and to develop positive attitudes toward integration. Those workshops and other events sponsored by FSU and FAMU helped create a more harmonious, collegial educational environment.

Because the board had hired black staff before the final implementation decision, some of the problems related to faculty and staff transfer were less intractable than they might have been. Sterling Bryant and his staff worked "day and night" in the months after the final court decree to ensure that "come hell or high water," no teachers, black or white, were displaced by the plan. Bryant had developed a positive rapport with both black and white teachers during his tenure in the county schools and tried to implement a teacher transfer policy based first on volunteers and then on criteria such as length of service, experience in integrated classrooms, and willingness to attend staff development and in-service education provided by the desegregation center as well as by FSU and FAMU. Still, there were a few white principals who resisted the new faculty racial quotas and even a few who chose early retirement rather than face the new era.[14]

Despite efforts to be fair, recalled Aquilina Howell, there was a conscious attempt to transfer those black teachers "who would be more acceptable to the white community." Understandably, some black teachers remained bitter over the county's "criteria" for faculty assignment. It was a selection process, they charged, that robbed the black schools of their best and brightest and sent the newest and least skilled white teachers into the historically black schools. But not all teacher assignment was so blatantly arbitrary. Many young "liberal" white teachers volunteered for transfer to black schools, while many seasoned white teachers protested their reassignment for reasons other than race. While blacks resented losing experienced teachers, they wanted the best of their ranks to be among the first faculties to be integrated, particularly at Leon and Kate Sullivan schools, where racist attitudes about black qualifications would be most intense.

Faculty reassignment achieved racial quotas mandated by the court, and with the help of the ad hoc committee, no teacher was assigned to a position more than one grade above or below the previous year's assignment. Despite this policy, numbers of black teachers did leave the profession. In 1971, the Florida Education Association reported that over a three-year period, Leon County was one of ten Florida counties with the greatest overall loss in the number of black teachers. Many of them "left voluntarily," the report concluded, while others had been "pushed aside."[15]

The negative consequences of dismantling the dual school system included the closing of black schools and the displacing and demoting of black principals. Like black children and black teachers, black principals paid the biggest price in righting the wrong that had been done to them. Lack of equal employment opportunities for displaced black principals was widespread across the South. Florida was no exception. In hearings before the U.S. Senate Select Committee on Equal Educational Opportunity in 1971, testimony revealed that 27 percent of the state's black principals had lost their jobs in 1970. Gilbert Porter, former executive secretary of the Florida State Teachers Association, reported that the number of black high school principals dropped from 102 to 13 between 1965 and 1971.[16]

In December of 1972, the U.S. Commission on Civil Rights investigated Leon County as part of a report on school desegregation in communities across the South. While noting the community's "lengthy resistance to integration" and some of the problems resulting from faculty transfers, the report concluded on an optimistic note: "Leon County's relative success in desegregating its schools does not appear accidental, but rather the result of determined efforts by administrators, teachers, and parents both black and white. School staffs in Leon County were integrated without the displacement of black professionals that has marred the implementation of desegregation in many other cities."[17]

Despite the commission's assessment, the "implementation of desegregation" had taken its toll on black professionals in Leon County. Beginning in 1967, the closing of black schools cost many black principals, administrators, and coaches their jobs. For instance, when Lincoln High School closed in 1967, principal Freeman Lawrence, who held one of the most respected jobs in the black community, was transferred to Griffin Junior High School as principal. He later moved to a position in the board office. Herman Landers, the principal of Griffin, was transferred to Lincoln, which had been converted to an elementary school. When all-black Raney Junior High closed in 1968, Principal Willie Gardner became assistant principal at Griffin Junior High. George Williams, principal at Station One Junior High, was transferred to Concord Elementary School when his school closed in 1968. Concord Elementary, which was also all black, merged with a white rural school and finally closed in 1985. Fairfield Anderson, the principal of Lake McBride Elementary School until it closed in 1969, became assistant principal at all-black Nims Junior High School. James Ford, who had been principal of both Barrow Hill Elementary School, which closed in 1968, and Concord, was transferred to the board office in 1968. In 1971 he became assistant principal at Leon High School, the first black administrator in the county to be placed in a formerly all-white school. Although many whites considered Ford's appointment an honor, the former principal considered it "a necessity. Technically it was a demotion because now, I don't share in the knowledge of activities that govern education in the county. I'm in a subservient position when it comes to that kind of knowledge. When they had principals' meetings, [I] didn't go."[18]

The experience of black athletic coaches was much the same. In 1972, there were three integrated public high schools in Leon County, none of which had a black head coach for its major sports programs.[19]

Although Florida in general compared favorably with other southern states that experienced upheaval and violence during the long desegregation process, Leon County fought school integration as tenaciously as any community in Florida. The area was spared some of the worst excesses of racial demagoguery, thanks in large measure to the early stewardship of LeRoy Collins, but it never lacked leaders who fueled and exploited its worst fears and most deep-seated prejudices.

We may well wonder whether the schools in Leon County, indeed throughout Florida, would have desegregated earlier with less strife and with greater acceptance if there had been less resistance, fewer dire predictions, and less mean-spiritedness from those in positions to influence, shape, and lead public opinion and values. Despite the many impediments to progress, the forces of change eventually took root in Leon County, and the parochial, guarded nature of Tallahassee and its environs reluctantly yielded to their influences. As a result, the community accepted and incorporated ideas once antithetical to its very foundation.

Tallahassee's adjustment to an integrated school system took longer, and was in most ways harder, than the earlier struggles to desegregate restaurants, theaters, beaches, pools, and buses. But the change, when it finally came, was the most profound, the most difficult, and the most lasting. In the end, school desegregation affected the entire community on a personal, daily basis. It was the last frontier of the black struggle for civil rights. Never again would the barriers to black equality be as apparent, the battles to be won as clear-cut, the evils of racism as lucid.

From the beginning, school segregation had cost the county and state millions of dollars. It also distracted and at times consumed elected officials, obscured important community concerns, drained the human and financial resources of the school system, condemned thousands of black children to an inferior education, and destroyed much of their community's educational heritage. At the same time it instilled prejudice and fear in the hearts of white children that no law or court order could completely erase.

But in September 1970, as the yellow school buses rumbled down the roads of Leon County, from the dusty unpaved streets of Chaires, through the tall timbered forests of Woodville, over the oak-lined, winding roads of Miccosukee, and onto the new asphalt highways of Tallahassee, it became clearer that a great battle had been won. And for the 26,000 blacks in this Florida community, a new decade, full of new possibilities and opportunities, had finally arrived.

Afterword

Reflecting on forty years of life in this city since the 1956 bus boycott, Daisy Young observed, "In spite of the gains that we have made in Tallahassee and throughout Florida, we have not arrived." After four decades of protests, litigation, court rulings, and desegregation, race still clearly matters in Tallahassee. Segregation may have been destroyed, but racism, as C. K. Steele noted in 1978, has in many ways just gone underground.[1]

From the early days of civil rights protest in Tallahassee, Steele saw the connection between segregation and other types of oppression, including economic inequality. Beginning in the late 1950s, he and other civil rights leaders picketed, boycotted, and bargained with business owners in Tallahassee to hire and promote blacks. Results were not very encouraging in this small town where the government was the main employer. Blacks did have money to spend and to deposit, however, and Steele continued to insist that the wholesale withdrawal of patronage from a business could be used as a lever to promote more equitable hiring policies.

Steele's economic strategy worked best when supported by a total community effort. But this unity seldom materialized because, like whites, blacks in Tallahassee were stratified along class lines. Despite their common experience of racial oppression, blacks often found that class lines undermined racial unity. Residents of the FAMU community, professors who worked for the university, state government employees, and other black professionals had little in common economically with the semiskilled, undereducated, lower-income blacks living in Frenchtown or in the county's rural areas. Black leaders found it harder to create a coalition for effective economic protest than they had in many of the civil rights battles in the 1950s and 1960s. Yet despite the growing disparity in status and fortune between middle- and lower-class blacks, a sense of continuation, if not continuity, characterized the push for racial equality in the post-movement years.

In the late 1960s, the Elberta Crate and Box Company was representative of workplaces in which employees were mostly black. It employed unskilled labor at low wages and afforded unsafe working conditions. Owned by former Tallahassee mayor Jack Simmons (the father-in-law of federal judge Harrold Carswell), the factory, locally notorious for its primitive working conditions, produced ammunition crates for shipment to Vietnam. In September 1969, more than 500 black workers at the plants in Tallahassee and Bainbridge, Georgia, struck for better wages, safer working conditions, and retirement and insurance benefits. According to the International Woodworkers Union, the base pay for the workers was $1.60 an hour, the federal minimum wage.

Almost immediately the strikers were supported by a contingent of FSU students, mostly white, who marched and picketed at the Tallahassee plant. Some were members of Students for a Democratic Society; others, the Tallahassee Coalition for Labor. On 14 October, C. K. Steele led a racially mixed group of supporters from Bethel Baptist Church to the capitol to demand that the state's Human Relations Commission intervene on behalf of the strikers. That afternoon, SCLC's Hosea Williams joined the protest and called on blacks to boycott white stores and to continue to march and demonstrate until workers' demands were met.

Meanwhile the crate company went to court seeking an injunction against the union and students, who, it claimed, had intimidated nonstriking workers. Circuit court judge Ben Willis granted the injunction, but the protests continued. On 30 October, Steele led another, larger group of marchers to the capitol in support of the workers and promised a massive march for 17 November in support of "raising the living wage of black workers everywhere." Five days later, workers returned to their jobs with higher wages and additional benefits.[2]

As in the past, blacks used a variety of tactics to fight wage and employment discrimination. In 1974, after years of protests over the failure of the city government to employ and promote minorities, local blacks asked the federal government to come to their aid. In the same year, the U.S. Justice Department sued the city of Tallahassee for work-related race discrimination. The government charged the city with engaging "in a pattern or practice of discrimination based on race in hiring . . . in violation of Title VII of the Civil Rights Act of 1964." On 10 April 1975, the U.S. District Court for the Northern District of Florida ordered the city to "hire, assign, promote, transfer and dismiss employees without regard to race or color." The city was directed to conform its employment policies to provisions set by the Equal Employment Opportunity Commission, and the court set out specific goals to be met by the city in order to "achieve the goal of employing a proportion of black employees in each job classification approximately the proportion in the civilian labor force."[3]

Originally, the court was to retain jurisdiction over the city's employment actions for five years, but in 1980, the court extended its jurisdiction to another three years because the city had not yet reached a percentage in black hiring commensurate with the minority population. In December 1982, the city moved for a dissolution of the decree, and the court agreed that the objectives had been achieved. Sixteen years later, 34 percent of all city employees were black, while blacks comprised 19 percent of the city's top-level administrative positions in 1998.

On the political front, in 1966, for the first time since Reconstruction, four blacks were elected as Democratic Party committeemen from Leon County. But until 1971, no blacks had been elected to serve in any city or countywide office, including the school board and both city and county commissions. Finally, in the same year, James Ford, the vice principal at Leon High School, became the first black elected to the city commission. Ford's main opponent in the four-person ballot group two citywide race was incumbent W. H. Cates, who had served four terms on the commission.

Before the primary, the *Tallahassee Democrat* described Ford as a "mature Negro of several generations background in Tallahassee and concern for the general welfare of his community. We are impressed that he may be the best qualified Negro ever to offer for public office in Tallahassee. We would expect him to serve, if elected, as a proper representative of his racial minority without antagonistic attitudes toward the majority that might result in more frustration and discord than genuine advancement of either racial justice or community betterment." Running for a seat on the commission in ballot group one, Raleigh Jugger Jr., another black candidate, did not fare as well in the *Democrat*. "An intense Negro student leader of the Malcolm X Liberation Front," the editors wrote, "with interests too narrow for representation of all the people, and perhaps not even broad enough for his own race."[4]

Despite the fact that two blacks were running in a citywide race, only 43 percent of registered voters came to the polls. Ford made it into a runoff with Cates, and Jugger came in a distant but surprising third in a field of six candidates. Ford said he had made it clear that "he was not running as a black candidate but in a desire to represent all citizens." His campaign was centered around a variety of issues "that white folks cared about," Ford recalled. "If you are going to get elected, that's what you have to do." Indeed, many of Ford's backers were white liberals from FSU and from the small contingent of townspeople who belonged to the Tallahassee Good Government Association, the Liberal Forum, and the Tallahassee Council on Human Relations.[5]

"Every politician knows the 'silent vote' is a weak crutch to lean on because it seldom finds its voice on election day," Malcolm Johnson wrote after the primary, "but when you're a black candidate in a town where eighty-one percent of the voters are white, it's about the only prop for your hope." Despite Johnson's forecast that Ford "didn't have much chance" of unseating Cates, Tallahassee woke up to its first black commissioner on 24 February 1971. Ford defeated Cates by 895 votes.[6]

The "winds of change blow through old city hall," announced the *Democrat*, noting not just Ford's victory but that of a white environmentalist who had defeated incumbent commissioner George Taff. But Ford was only one black on the five-person commission, and true to his word, he sought to serve his entire constituency, focusing on issues as diverse as government consolidation, the city's need for a civic center, and improved recreation facilities for children in black neighborhoods. Throughout Ford's four terms on the commission, some blacks criticized him for being insensitive to the needs of his people particularly when it came to city hiring policies. "There are moments when I've felt abandoned by blacks or that blacks were not being fair to me," Ford told a reporter in 1975. "I think it's because they couldn't understand some of the things I've done or the reasons. . . . I can't always jump in and push for something. I have to assess the commission's mood and the timing."[7]

Ford remained Tallahassee's lone black city commissioner until 1984. The first black county commissioner was not elected until 1986, and it was 1990 before the first black school board member was elected in a regular election. Part of the difficulty for black candidates was that blacks composed less than 30 percent of the electorate, and all city and county elections were at large. A number of blacks ran for office—C. K. Steele was defeated in a school board race in 1972—but not until a successful NAACP suit led to single-member districts for school board and county commission seats were blacks elected to those offices. The first black county commissioner, FAMU dean Henry Lewis, was elected in 1986.

Even though blacks were elected in the new single-member districts, they were not immune from the frustrations that dogged James Ford. Curtis Richardson, the first black elected to the school board after the NAACP suit, was in office for only four years before residents of his district accused him of not doing enough for the south-side schools he represented, which were predominantly black and poor white. Richardson defended his record of helping to improve specific schools, but like Ford, he insisted that he had to look at what was best for "an entire school system."[8]

Although there were moves to create single-member districts for the city commission, the offices remained at large. In 1984, Jack McLean, a liberal black attorney with a wide cross section of community support, defeated a well-financed conservative black candidate who was backed by the chamber of commerce and some well-heeled developers. A few other blacks have been elected to the city commission since 1984, leading some to dispute the need for single-member districts to ensure minority participation at the local level.

By 1970, as Tallahassee began its adjustment to a single public school system, integration at Florida State was no longer an anomaly. In 1962, the first black undergraduate enrolled at the university, and two black graduate students did so as well. Over the next few years, the number of blacks slowly increased. The first black FSU students included Phillip Hadley, who enrolled after graduating from Leon High School in 1965, and Jane Marks, the daughter of K. S. Dupont, one of the leaders of the bus boycott. All of the first black students at Florida State endured harassment, intimidation, and loneliness. "We were, in effect, the sacrificial lambs," one early graduate remembered. But the campus, while not congenial, was not violent, and some faculty, campus ministers, administrators, and white students helped ease the transition to integration. By 1970, there were 396 black students enrolled at the 13,000-student university. One of them was Harold Knowles, who had returned to Tallahassee from DePauw University. Knowles was elected vice president of the black student union. Established in 1968, the organization was the first of its kind in Florida and one of the first in the Southeast. In the same year, the faculty senate established a recruitment program to increase the number of black students on campus. It worked. Between 1968 and 1970, black enrollment increased 500 percent.[9]

On 20 January 1970, thirty-five black students set up a barricade in a classroom building at Florida State University and demanded a meeting with university president Stanley Marshall. For twelve hours the students took over the exits, the elevator, and the sixth floor. The meeting was held the next morning at 5:30. Dissatisfied with Marshall's response to their demands for black professors, coaches, administrators, doctors, and specific services, the students met six days later with a more sympathetic faculty senate, which agreed to intervene on their behalf.

By 1971, after several demonstrations relating to antiwar protests, women's liberation, and black power, the national press had taken to calling FSU "the Berkeley of the South." In the same year, hundreds of black students marched to Marshall's office with additional grievances. The president addressed the students, who left only when FAMU officials arrived and warned them that adverse publicity could hinder Florida A&M's fight against merger with the predominantly white university. According to black student union president John Burt, the students then marched to Florida A&M, where they were heckled and called "Toms." While not all demands were met, Florida State University did respond to many of the black students' grievances. In 1972, the university became the third in the nation to set up an affirmative action program. In the same year, a black assistant basketball coach was hired and more black professors. Twenty-five years later, 11 percent of Florida State University students and 6 percent of faculty are black.[10]

Florida A&M University remains at the center of black life in Tallahassee as it has since 1887. Threats to merge FAMU with FSU were finally defeated during the administration of Gore's successor, Benjamin Perry. The loss of the FAMU Law School continues to rankle blacks, and there is some legislative support for establishing a new law school at the historically black institution.[11]

Throughout the 1970s, FAMU struggled to overcome the inequities of the past while maintaining an "open door" admissions policy that kept entry-level test scores and graduation rates at the bottom of the state university system. Stricter admissions qualifications and academic standards led to a decline in enrollment in the late 1970s and early 1980s. In 1985, under a new administration, Florida A&M embarked upon a campaign to raise academic standards, increase enrollment, and secure corporate sponsorship for new programs and facilities.

In 1992, Florida A&M attracted more black National Merit Scholars than Harvard University. Since then, the university has remained a favorite school of black National Merit Scholars. Enrollment doubled from 1985 to 1994, and the university now has the largest private endowment of any historically black public university. Although FAMU was first integrated in 1966, it remains a predominantly black institution. Despite a statewide mandate from the board of regents to diversify student enrollment at each of the ten state universities, FAMU's student body is 89 percent black.[12]

How can the effects of the civil rights movement best be measured? One

Notes

Abbreviations

FAMU   Florida Agricultural and Mechanical University
FLIC   Florida Legislative Investigation Committee
ICC   Inter-Civic Council
NAACP National Association for the Advancement of Colored People
FSU   Florida State University

Introduction

1. Key, *Southern Politics in State and Nation,* 83.

2. Fairclough, *Race and Democracy,* xii–xv.

3. M. S. Thomas, interview with the author, 16 June 1981, Tallahassee, Florida.

4. George W. Conoly, interview with Jackson Ice, 9 July 1978, Oral History of the Civil Rights Movement, Special Collections Department, Florida State University Libraries, Tallahassee, Florida. Richard Haley, "Statement to CORE-SEDF on Patricia Stephens Due," Congress of Racial Equality Papers, 1941–1967, microfilm ed., series (s) 5, "Departments and Related Organizations, 1946–1979," group "Local Chapters," file 332, "Florida, Tallahassee, July 1960–November 21, 1963, n.d.," at Florida State University Libraries, Tallahassee, Florida.

5. Chafe, *Civilities and Civil Rights.*

Chapter 1. A Long, Long Step Toward Victory

1. Wilhelmina Jakes Street, telephone interview with the author, 8 September 1993.

2. Ibid.

3. The title "executive secretary" was later changed to "field director." Robert Saunders, interview with the author, 26 June 1981, Tampa, Florida.

4. Saunders, interview with the author.

5. Poore, "Striking the First Blow," is the most complete account of the NAACP leader's life; see also Florida Department of Law Enforcement, Investigative Summary, FDLE CASE EI-91-25-016, Harry T. Moore, 24 March 1992, Tallahassee, Florida. The case was last reinvestigated in 1992. *Tallahassee Democrat*, 26, 27 December 1951. The results of the initial investigation are contained in Correspondence of Governor Fuller Warren, 1949–1953, FDLE CASE EI-91-25-016, series 235, boxes 63, 64, 65, Florida Archives, Tallahassee, Florida. Letters from Florida and throughout the United States are included along with telegrams and notification of protests related to Moore's murder and investigation.

6. James Hudson, interview with Jackson Ice, Oral History of the Civil Rights Movement, 15 July 1978.

7. J. Metz Rollins, interview with the author, 27 May 1981, Tallahassee, Florida; *Tallahassee Democrat*, 29 May 1956.

8. Eugene Morris, "Woman's Bus Ride Launched City Boycott," *Tallahassee Democrat*, 15 January 1990.

9. In April 1956, the U.S. Supreme Court had affirmed a federal appellate court ruling striking down segregated seating on the municipal buses of Columbia, South Carolina. Editorial, *Tallahassee Democrat*, 29 May 1956.

10. Tallahassee City Ordinance 741 (section 4), Correspondence of Governor LeRoy Collins, series 776, box 116, folder "Race Relations, 1957," Florida Archives, Tallahassee, Florida.

11. Rollins, interview with the author.

12. C. K. Steele, interview with Jackson Ice, 26 January 1978, Oral History of the Civil Rights Movement; Saunders, interview with the author. M. S. Thomas, interview with the author, 16 July 1981, Tallahassee, Florida.

13. Malcolm B. Johnson, interview with Jackson Ice, 12 July 1978, Oral History of the Civil Rights Movement.

14. Steele, interview with Jackson Ice, 16 February 1978.

15. King Solomon Dupont, interview with Jackson Ice, 21 July 1978, Oral History of the Civil Rights Movement.

16. Branch, *Parting the Waters*, 160; *Tallahassee Democrat*, 31 May 1956; Steele, interview with Jackson Ice, 26 January 1978.

17. *Tallahassee Democrat*, 30 May 1956; Steele, interview with Jackson Ice, 26 January 1978.

18. *Tallahassee Democrat*, 30, 31 May 1956; "ICC Diary," 1, City Exhibit 1, in *City of Tallahassee v. Inter-Civic Council*, Law No. 8502 (1957).

19. Editorial, *Tallahassee Democrat*, 30 May 1956; *Tallahassee Democrat*, 31 May 1956.

20. *Tallahassee Democrat*, 31 May 1956.

21. *Tallahassee Democrat*, 3 June 1956.

22. Ibid.

23. Ibid.; Steele, interview with Jackson Ice, 26 January 1978; Meiklejohn, "Company Wants to Halt Bus Run," *Tallahassee Democrat*, 4 June 1956.

24. Meiklejohn, "Company Wants to Halt Bus Run."

25. Ibid.; Steele, interview with Jackson Ice, 26 January 1978; Branch, *Parting the Waters,* 188; Gilliam, "The Montgomery Bus Boycott," 261–262.

26. *Tallahassee Democrat,* 4 June 1956.

27. Editorial, *Tallahassee Democrat,* 4 June 1956.

28. *Tallahasee Democrat,* 7 June 1956.

Chapter 2. To Walk in Dignity

1. William T. Mayo, interview with the author, 14 August 1981, Tallahassee, Florida.

2. M. S. Thomas, interview with the author.

3. Steele, interview with Jackson Ice, 26 January 1978; Conoly, interview with Jackson Ice; Killian and Smith, "Negro Protest Leaders," 250–257. The authors did not mention the leaders by name in the article; they did so only in the survey.

4. *Afro-American,* 16 June 1956.

5. Editorial, *Tallahassee Democrat,* 17 June 1956.

6. *Tallahassee Democrat,* 20 June 1956.

7. "ICC Diary," 2; Editorial, *Tallahassee Democrat,* 27 June 1956; Don Meiklejohn, "Glimmer of Hope Dawns in Negro Bus Boycott," *Tallahassee Democrat,* 26 June 1956.

8. *Tallahassee Democrat,* 26 June 1956.

9. Ibid. (quotation of Rollins); Steele, interview with Jackson Ice; Robert Saunders, "The Tallahassee Bus Protest Story," speech, in Robert and Helen Saunders Papers, series 1, box 5, folder 8, 1–6, Special Collections Department, University of South Florida Library, Tampa Campus.

10. Laura Dixie, interview with author, 30 July 1981, Tallahassee, Florida.

11. "ICC Diary," 2; *Tallahassee Democrat,* 30 June 1956; King Solomon Dupont, interview with Jackson Ice, 21 July 1978, Oral History of the Civil Rights Movement; *Tallahassee Democrat,* 30 June 1956, 1 July 1956.

12. "A Confidential Report," in Governor LeRoy Collins's Papers, Race Relations, 1955–58, box 139, Special Collections Department, University of South Florida Library, Tampa Campus.

13. Ibid., 1–2.

14. Ibid., 7–8.

15. Ibid., 2–5.

16. Ibid., 10–17.

17. Ibid., 5–7, 19–33.

18. Ibid., 14–15, 17–18.

19. Editorial, *Orlando Sentinel,* quoted in *Florida Flambeau,* 6 July 1956.

20. *Tallahassee Democrat,* 9 July 1956.

21. "ICC Diary," 3.

22. *Tallahassee Democrat,* 9 July 1956.

23. Steele, interview with Jackson Ice, 26 January 1978; "ICC Diary," 2.

24. *Tallahassee Democrat,* 10 July 1956; Tallahassee City Commission Minutes, special meeting, 10 July 1956.

25. *Tallahassee Democrat,* 19 July 1956.

26. *Tallahassee Democrat,* 7, 9 July 1956.

27. *Tallahassee Democrat,* 18, 22, 23 July 1956; Colburn and Scher, *Florida's Gubernatorial Politics,* 225.

28. Chap. 29746, Laws of Florida (1956), 302–305; *Tallahassee Democrat,* 24, 25, 27, 30 July 1956.

29. Street, telephone interview with author.

30. Colburn and Scher, *Florida's Gubernatorial Politics,* 75–76; David R. Colburn, "Florida's Governors Confront Brown," in Hall and Ely, *An Uncertain Tradition,* 326–354; Collins, interview with Jackson Ice; Wagy, *Governor LeRoy Collins of Florida,* 1–2, 74–75, 201–204; Statement of Governor LeRoy Collins, 2 July 1956, Correspondence of Governor LeRoy Collins, series 776, box 33, folder "Race Relations Statements"; *Tallahassee Democrat,* 9 July 1956; "ICC Diary," 2.

31. *Tallahassee Democrat,* 30 June 1956.

32. Ibid.

33. Ibid.; Editorial, *Tallahassee Democrat,* 16 August 1956.

34. *Tallahassee Democrat,* 2 August 1956; "ICC Diary," 2.

35. Edward Irons, interview with the author, 28 May 1981, Tallahassee, Florida.

36. *Tallahassee Democrat,* 27 August 1956; Padgett, "Steele and the Bus Boycott," 53.

37. Steele, interview with Jackson Ice, 26 January 1978; *Tallahassee Democrat,* 3 September 1956.

38. John W. Riley, interview with the author, 17 November 1982, Tallahassee, Florida.

39. Hudson, interview with Jackson Ice; *Tallahassee Democrat,* 20 September 1956; *Tallahassee Democrat,* 20 September 1956.

40. *Tallahassee Democrat,* 20 September 1956.

41. Irons, interview with the author; Emmett W. Bashful, interview with the author, 26 May 1981, Tallahassee, Florida.

42. This point has been corroborated by both black and white Tallahasseeans involved in the city's civil rights movement.

43. Rollins, interview with author.

44. Conoly, interview with Jackson Ice; Hudson, interview with Jackson Ice; Russell Anderson, interview with Jackson Ice, 28 June 1978, Oral History of the Civil Rights Movement.

45. Padgett, "Steele and the Bus Boycott," 96.

46. "Informant's Memorandum Reports," 31 July–2 September 1956, Correspondence of Governor LeRoy Collins, series 776, box 33, folder "Race Relations, July–December 1956." These anonymous reports appear in the correspondence of Governor LeRoy Collins, Florida Archives, Tallahassee, Florida. "A Confidential Report," written by Detective R. J. Strickland, appears in Collins's Papers in the Special Collections Department of the University of South Florida Library, Tampa Campus.

47. "A Memorandum Report," in "A Confidential Report," 9.

48. "Informant's Memorandum Reports," 26 August 1956, 29 August 1956.

49. Ibid., 8, 12, 19, 22, 26, August 1956; Gilliam, "The Montgomery Bus Boycott," 233.

50. "Informant's Memorandum Reports," 2 September 1956; 22, 26 August 1956.

51. *Tallahassee Democrat,* 18 October 1956.

52. *Afro-American,* 3 November 1956.

53. *Tallahassee Democrat,* 21 October 1956; *Afro-American,* 27 October 1956, 11 November 1956.

54. *Afro-American,* 3 November 1956; *Tallahassee Democrat,* 22 October 1956; Tallahassee City Commission Minutes, 23 October 1956.

55. Gilliam, "The Montgomery Bus Boycott," 274–275.

56. *Afro-American,* 3 November 1956.

57. Steele, interview with Jackson Ice, 26 January 1978.

Chapter 3. In the Wake of the Boycott

1. *Tallahassee Democrat,* 28 December 1956; Notes on the Meeting of the Bi-Racial Commission, 20 November 1956, Correspondence of Governor LeRoy Collins, series 776, box 33, folder "Race Relations, Governor's Advisory Commission." The Commission went through several reorganizations from 1956 to 1960. It was first known as the Fabisinski Committee, then as the Governor's Advisory Commission on Bi-Racial Problems, and finally as the Advisory Commission on Race Relations to Governor LeRoy Collins. In 1960, a new entity, The Governor's Commission on Race Relations, was created. *Tallahassee Democrat,* 4, 23 December 1956.

2. *Tallahassee Democrat,* 23, 24 December 1956.

3. *Tallahassee Democrat,* 24 December 1956; Steele, interview with Jackson Ice, 26 January 1978; Rollins, interview with the author.

4. *Tallahassee Democrat,* 27, 28 December 1956, 1 January 1957; Steele interview with Jackson Ice, 26 January 1978; Lois Brock Steele, interview with author, 23 November 1982, Tallahassee, Florida.

5. Lois B. Steele, interview with author; Steele, interview with Jackson Ice, 26 January 1978.

6. *Proclamation of Governor,* 1 January 1957, Correspondence of Governor LeRoy Collins, series 776, box 33, folder "Race Relations Statements"; *Tallahassee Democrat,* 1 January 1957.

7. *Tallahassee Democrat,* 5 January 1957; Collins, interview with Jackson Ice; LeRoy Collins, Opening Address, Silver Anniversary of the Tallahassee Bus Boycott, Florida A&M University, 27 May 1981; Editorial, *Tallahassee Democrat,* 2 January 1957; *Tallahassee Democrat,* 2 January 1957; *St. Petersburg Times,* 3 January 1957; *Tampa Tribune,* 3 January 1957.

8. *Tallahassee Democrat,* 3 January 1957, Steele, interview with Jackson Ice, 26 January 1978; Editorial, *Tallahassee Democrat,* 3 January 1957.

9. *Tallahassee Democrat,* 7, 8, 10 January 1957; 2 Race Relations Law Reporter (1957) at 460; "Ordinance No. 741," Correspondence of Governor LeRoy Collins, series 746, box 116, folder "Race Relations."

10. Collins, interview with Jackson Ice.

11. LeRoy Collins, interview with the author, 24 May 1983, Tallahassee, Florida; *Tallahassee Democrat,* 8 January 1957.

12. *Tallahassee Democrat,* 8 January 1957.

13. Ibid.

14. Editorial, *Tallahassee Democrat,* 8 January 1957.

15. Statement of Governor LeRoy Collins, 11 January 1957, Correspondence of Governor LeRoy Collins, series 776, box 116, folder "Race Relations"; *Tallahassee Democrat,* 11 January 1957.

16. *Tallahassee Democrat,* 17, 18 January 1957.

17. Editorial, *Tallahassee Democrat,* 18 January 1957.

18. *Tallahassee Democrat,* 18 January 1957, Steele interview with Jackson Ice, 26 January 1978.

19. *Tallahassee Democrat,* 9 February 1957.

20. "Transcript of Testimony, 18 February 1957," FLIC, series 1486, box 4, folder 29.

21. Ibid.

22. *City of Tallahassee v. Joseph Spagna, Leonard D. Speed and Johnny Herndon,* Law No. 8581 (1957).

23. *Tallahassee Democrat,* 4 March 1957; *City of Tallahassee v. Spagna, Speed, Herndon,* 2 Race Relations Law Reporter (1957) at 459.

24. Minutes of the Meeting(s) of the Governor's Advisory Commission on Bi-Racial Problems, 29 January 1957, 5 March 1957, Correspondence of Governor LeRoy Collins, series 776, box 117, folder "Race Relations, Governor's Advisory Commission."

25. *Tallahassee Democrat,* 10 April 1958.

26. Editorial, *Tallahassee Democrat,* 11 April 1958; *St. Augustine Record,* 10 April 1958; *St. Petersburg Times,* 10 April 1958.

27. *Tallahassee Democrat,* 17 February 1957; "Progress Report, 17 January 1957," FLIC, series 1486, box 1, folder 21; "Report to the Legislature."

28. *Tallahassee Democrat,* 18 February 1957; "Transcript of Testimony," 18 February 1957, FLIC, series 1486, box 4, folder 29.

29. "Transcript of Testimony, 18 February 1957," FLIC, series 1486, box 4, folder 29.

30. *Tallahassee Democrat,* 18 February 1957, "Transcript of Testimony, 18 February 1957," FLIC, series 1486, box 4, folder 29.

31. "Transcript of Testimony, 18 February 1957," FLIC, series 1486, box 4, folder 29.

32. *Tallahassee Democrat,* 7 February 1957.

33. *Tallahassee Democrat,* 24 February 1957.

34. Editorial, *Tallahassee Democrat,* 25 February 1957.

35. *Tallahassee Democrat,* 7, 26, 27 February 1957; Editorial, *Tallahassee Democrat,* 27 February 1957.

36. Editorial, *Tallahassee Democrat,* 27 February 1957.

37. *Tallahassee Democrat,* 22, 26 January 1957.

38. *Tallahassee Democrat,* 21 January 1957.

39. Minutes of Governor's Advisory Commission on Bi-Racial Problems, 29 January 1957, Correspondence of Governor LeRoy Collins, series 776, box 117, folder "Race Relations-Governor's Advisory Committee."

40. Ibid.

41. Program of the Institute of Non-Violence and Social Change, 26–31 May 1957, FLIC, series 1486, box 17, folder 46; "Inter-Civic Council of Tallahassee," *Tallahassee Democrat*, 27 May 1956.

Chapter 4. Race, Retrenchment, and Red-Baiting

1. Chap. 57–125, *Laws of Florida; Tallahassee Democrat*, 7 February 1958.

2. *Tallahassee Democrat*, 21 August 1956.

3. *St. Petersburg Times*, 8 February 1958; *Tampa Tribune*, 8 February 1958; *Tampa Tribune*, 8 February 1958.

4. *Tallahassee Democrat*, 10 February 1958; Oshinsky, *A Conspiracy So Immense*, 318, 319; *Tallahassee Democrat*, 10 February 1958; *Tampa Tribune*, 13 February 1958; Caxton Doggett to James Shaw (n.d.), in the private papers of James Shaw.

5. Walter Goodman, *The Committee* (New York, 1964), cited in Oshinsky, *A Conspiracy So Immense*, 118; *Tallahassee Democrat*, 10 February 1958; Johns, Charley, "Communist Penetration and Influence on Organizations Operating in the South and the State of Florida"; "Transcript of Testimony (Sylvia Crouch), 11 February 1958," FLIC, series 1486, box 4, folder 29.

6. "Transcript of Testimony (James Shaw), 11 February 1958," FLIC, series 1486, box 4, folder 29.

7. Ibid.; James Shaw, interview with the author, 11 November 1982, Tallahassee, Florida; "Transcript of Testimony (James Shaw), 11 February 1957," FLIC, series 1486, box 4, folder 29.

8. "Transcript of Testimony (James Shaw), 11 February 1957."

9. *Tampa Tribune*, 12, 13 February 1958.

10. *St. Petersburg Times*, 12 February 1958; *Tampa Tribune*, 13 February 1958; J. S. Shaw, telegram to William Tompkins, Assistant Attorney General, 13 February 1958; Tompkins to Shaw, 19 February 1958, in Shaw's private papers; Editorial, *Tallahassee Democrat*, 12 February 1958; Editorial, *Tampa Tribune*, 13 February 1958.

11. Mabel Norris Reese, Florida Council on Human Relations, to Hon. William G. O'Neill, 26 May 1961, FLIC, series 1486, box 12, folder 98, "Florida Council on Human Relations."

12. Lillian Shaw correspondence with the author, 15 May 1994.

13. FLIC, Progress Report, 17 January 1957, FLIC, series 1486, box 1, folder 29.

14. *Florida Times Union*, 12 February 1958; Stark, "McCarthyism in Florida," 36–37.

15. Robert Saunders to Roy W. Wilkins, 6 November 1959, Robert and Helen Saunders Papers, series 1, box 1, folder 5; *Gibson v. FLIC*, 8 Race Relations Law Reporter (1963) at 20–21; "Resolution on Communism Adopted at the Forty-second Annual

Convention of the NAACP," 30 June 1951, "Reaffirmation of Anti-Communist Resolution," 28 June 1952, FLIC, series 1486, box 14, folder 28; "Florida Supreme Court—*Gibson et al. v. FLIC*," 1 of 2 files.

16. *FLIC v. Theodore R. Gibson*, Case No. 16820 (1960), FLIC, series 1486, box 14, folder 28; "*Gibson v. FLIC*"; *Gibson v. FLIC*, 108 So. 2d 729 (1958); "Statement to Be Made by Father Gibson," 27 July 1960, FLIC, series 1486, box 14, folder 28.

17. *FLIC v. Gibson*, No. 16820; FLIC series 1486, box 14, folder 28; "*Gibson v. FLIC*"; *Gibson v. FLIC*, 108 So. 2d 729 (1958); 126 So. 2d 129 at 131 (1960).

18. Report of the FLIC to the 1959 Legislature, part 2, FLIC, series 1486, box 1, folder 2.

19. Chap. 61–62, *Laws of Florida* (vol. 1); chap. 63–545, *Laws of Florida* (vol. 1).

20. Report of the FLIC to the 1961 Session of the Legislature, FLIC, series 1486, box 1, folder 29; Stark, "McCarthyism in Florida," 81.

21. Report of the FLIC to the 1959 and 1961 Session(s) of the Legislature, FLIC, series 1486, box 1, folder "Report to the Legislature"; George W. Gore to Charley Johns (n.d.); R. J. Strickland to George W. Gore, 10 February 1962; George W. Gore to R. J. Strickland, 15 February 1962, FLIC, series 1486, box 13, folder "Florida Agricultural and Mechanical University"; Superintendent Amos Godby to Charley Johns, 15 November 1961, FLIC, series 1486, box 2, folder "Correspondence Files: November 1961–1965"; *St. Petersburg Times*, 2 July 1993; Report from the FLIC to the State Board of Control and State Board of Education, Investigation of University of South Florida, August 1962, FLIC, series 1486, box 1, folder "Report to the State Board of Control Regarding the University of South Florida."

22. LeRoy Collins, "How It Looks from the South," *Look*, 27 May 1958, 95–97.

23. Governor's Statement, 28 September 1956, Correspondence of Governor LeRoy Collins, series 776, box 33, folder "Race Relations Statements"; Collins, interview with the author; *Tallahassee Democrat*, 12, 13 October 1956; Editorial, *Tallahassee Democrat*, 12 October 1956.

24. *Presbyterian Outlook* 139:38 (28 October 1957), in Governor LeRoy Collins Papers, box 47, "Speeches, Addresses, Messages"; Collins, interview with the author.

25. Collins was apparently unaware that at least three people had lost their jobs in Madison because they supported Dr. Coggins; the individuals included a Presbyterian minister and the editor of the local newspaper, who was a deacon in the Presbyterian Church. *Outlook*, 7, 14 January 1957; Collins, "How It Looks from the South," 95–97.

26. *Tallahassee Democrat*, 2 September 1952.

27. *Tallahassee Democrat*, 11 January 1956.

28. Ibid.

29. *Tallahassee Democrat*, 15 February 1956; Minutes of the Tallahassee City Commission, 14 February 1956; *Tallahassee Democrat*, 15 February 1956.

30. Carswell drafted the club's articles of incorporation but asked that his name be withdrawn from membership in the club on 12 February 1957. See "Testimony of Julian Proctor," in U.S. Senate, Committee on the Judiciary, *George Harrold Carswell*, 258 (hereinafter cited as *Carswell Hearings*). Charles U. Smith, "Return City's Golf Course to Its Original Owners," *Tallahassee Democrat*, 16 October 1989.

31. *Tallahassee Democrat,* 3 May 1959.

32. *Tallahassee Democrat,* 6 May 1959.

33. Roy Wilkins to LeRoy Collins, 6 May 1959, Correspondence of Governor LeRoy Collins, series 776, box 117, folder "Race Relations-Leon County Incident"; Statement by Governor LeRoy Collins, 15 June 1959, Correspondence of Governor LeRoy Collins, series 776, box 117, folder "Race Relations, Leon County Incident."

34. *Tallahassee Democrat,* 15 December 1955; Lawson, Colburn, and Paulson, "Groveland: Florida's Little Scottsboro," *Florida Historical Quarterly* 65 (July 1986): 1–26; Wagy, *Governor LeRoy Collins of Florida,* 65–68.

35. *Tallahassee Democrat,* 14, 15 June 1959.

36. *Tallahassee Democrat,* 22 June 1959; *St. Petersburg Times,* 23 June 1959.

37. *St. Petersburg Times,* 23 June 1959; *Tampa Tribune,* 23 June 1959.

38. *Tallahassee Democrat,* 29 June 1959.

39. *Tallahassee Democrat,* 2 May 1959.

40. Ibid.

Chapter 5. The Sit-Ins Begin

1. Patricia Stephens Due, interview with the author, 23 June 1981, Miami, Florida; White, "The Tallahassee Sit-Ins," 75–77; Robert M. White, telephone interview with author, 9 September 1994; "NOTICE" (n.d. 1957?), in FLIC, series 1486, box 19, folder 13, "Students and Universities."

2. Richard Haley, "Informal Report on Tallahassee CORE, October 1959 to June 1960," 11 June 1960, 2, Congress of Racial Equality Papers, 5:29.

3. Ibid.; Due, interview with the author, 23 June 1981.

4. Haley, "Informal Report," 2, Congress of Racial Equality Papers, 5:29.

5. Ibid.

6. Meier and Rudwick, *CORE,* 102–103.

7. Due, interview with the author; Stephens, "Tallahassee: Through Jail to Freedom," 74.

8. Due, interview with the author, 23 June 1981; *Henry M. Steele et al. v. City of Tallahassee,* Law No. 9627 (1960).

9. Steele, interview with Jackson Ice, 26 January 1978.

10. Haley, "Informal Report," 3, Congress of Racial Equality Papers, 5:29.

11. Haley, "Informal Report," 3, 5, Congress of Racial Equality Papers, 5:29.

12. [Collins] Press Conference Transcript, 3 March 1960, Governor LeRoy Collins Papers, box 424, "Research and Clippings, various."

13. Editorial, *Tallahassee Democrat,* 4 March 1960.

14. Due, interview with the author, 23 June 1981.

15. Ibid.; Haley, "Informal Report," 3; *Tallahassee Democrat,* 13 March 1960; White, "The Tallahassee Sit-Ins," 122.

16. Roger K. Steinhauer, "Challenge and Risk: The Story of Canterbury House," typescript, n.d., copy in unmarked boxes, Ruge Hall, Tallahassee, Florida.

17. Ibid., Killian, *Black and White,* 105; Killian, taped correspondence with Jackson

Ice; Clifton Lewis, interview with Jackson Ice, 23 July 1978, Oral History of the Civil Rights Movement.

18. Oscar (Bob) Brock, telephone interview with the author, 22 September 1994.

19. The Mayor of Tallahassee is chosen annually from among the city commissioners and by them. Brock, telephone interview with the author.

20. Ibid.; *Tallahassee Democrat,* 13 March 1960; Due, "Tallahassee: Through Jail to Freedom," 77.

21. *Florida Flambeau,* 15 March 1960.

22. *Tallahassee Democrat,* 13 March 1960; Haley, "Informal Report," 3; Patricia Stephens to James Robinson, n.d., Congress of Racial Equality Papers, 5:29.

23. Due, interview with the author, 23 June 1981; White, "The Tallahassee Sit-Ins," 124–125.

24. Due, interview with the author, 23 June 1981; *Tallahassee Democrat,* 13 March 1960; *Florida Flambeau,* 15 March 1960; Patricia Stephens to James Robinson, n.d., Congress of Racial Equality Papers, 5:29.

25. Brock, telephone interview with the author.

26. Virginia Delavan, correspondence with the author, 2 October 1994; Delavan, "Editor and Friends Land in Jail for Talking to Negroes," *Florida Flambeau,* 15 March 1960; Due, interview with the author, 23 June 1981; Georgiana Fry Vines, correspondence with the author, 9 November 1994.

27. Haley, "Informal Report," 4, Congress of Racial Equality Papers, 5:29; C. U. Smith, interview with Jackson Ice.

28. *Florida Flambeau,* 15 March 1960; *Tallahassee Democrat,* 13 March 1960; Editorial, *Tallahassee Democrat,* 14 March 1960.

29. *Florida Flambeau,* 15 March 1960; Delavan, "Editor and Friends Land in Jail."

30. Delavan, "Editor and Friends Land in Jail"; Delavan correspondence with author.

31. *Tallahassee Democrat,* 13 March 1960; White, "The Tallahassee Sit-Ins," 128.

32. Financial Report, 3 May 1960, Congress of Racial Equality Papers, 5:29. The report revealed that as of 7 March 1960, there was $168.05 in the CORE account in the Lewis State Bank; see Congress of Racial Equality Papers, 5:29. James Robinson to Richard Haley, 28 March 1960, Congress of Racial Equality Papers, 5:29; *Tallahassee Democrat,* 14 March 1960.

33. *Tallahassee Democrat,* 14, 17 March 1960.

34. *Tallahassee Democrat,* 15 March 1960.

35. *Tallahassee Democrat,* 15, 17 March 1960.

36. *Tallahassee Democrat,* 18 March 1960; Delavan, correspondence with the author; *Florida Flambeau,* 18, 22 March 1960; *Free Flambeau,* 21 March 1960, Congress of Racial Equality Papers, 5:29, "Local Chapters."

37. *Florida Flambeau,* 18 March 1960; *Tallahassee Democrat,* 16 March 1960.

38. *Tallahassee Democrat,* 15 March 1960.

39. Report of the FLIC to the 1961 Session of the Legislature, FLIC, series 1486, box 1, folder 29.

40. Anne Braden to Jim Robinson, Gordon Carey, and Marvin Rich, 12 May 1960,

Congress of Racial Equality Papers, 5:226, "Miscellany"; James Robinson to Anne Braden, 14 May 1960, Congress of Racial Equality Papers, 5:226; Anne Braden to Jim Robinson, Gordon Carey, and Marvin Rich, 12 May 1960, Congress of Racial Equality Papers, 5:226.

41. Steele, interview with Jackson Ice, 26 January 1978; Paul Piccard, interview with Jackson Ice, 31 July 1978, Oral History of the Civil Rights Movement; Killian, *Black and White*, 112.

42. Haley, "Informal Report," 6, Congress of Racial Equality Papers, 5:29; White, "The Tallahassee Sit-Ins," 132–134; Killian, taped correspondence with Jackson Ice; Steele, interview with Jackson Ice, 26 January 1978.

43. Killian, taped correspondence with Jackson Ice.

44. Ibid.; Collins, interview with the author.

45. Killian, taped correspondence with Jackson Ice.

46. Haley, "Informal Report," 7–8, Congress of Racial Equality Papers, 5:29; Killian, interview with the author, 17 February 1983.

47. Haley, "Informal Report," 7–8, Congress of Racial Equality Papers, 5:29; White, "The Tallahassee Sit-Ins," 130–132.

48. *Tallahassee Democrat*, 20 March 1960.

49. *Tallahassee Democrat*, 17 March 1960; Howard Dixon, interview with the author, 24 June 1981, Miami, Florida; *Tallahassee Democrat*, 18 March 1960; Patricia Stephens to James Robinson, [?] March 1960, Congress of Racial Equality Papers, 5:29.

50. *Tallahassee Democrat*, 18 March 1960.

51. Ibid.

52. This action delighted national CORE officials and put Tallahassee in the spotlight of civil rights activities. Stephens to Robinson, 19 April 1960, Congress of Racial Equality Papers, 5:29.

53. Barbara Joan Broxton, "Jailhouse Notes," *Southern Patriot* 18:5 (May 1960): 1–3; Due, interview with the author, 23 June 1981.

54. Due, interview with the author, 23 June 1981; Robinson to Mr. and Mrs. Hamilton, 3 April 1960, Congress of Racial Equality Papers, 5:29.

55. Broxton, "Jailhouse Notes," 3; Stephens, "Tallahassee: Through Jail to Freedom," 78–79; Henry Steele, interview with the author, 23 November 1982, Tallahassee, Florida.

56. Martin Luther King Jr. to the eight jailed students, 19 March 1960, in the private papers of Patricia Stephens Due.

57. Stephens to Robinson, 18 April 1960, Congress of Racial Equality Papers, 5:29.

58. Broxton, "Jailhouse Notes," 3.

59. Robinson to Stephens, 19 April 1960, Congress of Racial Equality Papers, 5:29; Stephens to Marvin Rich, 29 April 1960, Congress of Racial Equality Papers, 5:29.

60. "Text of Collins Address," *Miami Daily News*, 21 March 1960.

61. Ibid.

62. Ibid.

63. Ibid.

1. Robert Strozier to LeRoy Collins, 20 March 1960, Governor Leroy Collins Papers, box 45, "Race Relations, Reaction to 3/20/60 speech favorable, R–S"; Wayne Reitz to LeRoy Collins, 21 March 1960, box 44; LeRoy Collins to James Hudson, 12 April 1960, box 43; Doris and Irving Van Brunt to LeRoy Collins, 22 March 1960, box 46. Letters favorable to the governor's speech are arranged alphabetically in boxes 40–46. Letters unfavorable are in box 47.

2. *Tallahassee Democrat,* 21 March 1960.

3. James R. Robinson to Patricia Stephens, 28 March 1960, in the private papers of Patricia Stephens Due; Marvin Rich to "Dear Friend," 21 March 1960, Congress of Racial Equality Papers, 5:29.

4. *Miami Daily News,* 21 March 1960; *Florida Times Union,* 21 March 1960.

5. *Tallahassee Democrat,* 21 March 1960; Collins, interviews with the author and with Jackson Ice; Executive Committee of the Tallahassee Council on Human Relations to Fellow Faculty Members, 19 March 1960, Malcolm Johnson Papers, box 609, folder D21, "Civil Rights," Special Collections Department, Florida State University Libraries, Tallahassee, Florida; *Tallahassee Democrat,* 21 March 1960.

6. Wagy, *Governor LeRoy Collins of Florida,* 139–143. The Florida Democratic Party was already deeply divided over the reapportionment battle in the legislature and was further fragmented by Collins's moderate racial views. See Wagy, 104–119.

7. Richard Haley to Gordon Carey, 15 June 1960; Len Holt to Robinson, 10 May 1960; "Reasons for and Against Sit-Ins" (n.d.), Congress of Racial Equality Papers, 5:29.

8. *Tallahassee Democrat,* 22, 25 March 1960.

9. Haley to Carey, 15 June 1960, Congress of Racial Equality Papers, 5:29.

10. Holt to Robinson, 10 May 1960, Congress of Racial Equality Papers, 5:29.

11. Minutes of the Florida Board of Control, 25 March 1960, Florida Archives, Tallahassee, Florida; George W. Gore to James Hudson, 28 March 1960, James Hudson Papers, Black Archives, Florida A&M University, Tallahassee, Florida.

12. Editorial, *Tallahassee Democrat,* 28 March 1960; "Chronology of Demonstrations," Governor LeRoy Collins Papers, series 756, box 117, folder "Race Relations, Governor's Advisory Commission."

13. Lillian Shaw, interview with the author, 11 November 1982, Tallahassee, Florida.

14. Killian, taped correspondence with Jackson Ice.

15. *Tallahassee Democrat,* 15 April 1960; *Florida Flambeau,* 22 April 1960.

16. Killian, *Black and White,* 116; Killian, taped correspondence with Jackson Ice; *Tallahassee Democrat,* 15 April 1960.

17. *Florida Flambeau,* 22 April 1960.

18. Killian, *Black and White,* 116–117.

19. Killian, taped correspondence with Jackson Ice.

20. Haley to Carey, 14 October 1960, Congress of Racial Equality Papers, 5:29.

21. White, "Tallahassee Sit-Ins," 145.

22. Tallahassee City Commission Minutes, 10 May 1960, 162.

23. *Tallahassee Democrat*, 1, 3, 9, 16, 24 May 1960; *St. Petersburg Times*, 23, 24 May 1960.

24. Wagy, *Governor LeRoy Collins of Florida*, 141; *St. Petersburg Times*, 24 May 1960; Bartley and Graham, *Southern Elections*, 59; Collins, interview with the author; *Tallahassee Democrat*, 25 May 1960.

25. Rich to Stephens, 5 May 1960, Congress of Racial Equality Papers, 5:29.

26. "Five CORE members Released from Jail," CORE press release, 6 May 1960, Congress of Racial Equality Papers, 5:130, "Public Accommodations: Variety Store Projects"; White, "The Tallahassee Sit-Ins," 146; Due, interview with the author, 23 June 1981.

27. *Tallahassee Democrat*, 6 May 1960.

28. *Tallahassee Democrat*, 8 May 1960.

29. Ibid.

30. Ibid.

31. Ibid.

32. *Florida Flambeau*, 10 May 1960; *FAMUAN*, 27 May 1960; *Robert K. Armstrong et al. v. City of Tallahassee*, Law No. 9675 (1960). The writ of certiorari was denied (365 U.S. 834) as it was for *Steele*, the companion case. *Tallahassee Democrat*, 12 May 1960.

33. *Florida Flambeau*, 10 May 1960; Killian, *Black and White*, 110; Brock, telephone interview with the author.

34. *Tallahassee Democrat*, 8 May 1960.

35. Congress of Racial Equality Papers, 5:29, are filled with press releases, news articles, schedules, and personal correspondence related to the speaking tour.

36. William Larkins to Rich, 17 June 1960, Congress of Racial Equality Papers ("Assistant to National Director's File, 1942–1965"), 2:27 ("Larkins, William H").

37. Robert White to Gordon Carey, 2 July 1960; Carey to William Larkins, 28 June 1960, Congress of Racial Equality Papers, 5:29; Due, interview with the author, 23 June 1981; *Black Dispatch*, 10 June 1960, in Congress of Racial Equality Papers, 5:29; Carey to Larkins, 28 June 1960; Larkins to [?], 23 June 1960, Congress of Racial Equality Papers, 5:29.

38. Tallahassee CORE, financial report, 3 May 1960, 9 May 1960, 8 August 1960; Rich to Daisy Young, 16 August 1960, Congress of Racial Equality Papers, 5:29; White, "The Tallahassee Sit-Ins," 151; Robert Armstrong to Carey, 2 July 1960, Congress of Racial Equality Papers, 5:29.

39. *FAMUAN*, 27 May 1960. Miles noted that Haley's selection was "not in keeping with criteria for awards." Tallahassee CORE, press release, 1 June 1960, Sit-Down News Letter (CORE), 7 June 1960, both in private papers of Patricia Stephens Due; *CORE-LATOR* 82 (June 1960), Congress of Racial Equality Papers, 6:1; George W. Gore to Warren C. Middleton, 23 November 1960; Middleton to Gore, 30 November 1960; Middleton to Haley, 30 November 1960, Congress of Racial Equality Papers, 5:29.

40. Riley, interview with the author; Summary of Meeting Held 4 June 1960, Correspondence of Governor LeRoy Collins, series 756, box 117, folder 3, "Governor's Commission on Race Relations."

41. *CORE of the Matter* 1:1 (July 1960), copy in Congress of Racial Equality Papers, 5:29; Robert W. Saunders to Haley, 11 November 1960, Congress of Racial Equality Papers, 5:250; "Haley, Richard, August 5, 1960–October 16, 1966."

42. Richard Haley, "The Present Situation: A Report to Tallahassee CORE," 14 October 1960, in Congress of Racial Equality Papers, 5:250.

43. White to Carey, 2 July 1960, Congress of Racial Equality Papers, 5:29; Carey to Young, 10 June 1960; Carey to White, 20 July 1960; *Chicago Daily Defender,* 6 June 1960; 11 June 1960, in Congress of Racial Equality Papers, 5:29; White to Carey, 9 June 1960, Congress of Racial Equality, 5:29.

44. Carey to Young, 10 June 1960, Congress of Racial Equality Papers, 5:29.

45. Larkins to Carey, 10 November 1960, Congress of Racial Equality Papers, 5:29; *CORE of the Matter* 1:1 (July 1960), in Congress of Racial Equality Papers, 5:29.

46. "Statement by Cody Fowler, Chairman, Governor's Commission on Race Relations," 27 May 1960, Governor LeRoy Collins Papers, series 756, box 117, folder 2, "Race Relations, Governor's Advisory Commission."

47. Cody Fowler, Chairman of the Commission on Race Relations, memorandum, 17 October 1960, in Saul A. Silverman to Malcolm Johnson, Malcolm Johnson Papers, file D21, box 609, "Civil Rights."

48. Davis Thomas, interview with the author, 6 October 1992, Tallahassee, Florida.

49. Larkins to Carey, 10 November 1960, Congress of Racial Equality Papers, 5:29; Carey to Larkins, [?] November 1960, Congress of Racial Equality Papers, 5:29; Larkins to Carey, 10 November 1960, Congress of Racial Equality Papers, 5:29; Haley to Carey, 14 October 1960; "The Present Situation," Congress of Racial Equality Papers, 5:250.

50. Gordon Blackwell correspondence with the author, 3 April 1986.

51. Ibid.

52. Carey to Rolf Knauer, 2 November 1960, Congress of Racial Equality Papers, 5:29; Carey to Haley, 11 December 1960, Congress of Racial Equality Papers, 5:250; Haley to Stephens, 20 October 1960, Congress of Racial Equality Papers, 5:29; Haley, "The Present Situation"; Haley to Carey, 14 October 1960, Congress of Racial Equality Papers, 5:250.

53. Minutes of the initial meeting of the Tallahassee Committee of the Florida Legislative Project, 1 October 1960, Congress of Racial Equality Papers, 5:29; Due, interview with the author, 23 June 1981.

54. *Tallahassee Democrat,* 7, 8 December 1960; Frank Trippet, "Mean Look," *St. Petersburg Times,* 8 December 1960; Saul A. Silverman to Bill Durden, "Summary of the Picket Incidents in Tallahassee on December 6, 7, and 8, 1960," Correspondence of Governor LeRoy Collins, series 756, box 117, folder 2, "Race Relations, Governor's Advisory Commission"; Trippet, *St. Petersburg Times,* 8 December 1960.

55. U.S. Commission on Civil Rights, *The Fifty States Report.*

1. Evans, *Time for Florida; Tallahassee Democrat*, 3 January 1961.

2. Farris Bryant to Miriam B. Cohen, 7 September 1962, Evans to H. R. Edwards, 31 May 1962, both in Correspondence of Governor Farris Bryant, series 756, box 113, folder "Race Relations, 1962"; *Tallahassee Democrat*, 30 December 1960; Evans, *Time for Florida*; Bryant to Cohen; Correspondence of Governor Farris Bryant, series 756, box 113, folder "Race Relations, 1962."

3. William Larkins to Gordon Carey, 2 January 1961, Congress of Racial Equality Papers, 5:29.

4. Ibid.

5. *City of Tallahassee v. Benjamin F. Cowins, City of Tallahassee v. Patricia G. Stephens,* Laws No. 76569 and 76570; "A Statement of Facts Concerning the Outbreak of Violence at the Sit-In at Neisner's, March 4 1961," in personal papers of Patricia Stephens Due; *Tallahassee Democrat*, 5 March 1961.

6. *City of Tallahassee v. Cowins, City of Tallahassee v. Patricia Stephens,* Laws No. 76569 and 76570 (1961).

7. *Benjamin F. Cowins v. City of Tallahassee, Patricia G. Stephens v. City of Tallahassee,* "Appeal from Judgements and Sentences of Municipal Court of Tallahassee, Florida," Law No. 10017 (1961); Richard Haley to Marvin Rich, 11 December 1961, Congress of Racial Equality Papers, 5:250.

8. Haley to George W. Gore, 11 December 1961, Congress of Racial Equality Papers, 5:29.

9. Haley to Rich, 11 December 1961, Congress of Racial Equality Papers, 5:250; Haley to Samuel Adams, 11 December 1961, Congress of Racial Equality Papers, 5:250.

10. Haley to Carey, 17 November 1961, Congress of Racial Equality Papers, 5:29; Riley, interview with the author.

11. "Sour Grapes" (open letter), 4 November 1961, Congress of Racial Equality Papers, 5:29.

12. "Rights and Teachers" (open letter), Congress of Racial Equality Papers, 5:29.

13. Daisy Young, interview with the author, 6 June 1981, Tallahassee, Florida.

14. Haley to Tallahassee CORE, 11 November 1961, Congress of Racial Equality Papers, 5:29; Benjamin Cowins to James McCain, 6 November 1962, Congress of Racial Equality Papers, 5:332, "Tallahassee, Florida, July 1960–Nov. 21, 1963, n.d."

15. "A Plea from the Heart of Charles Kenzie Steele, Sr.," 26 May 1961, Congress of Racial Equality Papers, 5:332.

16. Poland to Anne Braden, 28 May 1961, Carey to McCain, 14 April 1961, press release, Tallahassee CORE, [n.d.], *CORE of the Matter*, 25 May 1961, Poland to Carey, 24 May 1961, all in Congress of Racial Equality Papers, 5:29.

17. Carey to Poland, 21 April 1961, Congress of Racial Equality Papers, 5:29; "Pledge to Fast on Fridays, Fast for Equality," 20 May 1961, Congress of Racial Equality Papers, 5:29; Jim Peck, "Freedom Ride," *CORE-LATOR* 89 (May 1961): 1–4; Meier and Rudwick, *CORE*, 136–140.

18. Ibid., 4–7; *CORE-LATOR*, 90 (June 1961): 1–2, Congress of Racial Equality Papers, 6:1; Meier and Rudwick, *CORE*, 139–142; Branch, *Parting the Waters*, 477–478.

19. Farris Bryant, interview with the author, 8 July 1982, Jacksonville, Florida.

20. *Southern Patriot* 19:7 (September 1961): 3, in the private papers of Patricia Stephens Due.

21. Collins, interview with Jackson Ice.

22. Farris Bryant, interview with the author; *Israel Dresner et al. v. City of Tallahassee*, 8 Race Relations Law Reporter (1963) at 1341; 9 Race Relations Law Reporter (1964) at 579; *Tallahassee Democrat*, 16 June 1961; *Tallahassee Democrat*, 16 June 1961.

23. Rick Tuttle, "Bryant Is Foiled in Own Backyard," *St. Petersburg Times*, 17 June 1961.

24. *Tallahassee Democrat*, 17, 21 June 1961.

25. *Tallahassee Democrat*, 23 June 1961.

26. Ibid.

27. John Rudd, interview with Jackson Ice, 18 July 1978, Tallahassee, Florida, Oral History of the Civil Rights Movement.

28. *David H. Brooks et al. v. City of Tallahassee et al.*, 6 Race Relations Law Reporter (1961) at 1099–1100; *Priscilla G. Stephens v. City of Tallahassee*, Law No. 10085 (1962); *Israel Dresner et al. v. City of Tallahassee*, Law No. 10084 (1962).

29. Haley to Carey, 11 December 1961, Haley to Carey, 19 November 1961, both in Congress of Racial Equality Papers, 5:29.

30. Haley to Carey, 16 November 1961, Congress of Racial Equality Papers, 5:29; Fairclough, *To Redeem the Soul of America*, 102–106.

31. Haley to David Brooks, 4 December 1961, Congress of Racial Equality Papers, 5:29.

32. Carey to Tallahassee CORE, 21 December 1961, Carey to Haley, 1 November 1961, both in Congress of Racial Equality Papers, 5:29.

33. Meier and Rudwick, *CORE*, 143–144; Carey to Members of the National Action Committee, ? March 1962, 23 March 1962, Congress of Racial Equality Papers, 5:494; "Howard Johnson's Project, November 9, 1957–June 27, 1963."

34. Due, interview with the author, 23 June 1981; Haley to Carey, 17 November 1961, Congress of Racial Equality Papers, 5:29.

35. CORE, press release, 11 October 1962, Congress of Racial Equality Papers, 5:332.

36. Miscellaneous letters to Farris Bryant on Bill of Rights Campaign (October 1962); Correspondence of Governor Farris Bryant, series 756, box 113, folder RR-1962; Bryant's correspondence, box 113, RR-1961, contains miscellaneous letters and memorandum on the Southern Governors' Conference and on Bryant's stand on civil rights issues.

37. Young, interview with the author.

38. Steele, interview with Jackson Ice, 26 January 1978. In their works on Martin Luther King and the Southern Christian Leadership Conference, historians David Garrow and Adam Fairclough note Steele's presence at many important civil rights protests and meetings outside Tallahassee; "Deacon Board of Bethel Baptist Church Leave Direction," in Padgett, "C. K. Steele: A Biography," appendix E, 297–301; 180, 196.

39. Haley to James Farmer, 29 October 1962, Congress of Racial Equality Papers, 5:332; Saul A. Silverman to Bill Durden (memo to Fowler Commission), Correspondence of Governor Farris Bryant, series 756, box 114, folder "Race Relations: Fowler Commission."

40. Davis Thomas, interview with the author.

Chapter 8. Struggle Without End

1. Patricia Stephens Due to Marvin Rich, 28 March 1963, Congress of Racial Equality Papers, 5:332.

2. Editorial, *Tallahassee Democrat,* 30 May 1963.

3. Samuel Teague, interview by Jackson Ice, 18 August 1978, Oral History of the Civil Rights Movement.

4. Ibid.

5. *Tallahassee Democrat,* 29 May 1963; Austin Hollady, interview with the author, 18 June 1993, Tallahassee, Florida.

6. *Tallahassee Democrat,* 31 May 1963.

7. *Tallahassee Theatres, Inc. et al. v. Patricia Stephens Due,* Temporary Restraining Order Modification, Race Relations Law Reporter (1963) at 636–638.

8. CORE, press release, Congress of Racial Equality Papers, 5:332; Haley to McCain, 5 June 1963, Congress of Racial Equality Papers, 1:42.

9. As quoted from CORE papers in Robnett, *How Long? How Long?* 167.

10. *Tallahassee Democrat,* 26 June 1963; Tallahassee City Commission Minutes, 25 June 1963, 189.

11. Tallahassee City Commission Minutes, 9 July 1963, 202.

12. Patricia Stephens Due to Dena Ray, 12 September 1963, Congress of Racial Equality Papers, 5:29; *Miami Herald,* 24 August 1963.

13. Clifton Lewis, interview with the author.

14. *Constitutional Principle vs. Community Practice: A Survey of the Gap in Florida: Report of the Florida Advisory Committee to the U.S. Commission on Civil Rights* (Washington, D.C., August 1963), 1.

15. Ibid., 4–5.

16. Ibid.

17. Ibid., 38–39.

18. Ibid.

19. Ibid., 39.

20. *Tallahassee Democrat,* 10 September 1963.

21. George Lewis II to Sam Teague, 10 September 1963, Malcolm Johnson Papers, box 609, folder D22, "Civil Rights."

22. Editorial, *Tallahassee Democrat,* 11 September 1963.

23. Garrow, *Bearing the Cross,* 268, 287.

24. *Tallahassee Democrat,* 16 September 1963.

25. Ibid.

26. *Tallahassee Democrat,* 17 September 1963; CORE, press release, 19 September

1963, Congress of Racial Equality Papers, 5:332; *Tallahassee Democrat,* 17 September 1963.

27. *Tallahassee Democrat,* 20 September 1963.

28. *Tallahassee Democrat,* 21 September 1963.

29. *Patricia Stephens Due et al. v. Tallahassee Theatres, Inc. et al.,* 160 So. 2d 160 (1964); *Stephens v. Theatres,* No. 21121, Appeal from the U.S. District Court (26 June 1964), 9 Race Relations Law Reporter (1964) at 904–908.

30. *Harriet Louise Adderley et al. v. State of Florida,* 385 U.S. 39, 87 S. Ct. 242, 17 L. Ed. 2d 149 (1966); Abraham, *Freedom and the Court,* 356–367; 11 Race Relations Law Reporter (1966) at 1651–1658.

31. Tallahassee City Commission Minutes, 8 October 1963, 251.

32. Ibid., 251–252.

33. "Statement to the Press," 11 October 1963, Malcolm Johnson Papers, box 609, folder D22.

34. Resolution, Malcolm Johnson Papers, box 609, folder D22; *Tampa Tribune,* 13 October 1963; Guyte F. McCord Jr. et al. to Honorable Sam Teague, 18 October 1963, Malcolm Johnson Papers, box 609, folder D22.

35. *Florida Flambeau,* 18 October 1963.

36. *Florida Flambeau,* 17 October 1963, 18 October 1963, *Tallahassee Democrat,* 17 October 1963.

37. *Florida Flambeau,* 21 October 1963; *Tallahassee Democrat,* 17 October 1963.

38. CORE, press release, 21 November 1963, Congress of Racial Equality Papers, 5:29; *Tallahassee Democrat,* 3, 4 November 1963; *Florida Flambeau,* 11 November 1963.

39. Press release (Florida Civil Liberties Union), 24 October 1963, copy in Malcolm Johnson Papers, box 609, folder D21; *Tallahassee Democrat,* 7 December 1963; *Patricia Stephens Due et al. v. Florida Agricultural and Mechanical University et al.,* 8 Race Relations Law Reporter (1963) at 1396–1402, 1696–1698.

40. Judy Benninger Brown, interview with the author, 9 July 1982, Gainesville, Florida.

41. Ibid.

42. Ibid.

43. *Miami Herald,* 24 March 1964.

44. Robert Saunders to Bayard Harrison, 11 October 1963, Robert Saunders to Charles F. Wilson, 20 November 1963, Robert and Helen Saunders Papers, series 1, box 1, folder 9, "Correspondence, 1963."

45. Alfred[?] to Robert Saunders, 4 February 1964, Robert and Helen Saunders Papers, series 1, box 2, folder 1, "Correspondence, 1964."

46. Rutledge H. Pearson to State Conference Officers, 4 March 1964, Robert and Helen Saunders Papers, series 1, box 2, folder 3, "Correspondence, 1965."

47. Garrow, *Bearing the Cross,* 316; Fairclough, *To Redeem the Soul of America,* 184; Robert Saunders, "Report of Tallahassee March," 29 March 1964, Robert and Helen Saunders Papers, series 1, box 2, folder 3; Patricia Stephens Due, "Report on the March on Tallahassee," 1 April 1964, Congress of Racial Equality Papers, 5:332.

48. Due, Report, Congress of Racial Equality Papers Addendum, F:111:152; Due to McCain, Congress of Racial Equality Papers, 5:332.

49. Haley to Julius Hamilton, 11 November 1963, Congress of Racial Equality Papers, 2:19, "H-General File, June 11, 1962–November 20, 1964."

50. Due, Report, Congress of Racial Equality Papers, 5:332.

51. Ibid., John Evans to Farris Bryant, 17 March 1964; Brooks and Steele to Terry Lee (Coordinator Board of Commissioners), 20 March 1964; Lula Mullikin (secretary to Board of Commissioners) to Brooks, 24 March 1964, Correspondence of Governor Farris Bryant, series 756, box 114, folder 2; Saunders, "Report"; Saunders to Arvah Hopkins [? March 1964], Hopkins to Saunders, [? March 1964), both in Robert and Helen Saunders Papers, series 1, box 2, folder 3; Due, "Report," Congress of Racial Equality Papers, 5:332; Due to McCain, 28 March 1964, Congress of Racial Equality Papers Addendum, F:111:152.

52. Due, telegram to James Farmer, 26 March 1964, Congress of Racial Equality Papers Addendum, F:11 (chapter files, 1958–1967) :44 (Florida, Tallahassee CORE, January 17–April 17, 1964); Due, "Report," Congress of Racial Equality Papers, 5:332; Due to McCain, 28 March 1964, Congress of Racial Equality Papers Addendum, F:111:152.

53. Due to McCain, 28 March 1964, CORE Addendum, F:111:152.

54. *Washington Newsletter from George Smathers,* 1 July 1964, Correspondence of Governor Farris Bryant, series 756, box 22, folder 1, "Civil Rights."

55. *Tampa Tribune,* 4 July 1964.

56. Editorial, *Tallahassee Democrat,* 3 July 1964.

Chapter 9. Ballots and Backlash

1. *Tallahassee Democrat,* 11 July 1964; Farris Bryant to Leo L. Rockwell, 23 July 1964, Correspondence of Governor Farris Bryant, series 756, box 22, folder "Civil Rights"; *Tallahassee Democrat,* 6 July 1964.

2. Chap. 3850, *Laws of Florida* (1889); chap. 63–98, *Laws of Florida* (1937). Language in the law was such that poll taxes continued to be charged by some communities in local elections. Consequently, in 1941 the legislature strengthened and clarified the language, abolishing the tax. Chap. 193, *Laws of Florida* (1941).

3. *Daily Democrat,* 1 May 1944; Calhoun, "A Century of Silence"; *Daily Democrat,* 1 May 1944.

4. U.S. Commission on Civil Rights, *1961 Report: Vol. 1, Voting,* 260–261; U.S. Commission on Civil Rights, *Excerpts from the 1961 Report,* 17; U.S. Commission on Civil Rights, *1961 Report: Vol. 1, Voting,* 28–29.

5. Susan Mitchell Ausley, interview with Jackson Ice, 30 July 1978, Oral History of the Civil Rights Movement.

6. Ibid.

7. Ibid.

8. Benninger-Brown, interview with the author.

9. Leon County Health Department Summons, FLIC, series 1486, box 17, folder "CORE"; Due to McCain, 13 May 1964, Congress of Racial Equality Papers Addendum, F:111:152; Due to Attorney General Kynes, 29 June 1964; FLIC, series 1486, box 17, folder "CORE"; Benninger-Brown, interview with the author; Benninger to Marvin Rich, 24 June 1964, Congress of Racial Equality Papers, 5:332.

10. *Tallahassee Democrat,* 8 February 1964.

11. Ibid.

12. Due to McCain, 19 February 1964, Congress of Racial Equality Papers Addendum, F:111:152; Ausley, interview with Jackson Ice; *Tallahassee Democrat,* 19 February 1964.

13. *Tallahassee Democrat,* 16 February 1964.

14. *Tallahassee Democrat,* 18, 19 February 1964.

15. Due to McCain, 7 May 1964, Congress of Racial Equality Papers Addendum, F:111:152; *Miami Herald,* 3, 29 April 1964, 26 May 1964; *St. Petersburg Times,* 18, 22 May 1964; *Tallahassee Democrat,* 27 May 1964.

16. Editorial, *Tallahassee Democrat,* 3 May 1964.

17. Due to McCain, 29 February 1964, Congress of Racial Equality Papers Addendum, F:111:152; Big Bend Voter Education Campaign to FAMU Faculty and Staff, 13 March 1964; Big Bend Voter Education Campaign to Dr. George Gore, n.d., Congress of Racial Equality Papers Addendum, F:111:152.

18. Due to McCain, 29 February 1964, Congress of Racial Equality Papers Addendum, F:113:152; Due to McCain, 28 March 1964, Congress of Racial Equality Papers Addendum, F:111:52.

19. Due to McCain, 13 May 1964, Congress of Racial Equality Papers Addendum, F:111:52.

20. *Tallahassee Democrat,* 27 May 1964.

21. Due to National CORE Convention, 27 June 1964; CP, 5:27.

22. Due to McCain, 13 January 1964, Congress of Racial Equality Papers Addendum, F:111:152; Due to McCain, 27 January 1964, Congress of Racial Equality Papers Addendum, F:111:152; Due, interview with the author, 24 June 1981.

23. Due to McCain, 23, 27 January 1964, Congress of Racial Equality Papers Addendum, F:111:152; Due to McCain, 1 February 1964, Congress of Racial Equality Papers Addendum, F:111:152.

24. Due to McCain, 1 February 1964.

25. Ibid.

26. "North Florida Citizenship Education Project: Report July 20–27, 1964"; Due to George Appleton, CORE Scholarship, Education, and Defense Fund et al., 23 July 1964, Congress of Racial Equality Papers, 5:27; Benninger (for Patricia Stephens Due) to Appleton et al., 27 July 1964, Congress of Racial Equality Papers Addendum, F:111:152; Due, interview with the author, 24 June 1981; Benninger-Brown, interview with the author.

27. Benninger-Brown, interview with the author. Of the major Florida newspapers, the *St. Petersburg Times* provided the most detailed coverage of the North Florida Citizenship Education Project during the summers of 1964 and 1965, including the

arrests of workers. National CORE's publication *CORE-LATOR,* and the local Quincy CORE publications, the *Gadsden County Free Press,* and the *Florida Free Press,* provided continued coverage of voter registration activities throughout North Florida.

28. "Staff Orientation, North Florida Citizenship Education Project, 7–11 July 1964," Congress of Racial Equality Papers, 5:27; Due, "A Project Summary of Registration Figures," Congress of Racial Equality Papers, 5:27.

29. Mike Geison to Due, Judy Benninger, James McCain, and Richard Haley, 8 August 1964, Congress of Racial Equality Papers Addendum, F:111:152; Benninger-Brown, interview with the author.

30. Due, interview with the author, 24 June 1981.

31. "Testimony of Ernst H. Rosenberger," *Carswell Hearings,* 150, 100–171; "Testimony of John Lowenthal," *Carswell Hearings,* 139–147.

32. Bruce Huston and Mike Geison, "Field Report, Harassment, Madison County, July 13–20, 1964," Benninger to Marvin Rich, "Brief Report on Intimidations," 23 July 1964, Due to McCain et al., 31 July 1964, Due to McCain et al., 6 September 1964, all in Congress of Racial Equality Papers, 5:27; Benninger-Brown, interview with the author.

33. Due, "A Project Summary of Registration Figures," 6 September 1964, Congress of Racial Equality Papers, 5:27; Benninger to Due, [?] October 1964, Congress of Racial Equality Papers, 5:27.

34. *Wechsler v. County of Gadsden,* 351 F. 2d 311 (1965).

35. Benninger-Brown, interview with the author.

36. Ibid.

37. Ibid.; Due to McCain, 27 January 1964, Congress of Racial Equality Papers Addendum, F:111:152.

38. Morris, *The Florida Handbook,* 1987–1988, 629.

39. USCCR, *Political Participation,* (1968), 12–13.

40. *Tallahassee Democrat,* 1, 4 May 1966.

41. Rudd, interview with Jackson Ice.

42. Ibid.

43. *Tallahassee Democrat,* 17 February 1966; Editorial, *Tallahassee Democrat,* 17 February 1966.

44. *Tallahassee Democrat,* 18, 21 February 1966.

45. *Tallahassee Democrat,* 22, 23 February 1966; Rudd, interview with Jackson Ice.

46. *Florida Times-Union,* 8 November 1966; *St. Petersburg Times,* 7, 9 November 1966; Editorial, *St. Petersburg Times,* 9 November 1966; *Tampa Tribune,* 8 November 1966; *Tallahassee Democrat,* 9 November 1966; "Governor, General Election, November 8, 1966," Bureau of Election Results. The vote in Leon County was: High, 10,773; Kirk, 10,682.

Chapter 10. The Limits of Change

1. *Tallahassee Democrat,* 5, 6 July 1964.

2. Editorial, *Tallahassee Democrat,* 14 June 1966.

3. Don Pride, "Ole Swimmin' Hole Ain't What It Used To Be," *St. Petersburg Times,*

24 July 1966; Clifton Lewis, interview with Jackson Ice; *Tallahassee Democrat,* 27 July 1966.

4. *Tallahassee Democrat,* 15, 31 March 1967, 26 April 1967.

5. Tallahassee City Commission Minutes, 9 December 1941.

6. Tallahassee City Commission Minutes, 21 August 1945, 43, 10 April 1947, 331.

7. Tallahassee City Commission Minutes, 14 October 1948, 84.

8. R. L. Anderson to George W. Gore, 2 October 1950; George W. Gore Papers, box 1, folder 5, Black Archives, Florida A&M University, Tallahassee, Florida; Minutes of the A&M Hospital Advisory Board, 8 September 1952, in Governor LeRoy Collins Papers, box 62, folder "A&M Hospital Board"; H. B. Foote, "Evolution of the Development of a Pay Patient Census at the Florida A&M College Hospital," memo to Hospital Board, n.d., Governor LeRoy Collins Papers, box 62, folder "A&M Hospital Board."

9. LeRoy Collins to R. H. Bradford, 26 March 1953, Governor LeRoy Collins Papers, box 62, folder "A&M Hospital Board"; Neyland, *Centennial History,* 297.

10. Minutes of the Leon County Commission, 22 March 1954, 7 December 1954, County Court House, Tallahassee, Florida.

11. *Tallahassee Democrat,* 24 June 1964; Anderson, interview with Jackson Ice, 28 June 1978.

12. Neyland, *Centennial History,* 296.

13. The creation of the FAMU Law School is discussed in Chapter 11; Colburn, *Florida's Gubernatorial Politics,* 227; Editorial, *Tampa Tribune,* 2 February 1959.

14. *Tallahassee Democrat,* 11 April 1959.

15. Thomas Miller Jenkins to George W. Gore Jr., 15 July 1963, FAMU Law School files, Black Archives, Florida A&M University, Tallahassee, Florida, box 7.

16. Minutes of the Board of Regents, 3 May 1965, Florida Archives, Tallahassee, Florida; Editorial, *Tallahassee Democrat,* 29 March 1964; Editorial, *Pensacola News,* 31 August 1964; Gordon W. Blackwell to George Gore Jr., 26 May 1964, FAMU Law School files, box 7.

17. Minutes of the Board of Regents, 19 July 1965.

18. *Florida Flambeau,* 4 November 1968; *FAMUAN,* November 1967.

19. *FAMUAN,* November 1967.

20. Ibid.

21. *Tallahassee Democrat,* 3 April 1968; *Florida Flambeau,* 3 April 1968.

22. Rudd, interview with Jackson Ice.

23. *Tallahassee Democrat,* 8 April 1968.

24. *Tallahassee Democrat,* 5 April 1968; *Florida Flambeau,* 11 April 1968.

25. *Tallahassee Democrat,* 6 April 1968.

26. *Tallahassee Democrat,* 8 April 1968.

27. *Tallahassee Democrat,* 23 May 1968; *St. Petersburg Times,* 24 May 1968.

28. Larry Campbell, interview with the author, 25 March 1995, Tallahassee, Florida; *Tallahassee Democrat,* 27 June 1968; *St. Petersburg Times,* 26, 28 May 1968; *Tallahassee Democrat,* 26 May 1968.

29. Neyland, *Centennial History,* 430; James M. Abraham, "Ushering Florida A&M Through the Age of Desegregation," *Tallahassee Democrat,* 20 February 1994.

30. Neyland, *Centennial History,* 430–431.

31. Minutes of the Board of Regents, 6 May 1968, 433.

32. Ibid.

33. Minutes of the Board of Regents, 1 July 1968, 447; Neyland, *Centennial History,* 306, 307.

34. Minutes of the Board of Regents, 1 July 1968, 461; Hendricks Chandler, interview with the author, 8 April 1995, Tallahassee, Florida.

35. On 20 November 1970, one month after the district court denied its petition for a rehearing, the defense for Colbert and Oliver appealed in a consolidated case to the Florida Supreme Court. The defense charged that Colbert and Oliver had confessed to the crime without benefit of counsel in a coercive atmosphere, that law enforcement had failed to take them before a magistrate within proper time, and that the trial court had erred in allowing the prosecution to impeach its own witness when she gave "testimony diametrically opposed to testimony previously given under oath." *Colbert v. State,* Case No. 40-459, Jurisdictional Brief of Respondent in Opposition to Petition for Writ of Certiorari, Brief in Support of Petition for Certiorari, *Oliver v. State of Florida,* 250 So. 2d 888, 16 A.L.R. 4th 427; Campbell, interview with the author. On 7 July 1971, the Florida Supreme Court granted the request for certiorari, overturned the convictions of the two men, and ordered a new trial in a different venue. Oliver and Colbert were subsequently found not guilty and were released from prison.

36. *Tallahassee Democrat,* 26 May 1968.

Chapter 11. Justice Delayed

1. Florida, *Acts and Resolutions* (1895), 96; Margo, *Race and Schooling,* 21.

2. Florida. *Biennial Report of the Superintendent of Public Instruction (BRSPI), 1931–1932* (Tallahassee, 1932), 166, 168, 356, 400.

3. Minutes of the Board of Control, 14 October 1945, 158–159; 15 April 1946, 382; 10 May 1946, 417–418; 8 June 1946, 477–478; 17 February 1947, 211; 19 June 1947, 383. After 1947, the names of the recipients were not published in the minutes. Minutes of the Board of Control, 21 December 1949. Chandler, *Dreams and Political Realities,* 226.

4. *Sweatt v. Painter,* 339 U.S. 629 (1950).

5. *Brown v. Board of Education,* 347 U.S. 483, at 486–496, 493 (1954).

6. Ralph E. Odum, "Review of Public School Desegregation in Florida," speech, 23 May 1960, St. Augustine, Florida, Correspondence of Governor Farris Bryant, series 756, box 114, folder "Race Relations"; *Tallahassee Democrat,* 17–19 May 1954; *Tampa Tribune,* 17 May 1954; Editorial, *Tampa Tribune,* 19 May 1954.

7. *Tallahassee Democrat,* 18, 19 May 1954; Editorial, *Tallahassee Democrat,* 20 May 1954.

8. Kluger, *Simple Justice,* 751–752.

9. *Tallahassee Democrat,* 17, 18, 19, 23 May 1954.

10. *Tallahassee Democrat,* 18 May 1954.

11. Killian, taped correspondence with Jackson Ice.

12. Ibid.

13. Florida, Amicus Curiae Brief (1954), 29–33.

14. Odum, "Review of Public School Desegregation."

15. Killian, taped correspondence with Jackson Ice; Smith and Parks, "Desegregation in Florida," 56.

16. Florida, Amicus Curiae Brief (1954), Appendix A, 99–152.

17. Florida, Amicus Curiae Brief (1954), 51.

18. Ibid., 20–21.

19. Ibid., 59–65, 91–97; Killian, taped correspondence with Jackson Ice.

20. *Brown v. Board of Education,* 349 U.S. 294 at 298, 299 (1955).

21. Id. at 300, 301.

22. Editorial, *Tallahassee Democrat,* 1 June 1955; Ervin, interview with the author; Wagy, *Governor LeRoy Collins of Florida,* 86–87; Killian, *Black and White,* 85–87.

23. "End to Construction of Segregated Schools Demanded by Florida NAACP," press release, 24 February 1955; NAACP, Library of Congress, "Desegregation Schools, Branch Action FL-1953-1955," group 2, box A226; Tomberlin, "The Negro," 85; Minutes of the Leon County Board of Public Instruction (hereinafter referred to as Board Minutes), May–June 1954, Leon County School Board Office, Tallahassee, Florida; *Tallahassee Democrat,* 3 June 1955; Florida, chap. 29746, *Laws of Florida* (1955).

24. Florida, chap. 29746, *Laws of Florida* (1955).

25. Cooper, "*Brown v. Board of Education,*" 6–7.

26. *Miami Herald,* 20 September 1955.

27. *Hawkins v. Board of Control,* "On Petition for Writ of Certiorari," 350 U.S. 413 (1956); *Tallahassee Democrat,* 13, 14 March 1956.

28. *Hawkins v. Board of Control,* 93 So. 2d 354, at 359, 360, 367 (1957).

29. Id. at 361.

30. Id. at 362; *Southern School News,* April 1957, 6.

31. FLIC, "Transcripts of Testimony (Virgil D. Hawkins), February 4, 5, 1957," s. 1486 Box 3, 7 February 1957, Box 4.

32. Jack Gant, interview with author, 23 December 1997, Tallahassee, Florida.

33. FLIC, "Transcripts of Testimony (Virgil D. Hawkins)," box 3.

34. Cooper, "*Brown v. Board of Education,*" 17 n. 75.

35. Ibid., 11.

36. *Hawkins v. Board,* 162 F. Supp. 851 (1958) at 853; *Southern School News,* July 1958, 15; *Southern School News,* July 1962, 14; Editorial, *Florida Flambeau,* 5 September 1962.

37. Florida, *A Report of the Special Committee,* Correspondence of Governor LeRoy Collins, series 776, box 33, "Race Relations, Governor's Advisory Council."

38. Ibid.

39. Editorial, *Tallahassee Democrat,* 17 July 1956.

40. *Tallahassee Democrat,* 18 July 1956.

41. Editorial, *Tallahassee Democrat*, 31 July 1956.

42. U.S. Commission on Civil Rights, *Legal Developments in the Southern States* (Washington, D.C.: Government Printing Office, 1961), 233; *Tallahassee Democrat*, 18 June 1956; Ervin, interview with the author; Odum, "A Review of Public School Desegregation."

43. *Tallahassee Democrat*, 31 July 1956.

44. *Tallahassee Democrat*, 22 July 1956, 27 July 1956; *Southern School News*, September 1956, 13; *Tallahassee Democrat*, 30 July 1956.

45. *Tallahassee Democrat*, 8 January 1957.

46. *Newsweek*, 21 January 1957, 31; *Southern School News*, February 1957, 13.

47. "Excerpts from Report of Saul A. Silverman, Staff Assistant to the Fowler Commission on Race Relations," in *Florida Across the Threshold*, 57–60; Minutes of the Governor's Advisory Commission on Bi-Racial Problems, 5 March 1957, Correspondence of Governor LeRoy Collins, series 776, box 117, "Race Relations, Governor's Advisory Commission."

48. Florida, *Acts and Resolutions* (1957), 1217–1222; Florida, *Biennial Report of the Attorney General* (1958); *Tallahassee Democrat*, 21 April 1957; Minutes of the Governor's Advisory Commission on Bi-Racial Problems, 30 April 1957, Correspondence of Governor LeRoy Collins, series 776, box 117, folder "Race Relations, Governor's Advisory Commission."

49. "Statement by Governor Collins, Re: Interposition," Correspondence of Governor LeRoy Collins, series 776, box 116, folder "Race Relations." Collins, Statement on Interposition Resolution, 19 April 1957, Correspondence of Governor LeRoy Collins, series 776, box 117, folder "Race Relations, Governor's Advisory Commission."

50. "News Release Re: Sustaining of 'Last Resort' Bill Veto," 7 June 1947, Correspondence of Governor LeRoy Collins, series 776, box 116, folder "Race Relations"; *Southern School News*, November 1957, 14.

51. "Statement by Governor Collins," 12 October 1957, Correspondence of Governor LeRoy Collins, series 776, box 116, folder "Race Relations"; *Southern School News*, November 1957, 14, "Suggestion for Congressional Implementation of Supreme Court Desegregation Decision," "Editorial Comments on Congressional Implementation Plan," "Collins' Plan," all in Governor LeRoy Collins Papers, box 136, "Education-School Desegregation—Collins' Plan."

52. LeRoy Collins, interview with Lawrence Spivak on "Meet the Press," 25 May 1960, Transcript in Correspondence of Governor LeRoy Collins, series 776, box 116, folder "Race Relations."

53. Report of the Advisory Commission on Race Relations to Governor LeRoy Collins, 16 March 1959, Correspondence of Governor LeRoy Collins, series 776, box 117, folder "Race Relations—Governor's Advisory Commission."

54. *Tallahassee Democrat*, 26 February 1959.

55. Richard Ervin to LeRoy Collins, "Legislative Recommendations of the Attorney General" (1959), Correspondence of Governor LeRoy Collins, series 776, box 116, folder "Race Relations."

56. *Gibson v. Board of Public Instruction of Dade County, Florida et al.*, 272 F. 2d 763 (1959).

57. *Southern School News*, April 1959, 15.

58. Colburn and Scher, *Florida's Gubernatorial Politics*, 227; *Southern School News*, April 1961, 4.

Chapter 12. The Plaintiff's Burden

1. "Resolutions of the Inter-Civic Council of Tallahassee, Inc., Respecting Compliance with the United States Supreme Court Mandates on Racial Desegregation in Public Schools," 28 April 1957, in Leon County Board of Public Instruction files, "Integration," Tallahassee, Florida (hereinafter cited as Board Files).

2. L. L. Fabisinski to Amos Godby, 1 May 1957, "Draft reply to Inter-Civic Council, Inc., 30 April 1957," "Excerpt to be Included in the Minutes of Regular Board Meeting on May 7, 1957," all in Board Files.

3. C. K. Steele to Amos Godby, 20 August 1957, Board Files.

4. Godby to Steele, 9 September 1957, Steele to Godby, 14 September 1957, both in Board Files.

5. C. K. Steele to Walter T. Moore, 17 November 1961, Board Files; Board Minutes, 5 December 1961; "Status of School Desegregation in the Southern and Border States," November 1961, Robert and Helen Saunders Papers, series 1, box 2, folder 3, "Court Decisions and Laws."

6. *Clifford N. Steele et al. v. Board of Public Instruction of Leon County*, Tallahassee Civil Action No. 854 (1962), copy in Board Files.

7. Ibid.

8. Ibid.; Deposition of Walter T. Moore Jr. (1 June 1962), copy in Board Files.

9. Deposition of Walter T. Moore Jr. (1 June 1962), Deposition of Amos P. Godby (1 June 1962), both in Board Files.

10. *Tallahassee Democrat*, 9 October 1962; *Southern School News*, January 1963, 10.

11. Details of Carswell's life and his professional career are contained in *Carswell Hearings*, 27–29 January and 2–3 February 1970.

12. *Augustus v. Board*, 306 F. 2d 862 (1962); *Augustus v. Board*, 8 Race Relations Law Reporter (1963) at 59.

13. *Southern School News*, April 1963, 14; *Southern School News*, December 1962, 13.

14. *Southern School News*, December 1962, 13.

15. *Southern School News*, April 1963, 14.

16. U.S. Commission on Civil Rights, *The Diminishing Barrier*, 43 ("Leon County").

17. *Southern School News*, December 1964, 1; U.S. Commission on Civil Rights, *1964 Staff Report: Public Education*, 59.

18. Leon County Public Schools (LCPS,) Application(s) for Pupil Assignment, [for] Hadley, Phillip, Holifield, Marilyn, Knowles, Harold, Board Files.

19. Amos Godby to Leon County Board of Public Instruction, 21 May 1963, all in Board Files.

20. Amos Godby to Frank Stoutamire, 27 August 1963, in Board Files.

21. U.S. Commission on Civil Rights, Florida Advisory Committee, *Report on Florida*, 10–20.

22. Robert Stevens correspondence with the author, 14 January 1994.

23. Ibid.; *Tallahassee Democrat*, 8 September 1963; *Tampa Tribune*, 8 September 1963.

24. Christene Knowles Rhodes, interview with the author, 14 June 1984, Apalachicola, Florida; Harold Knowles, interview with the author, 30 May 1984, Tallahassee, Florida.

25. Rhodes, interview with the author.

26. James Ford, interview with the author, 9 February 1998, Tallahassee, Florida.

27. Aquilina Howell, interview with the author, 6 April 1994, Tallahassee, Florida.

28. Rhodes, interview with the author; Knowles, interview with the author.

29. Knowles, interview with the author; Antoine Bell, "Entering the Lion's Den," *Tallahassee Democrat*, 30 May 1988.

30. Knowles, interview with the author; Stevens correspondence with the author, 14 January 1994.

31. Mike Conley, interview with the author, 8 November 1993, Tallahassee, Florida; Stevens correspondence with the author, 14 January 1994; Knowles, interview with the author.

32. Knowles, interview with the author.

33. Ibid.

34. Ibid.

35. Ibid.

36. Ibid.

37. Rhodes, interview with the author.

38. Ibid.

39. Knowles, interview with the author.

40. *Goss v. Board of Education*, 373 U.S. 683 (1963); *Griffin v. County School Board of Prince Edward County, Virginia*, 377 U.S. 218 (1964).

41. *Carswell Hearings*, 223–224; *Tallahassee Democrat*, 27 May 1964.

Chapter 13. Deliberate Speed

1. *Civil Rights Act of 1964*, P.L. 88–352, Title IV, Sec. 407, 601 (quoted).

2. U.S. Commission on Civil Rights, *Southern School Desegregation, 1966–1967*, 15–18; Tomberlin, "The Negro and Florida's System of Education," 237.

3. Mary Louise Ruff Ellis, interview with the author, 23 November 1997, Tallahassee, Florida.

4. *Carswell Hearings*, 120–121, 135; *Steele v. Board*, Tallahassee Civil Action No. 854, Board Files.

5. *Steele v. Board*, 10 Race Relations Law Reporter (1965–66) at 606–609; *Carswell Hearings*, 230; *Steele v. Board*, 371 F. 2d 395 (1967).

6. *Southern School News*, June 1965, 10.

7. *Tallahassee Democrat*, 4 August 1965; U.S. Commission on Civil Rights, *Survey of*

School Districts in the Southern and Border States, 1965–1966, 27–28; *Miami Herald,* 17 February 1966.

8. U.S. Commission on Civil Rights, *Southern School Desegregation, 1966–1967,* 3; Tomberlin, "The Negro and Florida's System of Education," 242.

9. Rhodes, interview with the author.

10. Ibid.

11. Ibid.

12. [Petition] to Leon County School Board (October 4, 1966), Board Files.

13. *Florida Flambeau,* 28, 29 November 1966; Rhodes, interview with the author.

14. *Florida Flambeau,* 23, 28 November 1966.

15. Ibid., 22, 29 November 1966; Kent Spriggs, interview with the author, 26 January 1983, Tallahassee, Florida.

16. *Tallahassee Democrat,* 29 November 1966; Board Minutes, 29 November 1966.

17. Editorial, *Tallahassee Democrat,* 30 November 1966; *Tallahassee Democrat,* 30 November 1966; Board Minutes, 29 November 1966.

18. *United States v. Jefferson County Board of Education,* 372 F. 2d 836 (1966).

19. Id. at 847, 896.

20. Id. at 889, 890, 896.

21. U.S. Commission on Civil Rights, *Southern School Desegregation, 1966–1967,* 43, 117–120.

22. *United States v. Jefferson County Board of Education,* 372 F. 2d 836 at 852, 890, 891, 892–900 (1966).

23. *Steele v. Board,* 371 F. 2d 395 (1967).

24. Board Minutes, 24 March 1967; "A Proposed Plan for Desegregation of Schools in Leon County 1967–78," Board Files; *Steele v. Board,* 12 Race Relations Law Reporter (1967–1968) at 804.

25. Ford, interview with the author.

26. James T. Campbell, "Florida School Desegregation Moves Forward," Florida Schools (January 1969), Board Files.

Chapter 14. Root and Branch

1. Graham Carothers, interview with the author, 19 November 1993, Tallahassee, Florida.

2. Ibid.

3. *Green v. County School Board of New Kent County,* Virginia 88 Sct. 1689 (1968).

4. *Brown v. Board of Education of Topeka,* 349 U.S. 294 (1955).

5. Andy Lindstrom, "Memories Live on at Old Lincoln," *Tallahassee Democrat,* 19 February 1995. Both white Godby Junior High and Rickards Junior High were converted to high schools in the mid-1960s.

6. *Carswell Hearings,* 227.

7. Carothers, interview with the author; *Carswell Hearings,* 2, 3, 5, 72, 107.

8. *Alexander v. Holmes County Board of Education,* 396 U.S. 19 (1969) at 20.

9. *Steele v. Board*, 421 F. 2d 1382 (1969); *Steele v. Board*, "Opposition to Extension of Time for Filing Report to Court," Board Files; *Steele v. Board*, "On Petition for Recall," 421 F. 2d 1382 (1970).

10. *Steele v. Board*, Tallahassee Civil Action No. 854, 30 January 1970, Board Files; Howell, interview with the author.

11. Sterling Bryant, interview with the author, 21 March 1994, Tallahassee, Florida.

12. U.S. Commission on Civil Rights, *The Diminishing Barrier*, 44; Board Minutes, 12 May 1970; the board's files contain various telegrams, petitions, and letters from black citizens' groups opposing the closing of the school. *Steele v. Board*, Tallahassee Civil Action No. 854; "Order," 29 June 1970, Board Files; *Tallahassee Democrat*, 5 July 1970. "Lincoln Elementary School Report," 31 July 1970. *Tallahassee Democrat*, 5 August 1970; U.S. Commission on Civil Rights, *The Diminishing Barrier*, 45.

13. Hettie Cobb, "Public Schools Losing $$$ to Private System"; *Tallahassee Democrat*, 11 August 1970; U.S. Commission on Civil Rights, *The Diminishing Barrier*, 46, 158.

14. Sterling Bryant, interview with the author.

15. U.S. Commission on Civil Rights, *The Diminishing Barrier*, 45; U.S. Senate, *Hearings Before the Select Committee on Equal Educational Opportunity*, 5365–5366.

16. United States Senate, *Hearings Before the Select Committee on Equal Educational Opportunity of the United States Senate*, Ninety Second Congress, First Session on Equal Educational Opportunity. Part 10—Displacement and Present Status of Black School Principals in Desegregated School Districts (Washington, 1971), 5383.

17. U.S. Commission on Civil Rights, *The Diminishing Barrier*, 48–49.

18. Ford, interview with the author.

19. U.S. Commission on Civil Rights, *The Diminishing Barrier*, 49.

Afterword

1. Daisy Young, interview on "The Bus Stops Here," 8 November 1996, Florida Public Television; C. K. Steele, "Non-violent Resistance: The Pain and the Promise," speech delivered at the Black Studies Program, Florida State University, Tallahassee, Florida, 27 September 1978.

2. *Tallahassee Democrat*, 14, 22, 30 October 1969; *Florida Flambeau*, 5 November 1969; *Tallahassee Democrat*, 4 November 1969.

3. *United States of America v. City of Tallahassee*, "Consent Decree," Civil Action No. TCA-74-209 (1975).

4. *Tallahassee Democrat*, 14 February 1971.

5. *Tallahassee Democrat*, 16, 17 February 1971; Editorial, *Tallahassee Democrat*, 21 February 1971, Hallie Boyles, "Weather Cooperating in City Runoff Vote," 23 February 1971; Ford, interview with the author; Malcolm Johnson, "Silent Vote a Poor Crutch," *Tallahassee Democrat*, 19 February 1971.

6. Johnson, "Silent Vote," *Tallahassee Democrat*, 19 February 1971; Hallie Boyles, "Black City Commissioner," *Tallahassee Democrat*, 24 February 1971.

7. "Winds of Change Blow Through Old City Hall," *Tallahassee Democrat,* 27 February 1971; Ford, interview with the author; Pat Harbolt, "Ford Believes in Providing Basics," *Tallahassee Democrat,* 26 April 1975.

8. Averil Guiste, "Supporter's Expectations Dog Richardson," *Tallahassee Democrat,* 1 November 1994.

9. *Tallahassee Democrat,* 15 February 1966; Browning Brooks, "Building the Bridge: Florida State's Thirty-Year Journey into Racial Diversity," *Tallahassee Democrat,* part one, 20 September 1992; Knowles, interview with the author; Brooks, "Building the Bridge," part one.

10. Brooks, "Building the Bridge," part two, *Tallahassee Democrat,* 21 September 1992.

11. The Florida State Normal College for Colored Students was founded in 1887. The school became Florida Agricultural and Mechanical College for Negroes in 1909 and Florida Agricultural and Mechanical University in 1953.

12. A separate scholarship fund, the National Achievement Scholars, is reserved for outstanding black high school students nationwide. National Merit Scholars can be either white or black.

13. Steele, "Non-violent Resistance: The Pain and the Promise."

Bibliography

Manuscripts and Archival Materials

Board Files, Leon County Board of Public Instruction, Tallahassee, Florida.

Governor Farris Bryant Correspondence, Florida State Archives, Tallahassee, Florida.

Doak Campbell Papers, Special Collections Department, Florida State University Libraries, Tallahassee, Florida.

Governor LeRoy Collins Correspondence, Florida State Archives, Tallahassee, Florida.

Governor LeRoy Collins Papers, Special Collections Department, University of South Florida Library, Tampa, Florida.

Congress of Racial Equality Papers, 1941–1967, and Addendum, 1944–1968 (Microfilm), Florida State University Libraries, Tallahassee, Florida.

First Presbyterian Church Session Minutes, 1953–1956, Tallahassee, Florida.

Florida A&M University Hospital Records and Papers, Black Archives, Florida A&M University, Tallahassee, Florida.

Florida A&M Law School Records and Papers, Black Archives, Florida A&M University, Tallahassee, Florida.

Florida Legislative Investigation Committee Papers, Florida State Archives, Tallahassee, Florida.

George W. Gore Papers, Black Archives, Florida A&M University, Tallahassee, Florida.

James Hudson Papers, Black Archives, Florida A&M University, Tallahassee, Florida.

Malcolm Johnson Papers, Special Collections Department, Florida State University Libraries, Tallahassee, Florida.

National Association for the Advancement of Colored People Papers, Library of Congress, Washington, D.C.

National Association for the Advancement of Colored People Papers (Microfilm), Florida State University Libraries, Tallahassee, Florida.

Papers, Reports, and Miscellaneous Documents, Ruge Hall, Tallahassee, Florida.

Helen and Robert Saunders Papers, Special Collections Department, University of South Florida Library, Tampa, Florida.

Silver Anniversary Observance of the Beginning of the Tallahassee Bus Boycott, Florida A&M University, Tallahassee, Florida, 27 May 1981. Speeches.

Robert Strozier, Biography, Special Collections Department, Florida State University Libraries, Tallahassee, Florida.

Governor Fuller Warren Correspondence, Florida State Archives, Tallahassee, Florida.

Interviews

Benninger-Brown, Judy. Interview with the author. 9 July 1982. Gainesville, Florida.

Blackwell, Gordon. Correspondence with author. 3 April 1986.

Brock, Oscar (Bob). Telephone interview with the author. 13 September 1994.

Bryant, Farris. Interview with the author. 8 July 1982. Jacksonville, Florida.

Bryant, Sterling. Interview with the author. 21 March 1994. Tallahassee, Florida.

Campbell, Larry. Interview with the author. 23 March 1995. Tallahassee, Florida.

Carothers, Graham. Interview with the author. 19 November 1993. Tallahassee, Florida.

Chandler, Hendrix. Interview with the author. 8 April 1995. Tallahassee, Florida.

Collins, LeRoy. Interview with the author. 24 May 1983. Tallahassee, Florida.

Conley, Mike. Interview with the author. 8 November 1993. Tallahassee, Florida.

Delavan, Virginia. Correspondence with the author. 2 October 1994.

Dixie, Laura. Interview with the author. 30 July 1981. Tallahassee, Florida.

Dixon, Howard. Interview with the author. 25 June 1981. Miami, Florida.

Due, John. Interview with the author. 24 June 1981. Miami, Florida.

Due, Patricia Stephens. Interview with the author. 24 May 1981. Tallahassee, Florida.

Due, Patricia Stephens. Interviews with the author. 23, 24 June 1981. Miami, Florida.

Ellis, Mary Louise Ruff. Interview with the author. 16 November 1997. Tallahassee, Florida.

Ervin, Richard. Interview with author. 4 August 1981.

Ford, James. Interview with the author. 9 February 1998. Tallahassee, Florida.

Gant, Jack. Interview with the author. 22 December 1997. Tallahassee, Florida.

Hollady, Austin. Interview with the author. 18 June 1993. Tallahassee, Florida.

Howell, Aquilina. Interview with the author. 6 April 1994. Tallahassee, Florida.

Interviews with Jackson Ice. In *Oral History of the Civil Rights Movement*, Special Collections Department, Florida State University Libraries, Tallahassee, Florida.

Irons, Edward. Interview with the author. 28 May 1981. Tallahassee, Florida.

Kenon, Reuben R. Interview with the author. 20 February 1995. Lake City, Florida.

Killian, Lewis. Interview with the author. 17 February 1983. Tallahassee, Florida.

Knowles, Harold. Interview with the author. 30 May 1984. Tallahassee, Florida.

Lewis, Clifton. Interview with the author. 6 November 1994. Tallahassee, Florida.

Lewis, George. Interview with the author. 6 November 1994. Tallahassee, Florida.

Maige, Robert. Telephone interview with the author. 23 November 1994.

Mayo, William T. Interview with the author. 14 August 1981. Tallahassee, Florida.

Peacock, Burl. Interview with the author. 13 October 1994. Tallahassee, Florida.

Rhodes, Christene Knowles. Interview with the author. 14 June 1984. Apalachicola, Florida.

Riley, John. Interview with the author. 17 November 1982. Tallahassee, Florida.

Rollins, Metz. Interview with the author. 27 May 1981. Tallahassee, Florida.

Saunders, Robert W. Interview with the author. 26 June 1981. Tampa, Florida.

Shaw, James. Interview with the author. 11 November 1982. Tallahassee, Florida.

Shaw, Lillian. Interview with the author. 11 November 1982. Tallahassee, Florida.

Spriggs, Kent. Interview with the author. 26 January 1983. Tallahassee, Florida.

Steele, Henry. Interview with author. 23 November 1982, Tallahassee, Florida.

Steele, Lois B. Interview with the author. 23 November 1982. Tallahassee, Florida.

Stephens, Robert. Correspondence with the author. 14 January 1994.

Street, Wilhelmina Jakes. Telephone interview with the author. 8 September 1993.

Teague, Sam. Interview with the author. 23 January 1984. Tallahassee, Florida.

Thomas, Davis. Interview with the author. 6 October 1992. Tallahassee, Florida.

Thomas, M. S. Interview with the author. 16 July 1981. Tallahassee, Florida.

Vines, Georgiana Fry. Correspondence with the author. 9 November 1994.

White, Robert M. Telephone interview with the author. 9 September 1994.

Willis, Ben C. Interview with the author. 7 August 1981. Tallahassee, Florida.

Young, Daisy O. Interview with the author. 6 June 1981. Tallahassee, Florida.

Government Documents

Arrington, Karen McGill. *With All Deliberate Speed, 1954–19——*. Washington, D.C.: U.S. Commission on Civil Rights, 1981.

Florida. Acts and Resolutions, Laws of Florida, 1885, 1956, 1957.

——. *Biennial Report of the Superintendent of Public Instruction, State of Florida, 1896–1897*. Tallahassee Department of Public Instruction, 1897.

——. *Biennial Report of the Superintendent of Public Instruction, State of Florida, for the Two Years Ending 1908–1910*. Tallahassee: Department of Public Instruction, 1910.

——. *Biennial Report of the Superintendent of Public Instruction, State of Florida, 1931–1932*. Tallahassee: Florida Department of Public Instruction, 1932.

——. *Biennial Report of the Superintendent of Public Instruction, State of Florida, 1954–1956*. Tallahassee: Florida Department of Public Instruction, 1956.

——. Constitution. 1885.

——. *Journal of the Proceedings of the Constitutional Convention of the State of Florida*, 1885.

——. *Laws of Florida, 1889–1910, 1937–1970*.

——. *A Report of the Special Committee Appointed by the Governor and Cabinet of Florida to Recommend Legislative Action Relating to Public Education*. Tallahassee, 1956.

Florida. Board of Control. Minutes, 1945–1965. Florida State Archives, Tallahassee, Florida.

——. *Study on Desegregation*. 2 vols. Tallahassee, May 1956.

Florida. Board of Regents. Minutes, 1966–1970. Florida State Archives, Tallahassee, Florida.

Florida. Department of State, Division of Elections, Bureau of Election Records, Election Results, Tabulations, 1946–1970. County Courthouse, Tallahassee, Florida.

Florida. Office of the Attorney General. *Report of the Attorney General to the Governor and the 1957 Legislature.* Tallahassee, 1957.

———. *Report of the Attorney General to the Governor and the 1959 Legislature.* Tallahassee, 1959.

Leon County. Board of Public Instruction. Minutes, 1954–1965. Leon County School Board Office, Tallahassee, Florida.

———. Commission Minutes, 1954–1965. Leon County Court House, Tallahassee, Florida.

Tallahassee City Commission Minutes, 1944–1974. City Hall, Tallahassee, Florida.

U.S. Commission on Civil Rights. *Civil Rights Under Federal Programs: An Analysis of Title VI.* Washington, D.C.: Government Printing Office, 1965.

———. *The Diminishing Barrier: A Report on School Desegregation in Nine Counties.* Washington, D.C.: Government Printing Office, 1972.

———. *The Fifty States Report.* Washington, D.C.: Government Printing Office, 1961.

———. *1961 U.S. Commission on Civil Rights Report: Vol. 1, Voting.* Washington, D.C.: Government Printing Office, 1961.

———. *1961 U.S. Commission on Civil Rights Report: Vol. 2, Education.* Washington, D.C.: Government Printing Office, 1961.

———. *1963 Staff Report: Public Education.* Washington, D.C.: Government Printing Office, 1963.

———. *1964 Staff Report: Public Education.* Washington, D.C.: Government Printing Office, 1964.

———. *Political Participation: A Study of the Participation by Negroes in the Electoral and Political Process in Ten Southern States Since Passage of the Voting Rights Act of 1965.* Washington, D.C.: Government Printing Office, 1968.

———. *Report: Public Education.* Washington, D.C.: Government Printing Office, 1961.

———. *Southern School Desegregation, 1966–1967.* Washington, D.C. Government Printing Office, 1967.

———. *Survey of School Districts in the Southern and Border States, 1965–1966.* Washington, D.C.: Government Printing Office, 1966.

———. *The Voting Rights Act: The First Months.* Washington, D.C.: Government Printing Office, 1965.

———. *The Voting Rights Act: Ten Years After.* Washington, D.C.: Government Printing Office, 1975.

———. *With Liberty and Justice for All: An Abridgement of the Report of the United States Commission on Civil Rights.* Washington, D.C.: Government Printing Office, 1959.

U.S. Commission on Civil Rights. Florida Advisory Committee to the United States Commission on Civil Rights. *Report on Florida.* Washington, D.C.: Government Printing Office, 1963.

U.S. Department of Commerce. *1940 Census of Population. Vol. 11: Characteristics of the Population.* Washington, D.C.: Government Printing Office, 1942.

―――. *1950 Census of Population. Vol. 2, Characteristics of the Population, Part 10, Florida.* Washington, D.C.: Government Printing Office, 1952.

―――. *1960 Census of Population. Vol. 1, Characteristics of the Population, Part 11, Florida.* Washington, D.C.: Government Printing Office, 1962.

―――. *1970 Census of Population. Vol. 1, Characteristics of the Population, Part 11, Florida.* Washington, D.C.: Government Printing Office, 1972.

―――. *1970 Census of the Population and Housing, Census Tracts, Tallahassee, Fla.* Washington, D.C.: Government Printing Office, 1972.

―――. *1980 Census of the Population and Housing, Census Tracts, Tallahassee, Fla.* Washington, D.C.: Government Printing Office, 1983.

―――. *1990 Census of Population,* Social and Economic Characteristics, Florida. Washington, D.C.: Government Printing Office, 1993.

U.S. Senate. Committee on the Judiciary. *George Harrold Carswell, Hearings Before the Committee on the Judiciary, 91st Cong., 2d sess.* Washington, D.C.: Government Printing Office, 1970.

―――. *Hearings Before the Select Committee on Equal Educational Opportunity of the United States Senate, 92d Cong., 1st sess. Displacement and Present Status of Black School Principals in Desegregated Schools.* Washington, D.C.: Government Printing Office, 1971.

Court Cases

Adderley v. State of Florida, 385 U.S. 39 (1966).

Alexander v. Holmes County Board of Education, 396 U.S. 19 (1969).

Augustus v. Board of Public Instruction of Escambia County, Florida, 306 F. 2d 862 (1962).

―――. 6 Race Relations Law Reporter 73 (1960).

―――. 6 Race Relations Law Reporter 689 (1961).

―――. 7 Race Relations Law Reporter 669 (1962).

Brooks v. City of Tallahassee et al., 6 Race Relations Law Reporter (1961).

Brown v. Board of Education of Topeka, 347 U.S. 483 (1954).

―――. 349 U.S. 294 (1955).

Cities Transit, Inc. v. City of Tallahassee, Law No. 590 (Fla. 1956).

City of Tallahassee v. Benjamin F. Cowins; City of Tallahassee v. Patricia G. Stephens. Law No. 76569 and 76579 (Fla. 1961).

―――. Law No. 10017 (Fla. 1961).

City of Tallahassee v. Cities Transit, Law No. 15137 (Fla. 1956).

City of Tallahassee v. Inter-Civic Council, Law No. 8502 (Fla. 1957).

Colbert v. State of Florida, 239 So. 2d 637 (1970).

―――. 250 So. 2d 888 (1970).

―――. Petition for Writ of Certiorari (Fla. 1970).

―――. Case No. 40, 459 (Fla. 1970).

Dresner v. City of Tallahassee, Law No. 10084 (Fla. 1961).

―――. Law No. 10084 (Fla. 1962).

————. Case No. 31, 1211 (Fla. 1961).

————. 375 U.S. 136 (1963).

————. 8 Race Relations Law Reporter (1963).

————. 9 Race Relations Law Reporter (1964).

Florida Legislative Investigation Committee v. Theodore R. Gibson, Law No. 16820 (Fla. 1960).

Gibson v. Board of Public Instruction of Dade County, Florida, 272 F. 2d 763 (1959).

Gibson v. Florida Legislative Investigation Committee, 108 So. 2d 729 (1958).

————. 126 So. 2d 129 (1960).

————. 372 U.S. 539 (1963).

————. 8 Race Relations Law Reporter (1963).

Goss v. The Board of Education of the City of Knoxville, Tennessee et al., 373 U.S. 683 (1963).

Green v. County School Board of New Kent County, Virginia, 391 U.S. 430 (1968).

Griffin v. County School Board of Prince Edward County, 377 U.S. 218 (1964).

Inter-Civic Council of Tallahassee v. City of Tallahassee, Civil Action No. 584 (Fla. 1956).

Oliver v. State of Florida, 16 A.L.R. 4th 427 (Fla. 1971).

Smith v. Allwright, 321 U.S. 649 (1944).

Leonard D. Speed, Joseph Spagna and Johnny Herndon v. City of Tallahassee, Law No. 8581 (Fla. 1957).

————. 356 U.S. 913 (1958).

————. 3 Race Relations Law Reporter (1958).

State ex rel. Hawkins v. Board of Control, 47 So. 2d 608 (1950).

————. Brief of Respondents (1950).

————. 83 So. 2d 20 (1955).

————. 162 F. Supp. 851 (N.D. Fla. 1958).

————. Final Judgment No. 643 (Fla. 1958).

State v. Virgil D. Hawkins, Brief of Respondents, 1950.

Clifford N. Steele et al. v. Board of Public Instruction of Leon County, Civil Action No. 854 (1962–1970).

————. Deposition of Defendants (1962).

————. 8 Race Relations Law Reporter (1963).

————. 10 Race Relations Law Reporter (1965–66).

————. 12 Race Relations Law Reporter (1967–68).

Priscilla G. Stephens v. City of Tallahassee, Law No. 10085 (1962).

Patricia Stephens Due v. Tallahassee Theatres, Inc., 160 So. 2d 169 (1964).

Sweatt v. Painter, 339 U.S. 629 (1950).

Tallahassee Theatres Inc. v. Patricia Stephens Đue, 8 Race Relations Law Reporter (1963).

Wechsler v. County of Gadsden, 351 F. 2d 311 (1965).

Newspapers

Afro-American. 1956–1957.

CORE-LATOR. 1956–1965.

Core of the Matter. 1960–1961.

Democrat. 1937–1945.

FAMUAN. 1956–1961.

Florida Flambeau. 1957–1970.

Florida Free Press. 1964.

Florida Information Exchange. 1960–1961.

Florida Times-Union. 1954–1970.

Gadsden County Free Press. 1964–1965.

Miami Daily News. 1954–1970.

Miami Herald. 1954–1970.

Race Relations Law Reporter. 1959–1970.

St. Petersburg Times. 1954–1970.

Southern Patriot. 1960–1961.

Tallahassee Daily Democrat. 1909–1915.

Tallahassee Democrat. 1950–1997.

Tampa Morning Tribune. 1954–1957.

Tampa Tribune. 1954–1966.

Books and Articles

Abraham, Henry J. *Freedom and the Court: Civil Rights and Liberties in the United States.* New York: Oxford University Press, 1972.

Bartley, Numan V. *The Rise of Massive Resistance: Race and Politics in the South During the 1950's.* Baton Rouge: Louisiana State University Press, 1969.

Bartley, Numan V., and Hugh D. Graham. *Southern Elections: County and Precinct Data, 1950–1972.* Baton Rouge: Louisiana State University Press, 1978.

Bass, Jack, and Walter DeVries. *The Transformation of Southern Politics: Social Change and Political Consequence Since 1945.* New York: Basic Books, 1976.

Bassiouni, M. Cherif. *The Law of Dissent and Riots.* Springfield, Ill.: Thomas, 1971.

Berman, Daniel M. *It Is So Ordered: The Supreme Court Rules on School Segregation.* New York: Norton, 1966.

Black, Earl. *Southern Governors and Civil Rights: Racial Segregation as a Campaign Issue in the Second Reconstruction.* Cambridge, Mass.: Harvard University Press, 1976.

Blaustein, Albert P., and Clarence C. Ferguson, Jr. *Desegregation and the Law: The Meaning and Effect of the School Segregation Cases.* New Brunswick, N.J.: Rutgers University Press, 1957.

Branch, Taylor. *Parting the Waters: America in the King Years, 1954–63.* New York: Simon and Schuster, 1988.

Bureau of Economic and Business Research, University of Florida. *Florida Statistical Abstract, 1967.* Gainesville: University of Florida Press, 1968.

———. *Florida Statistical Abstract, 1971.* Gainesville: University of Florida Press, 1972.

Button, James W. *Blacks and Social Change: Impact of the Civil Rights Movement in Southern Communities.* Princeton, N.J.: Princeton University Press, 1989.

Carson, Clayborne. *In Struggle: SNCC and the Black Awakening of the 1960's*. Cambridge, Mass.: Harvard University Press, 1981.

Carson, Clayborne, David J. Garrow, Geral Gill, Vincent Harding and Darlene Clark Hine, eds. *The Eyes on the Prize: Civil Rights Reader: Documents, Speeches, and Firsthand Accounts from the Black Freedom Struggle, 1954–1990*. New York: Penguin, 1991.

Cash, W. J. *The Mind of the South*. New York: A. A. Knopf, 1941.

Cecelski, David S. *Along Freedom Road: Hyde County, North Carolina, and the Fate of Black Schools in the South*. Chapel Hill: University of North Carolina Press, 1994.

Chafe, William H. *Civilities and Civil Rights: Greensboro, North Carolina, and the Black Struggle for Freedom*. New York: Oxford University Press, 1980.

Chandler, Hendrix. *Dreams and Political Realities: A Twentieth-Century History of Florida's University System*. Tallahassee: Board of Regents, 1983.

Colburn, David R. *Racial Change and Community Crisis: St. Augustine, Florida, 1877–1980*. New York: Columbia University Press, 1985.

Colburn, David R., and Jane L. Landers, ed. *The African American Heritage of Florida*. Gainesville: University Presses of Florida, 1995.

Colburn, David R., and Richard K. Scher. *Florida's Gubernatorial Politics in the Twentieth Century*. Gainesville: University Presses of Florida, 1980.

———. "Race Relations and Florida Gubernatorial Politics Since the *Brown* Decision." *Florida Historical Quarterly* 55 (October 1976): 153–169.

Collins, LeRoy. *Forerunners Courageous: Stories of Frontier Florida*. Tallahassee: Colcade Publishers, 1971.

Cooper, Algia R. "*Brown v. Board of Education* and Virgil Darnell Hawkins: Twenty-eight Years and Six Petitions to Justice." *Journal of Negro History* 64:1 (Winter 1979): 1–201.

Crawford, Vicki, Jacqueline Anne Rouse, and Barbara Woods. *Women in the Civil Rights Movement: Trailblazers and Torchbearers, 1941–1965*. Brooklyn: Carlson, 1990.

Cushman, Robert F. *Cases in Civil Liberties*. New York: Appleton-Century-Crofts, 1968.

A Desegregation Plan for the Leon County Public Schools by the Florida Desegregation Consulting Center. Coral Gables, Fla.: University of Miami, 1970.

Dittmer, John. *Local People: The Struggle for Civil Rights in Mississippi*. Urbana: University of Illinois Press, 1994.

Dodd, Hurley. "The Sit-In Demonstrations and the Dilemma of the Negro College President." *Journal of Negro Education* 30 (Winter 1961): 1–3.

Ellis, Mary Louise, William Warren Rogers, and Joan Morris. *Favored Land: A History of Tallahassee and Leon County*. Norfolk: Donning, 1988.

Evans, John E. *Time for Florida: Report on the Administration of Farris Bryant, Governor, 1961–1965*. Jacksonville: 1965.

Evans, Sara. *Personal Politics: The Roots of Women's Liberation in the Civil Rights Movement and the New Left*. New York: Knopf, 1979.

Fairclough, Adam. *Race and Democracy: The Civil Rights Struggle in Louisiana, 1915–1972.* Athens: University of Georgia Press, 1995.

———. *To Redeem the Soul of America: The Southern Christian Leadership Conference and Martin Luther King, Jr.* Athens: University of Georgia Press, 1987.

Farmer, James. *Lay Bare the Heart: An Autobiography of the Civil Rights Movement.* New York: Arbor House, 1985.

Fendrich, James Max. *Ideal Citizens: The Legacy of the Civil Rights Movement.* Albany: State University of New York Press, 1993.

Florida A&M University. *Rattler.* Year Book. 1957–1965.

Florida Across the Threshold: The Administration of Governor LeRoy Collins, January 4, 1955, to January 3, 1961. Tallahassee, 1961.

Gannon, Michael V. *Florida: A Short History.* Gainesville: University Presses of Florida, 1993.

———, ed. *The New History of Florida.* Gainesville: University Presses of Florida, 1996.

Garrow, David H. *Bearing the Cross: Martin Luther King, Jr., and the Southern Christian Leadership Conference.* New York: W. Morrow, 1986.

———. *Protest at Selma: Martin Luther King, Jr., and the Voting Rights Act of 1965.* New Haven, Conn.: Yale University Press, 1978.

———, ed. *The Montgomery Bus Boycott and the Women Who Started It: The Memoir of Jo Ann Gibson Robinson.* Knoxville: University of Tennessee Press, 1987.

———, ed. *The Walking City: The Montgomery Bus Boycott, 1955–1956.* Brooklyn, N.Y.: Carlson, 1989.

Giddings, Joshua R., ed. *The Exiles of Florida.* Facsimile ed. Gainesville: University of Florida Press, 1964.

Gilliam, Thomas J. "The Montgomery Bus Boycott of 1955–56," in *The Walking City: The Montgomery Bus Boycott, 1955–56.* Edited by David H. Garrow. Brooklyn, N.Y., 1989.

Goldfield, David R. *Black, White, and Southern: Race Relations and Southern Culture, 1940 to the Present.* Baton Rouge: Louisiana State University Press, 1990.

Graham, Hugh Davis. *The Civil Rights Era: Origins and Development of National Policy, 1960–1972.* New York: Oxford University Press, 1990.

Hall, Kermit L., and James W. Ely, Jr., eds. *An Uncertain Tradition: Constitutionalism and the History of the South.* Athens: University of Georgia Press, 1988.

Hamburger, Susan. "The 1968 Tallahassee Riots Following the Assassination of Martin Luther King, Jr." *Apalachee* 9 (1984): 57–66.

Hamilton, Charles V. *The Bench and the Ballot: Southern Federal Judges and Black Voters.* New York: Oxford University Press, 1973.

Hartsfield, Annie M., and Elston E. Roady. *Florida Votes, 1920–1962: Selected Election Statistics.* Tallahassee: Institute of Government Research, Florida State University, 1963.

———. *Florida Votes, 1920–1970.* Tallahassee: Institute for Social Research, Florida State University, 1972.

Havard, William C., ed. *The Changing Politics of the South*. Baton Rouge: Louisiana State University Press, 1972.

Hill, Herbert, and Jack Greenberg. *Citizens Guide to Desegregation: A Study of Social and Legal Change in American Life*. Westport, Conn.: Greenwood Press, 1979.

Hole, Judith, and Ellen Levine. *Rebirth of Feminism*. New York: Quadrangle Books, 1971.

Jacobstein, Helen L. *The Segregation Factor in the Florida Democratic Gubernatorial Primary of 1956*. Social Science Series 47 (Gainesville: University of Florida, 1972).

Key, V. O., Jr. *Southern Politics in State and Nation*. Rev. ed. Knoxville: University of Tennessee Press, 1984.

Killian, Lewis M. *Black and White: Reflections of a White Southern Sociologist*. Dix Hills, N.Y.: General Hall, 1994.

———. *The Impossible Revolution? Black Power and the American Dream*. New York: Random House, 1968.

Killian, Lewis M., and Charles U. Smith. "Negro Protest Leaders in a Southern Community." *Social Forces* 38:3 (March 1960): 250–257.

King, Martin Luther. *Stride Toward Freedom: The Montgomery Story*. New York: Harper, 1958.

———. *Where Do We Go from Here: Chaos or Community?* New York: Harper and Row, 1967.

Ladd, Everett Carll. *Negro Political Leadership in the South*. Ithaca, N.Y.: Cornell University Press, 1966.

Lawson, Steven F., David R. Colburn, and Darryl Paulson. "Groveland: Florida's Little Scottsboro." *Florida Historical Quarterly* 65:1 (July 1986): 1–26.

Lewis, Anthony. *Portrait of a Decade: The Second American Revolution*. New York: Random House, 1964.

Lewis, David L. *King: A Biography*. Urbana: University of Illinois Press, 1978.

Littlefield, Jr., Daniel F. *Africans and Seminoles: From Removal to Emancipation*. Westport, Conn.: Greenwood Press, 1977.

Margo, Robert A. *Disenfranchisement, School Finance, and the Economics of Segregated Schools in the United States South, 1890–1910*. New York: Garland, 1985.

———. *Race and Schooling in the South, 1880–1950: An Economic History*. Chicago: University of Chicago, 1990.

McAdam, Doug. *Political Process and the Development of Black Insurgency, 1930–1970*. Chicago: University of Chicago Press, 1982.

Matthews, Donald R., and James W. Prothro. *Negroes and the New Southern Politics*. New York: Harcourt, Brace and World, 1966.

Meier, August, and Elliott Rudwick. *CORE: A Study in the Civil Rights Movement, 1942–1968*. New York: Oxford University Press, 1973.

Meier, August, Elliott Rudwick, and F. Broderick. *Black Protest Thought in the Twentieth Century*. Indianapolis: Bobbs-Merrill, 1971.

Morris, Aldon D. *The Origins of the Civil Rights Movement: Black Communities Organizing for Change*. New York: Free Press, 1986.

Morris, Allen. *The Florida Handbook, 1959–1960*. Tallahassee: Peninsular, 1960.

———. *The Florida Handbook, 1963–1964.* Tallahassee: Peninsular, 1964.

———. *The Florida Handbook, 1967–68.* Tallahassee: Peninsular, 1968.

Neyland, Leedell W. *Florida Agricultural and Mechanical University: A Centennial History, 1887–1987.* Tallahassee: Florida A&M University Foundation, 1987.

Neyland, Leedell W., and John W. Riley. *The History of Florida Agricultural and Mechanical University.* Gainesville: University of Florida Press, 1963.

Norrell, Robert J. *Reaping the Whirlwind: The Civil Rights Movement in Tuskegee.* New York: Knopf, 1985.

Oates, Stephen B. *Let the Trumpet Sound: The Life of Martin Luther King, Jr.* New York: Harper and Row, 1982.

Oshinsky, David M. *A Conspiracy So Immense: The World of Joe McCarthy.* New York: Free Press, 1983.

Paulson, Darryl, and Paul Hawkes. "Desegregating the University of Florida Law School: *Virgil Hawkins v. The Florida Board of Control.*" *Florida State University Law Review* 12 (1984): 59–71.

Peck, James. *Freedom Ride.* New York: Simon and Schuster, 1962.

Porter, Kenneth W. *The Black Seminoles: A History of a Freedom-Seeking People.* Gainesville: University Press of Florida, 1996.

Price, Hugh D. *The Negro and Southern Politics: A Chapter of Florida History.* New York: New York University Press, 1957.

Raines, Howell. *My Soul Is Rested: Movement Days in the Deep South Remembered.* New York: Putnam, 1977.

Robnett, Belinda. *How Long? How Long?: African-American Women in the Struggle for Civil Rights.* New York: Oxford University Press, 1997.

Salamon, Lester. "Leadership and Modernization: The Emerging Black Political Elite in the American South." *Journal of Politics* 35 (1973): 615–646.

Sherrill, Robert. *Gothic Politics in the Deep South: Stars of the New Confederacy.* New York: Goosman Publishers, 1968.

Sitkoff, Harvard. *The Struggle for Black Equality, 1954–1992.* New York: Hill and Wang, 1993.

Smith, Charles U. "Student Activism, Benign Racism, and Scholarly Irresponsibility." *Research Bulletin* 20:7 (September 1974): 65–76.

———, ed. *The Civil Rights Movement in Florida and the United States: Historical and Contemporary Perspective.* Tallahassee: Father and Son, 1989.

Smith, Charles U., and A. S. Parks. "Desegregation in Florida: a 'Progress Report.'" *Quarterly of Higher Education Among Negroes* 25:1 (January 1957): 54–60.

Southern Regional Council. *Special Report: The Student Protest Movement.* Winter 1960.

Statistical Abstract of Florida Counties. Jacksonville: Florida Chamber of Commerce, 1944.

Stephens, Patricia. "Tallahassee: Through Jail to Freedom." In *The Students Report.* New York: CORE, 1960.

Tanne, Leslie, ed. *Voices from Women's Liberation.* New York: New American Library, 1971.

Tebeau, Charlton W. *A History of Florida*. Coral Gables, Fla.: University of Miami Press, 1971.

Viorst, Milton. *Fire in the Streets: America in the 1960's*. New York: Simon and Schuster, 1979.

Wagy, Tom R. *Governor LeRoy Collins of Florida: Spokesman of the New South*. University: University of Alabama Press, 1985.

Walker, Jack L. "The Functions of Disunity: Negro Leadership in a Southern City." *Journal of Negro Education* 32 (Summer 1963): 227–236.

Wasby, Stephen L., Anthony A. D'Amato, and Rosemary Metrailer. *Desegregation from Brown to Alexander: An Explanation of Supreme Court Strategies*. Carbondale: Southern Illinois University Press, 1977.

Watters, Pat, and Reese Cleghorn. *Climbing Jacob's Ladder: The Arrival of Negroes in Southern Politics*. New York: Harcourt, Brace and World, 1967.

West, Cornel. *Race Matters*. New York: Vintage Books, 1993.

White, G. Edward. *Earl Warren, A Public Life*. New York: Oxford University Press, 1982.

Wilkinson, J. Harvie III. *From Brown to Bakke: The Supreme Court and School Integration, 1954–1978*. New York: Oxford University Press, 1981.

Wilson, William Julius. *The Declining Significance of Race: Blacks and Changing American Institutions*. Chicago: University of Chicago Press, 1980.

———. *The Truely Disadvantaged*. Chicago: University of Chicago Press, 1987.

Theses and Dissertations

Calhoun, Mary C. "A Century of Silence: A Survey of Black Politicians in Tallahassee, Leon County, from Reconstruction to the Present." November 29, 1988.

Padgett, Gregory. "C. K. Steele, A Biography." Ph.D. dissertation, Florida State University, 1994.

———. "C. K. Steele and the Tallahassee Bus Boycott." Master's thesis, Florida State University, 1977.

Poore, Caroline. "Striking the First Blow: Harry T. Moore and the Fight for Black Equality in Florida." Master's thesis, Florida State University, 1992.

Stark, Bonnie. "McCarthyism in Florida: Charley Johns and the Florida Legislative Investigation Committee, July 1956 to July 1965." Master's thesis, University of South Florida, 1985.

Thomerlin, Joseph A. "The Negro and Florida's System of Education: The Aftermath of the *Brown* Case." Ph.D. dissertation, Florida State University, 1967.

White, Robert M. "The Tallahassee Sit-Ins and CORE: A Nonviolent Revolutionary Submovement." Ph.D. dissertation, Florida State University, 1964.

Index

of, 116; Freedom Riders and, 135, 136;
inaugural address of, 128; Lowry v., 214;
move by, 127; political prospects of, 111
Bryant, Sterling, 253, 255–56
Bryant administration, 129, 141, 161, 168
Burns, Haydon, 171, 172–73, 181–82
Burress, Spencer, 110
Burt, John, 264
Bus boycotts. *See* Cities Transit boycott;
Montgomery bus boycott
Business and Civic League of Quincy, 174
Businessman's League, 189
Byrons-Jackson sit-in (1959), 82, 83

Caldwell, Millard, 116, 199
Calhoun, Edna, 10
Camp, Spurgeon, 185
Campbell, Doak, 62, 63, 98
Campbell, James, 248
Campbell, Larry, 192, 194
Campbell, Whit, 174
Canterbury House, 92, 94, 119
Cape Canaveral, 128
Capital City Bank, 21
Capital City Country Club, 74–75, 76–77,
252, 274 (n. 30)
Carey, Gordon R.: airport restaurant
and, 136; on biracial commission, 124;
Cowins's suspension and, 131; on delay,
123; Haley and, 87, 96, 111, 115, 126, 139,
140; Larkins and, 129; Miami CORE and,
82; North Carolina activists and, 88;
Poland and, 133, 134; on "reactivation,"
125; Tallahassee CORE and, 85, 86,
121, 140
Carlton, Doyle, Jr., 116
Carmichael, Stokely, 191
Carothers, Graham, 250, 252
Carothers, Milton, 114
Carraway, Wilson, 76, 113, 188–89, 190
Carrousel Restaurant, 141
Carswell, Harrold: airport integrated by,
138; Capital City Country Club and, 76,
252, 274 (n. 30); on Council of Human
Relations, 69; courtroom segregation
and, 145; FAMU-ACLU suit and, 157;
father-in-law of, 260; freedom-of-choice

plan and, 247, 249; on public pools, 184;
school reassignment requests and, 229;
Steele and, 226, 227–28, 237, 240–41, 243,
250, 252; theater demonstrators and, 154;
U.S. Supreme Court and, 76, 177, 251–52;
Wechsler case and, 177
Carter, Charles: arrest of, 48; on
black patronage, 23; on boycott, 13;
exoneration of, 52; on former bus
routes, 36–37; on lost revenue, 44;
ministerial delegation and, 14; "official
statement" on, 21–22; on segregation
ordinances, 19–20
Castro, Fidel, 118
Cates, Bob, 184, 185
Cates, W. H., 75, 261, 262
Central High School, 218
Chafe, William, 8, 124
Chaires, Fla., 28–29, 258
Chapel of the Resurrection, 92, 100–
101, 114
Charlotte County, Fla., 242
Chicago, 118, 120, 193
Choate, Emmett, 51
Christianity: Canterbury House and,
92; Collins on, 74; DeVane on, 55;
Fellowship of Reconciliation and, 81;
Fowler on, 123; Godby and, 224; ICC
and, 27; Rudd on, 118, 137; Strozier and,
115; University of South Florida and, 73;
Waller on, 101
Cities Transit boycott (1956), 1, 9–46, 216;
arrests initiating, 6, 10; CORE and, 86;
economic consequences of, 7, 20, 23,
27, 49; effectiveness of, 138, 140; FLIC-
NAACP conflict and, 7, 66; professional
risks of, 90; Simon and, 70; social
consequences of, 3–5, 47–64, 65; store
boycott and, 103; mentioned, 73, 80,
89, 159
Civic League, 26, 75, 79, 185
Civil Rights Act (1957), 164
Civil Rights Act (1960), 164
Civil Rights Act (1964), 183; Bryant and,
163; Gadsden County voter registration
and, 175; hiring discrimination and, 261;
hospitals and, 187; lax enforcement of,

Dupont, King Solomon: on bus riding, 42; candidacy of, 60–61, 62, 179; on city proposal, 22; daughter of, 263; on deed offers, 38; ICC and, 16; on Montgomery boycott, 18; on transport alternatives, 29

Easterwood, H. G., 75–76, 180
Eastland, James, 201
Economy Cab Company, 45
Eisenhower, Dwight D., 226
Elberta Crate and Box Company, 260
Elementary and Secondary Education Act (1965), 238
Ellis, Roscoe, 191
Episcopal Church, 92, 107, 114, 149
Equal Employment Opportunity Commission, 261
Erasing the Color Line (CORE), 87
Ervin, Richard: Advisory Committee and, 149; on *Brown*, 102, 201, 203, 208; on desegregation, 206, 220–21; on ICC carpool, 37; ideology of, 197–98; on interposition bill, 216, 217–18; Killian and, 102, 204, 205; on law testing, 47; Messer and, 33
Escambia County, Fla., 226, 227, 228, 240, 241
Evans, E. G., 152
Evans, John, 168
Evers, Medgar, 152

Fabisinski, L. L., 57, 214, 224
Fabisinski Committee. *See* Florida Advisory Commission on Race Relations to Governor LeRoy Collins
Fair Deal, 171
Fairclough, Adam, 4, 89, 282 (n. 37)
FAMU High School, 229, 232, 235, 240
FAMUAN, 191
Farmer, James, 122, 129, 134, 159, 161
"Fast for equality," 133–34
Federal Bureau of Investigation, 118, 122, 146, 176
Federal Correctional Institution (Tallahassee), 112
Fellowship of Reconciliation, 63, 81
Ferguson, Chester, 188, 195

Fifth Circuit Court of Appeals. *See* U.S. Fifth Circuit Court of Appeals
"Fighting Fund for Freedom Campaign," 84
First Amendment, 71, 72, 99
First Christian Church, 40
First Presbyterian Church, 40–41
Florida A&M College Hospital, Health Center, and Nursing School, 96, 185–86, 187, 188, 190
Florida A&M University: building program of, 203; bus route to, 23, 36–37, 42, 48; CORE Chapter at, 5, 141; Cowins suspension and, 131; demonstration high school of, 229, 232, 235, 240; earlier names of, 296 (n. 11); emergency closing of, 193, 194; golf course near, 76; graduate offerings of, 211, 213; Improvement Committee of, 195; lawsuit against, 157; Lee Hall at, 12, 191–92; Lewises and, 25; local conservatism and, 3; NAACP Student Chapter at, 5, 13, 40, 84; Poland and, 133; police investigation of, 31; proposed FSU merger with, 190–91, 194, 195, 264; public schools and, 253, 255, 256; remonstration to, 111; "Senior Day" at, 112; vocational education at, 26. *See also* Florida A&M University faculty; Florida A&M University Law School; Florida A&M University students
Florida A&M University faculty: activism of, 26; Big Bend Project and, 172; bus boycott and, 38, 39–40; class status of, 260; discipline proposed for, 99; FLIC and, 59, 66; FSU faculty and, 85; injured students and, 96; negotiation experience of, 15; newcomers to, 2; proposed investigation and, 155; Tallahassee Council on Human Relations and, 25, 69, 70; Whites and, 86; Woolworth sit-in and, 90
Florida A&M University Law School: closing of, 183, 188–90, 264; founding of, 199; Hawkins and, 209, 212, 213; Lindsey and, 20
Florida A&M University students: affidavit on, 120; bus boycott and, 1, 6, 9–13, 14,

71; Hawkins and, 209–10, 211–12, 213; murder defendants and, 289 (n. 35); seat assignment plan and, 57, 58; sit-in demonstrators and, 118–19

Florida Theater, 144, 146–47, 152

Florida Times Union, 110

Flucas, Laura, 44

Foote, H. B., 186

Ford, James: assistant principalship of, 257; election of, 181, 261, 262; Richardson and, 263; on schools, 232, 248

Ford Fellowships, 158

Fort Lauderdale, 13

Fort Pierce Rotary Club, 216

Fortas, Abe, 155

"Four Point Program," 214, 215

Fourteenth Amendment: Collins's plan and, 219; Gibson and, 71, 72; Hawkins and, 209–10; legality of, 141; Leon County School Board and, 226; seat assignment plan and, 57; segregated education and, 200, 221; sit-in demonstrators and, 117

Fowler, Cody, 123, 128

"Freedom Highways," 140

Freedom House, 174, 176

"Freedom Ride" (1961), 129, 134–39

Freedom Riders Coordinating Committee, 135

"Freedom Schools," 245

"Freedom Summer" (1964), 173

Free Flambeau, 99

Frenchtown: bus route of, 23, 36–37, 42, 48; economic status in, 260; housing in, 255; voter registration office in, 166

Fry, Georgiana, 95–96, 97

Gadsden County: black electorate of, 165, 177; cross burning in, 176; gubernatorial vote in, 182; official harassment in, 168; presidential vote in, 178; schoolchildren of, 202; voter registration in, 166, 167, 173–74, 176–77

Gadsden County Free Press, 287 (n. 27)

Gadsden NAACP, 174

Gaines, Mary Ola, 89, 90

Gaines v. Canada (1938), 209

Gainesville, Fla., 158, 160, 168, 226

Gainesville CORE, 178

Gainesville Women's Liberation, 178

Gaither, Alonzo "Jake," 21

Gaither Golf Course, 76

Gandhi, Mahatma, 81, 82–83, 133

Gandhi Award, 120

Gardner, Willie, 257

Garrow, David, 282 (n. 37)

Gates, Robert, 204

Georgia: *Brown* decision and, 201; Freedom Riders in, 134; interposition bill of, 216; school integration in, 246; travel tests in, 139; voter registration in, 178–79

Gerstein, Dick, 73

Geschwender, James, 156

Gibson, Theodore, 71–72

Gibson v. Dade County (1956), 221–22

Glenn, John, 147

Godby, Amos: black students and, 229, 233; ICC petitions to, 223–24; irate father and, 234; C. Knowles and, 231; lawsuit against, 225, 226; Stevens and, 230

Godby Junior High School, 294 (n. 5)

Goldwater, Barry, 175, 177, 178, 179

Good Shepherd's Group, 174

Gooden, R. N., 254

Gordon, Spiver, 178, 184

Gore, George W.: alleged picketing ban of, 153; bus boycott and, 38–40; on campus speakers, 191; committee appointed by, 194; Cowins suspension and, 131; on demonstrations, 112; FLIC and, 59; on Haley contract, 121; hospital issue and, 186, 188; at King memorial, 193; law school issue and, 189, 190; police investigation of, 31; resignation of, 195–96; rioters and, 192, 194; sit-in demonstrators and, 98, 119; "sleep-in" and, 157; women bus riders and, 12; Young and, 132

Gore, Pearl Winrow, 31

Goss v. Knoxville (1963), 236

Governor's Advisory Commission on Bi-Racial Problems. *See* Florida Advisory Commission on Race Relations to Governor LeRoy Collins

Hunter, Stephen, 137
Hurley, Ruby, 160, 162

Ice, Jackson, 112, 113–14
Institute on Nonviolence and Social
    Change: Montgomery, 47–48;
    Tallahassee, 63
Inter-Civic Council, 5, 84, 86, 89, 159;
    anniversary celebration of, 63; arrested
    members of, 37, 43; Atkinson on,
    60; Bashful and, 59; Big Bend Voter
    Education Project and, 167; cash
    donations to, 17, 41; church youth and,
    40; Cities Transit closing and, 29; city hall
    meeting and, 27, 28; civil disobedience
    and, 32–33; closed-door meeting and,
    21; Collins and, 50, 51; Community Day
    and, 79; "conservative" blacks and, 27,
    31; CORE and, 90, 139; divisions in, 43;
    economic boycott and, 133; Executive
    Committee of, 16, 22, 27, 223–24;
    FAMU Law School and, 189; FLIC
    and, 70; founding of, 15; "franchise
    interpretation" and, 22; FSU students
    and, 61, 62; "full integration" demands
    of, 23; on Gore, 39; joint meeting with,
    111; lawsuit against, 44–45; Lewis State
    Bank and, 26; Montgomery ruling
    and, 47–48; partial compromise with,
    36; police infiltration of, 30, 41; "Ride
    the Bus Integrated" campaign of, 49;
    "Rights and Teachers" and, 132; Rudd
    and, 19, 58; "school holiday" and, 244;
    seat assignment plan and, 52, 55, 56;
    Strickland on, 31, 42; Tallahassee NAACP
    and, 85; Transportation Committee of,
    18; unwritten communications of, 19–
    20; "Vigil for Poverty" and, 196; violence
    against, 54; voter registration by, 38, 166;
    white fear of, 25
International Woodworkers Union, 260
Interracial Action Institute (1959), 81,
    82–83
Interstate Commerce Commission, 87, 135,
    136, 139, 141
Irons, Bessie, 37, 44
Irons, Edward, 32, 39–40

Isbell, Hubert, 137
Islam, 31
Israelites, 148

Jackson, Miss., 134, 152, 155
Jacksonville, Fla.: desegregation in, 140;
    newspaper of, 110; racial crisis in, 124,
    171; student teaching in, 157; TV station
    of, 107
"Jailhouse Notes" (B. Broxton), 106
Jake Gaither Golf Course, 76
Jakes, Wilhelmina: arrest of, 9–10;
    exculpation of, 18–19; at home, 11, 13;
    Strickland and, 35; student rally and, 12
Jefferson County, Fla., 74, 166, 176
Jefferson County case (1966), 245–46, 247,
    249, 251
Jemison, T. J., 63
Jenkins, Thomas M., 189
Johns, Charley: on Communist Party,
    65–66; gubernatorial race of, 203, 206;
    on integration, 201; Killian survey and,
    204–5; J. B. Matthews and, 67; pupil
    assignment and, 208; J. S. Shaw and,
    68; "watchdog" committee proposal
    of, 35
Johns Committee. *See* Florida Legislative
    Investigation Committee
Johnson, Dewey, 56, 110, 111, 112
Johnson, Lyndon B., 162, 171, 175, 178, 181
Johnson, Malcolm, 3, 21, 110; on Advisory
    Committee, 151; on black leadership,
    16; on *Brown II,* 208; on bus boycott,
    23, 27; on city commission races, 60, 61,
    180, 262; on civic responsibility, 36; on
    Civil Rights Act, 162, 171; closed-door
    meeting and, 20–21; on Collins, 51, 54;
    on complete integration, 28; on cross
    burning, 51; on Fabisinski Committee,
    215; on FLIC, 69; on interposition bill,
    218; on Madison County women, 74; on
    public pools, 184; on school boycott, 245;
    on segregation debate, 201–2; on "Senior
    Day," 112; on sit-ins, 91; on student bus
    riders, 13, 58; on theater demonstration,
    145; on white rioters, 96
Jones, Elbert W., 16

Hawkins and, 66, 212; J. B. Matthews on, 67; Legal Defense Fund of, 222, 251; Miami Chapter of, 51, 71; Orr and, 216; school desegregation suits of, 19; sit-in demonstrators and, 117; Tallahassee march and, 162; *Tampa Tribune* on, 69; women bus riders and, 10–11, 35. *See also* National Association for the Advancement of Colored People Florida Chapter; National Association for the Advancement of Colored People Tallahassee Chapter

National Association for the Advancement of Colored People Florida Chapter: Church Committee for Florida, 160; civil rights organizations and, 159, 160; CORE and, 174; FLIC and, 58, 72, 84; school segregation and, 208, 223; Tallahassee march and, 161; voter registration by, 164, 166; weakness of, 11

National Association for the Advancement of Colored People Tallahassee Chapter: Big Bend Voter Education Project and, 167; bus boycott and, 13, 15; Conoly and, 27; Dixie and, 29; economic boycott and, 111, 133; Educational Improvement Committee, 244, 245; FLIC and, 58, 59, 72; ICC and, 85; in 1930s, 4; "Rights and Teachers" and, 132; School Board and, 84, 225, 243; single-member district suit of, 262–63; Woolworth sit-in and, 89

National Baptist Convention, 42
National Broadcasters Association, 222
National Guard: Alabama, 134; Florida, 193
National Merit Scholars, 264, 296 (n. 12)
National Negro Congress, 67
National Youth Administration, 30
Neisner's Department Store, 122, 130
New Deal, 30, 171
New Orleans, 134
New Southerner, 30
New York City, 132–33, 141, 166–67
New Zion Baptist Church, 52
Neyland, Leedell, 194
Nims Junior High School, 257
Nixon, Richard M., 251

Nixon administration, 252
Non-Partisan Voter's Crusade, 132
North Carolina, 88, 113, 124, 140, 242
North Carolina A&T College, 87, 124
North Carolina Textile Workers' Union, 67
North Florida Citizenship Education Project, 173–78, 286–87 (n. 27)
North Florida Presbytery, 40
Northern District Court. *See* U.S. District Court, Northern District of Florida
Norwood, Edwin, 179, 181

O'Bryan, William A., 225, 227, 250
Ocala, 148, 149, 158
Odham, Brailey, 171, 172
Odum, Ralph, 204, 205, 207, 210, 222
Oglesby, Ross R., 99, 119, 156
Oklahoma City Black Dispatch, 121
"Old South" region, 165
Oliver, Billy Ray, 194, 196, 289 (n. 35)
Oliver Brown v. Board of Education. See *Brown v. Board of Education of Topeka* (1954)
O'Neal, Frank, 160
Orchard Villa Elementary School, 220
Orr, John, 216

Palm Beach County, 83, 84
Palm Beach County School Board, 83
Parker, John J., 202
Parker, Richard, 124
Parker, Robert, 76
Parks, Rosa, 12
Patricia Stephens Due v. Tallahassee Theatres, Inc. (1964), 154
Patterson, Carrie: arrest of, 9–10; exculpation of, 18–19; at home, 11, 13; Strickland and, 35; student rally and, 12
Peacock, Burl, 18, 192
Peck, James, 134
Pensacola, 226
Pepper, Claude, 216
Pepper, Frank, 94
Perkins, W. R., 43
Perry, Benjamin L., 62, 119, 120, 264
Perry, John, 101, 102

U.S. National Youth Administration, 30
U.S. Office of Education, 238, 239, 240, 241
U.S. Reserve Officers' Training Corps, 191
United States Steel and Coal Corporation, 16
U.S. Supreme Court: Carswell and, 76, 177, 251–52; Collins on, 53, 54, 217; on Columbia buses, 19, 268 (n. 9); DeVane on, 55; Fabisinski Committee on, 215; Freedom Riders and, 138; on Gibson, 71–72; Governor's Advisory Commission on Race Relations on, 220; Hawkins case and, 210, 211, 213; interposition bill and, 215, 216, 217; on interstate transport, 81–82, 129; jail demonstrators and, 154–55; KKK on, 38; Montgomery boycott and, 32, 45–46, 47, 48, 49; NAACP cases and, 199; New Kent County School Board and, 250; school desegregation and, 221, 236, 240; sit-in demonstrators and, 104, 119, 133; student bus riders and, 13, 57–58; on Texas primaries, 164; theater demonstrators and, 5
United States v. Jefferson County Board of Education (1966), 245–46, 247, 249, 251
University Inn, 155–56
University of Alabama, 152, 158
University of Florida, 152, 154, 157–58, 214, 226; SDS Chapter of, 178. *See also* University of Florida Law School
University of Florida Law School: black attendance at, 188, 190, 199; Hawkins and, 66, 209–10, 211–13; white attendance at, 189
University of Miami Florida School Desegregation Center, 252–53, 256
University of North Carolina Woman's College, 124, 125
University of South Florida, 73
University Religious Council, 156

Vietnam, 260
"Vigil for Poverty" (1968), 196
Virginia, 216, 236, 242, 250
Voter registration, 89; CORE and, 82, 158–59, 173 (*see also* Big Bend Voter Education Project; North Florida Citizenship Education Project); ICC and, 38, 166; Irons on, 32; in Leon County, 164–65, 166, 167, 172, 179
Voting Rights Act (1965), 178–79, 183

Waldron, Martin, 126–27
Walker, W. May: on bus riders, 57; Gibson and, 71; law school case and, 189; rape case and, 77, 78, 79
Wallace, George, 152
Waller, Harcourt, 92, 97, 100–101, 114, 145
Warren, Earl, 155, 200, 207
Warren, Fuller, 214
Warren, Katherine, 97
Washington, D.C.: Freedom Riders in, 129, 134, 135; march on, 149, 152; Poor People's Campaign in, 196; prayer pilgrimage to, 52; race riots in, 193; school segregation in, 207
Washington, G. W., 115
Watertown, N.Y., 119
Watkins, Steve, 180
Way, Flo, 74
Wechsler, Stuart, 176–77
West, Don, 30
White, Robert, 86, 90, 122
White, Rosemary "Posey," 86
White Citizens Council of Leon County, 49, 50, 51, 61, 94
Wilkins, Roy, 11, 17, 77
Williams, Aubrey, 30
Williams, George, 257
Williams, Hosea, 260
Williams, Hugh: Berkowitz and, 185; candidacy of, 168, 169, 170; on recreation program, 183–84; Woolworth demonstrations and, 89, 104, 126
Williams, J. T., 76
Williams, M. C., 16
Willis, Ben C.: Crowe case and, 196; Elberta strike and, 260; "exploratory conference" and, 20; jail demonstrators and, 153; protest limitations of, 147, 156; sit-in demonstrators and, 118, 131; Priscilla Stephens and, 138; theater demonstrators and, 147, 154
Wilson, Charles, 225

Wilson, Rosa, 97

Woman's College of the University of North Carolina, 124, 125

Woodville, Fla., 258

Woolworth Company, 105, 110, 119

Woolworth picket (1960), 126–27

Woolworth sit-ins. *See* Woolworth sit-in, Greensboro (1960); Woolworth sit-in, Tallahassee (1960); Woolworth sit-in, Tallahassee (1962)

Woolworth sit-in, Greensboro (1960), 5, 85, 87, 93; Blackwell and, 124–25; Chafe on, 8; Communism and, 100; Pat Stephens and, 94

Woolworth sit-in, Tallahassee (1960), 88–90, 93–94; court case on, 103–4, 117–18; stockholders and, 119; theater demonstrations and, 147

Woolworth sit-in, Tallahassee (1962), 142

Works Progress Administration, 75

World Court, 25

World Federalist Organization, 25

Wortham, Curtis Lee, 194

WTVT Tampa, 57

Young, Daisy: on black educators, 142; bus boycott and, 12; Gore and, 132; ICC and, 15; on Killian-Grigg proposal, 103; leadership by, 143; march planning subcommittee and, 160; on racial progress, 259; raises for, 40; "school holiday" and, 244; Tallahassee CORE and, 85, 86, 122; Woolworth sit-in and, 90

Young Men's Christian Association, 97